Thomas Cromwell

Thomas Cromwell

THE RISE *and* FALL *of* HENRY VIII's
most NOTORIOUS MINISTER

ROBERT HUTCHINSON

Weidenfeld & Nicolson

LONDON

For Sue and Mike

First published in Great Britain in 2007
by Weidenfeld & Nicolson

1 3 5 7 9 10 8 6 4 2

A CIP catalogue record for this book
is available from the British Library.

ISBN-13: 978 0 297 84642 0
ISBN-10: 0 297 84642 6

Typeset at The Spartan Press Ltd,
Lymington, Hants

Printed in Great Britain by Clays Ltd, St Ives plc

The Orion Publishing Group's policy is to use papers that
are natural, renewable and recyclable products and made
from wood grown in sustainable forests. The logging and
manufacturing processes are expected to conform to the
environmental regulations of the country of origin.

Weidenfeld & Nicolson

The Orion Publishing Group Ltd
Orion House
5 Upper Saint Martin's Lane
London, WC2H 9EA

www.orionbooks.co.uk

Contents

Illustrations

Acknowledgements

This book could not have been written without the help and active support of many friends and colleagues, not least my dear wife, who has been forced to consider every single enviable and unenviable facet of Thomas Cromwell's complex character over more hours than I (and she) would probably care to admit. It could not have been written without her abundant kindness, uninterrupted patience and unstintingly loyal support.

Much of the material for this book has been drawn from contemporary sources, and I believe it is vital to consider the protagonists' actual words in this extraordinary human drama of greed, corruption and ambition. My thanks, as ever, are due to all those whose great kindness has enabled me to track down documents and rare books. In particular, I would like to thank Robin Harcourt Williams, Librarian and Archivist to the Marquis of Salisbury at Hatfield House; Bernard Nurse, Librarian, and Adrian James, Assistant Librarian, of the Society of Antiquaries of London; the ever-willing and helpful staff at the National Archives, Kew, the Manuscripts and Rare-Book Departments at the British Library; Kay Walters and her team at the incomparable library at the Athenæum; the Revd Father Jerome Bertram for much help, as always, with Latin translations; Ian Drury of Weidenfeld & Nicolson for all his encouragement; Ilona Jasiewicz, former Managing Editor, for her manifold kindnesses and patient assistance; Tom Wharton, her successor; Lisa Rogers for her painstaking care, attention to detail and considerable editing skills; Alison Waggitt for the index; and finally Marcel Hoad and his team at Fowlers for their invaluable administrative support in so many ways.

To all these kind people, I would like to pass on my grateful thanks. I must point out, however, that any errors or omissions are entirely my own responsibility.   Robert Hutchinson, West Sussex, 2006

Prologue

This was the cause why he was envied of the nobility, being by birth so much beneath them and by preferment so high above most of them. Besides, many of his advancements were interpreted not so much as honours to him as injuries to others, as being either in use improper or in equity unfit or in right unjust or in conscience unlawful for him to accept.

THOMAS FULLER, *CHURCH HISTORY OF BRITAIN*, 1655[1]

Early on the morning of Saturday, 10 June 1540, Thomas Howard, Third Duke of Norfolk, summoned Sir Anthony Wingfield, the Captain of the King's Guard, to the Parliament House at Westminster. He ordered him to arrest Thomas Cromwell, Henry VIII's all-powerful Chief Minister, after dinner – then normally served around noon – later that day. The captain was astonished by the instruction, but Norfolk told him bluntly: 'You need not be surprised. The king orders it.'[2]

A few hours later, the Privy Council gathered at the Palace of Westminster for their meal. As the councillors entered the maze of buildings beside the River Thames, a sudden gust of wind blew off Cromwell's hat. It was the polite but bizarre custom during this period for all gentlemen to remove their hats when another had lost his. That day, the councillors rudely ignored the Minister's plight and kept their caps firmly on their heads. Looking around at their hostile faces, he commented: 'A high wind indeed it must have been to blow my bonnet off – and to keep all yours on.' Apparently blind, they had now become deaf as well and his quip went unacknowledged.

Cromwell must have recognised their silence as an omen of what was to come. His instincts were correct. They also shunned him at the dining table and he appeared isolated, if not wholly ostracised, as he consumed his dinner. When they departed for the nearby Council Chamber, he sat at an open window, as was his habit, listening to the clamorous petitions for justice from the raucous crowd waiting outside in the courtyard.

An hour later, at about three o'clock, the Lord Privy Seal rejoined the group and found them seated in silence around the Privy Council table. Cromwell must have detected an atmosphere of high tension within the chamber. He assumed they had already been discussing some of the issues listed for debate that afternoon, and while walking towards his vacant chair commented: 'You were in a great hurry, gentlemen, to get seated.'

Again, he was ignored.

He was just about to sit down at the head of the table when Norfolk jumped to his feet and, pointing an accusatory finger, shouted: 'Cromwell! Do not sit there! That is no place for you! Traitors do not sit amongst gentlemen.'[3]

After all the conspiracies against him during the past few months, the Minister, in his heart, must have anticipated that at some time soon and in some familiar place, his nemesis would strike. He instantly recognised that the terrible hour of reckoning had finally arrived.

Thomas Cromwell, the last and greatest of Henry's ministers, was an ambitious and totally corrupt statesman, very much a creature of the turbulent and violent Tudor times in which he lived. A frighteningly efficient administrator, he was, however, no mere pen-pushing bureaucrat. In truth, Cromwell was an opportunistic jack-the-lad, a ruffian on the make. This wholly self-made man, who desperately aspired to noble gentility, was also a devious, ruthless instrument of the state. Some said Cromwell was Machiavellian in his methods. His firm grip on the levers of power in Henry's realm was certainly often devoid of compassion.

Equipped with a remarkable gift of low animal cunning, a capacity for raw deceit, and employing extraordinary political skills and vision, he clawed his way up from rough, humble origins to become the most powerful man in England – ranking only below his fickle and sometimes malevolent sovereign. There were to be casualties aplenty on his perilous road to amassing his enormous wealth and domination of the state. Cromwell had no compunction whatsoever in trampling underfoot the mangled bodies of those he had exploited or crushed as he deftly and swiftly clambered to the slippery pinnacle of Tudor government.

'Scruples' was a word unaccountably missing from his vocabulary.

In sixteenth-century England, few other individuals, except those of the blood royal, made such an impact on everyday life as Thomas Cromwell.[4] Some of his government measures live on to affect us to this very day. The lawyer's carefully drafted legislation transformed Henry's nation into what we would now recognise as a totalitarian Stalinist state. Many would die barbarous deaths as a direct result of his policies as he directed the executioner's axe, targeting his victims with the sure hand of a skilled surgeon cutting out a cancerous growth. In Cromwell's simple, utilitarian philosophy of life – and death – the end *always* justified his means.

To many, not least Cardinal Reginald Pole, whom he tried to assassinate and whose family he manipulated and slaughtered, he was always that 'emissary of Satan' who perverted both the King and the ancient Catholic religion of the realm.[5] But despite grim warnings of the consequences of his actions, this loyal Minister always provided Henry VIII with exactly what he wanted: wealth, power and primacy – even though, at times, his policies would threaten the very throne of England.

Cromwell's dissolution of the monasteries – his audacious legal pillage that remains the greatest single act of privatisation in the history of Britain's governance – also abruptly ended their care of the poor and sick and the provision of education and spiritual comfort to thousands of pilgrims. An additional social by-product of the dissolution was the fashioning of a new affluent class of gentry through the redistribution of monastic wealth.

His necessity knew no laws. He gave the King absolute rule merely by proclamation, which drastically reduced any parliamentary scrutiny of government measures and provided a powerful carte blanche to the King and his sycophantic Council.[6] He willingly set the law above justice and distorted it into a potent weapon of the state for use against its enemies. Those accused of treason would no longer be entitled to trial by jury or their peers, and could now be condemned to die simply by parliamentary Act, their guilt and downfall sanctioned by Cromwell's legislators, many selected for their eager acquiescence to his will.

By Cromwell's hand, Henry became the supreme head of the Church in England 'on earth'; consequently, by law, the Pope became merely the Bishop of Rome. Cromwell ensured that the divine right of kings triumphed over the divine right of the descendants of St Peter.

His transformation of religion in England and Wales, including the state's iconoclastic assault on religious images and holy shrines (in the guise of eradicating idolatry), and the introduction of the Bible in English accelerated the Reformation in England and shunted many of the old beloved liturgies into the dim shadows of folk memory.

Cromwell also revolutionised the machinery of national and local government. His new corps of professional bureaucrats, employed for the first time outside the medieval confines of the royal household, laid the foundations of the Civil Service we know (and sometimes despise) today.

His widespread network of informers ensured that no man felt safe in his own home, nor so sure of himself as to dare to openly express his opinion, for fear of official retribution. The inquisitive fingers of state probed ever deeper into society. Government would now know when, where and to whom Henry's subjects were born and married, and when they died.[7]

Finally, his insidious propaganda, broadcast through dramatic spectacle or printed word, sought to mould and control the very minds and wills of the population on an unprecedented scale.

As a money-lender, lawyer, tax-imposing politician and religious reformer, it is scarcely surprising that Cromwell attracted unconcealed and virulent odium from both the jealous nobility around him at court and, at the other extreme, the lowliest human dregs of Henry's realm.

He was probably the most hated man in the kingdom.

John Tutton of Mere, near Glastonbury in Somerset, spoke 'great slanders' in March 1537 about Henry's Minister, maintaining that he was 'a stark heretic' and one of those 'wicked men' who constantly deceived the King and thus deserved a bad end.[8] In February 1538, John Hampson, decener[9] (or titheman) of Boarstall, Buckinghamshire, angrily told local constable Richard Hore that Cromwell, 'that traitor, has destroyed many a man and if I were as near to him as I am to you, I would thrust my dagger into the heart of him'.[10] In 1539, Thomas Molton said scornfully of Cromwell: 'There is one of the king's council . . . of such low birth that the world shall never be quiet and rest for so long as he continues.'[11] At the Minister's downfall the following year, the citizens lit bonfires in the streets in joyous celebration over his arrest.[12]

Cromwell's road to wealth and power was truly paved with bad intentions. For more than a decade he had walked the tightrope of his royal master's Tudor tantrums and vengeful spite and had survived – despite the best efforts of those around him to tear him down. Now the time had come for those countless scores against Cromwell to finally be settled.

CHAPTER ONE

The Most Hated Man in England

The Cardinal of York, seeing Cromwell's vigilance and diligence, his ability and promptitude, both in evil and good, took him into his service and employed him principally in demolishing five or six good monasteries.

SPANISH AMBASSADOR EUSTACE CHAPUYS, WRITING OF CROMWELL'S CAREER,

21 NOVEMBER 1535[1]

Tantalisingly little is known about Cromwell's early life: even his date of birth remains uncertain. He was born in or just before 1485, the son of Walter Cromwell, alias Smith, a failed small-time Tudor entrepreneur, of Putney, Surrey, south-west of London. Thomas's mother was the daughter of a yeoman called Glossop, and was living at the home of local attorney John Welbeck, possibly as a servant, when she married Walter in 1474.[2] Years later, Cromwell claimed his mother was aged fifty-two when he was born.[3]

Thomas's uncle was cook to William Warham, Archbishop of Canterbury. His grandfather, who had migrated from Norwell, Nottinghamshire, to Wimbledon, Surrey, in 1461, was probably involved in the cloth trade as a fuller, preparing wool in vats of human urine. Walter followed his father into the business, although he may earlier have been apprenticed to William Smith, who made armoured coats, called 'jacks', locally.

Probably because of declining demand for such warlike apparel after the end of the Wars of the Roses in 1487,[4] Cromwell's father moved into general blacksmithing and later owned both an inn, called the Anchor, and a brewery. These were built on a few acres of agricultural land west of Starling Lane, now Oxford Road, between today's Putney rail and East Putney District Line Underground stations. The family's cottage home and brewery were opposite the entrance to the aptly named Brewhouse Street, which still runs the short distance from Putney Bridge Road down to the River Thames, where a fishery existed in Cromwell's day.[5] An earlier home and Walter's smithy in Wandsworth Lane were pulled down in 1533.

Walter Cromwell was a drunken, quarrelsome scoundrel, always keen to challenge the authority of local government and, if possible, cheat his neighbours. Forty-eight times between 1475 and 1501 he was fined sixpence, or £10 in 2006 monetary values, for evading the Assize of Ale – the official method for testing the quality of all brewed beer before it was sold. He was probably watering it down. He also appeared in court several times, accused of overgrazing public pastures on Putney Common with his cattle and cutting too much furze and thorns for his fuel from the land there. In 1477 he was fined twenty pence for assaulting and drawing blood from William Michell.[6] Today, he would be a prime candidate for an Anti-Social Behaviour Order. Despite all these misdemeanours, Walter surprisingly became constable of Putney in 1495 and served many times as a juryman.

However, with old age his temper became more peevish. In October 1512 he was accused of leasing one virgate of land (up to 30 modern acres or 12.2 hectares) belonging to his brewery without permission and a year later, he lost his property in the adjacent parish of Wimbledon when he appeared again before the manor court, accused of fraudulently erasing evidences and terriers – property marker posts – of the local lord 'to the disturbance and disinheritance of the lord and his tenants'. The parish beadle was instructed to 'seize into the lord's hands all [Walter's] copyholds and tenements held of the lord . . . and [he had] to answer to the lord about the issues'.[7] Walter Cromwell was clearly the neighbour from hell.

Cromwell had two sisters: the elder, Katherine, probably born around 1477, and Elizabeth. Katherine married a Welshman called Morgan Williams[8] who came from a prosperous family who had settled in Putney. His brother John was a lawyer, accountant and steward to the local landowner, Lord Scales. Their son, Richard, was to legally change his name to Cromwell and work for his uncle, mainly in the suppression of the monastic houses in the 1530s, as well as becoming an unlikely soldier, chasing rebels in the North of England. Elizabeth married a sheep-farmer, William Wellifed, who folded his business into his father-in-law's. Their son Christopher was later financially supported by his famous uncle and educated alongside his own son Gregory.

Thomas did not get on with his father and, as he later admitted to Thomas Cranmer, Archbishop of Canterbury, had behaved like 'a ruffian . . . in his early days'.[9] Like father, like son. Eustace Chapuys, the gossipy Spanish ambassador, claimed in 1535 that in his youth Cromwell was 'ill-behaved and after an imprisonment was forced to leave the country'.[10] Whether it was this spell in jail or yet another quarrel with his malicious father that forced him to depart England's shores some time around 1502 is uncertain, but he certainly visited Flanders, Rome and elsewhere in Italy during his early travels.

There are several stories about Cromwell's wanderings around Europe, some probably apocryphal. The contemporary Italian author Matteo Bandello[11] recounts in his *Novelles* how Cromwell, now aged around eighteen, 'fleeing his father', joined the French army under Charles, Eighth Duc de Bourbon, to fight the Spanish as a mercenary foot soldier.

He had picked the wrong side.

A French advance in central Italy was halted at the Garigliano River, near Cassino, and on 28 December 1503 superior Spanish forces, commanded by Gonzalo Fernandez Cordoba, bridged the river upstream and surprised their enemies, miserably encamped on the marshy land on its west bank. In the ensuing battle the French troops were routed, losing their artillery, and the survivors (including Cromwell), now half-naked and starving, fell back to Rome.[12] In one daring stroke, the Spanish had captured control of southern Italy.

Cromwell eventually found his way to Florence and, still destitute, shrewdly sought help from the Anglophile merchant banker Francisco Frescobaldi, who kindly provided him with shelter and new clothes. After six months spent in his household as a clerk, Cromwell was generously given sixteen gold ducats, worth nearly £11,000 at 2006 prices, and a strong horse for his further adventures. Other versions of his early life maintain that he then worked as an accountant for a Venetian banker and as a merchant for a short period.[13] He was now fluent in Italian and French, well versed in Latin, and possessed a smattering of Greek.

He ended up in Antwerp sometime before 1512, working as a secretary or clerk for the English merchants based there, who sold their goods in the Flemish markets of Ghent and Bruges. Amongst some of these religiously nonconformist traders, he may have acquired ideas for the church reforms he put into practice in later life. He also moonlighted as a cloth merchant: in June 1536, George Eliot, an English mercer in Calais, recalled that he had experienced Cromwell's 'love and true heart' – friendship, that is – ever since they both attended the Syngsson Mart at the port of Middleburgh, 113 miles (182 km) south-west of Amsterdam in 1512.[14] He reportedly saved the life of Sir John Russell, later Earl of Bedford and Comptroller of the Royal Household, by rescuing him from French forces during the siege of Bologna the same year. He returned to Rome to pursue his commercial interests early in 1514 and the archives of the English Hospital record his stay there that June.

Cromwell then returned to London and by 1516 had married Elizabeth, daughter of Henry Wykes, another shearman, or cloth-worker, of Putney.[15] His brother had served as a gentleman usher to Henry VII. Elizabeth was the well-off young widow of Thomas Williams, a Yeoman of the Guard, and the couple settled in the eastern part of the City of London in a house in Fenchurch Street, with Cromwell becoming an agent, or 'fixer', for businessmen, as well as dealing in cloth himself, with a number of servants working for him.

He was now building up a useful network of contacts, and one of them, John Robinson, an alderman of the prosperous port of Boston, Lincolnshire, commissioned him in 1517–18 to travel to Rome to seek two indulgences from Pope Leo X[16] to relax the Lenten observances required by the Guild of Our Lady attached to St Botolph's Church, today still a towering landmark in the town.[17] Together with Geoffrey Chambers – ironically later to become one of the visitors charged with the task of destroying religious images – Cromwell travelled to Italy again, wearily prepared for the inevitable lengthy wait before being honoured by an audience with the pontiff.

Cromwell was ever the man of action. Unwilling to wrestle with Vatican bureaucracy, he tracked Pope Leo down on one of his hunting trips outside Rome. John Foxe, the Protestant polemicist, later described the meeting:

> At length, having knowledge that the Pope's holy tooth greatly delighted to new-fangled strange delicacies and dainty dishes, it came in [Cromwell's] mind to prepare certain fine dishes of jelly, after the best fashion, after our country manner here in England which to them of Rome was not known nor seen before.
>
> That done, Cromwell observing his time accordingly, as the Pope was newly come from hunting into his pavilion, he with his companion, approached with his presents brought in with a three man song (as we call it) in the English tongue and after the English fashion.[18]
>
> The Pope, suddenly marvelling at the strangeness of the song . . . asked them to be called in. Cromwell there showing his obedience and showing his jolly junkets, such as kings and princes only, he said in the realm of England, used to feed upon, desired to be accepted in benevolent part.[19]

The way to a pope's heart was clearly through his stomach. A convenient (and presumably expendable) cardinal tasted the strangers' sweetmeats and pronounced them not only safe to eat but entirely delectable. The Pope then consumed the delicacies and, enchanted by their flavour, ordered the indulgences to be approved by his personal signet stamp without further ado. On the tediously long journey back to England, a triumphant Cromwell is said to have learnt by heart the entire text of the Dutch humanist Desiderius Erasmus's Greek–Latin translation of the New Testament, first published in 1516.[20]

Back in London, Cromwell extended his business interests into money-lending at exorbitant rates and the law, and soon built up a client base amongst the rich and famous as both an open-handed creditor and a shrewd and perspicacious advocate.

In October 1520, Nicholas Cowper, Vicar of Cheshunt in Hertford-shire, sued Margaret Chawry, prioress of the neighbouring Benedictine nunnery, in a disagreement over tithes on a farm leased from her twelve years before. After hearings in the Consistory Court of Bishop of London Richard FitzJames, Cowper appealed to Rome,[21] and this brought the powerful Cardinal Thomas Wolsey, papal legate and Lord Chancellor of England, into the case. Wolsey requested that Cromwell assist in his judgment on the complex rights and wrongs of the dispute and the documents contain his precise annotations. It was the first time that they had dealings with each other, and it was the start of a fruitful relationship for the son of the Putney blacksmith and shearman.

In 1521, Cromwell acted for Charles Knyvett, who had the misfortune to resign as surveyor to Edward Stafford, Third Duke of Buckingham, just before he was executed by Henry for treason on 17 May that year. Knyvett now sought to recover the offices he had lost and forgiveness of £3,100 of debt he had been forced to incur on his master's behalf. Cromwell's carefully drawn up petitions pressing Knyvett's suit were dispatched both to the King and to Wolsey.[22] Unfortunately the plea was rejected, but Cromwell's name and the quality of his work had become known in government.[23]

The death of Buckingham also created other opportunities for Cromwell to exploit. He plainly snapped up some of the attainted noble's possessions, as eleven years later, in 1532, Robert ap Reynolds of Calais claimed with 'naughty words' that these had been bought from him, but that Cromwell still owed him 47 angels (or £17 13s.) for the goods. As the lawyer had by then risen in the world, Reynolds believed he now possessed ample wherewithal to pay him – with generous outstanding interest. Otherwise, he hinted darkly, he would have to reveal some unpleasant truths about him to the King and the Duke of Norfolk.[24] Blackmail was a tactic Cromwell understood very well and used frequently himself, but history is silent on the result of Reynolds's threat. He probably discovered, to his cost, that Cromwell was not a man to cross lightly.

By September 1522, Cromwell was prosperous enough to move house to larger premises 'against the gates' of the Priory of Austin Friars in Broad Street.[25] He was quickly elected secretary of the local ward committee that reported to its alderman on the workings of local government in the area.

Precisely how and when Cromwell first met Cardinal Wolsey face to face remains a matter for conjecture. It may be that Lord Henry Percy, a former member of the Cardinal's household who had borrowed substantial sums from Cromwell, was the conduit in arranging such a meeting.[26] Alternatively, the introduction could have come via Thomas Grey, Second Marquis of Dorset, who seems to have used Cromwell's legal expertise, or his continuing interests in the cloth trade,[27] and, moreover, employed Richard Williams, Cromwell's nephew, as one of his servants.[28] A third means may have been an introduction from the Italian merchant Antonio Bonvisi of Lucca, whose circle of affluent customers included Wolsey. Finally, there was Robert Cromwell, vicar of Battersea and overseer of the Cardinal's building works there,[29] who was a cousin to Thomas Cromwell, and it is entirely plausible that family affiliations could have been exploited.

The meeting probably occurred some time in late 1522 and, doubtless through Wolsey's influence, Cromwell was returned to Parliament the following year for an unidentified constituency, although Bath looks the most probable seat.[30] A draft of a speech by Cromwell – it is uncertain that he ever made it – contains an attack on proposals to invade France as logistically too dangerous, although it is hedged around with the prudent caveat that Cromwell was, of course, as committed as anyone to reclaiming the lost lands in France for the King. Loyally, he also harboured terrible fears about Henry's safety in leading the English host overseas:

> Only one thing . . . puts me in no small agony. I thought I heard my Lord Cardinal's grace say that our most gracious sovereign, more dear to any of his subjects . . . intends to go over [to France] in his royal person . . . Which thing I pray God for my part I never live to see. Most humbly beseeching his abundant and tender benignity of mercy and pardon of this my saying, for the humble and obedient love I owe unto his noble person,

causes me in this case to forget obeisance . . . I cannot consent to obey . . . this his pleasure, wherein lies the hazarding of this, his noble realm, and upon the which might follow (which God defend) the greatest calamity and affliction.[31]

Humble, obsequious Cromwell! To modern eyes, his words look uncomfortably fawning and cringing. But why shouldn't they have been? He knew his words would be read by Henry and that the King, whose household suffered under his uncertain temper, was always quick to take offence. Hence his flattering fears that his sovereign could fall sick or victim to the 'thousand dangers which chance in war'. Instead, he suggested, why not invade France's staunch ally Scotland and unite that kingdom with England, rather than wage war overseas, with inevitably vulnerable supply lines stretching across the English Channel? His sharp merchant's mind clearly saw less risk and more profit in this enterprise.

Cromwell's opposition both to the invasion of France and the cost of the war may appear strange for an ambitious man anxious to climb the ladder to fortune. But he may have been a player in a bigger, more devious plan either simply to halt approval of a new tax to pay for the war, or to lance the boil of opposition to the conflict within Parliament. Was he speaking as a surrogate voice, advocating Wolsey's personal opposition to Henry's foreign policy without risk to the Cardinal himself?

Parliamentary life did not appeal to Cromwell, which is surprising given his later skill at manipulating both Houses. He wrote a cynical, sneering letter on 27 August 1523 to an old friend, the merchant tailor John Creke, then staying in Bilbao in northern Spain, in which he passed on news of the debates within the Commons. He clearly viewed the fruitless proceedings with utter contempt:

> You shall understand that by long time I have endured a parliament which continued . . . the space of seventeen weeks,[32] where we communed [talked] of war, peace, strife, contention, debate, murmur, grudge, riches, poverty, penury, truth, falsehood, justice, equity, deceit, oppression, magnanimity, activity, force, moderation, treason, murder, felony, conciliation.

Also how a commonwealth might be edified and also contained within our realm.

Howbeit, in conclusion, we have done as our predecessors have been wont to do – that is to say, as well we might and left where we began.[33]

Cromwell added ruefully that Parliament had granted the King 'a right large subsidy [tax] the like of which was never granted in this realm'. It probably amounted to £800,000 for the royal exchequer, or £319 million at today's prices, to fund an invasion of France.

In 1524, Cromwell was appointed a subsidy commissioner to the Hundred of Ossulton, in Middlesex, a post that involved assessing the values of land and goods for taxation, and in the same year, his legal acumen was recognised by his election as a member of Gray's Inn. That February, he acted for the London alderman and mercer John Allen, who sold the manor of Kexby, 5 miles (8 km) east of York, to Wolsey. The lawyer's skills in conveyancing property were appreciated and he entered formal service with the Cardinal[34] some time later that summer. Within a year, he had become indispensable and was addressed as 'Councillor to my Lord Legate' and 'The Right Worshipful Mr Cromwell'. He had finally slipped into the shadows behind the seat of power.

There were similarities between the two men, although more than a decade separated them in age. Both came from modest roots: Wolsey was the son of a reasonably prosperous butcher in Ipswich. Both were ambitious and rapacious. Wolsey, however, had been educated at Magdalen College, Oxford, was made a Bachelor of Arts at the age of fifteen and was nicknamed the 'Boy Bachelor'. Cromwell, as we have seen, learnt his lessons in the University of Life with no formal schooling. He had received the toughest education of all: experience had taught him the mistakes to be avoided and the lessons to be applied later.

For his part, Henry, always apprehensive of the power of his turbulent and ambitious nobility and bored with the day-to-day business of running his realm, deliberately appointed commoners to the highest administrative posts in the land. Wolsey and Cromwell had no allegiance to any aristocratic power bloc and therefore appeared expendable without causing disruption to the delicate political balance between England's noble families. The King's Tudor low cunning ensured that, ostensibly at least, their loyalty would be to the sovereign who had created them and daily provided them with the enviable trappings of authority. But, inevitably, their influence and enrichment caused festering resentment amongst the nobility, who saw them as coarse, low-born usurpers of the power that, by rights, ought to have belonged to them. That snobbish animosity and hatred was to bring both ministers down.

Cromwell kept on his burgeoning legal practice, much of the business emanating from the English-held town of Calais on the north-west coast of France.[35] A number of illustrious England-based clients also came Cromwell's way, including the head of an increasingly influential clan, Thomas Boleyn, Viscount Rochford. His sister, the wife of Sir Robert Clere, retained Cromwell in 1527 in a dispute with Lady Feneux, the widow of a former Chief Justice of the King's Bench, over outstanding debts of £400. Cromwell told Boleyn that there was no remedy remaining in common law

> unless your lordship will move my lord's grace [Wolsey] to grant an . . .
> injunction to Lady Feneux [to] no further prosecute the [writ] of execution
> [repayment] and to allow no writ of *liberate*[36] to go out of Chancery until the
> whole matter be heard[37] . . . Your lordship thus doing, shall do the thing in
> my poor opinion which shall stand with reason and good conscience as
> knows the Holy Trinity, whom I most heartily beseech to preserve your
> lordship in long life, good health and much honour.

Rochford was, of course, the father of Anne Boleyn, and a few years later, Cromwell's final words to him were to take on a terribly hollow ring.[38]

Cromwell also developed his business as a money-lender, apparently specializing in loans to the gentry, merchants or those associated with the court. Thus, on 10 July 1527 a £100 mortgage was granted to Sir John Hussey, with 'certain parcels of plate' handed over as collateral.[39] That September, John Smith sought Cromwell's forbearance for 'a little while' in paying off his loan. He admitted he had been 'bolder' with him 'than with any friend and will [work] to deserve it' and sounded as if he was struggling financially. He thanked 'God for the fat oxen in the stall' but admitted he could have made more of his corn had he sold the crop at the beginning of the year.[40] Much later, in 1535, Cromwell wrote to his friend Thomas Allen at Rayleigh in Essex requesting the return of the £100 he had lent him:

> I looked to have heard from you and trusted not only to have . . . received from you now at Midsummer last past my £100, which of gentleness I lent you, but also sufficient bonds and surety for your brother the Archbishop of Dublin concerning the payment of 700 marks [£470] which he owes to the king's highness . . . For lack and default thereof, you have forfeited to the king's highness the sum of 1,000 marks [£670], which I think you ought to substantially look upon, for the king is no person to be deluded or mocked withal.
>
> Considering that for your sake, I so gently parted with my money, it seems to me that reason and good honesty requires [that] you should see me paid again.
>
> Praying that I may be advertised [informed] by this bearer what you mean and intend to do in the promises . . . And so heartily fare you well.
>
> THOMAS CROMWELL[41]

Friendship could only mean so much: business, after all, was business.

Whilst still active in his own right as a lawyer and money-lender, Cromwell's work for the Cardinal as a legal adviser and councillor revealed to him a new, undreamt-of world of riches. Wolsey's opulent lifestyle, wealth and love of pomp must have astonished Cromwell.

The Cardinal's household numbered nearly 500 members, including 'the tallest and [most] comely yeomen that he could get in all this realm'. George Cavendish, Wolsey's gentleman usher, relates that the Cardinal had three dining tables daily in his hall, presided over by three principal officers: a steward (always a dean or a priest) a treasurer (a knight) and a comptroller, who all carried white staves as badges of office. His kitchen staff was legion and included two clerks, a surveyor of the dresser, a clerk of the spicery, a yeoman of the scullery and three yeomen and two grooms of the cellar. There were also forty cup-bearers, carvers, waiters and sewers – who tasted Wolsey's food in case of poison. His two master cooks wore damask satin or velvet, with gold chains around their necks. Clearly someone else did the dirty work in the kitchen. Then there were the officers of his privy chamber and the fifty-four staff attached to his personal chapel: the private masses regularly included forty priests dressed in very rich copes, or Eucharistic vestments, accompanied by Wolsey's own choir of twelve boys and sixteen men. The Cardinal blatantly copied the uniforms of Henry's royal bodyguard, the Yeomen of the Guard, for those of his personal servants, who wore tunics of crimson velvet with the letters 'TC' – for *Thomas Cardinalis* – embroidered in gold, back and front.[42]

Cavendish describes Wolsey's daily procession to Westminster Hall from his palace at York Place to hear legal cases in the Chancery Court:

After mass he would return to his privy chamber . . . and would issue out, apparelled all in red, in the habit of a cardinal, which was either of fine scarlet or else of crimson satin, taffeta or caffa,[43] the best he could get for money. Upon his head, a round pillion;[44] he also had a tippet [cape] of fine sable around his neck, holding in his hand a very fair orange, [with] the . . . substance within taken out, wherein was vinegar and other confections against the pestilent airs, the which he most commonly smelt unto, passing among the press [of people] or . . . when he was pestered with suitors.

His procession formed up, led by a page bearing the Great Seal of England and another his cardinal's hat, and these were followed by tall priests carrying two large silver crosses, one symbolising his role as Archbishop of York and the other, a double cross like that of Lorraine, his position as papal legate, and two pillars of heavy silver. Then came his personal herald or pursuivant of arms, carrying a 'great mace of silver gilt'. Wolsey himself was humbly mounted on a mule, but this was richly trapped out in crimson velvet with gilt stirrups, and he was surrounded by his own foot guards, armed with gilded poleaxes.[45] His gentlemen ushers continually cried out: 'On, my lords and masters, on before – make way for my Lord's grace. Make way for his grace, the Cardinal Legate of York, Lord High Chancellor of this realm.' Quite a mouthful for those trying to clear a path through the great unwashed for their master.

He was indeed a prince of the Church – 'the proudest prelate that ever lived' – and the richest man in England after the King himself. Wolsey pillaged the goods of every bishopric he took over and even managed to extract financial profit from the treaties he negotiated. As Lord Chancellor, he received a commission for every favour conferred and levied a shilling in the pound on the value of all the wills proved by his administrators.[46] His annual income before he fell from power in 1529 is estimated at an incredible £50,000, or £17,500,000 in 2006 monetary values.

Here was a role model and mentor whom Cromwell, in all his grasping venality, could surely look up to.

Cromwell by this time was preoccupied with a rather vain pet scheme of Wolsey's: to build and endow two new secular colleges, one in Oxford and a second in his birthplace Ipswich, both to be called Cardinal's College. To provide the cash to fund these projects, Wolsey cast around for financial resources to avoid dipping into his own well-filled purse. He hit upon the alien and minor monasteries[47] and quickly obtained a papal dispensation from Pope Clement VII to suppress those said to be in decay. There were handy precedents for such dissolutions: Bishop Waynflete of Winchester had acquired two priories to support Magdalen College, Oxford, in the second half of the fifteenth century, and, as recently as 1524, Bishop Fisher of Rochester had seized two religious houses for the benefit of St John's College, Cambridge. Now Wolsey claimed that these small monasteries were ripe for suppression, as 'neither God was served, nor religion kept' within their crumbling walls.

On 4 January 1525, Cromwell and Sir William Gascoigne were instructed to investigate five monasteries and their wealth to establish their value.[48] Their commission named the first casualties amongst the minor religious houses – at Tickford,[49] Ravenstone and Medmenham in north Buckinghamshire, Poughley in Berkshire and Wallingford in Oxfordshire. The same day, Cromwell and John Smythe were appointed attorneys for Thoby, Stanesgate and Tiptree, all in Essex, which had already been granted to John Higden, the new dean of Cardinal's College, Oxford.

Eventually, twenty-nine religious houses were to be suppressed on Wolsey's orders; a total of around eighty monks, canons and nuns were all evicted without ceremony. The dissolutions yielded a net income of approximately £2,000, or nearly £700,000 at present-day prices, to fund the Oxford college alone.[50]

The prime agent in this plunder was Cromwell, who had fully demonstrated his skills at conveyancing properties and his remarkable attention to detail. He had to survey and value each monastic property, list its possessions and put them up for sale, then arrange for the disposal or lease of its lands. He was normally present at the surrender of each religious house. Moreover, he acted as a progress-chaser in the construction of the two colleges.

Of course, there were always opportunities for making money on the side for Cromwell and another of Wolsey's agents, Dr John Allen.[51] Some religious houses offered generous bribes to be spared from the indignity and inconvenience of suppression. Properties could also be rented out at a higher price than officially agreed, and the difference pocketed. Some of their choice goods and chattels could be appropriated and sold off for private profit. It is not surprising that Cromwell abandoned his cloth-trading business around this time: there were easier pickings and more lucrative methods of accumulating wealth.

Such under-the-table deals were not unusual in Tudor times, but the scale of the corruption caused ripples of disquiet, if not disgust. Sir William Knight, secretary to the King, wrote to Wolsey from Beaulieu in Essex in August 1527 to warn him that Henry shared that uneasiness: 'I have heard the king and noble men speak things incredible of the acts of Mr Allen and Cromwell – a great part whereof it shall be expedient that your grace do know, as at your coming, you shall, not only from me but by other faithful and loving servants.'[52] The constant temptation must have been irresistible, but Wolsey appears to have done nothing to stop the sleaze. He may have believed that the attacks on his servants were merely a weapon to discredit the suppressions; in any case, he was more than satisfied with the progress on his two colleges.

Cromwell was constantly beset by those wanting to cash in on the dissolutions. For example, Thomas Canner wrote to him on 14 January

1528, seeking the bells of Wallingford monastery for the people of Basingstoke in Hampshire, where he had been brought up. He enclosed a set of 'Oxford gloves' as a token for Cromwell's pains.[53]

The other side of this corrupt coin, of course, was that Cromwell became unpopular. The local gentry at Bayham, on the borders of East Sussex and Kent, assembled in disguise and temporarily forced the reinstatement of the ten Premonstratensian canons there. At nearby Tonbridge, the townsfolk petitioned against the closure of the Augustinian priory there, rejecting soothing promises of scholarships at the Oxford college. The new landlords of the monastic properties were more interested in profit and the tenants found themselves living under a harsher, more demanding regime. In August 1527, a 'sanctuary man'[54] was reported to be lying in wait to murder Cromwell, and Cardinal Pole later maintained that people thought Cromwell was in prison and would be punished for his crimes as Wolsey's agent.[55] Security precautions were needed and Cromwell fitted a strong chain to the front door of his home at Austin Friars so that 'no man not well known might enter'.

Undeterred, he continued with his duties – long hours in the saddle in all weathers, listing, verifying, evaluating. He wrote to Wolsey on 2 April 1528 from Oxford about his visit to Wallingford, reporting that all the goods and household implements had already been spirited away. More sanguinely, Cromwell described the progress in constructing Cardinal's College in the university town:

> The buildings of your college most prosperously and magnificently arise in such a way, that to every man's judgment, the like thereof [has] never been seen nor imagined, having consideration to the largeness, beauty, sumptuousness . . . and most substantial building of the same.
>
> Your chapel within the said college [is] most devoutly and virtuously ordered and the ministries within the same not only diligent in the service of God, but also the service done daily within the same, so devout, solemn and full of harmony that in my opinion, it has few peers.[56]

Cromwell regularly submitted his bureaucratic expenses for his work in setting up the new colleges. One claim, in April 1528, for his work in Ipswich included 56 shillings for vellum 'for drawing and flourishing letters . . . for the king's patents as [well] as my lord's deeds and charters; two dozen parchments which cost six shillings and one ream of paper, three shillings'. His personal expenses then amounted to a total of £11 19s. 8d, including 'my costs at Hampton Court and for my horses at diverse times in the sweating season'.[57] In June, Cromwell wrote to Thomas Arundell, one of the gentlemen of Wolsey's privy chamber, enquiring about the proposed constitution of Ipswich College and warning that it could not be formally established until legal matters had been cleared up in the Chancery Court: 'I trust, by the assistance of my lord the chief baron [of the exchequer, a judge], unto whom I will resort from time to time for his good counsel, to perform, fulfil and accomplish everything according to [Wolsey's] gracious pleasure in such ways as he should therewith be right well contented.'[58]

At last, William Capon, the first Dean of Cardinal's College, Ipswich, was appointed and, on 26 September 1528, he reported to Wolsey the arrival of the ecclesiastical vestments and plate, brought there by Cromwell, who was 'at great pains seeing [the] stuff carried hither safely and in preparing the hangings, benches etc. for the hall, which is now well trimmed'. Although building work was continuing, evensong was said in the college chapel, piously attended by Cromwell. The next day 'it rained continually', so the planned grand procession through the town had to be cancelled.[59]

On 18 January 1529, Cromwell wrote to Stephen Gardiner, Wolsey's secretary but later an arch-enemy, explaining his absence from the Cardinal's household, then at Richmond, as he was busy selling off Lesnes Abbey, at Bexley in Kent,

> where I saw one of the most piteous and grievous sights that ever I saw . . . the breach out of the Thames into the marshes at Lesnes which be all overflowed and drowned. At the last change, the tide was so high that there happened a new breach which has done as much [damage] there as will cost £300 the new making of the same.
>
> In so much that if my being there had not been to have encouraged the workmen and labourers, I assure you all the labour and money that has been spent heretofore, would have been clearly lost and cast away. And the

workmen . . . would have departed and left all at chance which should have been the greatest evil that ever happened to the country there.

Cromwell immediately took charge and 'with the advice of such wise men' directed the repairs to the sea defences. 'I trust all shall be well and the works there ended with good speed, God willing.'[60]

In addition to his work on setting up the colleges, as Wolsey's secretary Cromwell now exercised patronage on the Cardinal's behalf over ecclesiastical and official appointments. There was profit in this also. On 25 April 1528, Richard Bellyssis, master of Wolsey's mint at Durham, wrote to Cromwell, seeking his help in appointing him to a vacant post there: 'He had charge of the mint in his father's life and is very expert in fining, trying and coining. There is no-one else in the country fit for the post.' And if the appointment was made, Cromwell would have 'the promised gelding'.[61]

Cromwell was also keen to have loyal men around him in whom he could place absolute trust. He had recruited Ralph Sadler[62] to help him with the construction of the cardinal's colleges, and now wrote to Wolsey introducing Sadler and hoping he would be appointed to some post within the cardinal's household: 'I assure your grace, you are much bound to the gentleman, this bearer, for his good report in every place . . . He and such other[s] have done your grace much good. It shall be in my opinion therefore, right well done to give him thanks accordingly, for by my faith, he is right worthy.'[63] Sadler became Cromwell's clerk, and so began a distinguished career in government service.

But a family tragedy now intruded on Cromwell's busy life, diligently spent hunting the crock of gold at the end of Wolsey's rainbow.

Some time before 1529 his wife Elizabeth died, possibly from the fatal infectious fever called 'the sweating sickness' that swept England in 1528.[64] She had borne him two girls, Anne and 'little Grace', who both died young, possibly during the same epidemic, and a son, Gregory. He may also have had an illegitimate daughter.[65]

Gregory's education, at Pembroke Hall, Cambridge, was a topic that constantly troubled his father, who was determined to provide the boy with the formal learning that had been denied him. He may also have nurtured ambitious dreams of marrying his son into a noble family, seeing him as another pawn in his driving mission to climb the social ladder. Gregory's tutor, John Checking, frequently wrote to Cromwell with pleas for money. In May 1528, he sought compensation for 'his pains, which he did not intend to seek until the whole year commenced at mid-summer'[66] and on 28 June that year, he complained of being in debt 'and pressed for money'. He insisted: 'There is not a penny in the account but was not spent on your scholars.'

The following month a progress report was written on Gregory, who was in the country, 'where he works and plays alternatively. He is rather slow, but diligent.' His previous tutor Palgrave had taught him badly, with the pupil 'hardly [able] to conjugate three [Latin] verbs . . . though he repeated the rules by rote'. Checking would 'have to unteach him nearly all he has learned. He is now studying the things most conducive to the reading of authors, and spends the rest of the day in forming letters.'[67]

In October, the tutor begged Cromwell to send 'five yards of marble frieze[68] for a gabardine' for Gregory, 'to keep him from the cold this winter', and nine yards for his cousin Christopher Wellifed, who was studying with him; 'also a bed and a pair of sheets'. Checking wrote of 'various reports spread' in Cambridge about Cromwell, which he was glad had proved false – presumably rumours of his imprisonment – and ended with another plea for cash: 'The plague which sent us into the country has nearly consumed our money.'[69] With colder weather in November, the scholars had cloaks to warm them and also 'a blazing fire to keep them comfortable. Little Gregory is becoming great in letters. Christopher does not require much stirring up.'[70] Then came a near disaster: Christopher Wellifed 'did hinge a candle in a plate to look upon his book and so fell asleep and the candle fell into the bed straw' and burnt the bed, pillow and three overlays or blankets. Had not the chamber been 'ceiled and pargetted with plaster, we [might] have had more harm', reported Checking, claiming 40 shillings compensation.

In July 1529, Cromwell was clearly complaining about his son's lack of progress at his lessons and taunted Checking about his teaching skills. The tutor was incensed and protested that he had brought up many scholars, including six Masters of Arts and fellows of colleges. 'I could have seven scholars for the one that I have at present, if I could be troubled by them.'[71] Amid all this talk of education, Checking did not hesitate to seek Cromwell's good offices in support of a relative 'with my lord Cardinal' and promised him 'an ambling nag if successful'.[72]

The loss of Cromwell's wife and daughters may have prompted a sobering realisation of his own mortality, for on 12 July 1529 he signed his last will and testament,[73] describing himself proudly as 'Thomas Cromwell of London, gentleman'. He left his son £660 13s. 4d – increased from £400 in the first draft – together with a similar sum for the purchase of property in London for Gregory to live in. Rental income from tenements should be used for his education until he reached the age of twenty-two, 'during which time I heartily desire and require my said executors to be good to my said son and to see he lose no time but to see him virtuously ordered and brought up according to my trust'.

Cromwell may have harboured fears that he had sired a spendthrift and wastrel, and made provision accordingly. A further share of the Cromwell estate was to be trickled down to him: another £200 'of lawful English money' was to be paid to him at twenty-four. Amongst the bequests of household stuff to Gregory, the plate and other valuable items were to be 'put in safe keeping' until his twenty-second birthday. If he died before reaching this age, the goods and chattels were to be sold and the proceeds divided 'amongst my poor kinsfolk; that is to say amongst the children as well of my own sisters Elizabeth and Katherine, as of my late wife's sister Joan, wife to John Williamson'.

His servants were not forgotten for their loyal service. Ralph Sadler was to receive 200 marks, together with 'my second [best] gown, doublet and all my books'. Stephen Vaughan, 'sometime my servant', was bequeathed 100 marks and another gown, jacket and doublet. Cromwell added, in his own hand, bequests to other servants: William Brabazon, John Avery, Thurston 'my cook', William Body, Peter Mewtes, Richard Swift, George Wilkinson and John Hind, 'my horse-keeper'.

Piously, he instructed his executors to 'hire a priest, being a person of continent and good living to sing for my soul by the space of eight years next after my death and to give him for the same, £46 13s. 4d, that is to say, £6 13s. 4d yearly for his stipend'. He gave £1 to every order of friars within the City of London in payment for them praying for his soul. Being a generous soul, Cromwell also bequeathed £40 to be given to penniless maidens on their marriages, and £20 to be distributed to poor householders so they, too, could pray for his soul. Finally, he gave £10 to the prisoners of Newgate, Ludgate, the King's Bench Jail and the Marshalsea, across the river in Southwark.[74]

During his loyal service to Henry VIII, he was to fill some of those prisons with his own victims.

CHAPTER TWO

'Make or mar'

I am a £1,000 worse [off] than I was when your troubles began.

THOMAS CROMWELL TO CARDINAL WOLSEY FOLLOWING HIS DOWNFALL, 1530[1]

The blow may have been expected by some, but nonetheless, when it struck, the shock and awe were felt across all England. Cardinal Thomas Wolsey, prince of the Church, European statesman and Henry VIII's Lord Chancellor, had fallen from power.

His nemesis was Anne Boleyn, whom he described privately as the King's own 'night crow'.[2] The olive-skinned, dark-haired daughter of Sir Thomas Boleyn had been a maid of honour to Henry's queen, Catherine of Aragon, who was unlikely now ever to produce his longed-for legal son and heir. In the spring of 1526, the King, having drunk deeply of the sexual favours provided by Anne's elder sister Mary, fell desperately, ardently in love with the headstrong, determined Anne.

Egged on by an ever-ambitious paramour, Henry was soon obsessed and overwhelmed by his desire for her to be his queen. He had realised, with sudden, fearful insight, that his lack of healthy living sons was God's own terrible verdict on his existing aberrant marriage, as Catherine had briefly been wed to his fifteen-year-old elder brother Arthur before his death, probably from tuberculosis, in April 1502. To Henry, the holy teachings of the Bible – Leviticus, 20:21 – were as plain as a pikestaff: 'And if a man shall take his brother's wife, it is an unclean thing: he hath uncovered his brother's nakedness; they shall be childless.' So, as far as the King was concerned, for seventeen years he had been living in mortal sin with his dead brother's wife. Catherine vehemently denied that her first marriage was ever consummated and maintained defiantly that she had wed Henry as 'a virgin and an immaculate woman'.

Some claimed it was Wolsey who first put the idea of a flawed marriage into Henry's mind, in 1527. The contemporary historian Polydore Vergil reported:

> At a convenient moment, he [Wolsey] approached the king and with an appearance of affection and love of righteousness, warned him of the legal standing of such a marriage . . . It had no force or vigour because of the marriage Catherine had made with his brother and he urgently besought him no longer to live in such peril, since upon it directly depended the salvation of his soul, the legitimacy of the royal issue, the decency of his life.[3]

What Catholic king, particularly one granted the title *Fidei Defensor* – Defender of the Faith – by Pope Leo X in 1521, could resist such compelling arguments expressed by a papal legate? But in offering up this cunning theological argument, the Cardinal had unwittingly sown the poisoned seeds of his own destruction.

His idea was potentially arguable, but obtaining an annulment from Pope Clement VII was more problematical, though some had previously been granted to European royalty on even less certain grounds. After much diplomatic huffing and puffing with the Vatican, a legatine court, presided over by Wolsey and the gout-afflicted Cardinal Lorenzo Campeggio, sat in judgment on the 'King's Great Matter': the validity of his marriage to Catherine under canon law. During a series of dramatic hearings beginning in May 1529, in the great hall of the Dominican monastery at Blackfriars in London, the cardinals heard testimony from both the King and Queen and a host of learned and pious witnesses. Henry's lawyers produced reams of evidence with prurient panache. One told the court that if Arthur, Prince of Wales, had 'carnal conversation' with Catherine, the marriage with the King could not possibly be valid under God's law: 'I have here these two gentlemen of great credit who will swear that one morning the Prince came out of his chamber, saying, "Gentlemen, I come out glad this morning for I have been during the night six miles into Spain." '[4] Arthur was plainly a boastful youth, well endowed with Tudor sauce and swagger perhaps, though his words were unlikely truthfully to describe his manly attributes. But it was all to no avail. Catherine, all Spanish eloquence and piety, appealed to a higher jurisdiction and the case, still undecided, was referred to Rome. Campeggio pronounced on 23 July, the last day of the tribunal, that the delicate issue could only be settled after full consultation with the Curia in Rome. Vatican bureaucracy was famed for its procrastination and they were already away from their desks, enjoying a leisurely and protracted holiday from the Roman summer heat.

Henry watched the proceedings from the gallery above and stalked away, his face black with anger at Wolsey's failure to procure the desired verdict. The King's old friend and jousting partner Charles Brandon, First Duke of Suffolk, was also enraged. He hammered his fist on a table and cried out: 'By the Mass, now I see that the old saying is true: it was never merry in England while we had cardinals amongst us!'

Threatening storm clouds were still gathering around Wolsey's head in early autumn as Anne Boleyn mercilessly taunted Henry about his prospects of ever marrying her. The Cardinal's enemies exploited the King's keen sense of betrayal, impatience and disappointment with his Chief Minister.

On 9 October 1529, the dam of retribution against Wolsey finally burst. Attorney General Sir Christopher Hales preferred a Bill of Indictment for Praemunire[5] against Wolsey in the Court of King's Bench in Westminster Hall. Eight days later, the Dukes of Norfolk and Suffolk gleefully arrived at York House, Wolsey's new London palace, to demand the surrender of the Great Seal of England and his resignation as Lord Chancellor. Wolsey was ordered to remove himself to his fifteenth-century red-brick palace of Esher, in Surrey,[6] while his fate was decided, and he departed by barge from York House, still smarting from 'the sharp sword of the king's displeasure [that] had so penetrated his heart'. Well he might: his lands, offices and possessions were now all forfeit to the crown. On 26 October, a reluctant Sir Thomas More was appointed

Lord Chancellor, understandably apprehensive of taking on any role in the ever-pressing matter of the King's divorce.

Suddenly, with Wolsey ousted from power, Cromwell's carefully constructed world crumbled about his ears. Any chance of fulfilling his ambitions disappeared like fleeting dreams on awakening.

When the great and good meet their downfall, their supporters are frequently destroyed with them. Now, with Wolsey's protective patronage abruptly gone, the loathing that had encircled Cromwell after the dissolution of the religious houses became yet more threatening. Stephen Vaughan, his faithful friend in Antwerp, wrote on 30 October cautioning him that he was more hated for his master's sake than for anything he had done wrongfully to anyone. Reassuringly, he did not doubt that Cromwell's wisdom would see him out of danger.[7] Sir Thomas Rush, another of the Cardinal's servants, talked darkly of the evil being spoken about Cromwell in Ipswich: 'You will be astounded at the lies told of you in these parts.'[8]

George Cavendish,[9] one of Wolsey's gentlemen ushers, discovered Cromwell alone in the great chamber at Esher on All-Saints Day, 1 November 1529. Cromwell was in the sunlit bay of a tall window, leaning miserably on the sill and holding a Latin primer in his hand. He was devoutly 'saying of Our Lady's matins, which had been a very strange sight in him before'. Tears trickled down his chubby cheeks as he gravely muttered and mumbled the versicles, the *Venite*, followed by three groups of psalms, three lessons, and finally ending with a *Te Deum*,[10] which must have sounded a little lacklustre under the circumstances. Cavendish was plainly astonished at the spectacle. He enquired: 'Why, Master Cromwell, what means all this, your sorrow? Is my lord in danger, for whom you lament thus? Or is it for any loss that you have sustained by any misadventure?'

Cromwell looked completely downcast. 'No, no, it is my unhappy adventure. I am likely to lose all that I have travailed[11] for all the days of my life, for doing of my master, true and diligent services.' His appeals to the Virgin Mary for assistance could not have provided him with much solace, for he shrugged off all Cavendish's attempts at reassurance and comfort: 'This I understand right well. I am in disdain with most men for my master's sake and surely without just cause. An ill name once gotten will not be lightly put away. I never had any promotion by my lord to the increase of my living.'

At this last outrageous canard, he suddenly seemed to make up his mind on his next course of action. His earnest plea for heavenly help was at once subsumed by a desire to fight destiny and personally confront his many enemies. Self-pity was hastily banished and replaced by steely resolve: 'This much I say to you. I intend, God willing, this afternoon, when my lord has dined, to ride to London and so to the court, where I will either make or mar, or I come again. I will put myself in the prease[12] to see what any man is able to lay to my charge of untruth or misdemeanour.'[13]

Cavendish could only wish him good luck and Godspeed.

Meanwhile, elsewhere in that rambling palace, Wolsey heard three masses, made his confession to Dr Marshall, his chaplain, and returned to his privy chamber for dinner. Cromwell sat squirming at the table during this unhappy, tense meal and, always practical, strongly advised the Cardinal to now discharge his gentlemen and yeomen from service with 'good words and thanks' to give them courage to 'sustain your mishap in patient misery'. Simple gratitude would be their only reward: the coffers were empty, so they could not be paid off. Wolsey despondently agreed and told him to summon his household together in the great chamber, with the gentlemen positioned on the right, and the yeomen on the left. This Cromwell did immediately.

Wolsey entered the silent room, wearing a modest white rochet (a long lace surplice) over a bishop's purple cassock. Distressed, he could not bring himself to speak right away and was quickly overwhelmed by bitter tears of abject misery. The great churchman turned his face to the wall, ashamed of his emotion amid the uncomfortable and embarrassed throng of his retainers. Eventually, he wiped his eyes with his handkerchief, took a deep breath and told them:

It has come to this pass, that it has pleased the king to take all that ever I had into his possession, so that I have nothing left me, but my bare clothes upon my back, which [are] simple in comparison to those you have seen me have.

31

I would not stick [hesitate] to divide them among you, yes, and the skin of my back, if it might countervail[14] any thing in value among you.

Wolsey put on a brave front and regained a little of his hopeless optimism that he would eventually return fully to Henry's grace and favour:

I doubt not but that the king, considering the offence suggested against me by my mortal enemies to be of small effect, will shortly restore me again to my living, so that I shall be able to divide some part thereof, yearly among you, whereof you shall be well assured . . . the surplus of my revenues, whatever remains at the determination of my accounts, shall be, God willing, distributed among you.

I will never, hereafter, esteem the goods and riches of this uncertain world but as a vain thing, more than sufficient for the maintenance of my estate and dignity that God has or shall call me unto in the world during my life.

Such piety and new-found unworldliness must have been downright anathema to the thoroughly materialistic Cromwell, standing quietly and thoughtfully by his disgraced master's side. He broke the silence by telling the Cardinal:

Sir, there are diverse of these your yeomen that would be glad to see their friends, but they lack money.

Here are . . . your chaplains who have received at your hands great benefices and high dignities.

Let them therefore show themselves unto you, as they are bound by all humanity to do.

I think their honesty and charity is not so slender and void of grace that they would not see you lack where they may help to refresh you.

His words doubtless stunned the chaplains crowded in the chamber. Cromwell hastened on: although he had 'not received of your grace's gift one penny towards the increase of my yearly living', he would now happily donate his own cash to assist those worse off than himself in the Cardinal's household. Whereupon he dipped into his purse, produced £5 in gold and handed it to Wolsey. 'Now let us see what your chaplains will do. I think they will part with [give] you much more than I have done, who be able to give you a pound [to] my one penny.'

'Go to, masters,' he urged the helplessly entrapped chaplains, who then reluctantly, resentfully donated enough money for Wolsey to pay three months' wages to his yeomen and provide them with the equivalent of one month's board in cash. It was the first time that Cromwell had publicly displayed any antagonism towards the clergy. Was this merely a little barbed joke – so he could watch them squirm in front of their fallen master? Or was it an early harbinger of his attacks on the Church and its doctrine in the years ahead?

After some lengthy discussions in secret with Wolsey, he mounted his horse and, accompanied by his faithful clerk Ralph Sadler, left for London. He told Cavendish: 'You shall hear shortly of me and if I speed well, I will not fail to be here again within these two days.'

The mission seemed to promise a slim hope that Wolsey's lost fortunes could somehow be restored. If Cavendish and his fellow livery-men in the household believed that, they did not know or understand Thomas Cromwell.

His actions and motivations when he reached London remain a matter of conjecture. More pragmatic than his dejected master, he recog-nised the reality that Wolsey was now irretrievably down and had been counted out. For his own sake, it was high time he distanced himself from the fallen Cardinal if he were to have any chance of realising his hard-nosed ambitions of achieving wealth and status in the madhouse of Tudor politics.

His options were all too limited in a royal court that, from the queen-in-waiting downwards, was now packed with Wolsey's enemies, watchful for rich pickings from his downfall. Those who possessed the precious gift of patronage would plainly regard Cromwell with deep suspicion as the Cardinal's own creature. Cromwell nimbly overcame these ap-parently unassailable obstacles and managed to procure himself a seat in Parliament just two days before a new House of Commons was due to be sworn in, even though few vacancies were still available. Like any adroit politician in a tight spot, he called in the favours owed him and ruthlessly exploited his friendships. On arrival in the capital, he immediately dis-patched Sadler to interview his friend Sir John Gage,[15] MP for Sussex, Vice-Chamberlain of the Household and, most significantly, an ally of Wolsey's arch-enemy, the conniving Thomas Howard, Third Duke of Norfolk. Sadler told Cromwell that night:

> I spoke with Mr Gage and, according to your commandment, moved him
> to speak to my lord of Norfolk for the burgess's room [member's seat] of
> the Parliament on your behalf. He accordingly did so without delay, like a
> faithful friend and . . . Norfolk [told] Mr Gage that he had spoken with the
> king . . . and that his highness was very well contented you should become
> a burgess, so that you would order yourself . . . according to such
> instructions as the said Duke of Norfolk shall give you from the king.[16]

Norfolk would be happy to speak to Cromwell the next day about arrang-ing his election, Sadler dutifully reported.

The clerk had been very industrious at court on his master's behalf. He had talked with his friend Sir Thomas Rush, whose stepson Thomas Alvard held a parliamentary seat at Taunton in Somerset and who might be prepared to stand down in favour of Cromwell. This was speedily agreed, with the help of Sir William Paulet, Master of Wards,[17] who, irony of ironies, promptly released the seat as one of the boroughs previously controlled by Wolsey, as Bishop of Winchester.[18]

Cromwell was thus surprisingly returned to Parliament, mainly through the influence of Norfolk, who must have received pledges of eternal loyalty from Cromwell in return for assistance in manipulating House of Commons proceedings to his order.

Those promises would turn out to be entirely hollow. In the turbu-lent years that followed, the ambitious Duke would surely rue the day he extended a helping hand to Cromwell at a time when the autocrat's political career was in ruins and his life appeared consigned to the gutter.

Shortly afterwards, Cromwell returned to Esher with 'a much [more] pleasant countenance' and boasted to Cavendish that he had 'adventured to put in his foot where he trusted shortly to be better regarded, or ever the Parliament was finished'.[19] There were more secret discussions with

Wolsey and Cromwell left again late that night to return to London, as he could not afford to be absent from Parliament the next morning.

Norfolk was busy preparing a Bill of Attainder against Wolsey for debate as the first item of business for Parliament, after its opening session on 3 November. The Bill, nicknamed the 'Book of Articles' because of its vast bulk, was passed in the Lords on 1 December and sent down to the Commons for approval. But there it faltered, probably because of its unnecessarily virulent language and the wild claims it contained,[20] and the Attainder with its forty-six articles was dropped, probably by royal command, before Parliament was prorogued on 17 December. It had nevertheless achieved its principal political aim: the Cardinal's name and reputation had been thoroughly and salaciously blackened.

Wolsey, isolated, depressed and anxious, wrote constantly to Cromwell, imploring him for advice and assistance. Reading his appeals today, it is impossible not to feel at least a shred of sympathy for the once haughty and imperious Cardinal, now consigned to the shadows of public life. His letters indicate painfully just how far he had tumbled from his halcyon days as an arrogant, proud Minister. The extravagant pomp and circumstance of his own glittering court, those battalions of obsequious, richly attired retainers, were now transient memories, clouded by his deep despair. As with all suddenly deposed leaders, he must also have suffered the sour frustrations of suddenly vanished personal power and authority.

With the status and vast wealth drained from him, Wolsey swiftly degenerated into a frail, sick and lonely old man, fearful of what the future might hold for him. Gone were his peremptory commands and directives. Now Wolsey had been brought to his knees and was begging his former servant for help:

My own entirely beloved Cromwell:

I beseech you, as you love me and will ever do anything for me, repair hither this day, as soon as the Parliament is broken up, leaving apart all things for that time.

I would . . . communicate things to you, wherein for my comfort and relief, I would have your good, sad, discreet advice and counsel but also upon the same, commit certain things requiring expedition to you on my behalf.

From Esher, in haste, this Saturday in the morning with the rude hand and sorrowful heart of your assured friend.

With the shrewd understanding of what could bring Cromwell scurrying to his side, Wolsey added this postscript: 'I have also certain things concerning yourself, which I am sure you will be glad to hear and know. Fail not, therefore, to be here this night. You may return early in the morning again, if your need shall so require.'[21] But this emotional blackmail and coy coaxing did not tempt his former solicitor down from London. Cromwell, probably anxious to demonstrate that his allegiance to Wolsey was a thing of the past, ignored his increasingly frantic pleas to visit. The Cardinal, still not realising that the master–servant relationship had ended, wrote impatiently:

There [are] few things since my trouble that [have] more grieved me than your not coming hither at this time, for now is the season that you should do to me most good and acceptable pleasure in advancement of my pursuits.

Wherefore, at the reverence of God, tomorrow in the evening, be it never so late, take the pain to come hither, and having speech with the same but one hour, you shall depart that night or so early in the morning as you shall not be missed there.

For all love, leave me not now, thus destitute of all comfort.[22]

Henry meanwhile had vindictively forced Wolsey to surrender to the crown his London residence at York House and his country properties at The More and Tittenhanger in Hertfordshire. The King had even dismantled his new gallery at Esher and transported it, piece by piece, for incorporation into the new royal Palace of Westminster, knowing this would 'torment' Wolsey. If this were not enough, the Cardinal's waking hours were now filled with rumours that the royal grant of the Cluniac monastery of St Augustine at Daventry, Northamptonshire, was to be declared void. The priory was one of the largest and richest of those suppressed and its revenues were vital to the prosperity of his new Oxford college.[23] Were this income and his prized legacy to England's education system now to disappear?

Cromwell continued steadfastly to ignore his increasingly urgent pleas to visit.

Wolsey's letters take on the pathetic, fraught tones of an elderly, forlorn parent callously abandoned by their progeny:

> The ferdering [delay] and putting off of your coming hither has so increased my sorrow and put me in such anxiety of mind that this night my breath and wind, by sighing, was so short that I was, by the space of three hours, as one that should have died.
>
> If you love my life, break away this evening and come hither . . . [that] I may open my mind to you . . . which I cannot commit to writing . . .
>
> Take some pains now for me and forsake me not in this my extreme need and where as I cannot, God shall reward you. Now is the time to show whether you love me or not.[24]

Wolsey knew full well who was responsible for his downfall and was troubled that the poison of Anne Boleyn's disfavour still afflicted him. When Sir John Russell had recently supported the Cardinal when talking to the King, she had sulkily refused to speak to him for nearly a month.[25] Wolsey asked Cromwell to consult Sir Henry Norris, Groom of the Stool, 'if the displeasure of my Lady Anne be [some]what assuaged, as I pray God the same may be' and urged 'all possible means' be employed to 'attain her favour'.[26]

Anne was meanwhile tightening the grip of her sensual feminine power over a doting Henry. To prove the point for everyone to witness and marvel at, she mischievously caused a new motto to be embroidered on her servants' blue-and-purple livery coats: *Ainsi sera, groigne qui groigne*, bluntly declaring: 'This is how it will be, however much people grumble.'[27] She boasted that she would rather see Catherine of Aragon 'hanged, than have to confess she was her queen and mistress'.[28] There was no hope of any reconciliation with this headstrong girl, with her black eyes firmly fixed on the consort's throne.

Cromwell wrote comforting letters to the ailing Wolsey and helpfully suggested he should grant money to members of the Boleyn faction at court. When all else fails, bribery can subtly quench the hidden fires of antagonism. Anne's star was now shining dazzlingly at Henry's court and her family were basking in its radiance. On 8 December 1529, her father was created Earl of Wiltshire and Ormonde and her brother George, now Viscount Rochford, became a gentleman of the King's privy chamber. He received an annuity of £200 from the income of the bishopric of Winchester and another of £134 from the lands of St Alban's Abbey in Hertfordshire, also formerly in Wolsey's gift.[29] It must remain a matter of speculation whether Boleyn was allowed to believe the gift was instigated by Cromwell himself purely for his own advancement. It would certainly have been wise to hitch himself to the Boleyn bandwagon: on 24 January 1530, Wiltshire was appointed Lord Privy Seal and promoted to the King's Council.

Was the lawyer merely being discreet in the help he gave his former master or horribly duplicitous, comfortable in a casual betrayal of the Cardinal and ready to use his cash to further his own career? In truth, Cromwell appears to have trodden a precarious line between remaining ostensibly loyal, defending Wolsey in public with 'witty persuasions and deep reason[ing]', while craftily still insinuating his way into fresh circles of influence.[30] He was thus adept at playing both ends against the middle. It was probably Cromwell, perceptively sensing that Henry still had lingering affection for his fallen Minister, who engineered some improvements in Wolsey's living conditions.

Events looked to be taking on a happier complexion for the Cardinal. In January 1530, Wolsey, to his delight, received a tangible, thoughtful token of the King's continuing regard – the arrival of a troupe of four royal physicians, led by Henry's favourite and most trusted doctor, Sir William Butts,[31] to nurse him through an acute attack of dropsy.[32] The Cardinal commented that neither doctors nor medicine would be the cure for his sickness – only the King. The following month, he was allowed to leave his Esher episcopal palace for a small house called 'The Lodge' at Richmond in Surrey.

Most importantly, Cromwell obtained a pardon under the Great Seal for Wolsey on 12 February, probably only a few days after he entered the King's service as an adviser on parliamentary and legal affairs. Cavendish heard that Henry reputed him 'to be a very wise man and a meet instrument to serve his grace'. Cromwell's new role had another immediate benefit for his former master: two days later the Cardinal was restored to the archbishopric of York. Then, at the beginning of March, Wolsey was allowed to progress to a larger, much more comfortable residence alongside the Carthusian monastery at Sheen.

Moving ever closer to the royal court, Wolsey was buoyed by growing hopes that his humiliating trials were nearing their end. But as he sat peacefully in devout dialogue with the monks, or alone in 'godly contemplation'[33] amid the cloistered calm of the Charterhouse, his fate was unexpectedly and finally sealed by his powerful adversaries, still plotting in the corridors and chambers of Henry's palaces in and around London, downstream along the River Thames.

Norfolk, their chief protagonist, was painfully aware that if the Cardinal ever succeeded in clambering back to office, he would probably be the first to end up in the Tower of London to avenge his prime role in Wolsey's disgrace. Therefore, the Duke successfully conspired with his court allies to ensure that the prelate should 'go home to his benefice', to live out his days as a pious churchman as remotely as possible from the intrigues of the court or any hope of restoration to power. When Cromwell informed Wolsey of the decision, he answered ingenuously: 'Well then, Thomas, we will go to Winchester.' This was still too close to London and the Cardinal should immediately have perceived that it was his own political exile, pure and simple, that lay behind the pronouncement. Cromwell, the realist, understood this only too well and sought guidance from Norfolk. The Duke, resolute that his defeated opponent should live out his remaining days far from a still sympathetic Henry, insisted on York being Wolsey's final destination. Not a man for the polite nuances of diplomatic language, he told Cromwell bluntly: 'I think that the Cardinal your master makes no haste to go northward. Tell him if he go not away shortly but shall tarry, I shall tear him with my teeth. I would advise him to prepare himself as quickly as he can, or else he shall be sent forward.'[34]

Wolsey protested that he had no money for the journey and the King's Council grudgingly agreed to advance him a thousand marks (£670) from the pension due to him from the bishopric of Winchester. The King generously added a further £1000 (or £350,000 in modern spending power) out of his own Privy Purse. He handed the cash over to Cromwell to pass on to Wolsey, adding, reassuringly, that the Cardinal should be of good cheer. By now, Wolsey had unwisely recovered some of his old arrogance and pride, and demanded that he should travel in the style properly befitting an Archbishop of York. Cromwell therefore had to scurry around officials and reluctant donors, seeking loans to top up Wolsey's funds.[35]

On 5 April, the Cardinal left Richmond for York at the head of a procession of 160 horsemen, with a convoy of ships taking his remaining possessions up from London by sea. It was probably the last time that Cromwell met him face to face. On 28 April, Wolsey arrived at Southwell, Nottinghamshire, entering for the first time the church province he had ruled as metropolitan since August 1514.[36] He was not a happy man and wrote to Henry with more pleas for money: 'I have come into my diocese unfurnished, to my extreme heaviness, of everything that I and my poor folks should be entertained with . . . I have neither corn nor cattle, nor anything to keep household with.' Moreover, his houses were 'despoiled . . . and in such ruin and decay . . . that a great part of the portion assigned to me to live with for one year will scantily, in a very base and mean fashion, repair and make the same . . . to be inhabited.' He complained of being 'wrapped in misery and need on every side; not knowing where to be succoured or relieved but only at your highness' most merciful and charitable hands'.[37]

Henry did not deign to reply. Mercy and compassion were qualities held in very limited stocks by the Tudors. The court was alive with rumours, some clearly malicious, about Wolsey's return to extravagance. Sir John Gage told Cromwell on 13 April 'that he rode in such sumptuous fashion that some men thought he was of as good courage as in times past and that there was no impediment but lack of authority'. Cromwell wrote a stern letter to Wolsey advising him to 'quiet yourself' and be patient.

Sir, there be some that allege that your grace do keep too great a house and family [household] and that you are continually building.

For the love of God . . . as I often times have done, [I] most heartily beseech you to have respect to everything and considering the time, to refrain yourself for a season [from] all manner [of] buildings than mere necessity requires, which I assure your grace shall cease and put to silence some persons that speak much of the same.

Cromwell was now more confident of his future and his letter assumed an astonishingly presumptuous, impertinent tone as he lectured Wolsey on the realities of his exile. Forget the vain trappings of wealth, he urged, and concentrate on achieving those greater gifts bestowed by enjoying a simple, devoutly religious existence. Cromwell's conceited words must have been unbearable to read for a man who once aspired to wear the triple papal tiara of St Peter:

I do reckon your grace right happy that you be now at liberty to serve God and to learn how to experiment how you shall banish and exile the vain desires of this unstable world, which undoubtedly does nothing else but allure every person therein . . .

In studying and seeking, besides the great travails and afflictions that men suffer daily, most persons [having] been driven to extreme repentance and, searching for pleasure and felicity, find nothing but trouble, sorrow, anxiety and adversity.

Wherefore, in my opinion, your grace being as you are . . . [can] win a hundred times as much as ever you were possessed of.

His audacious hectoring over, Cromwell thanks the Cardinal 'for the geldings' sent to him, and apologises for not visiting him at Southwell because of 'importune business': 'Be assured I am and during my life shall be with your grace in heart . . . spirit, prayer and service to the uttermost of my poor and simple power. As Our Lord knows, whom I most heartily beseech to preserve your grace long life, good health and the increase of your heart's desire.'[38] These were silver-tongued words from a man now comfortably in the King's service. Wolsey could hardly complain about Cromwell's insolence as he was the only friend he now had at court. That so-called friend, always the opportunist, was now making money out of his misfortune.

Cromwell actively assisted the King in diverting revenues from the suppressed monasteries, originally granted to Wolsey's two colleges, to the purses of Henry's cronies at court. He also arranged for incomes from the see of Winchester and the monastery of St Alban's to be redistributed amongst the King's favourites. Wolsey wrote to the King's new secretary Stephen Gardiner, who had formerly worked for him, complaining that 'he did not deserve to have lost Winchester and St Alban's, having done no offence to the king'.[39]

It made no difference. George Cavendish reported:

> Both noblemen and others who had any patents of the king . . . do make earnest suit to Master Cromwell to solicit their causes to my lord [Wolsey] to get out of him his confirmations.
>
> And for his pains therein sustained, they promised, every man, not only to worthily reward him but also to show him such pleasures as should lie at all times in their several powers . . .
>
> Cromwell perceived an occasion given him by time to enrich himself . . . and having a great occasion of access to the king for the disposition of diverse lands, whereof he had the order and governance, by means whereof and by his witty demeanour, he grew continually in the king's favour.[40]

Wolsey could only bleat to Cromwell: 'I am greatly desirous to understand and hear from you how affairs stand and proceed, not only concerning my colleges but also my own poor estate, in the relief whereof my own undoubted trust is that you will, in all places and times, show yourself . . . my assured friend and only comfort.'[41]

Cromwell's skills at conveyancing had taken on a new meaning. A generous gratuity here, a small token of esteem there, and Cromwell had sorted out his affairs to the benefit of his new friends at court and the satisfaction of all except that sick old discarded servant of the crown, safely ensconced out of harm's way in the North.

Henry later suppressed Wolsey's college at Ipswich, dispersed its students and staff and appropriated its possessions and rents. Cardinal's

College, Oxford, continued but, with a characteristic twist of the royal knife, he decreed that its name should be changed to 'King Henry VIII's College'. Wolsey's personal heraldry was removed from the stained-glass windows and from over the doorways. In 1546, the foundation was reorganised and it became Christ Church, Oxford. Wolsey was grief-stricken, telling Cromwell in July 1530 that he was 'disposed and put from my sleep and meat in consequence of the news of the dissolution of my colleges . . . I cannot write [more] for weeping and sorrow'.[42]

He must have heard suggestions that his former solicitor was not entirely honest in dealing on his behalf. With typical bare-faced effrontery, Cromwell's last surviving letter to his former master, dated 18 October 1530, dared him to openly make any accusations of double-dealing. His words then become threatening:

> I am informed your grace [holds] me in some diffidence, as if I did dissemble with you, or procure anything contrary to your profit and honour. I much muse that your grace should think or repeat it secretly, considering the pains that I have taken.
>
> I beseech you to speak without feigning, if you have such conceit, that I may clear myself. I reckoned that [you] would have written plainly to me of such a thing, rather than secretly to have misrepresented me.
>
> But I shall bear your grace no less good will. Let God judge between us.
>
> Truly, your grace in some things over-shoots yourself. There is regard to be given [to] what things you utter and to whom.[43]

His warning about loose talk and unwise actions was perhaps timely. Wolsey was preparing at last to be enthroned as Archbishop of York on 7 November. He had summoned 'all the lords, abbots, priors, knights esquires and gentlemen of his diocese to be at his manor of Cawood[44] the 6 of November and so bring him to York with all manner of pomp and solemnity'.[45] It was plain he still yearned for his lost riches and the trappings of past glories and wrote to Henry, seeking 'the mitre and pall which he had formerly been accustomed to use in celebrating the divine office'. When he read this letter, the King marvelled greatly at Wolsey's 'brazen insolence', adding, 'Is there still arrogance in this fellow, who is so obviously ruined?'[46]

There were yet more serious charges to lay at Wolsey's door. His enemies claimed he was in secret communication with the Pope and was engaged in 'sinister practices made to the court of Rome for restoring him to his former estate and dignity',[47] as the King claimed in a letter to Sir Francis Bryan, his ambassador in France. Moreover, a papal brief had been issued against Henry at Bologna, forbidding, under pain of excommunication, his marriage to Anne Boleyn and ordering him to expel her from court. The brief could well be published during Wolsey's enthronement at York. Enough was enough, as far as Henry was concerned. Wolsey must now face a charge of high treason.

He was arrested at Cawood Castle, 12 miles (19 km) from York, as he sat down to dinner on Friday, 4 November and was moved to the Earl of Shrewsbury's home at Sheffield Park. There, Sir William Kingston, Constable of the Tower of London and Captain of the Guard, with twenty-four men, arrived on 22 November to take him into custody and escort him to the capital – and certain imprisonment, if not death. Wolsey laboured under a curious superstition about the name Kingston as, years before, he had been told by a fortune-teller that he would meet his end there. When in royal service he had always avoided the Surrey town on the banks of the Thames 'even though it was the nearest way for him to use to [go to] the court'. Now he saw the constable and blanched at his surname. '"Master Kingston," said he, rehearsing his name once or twice and with that clapped his hand on his thigh and gave a great sigh.'[48]

Adversity loosened Wolsey's tongue. He cautioned Cromwell that if ever he became a member of Henry's Council, 'I warn you to be well advised and assured what matter you put into his head, for you shall never put it out again . . . I have often kneeled before him in his Privy Chamber on my knees the space of an hour or two, to persuade him from his will and appetite, but I could never . . . dissuade him.'[49]

The sombre party with its corpulent, disconsolate prisoner proceeded south by easy stages and reached Leicester Abbey on Saturday, 26 November, where Wolsey fell sick. As he lay on what was to become his death bed, a messenger from the King arrived seeking information about the sum of £1500 reportedly missing from the inventory of his possessions rapidly taken at Cawood Castle. Despite his failing health, the Cardinal was enraged. Rather than defraud Henry of just one penny, he declared, 'I would rather it were molten and put into my mouth.' Kingston added his voice to the enquiries about the lost cash. 'I will not conceal it from the king,' said Wolsey, 'but will declare it to you or I die, by the grace of God. Take a little patience with me, I beseech you.'[50]

The Constable returned for his answer at six o'clock the next morning, 29 November 1530. Clearly, Wolsey was dying. He told Kingston, his words tinged with wry bitterness:

> I see the matter makes you much worse than you should be against me. How it is framed I know not.
>
> If I had served God as diligently as I have the king, he would not have given me over in my grey hairs.
>
> This is my just reward that I must receive for my worldly diligence and pains that I have had to do his service, only to satisfy his vain pleasure, not regarding my godly duty.[51]

Wolsey gave up the ghost about two hours later, still silent on the whereabouts of the missing £1500. He probably died from dysentery, although some 'reckoned he killed himself with purgations'.[52] He was aged around sixty. His body was quickly placed in a wooden coffin, dressed in fine vestments, a mitre on his head and a crosier across his body. The lid was left off, and the Mayor of Leicester was summoned to view the corpse, 'to avoid false rumours that might happen to say that he was not dead, but still living'.[53] Other dignitaries trooped in to confirm, in a macabre ritual, that Wolsey was not feigning death. His body was buried in the Lady Chapel of St Mary's Abbey, Leicester, at about four o'clock the next morning, amid a thunderstorm.

Back in London that same month, Cromwell had been involved in a quarrel with Sir John Wallop, who threatened and insulted him, possibly over his treatment of Wolsey, and had sought Henry's protection. Later, the Spanish ambassador, Eustace Chapuys, recounted how Cromwell had 'asked and obtained an audience from [the] king, whom he addressed in such flattering terms and eloquent language, promising to make him the richest king in the world'.[54]

With his king's patronage and protection, it was easy to shrug off an action against him in the Star Chamber, alleging extortion of £20, brought by the litigious Christopher Burgh, parson of Spennethorne and Hawkswell in Yorkshire and executor of his brother William, the former Warden of St Leonard's Hospital in York.[55]

After months of advising Henry, Cromwell knew that the way to his monarch's heart was through his purse. Although the appointment was officially kept secret for four months, in January 1531 he became a junior member of the King's Council.

CHAPTER THREE

Daily Round, Common Task

Cromwell is constantly rising in power, so much that he has now more influence with his master than [the] Cardinal ever had. Nowadays, everything is done at his bidding.

SPANISH AMBASSADOR EUSTACE CHAPUYS, IN LONDON, TO CHARLES V, 1535[1]

Thomas Cromwell inevitably became an inveterate conspirator within the magnificent surroundings of Henry's court. He was well aware that his new master was frustrated and angry over the interminable diplomatic negotiations with Rome regarding his divorce from Catherine of Aragon. What was almost as insufferable was that the King was also badly in need of money. Throughout Henry's long reign, both problems – being thwarted in obtaining his heart's desire and a distressingly empty exchequer – would always trigger outbursts of uncontrollable rage or petulance from a monarch accustomed to being denied nothing. Within the House of Commons there was a growing antipathy towards the clergy and the Mother Church that protected and nurtured them, not only loyally reflective of their sovereign's dissatisfaction, but also born out of mounting concerns about ecclesiastical power, wealth and influence on everyday life. These were factors that Cromwell would eventually harness to his own advantage and profit – but he knew he was swimming in dangerous waters, given both his sovereign's piety and uncertain temper.

After Wolsey's destruction, both Norfolk and Suffolk were eager to attack the wealthy clerical estate and reform it, root and branch. But change in the Church's infrastructure and administration was only one facet of the challenge mounted against it: other influential voices sought to radically transform its beliefs and doctrines. Beloved Anne Boleyn gave Henry her own annotated copy[2] of the exiled Lutheran reformer William Tyndale's[3] *Obedience of a Christian Man*, a controversial book published in Germany in 1528 that firmly asserted the monarch's privileges and duties and his inalienable right to the absolute allegiance of his subjects, based on the fourth commandment – 'Honour thy father and thy mother,' for, in Lutheran doctrine, paternal authority was the model of all power in society.[4] Whoever opposed the king, Tyndale wrote austerely, 'resists God, for they are in the room of God and they that resist shall receive damnation'. Even if a sovereign was 'the greatest tyrant in the world . . . he is to thee a great benefit of God and a thing wherefore you ought to thank God highly', he told his readers. Moreover, a king 'may at his lust do right and wrong and shall give account but to God only'.[5] Those were beliefs that would strike a glad chord in the heart of any Tudor monarch. Henry devoured the book, cover to cover, and commented approvingly, 'This book is for me and all kings to read.'[6] No author could hope for a more flattering review or generous endorsement.

Anne also probably gave him the polemic pamphlet 'A Supplication for the Beggars', also written in 1528 by the Gray's Inn lawyer Simon Fish. Hidden amongst the invective was his impertinent demand that the clergy should spend money on the needs of the poor rather than becoming fat on the income from others' open-handed piety. What was more, he claimed, the spirituality had installed its own separate state within Henry's realm, which now dangerously encroached upon the authority of the crown. Fish urged the King to seize the wealth of these 'strong, puissant and counterfeit holy . . . idle beggars and vagabonds which . . . by the craft and wiliness of Satan, are now increased under your sight, not only into a great number but also into a kingdom'.[7] Clearly he was not a lawyer who minced his words.

Cromwell had read both works[8] and divined the way the wind was blowing against both Church and priesthood. How much he subscribed to reformist Protestant beliefs at this stage in his career must remain a matter of conjecture. Adroitly, however, he must have been aware of Anne Boleyn's religious standpoint and had every reason to ally himself with her rising star at court.

Ironically, Tyndale, fired by his pompous, priggish fervour, was totally opposed to Henry's divorce and his attitude towards an issue so close to Henry's heart was to count against him. In 1531, he penned a heated retort to Lord Chancellor Sir Thomas More's eloquent arguments against challenging the authority of the Church and sent a copy to Henry for his approval, via Cromwell's friend in Antwerp, Stephen Vaughan. But the King was less than happy with the contents. He found Tyndale's 'Answer Unto Sir Thomas More' 'filled with seditious slanderous lies and fantastical opinions' and believed the author's sole objective was 'only to seduce, deceive and disquiet the people and commonwealth of this realm'. Henry later unsuccessfully sought Tyndale's extradition from the Low Countries on charges of heresy.

Cromwell was apprehensive that both he and Vaughan might be viewed as supporting Tyndale at a time when More and some of the bishops were enthusiastically persecuting – indeed burning – heretics in England. Was his climb to fame and fortune to be suddenly cut short by this overzealous Lutheran? He cautioned that Henry should quickly be made aware that Vaughan was 'a true, loving and obedient subject, bearing no manner [of] favour, love or affection to Tyndale, nor to his works in any manner, but utterly to condemn and abhor the same' – or else he would 'acquire the indignation of God and displeasure of your sovereign Lord'.

Back in November 1529, in the aftermath of Wolsey's downfall, the Commons had submitted a petition to Henry requesting that the bishops declare whether by 'the laws of God and Holy Church' the clergy should hold secular appointments, trade for profit, lease lands or hold more than one benefice.[9] John Fisher, the conservative Bishop of Rochester, complained bitterly that the Commons had been deafened by cries of 'down with the Church' from Members of Parliament who, he hinted threateningly, displayed a 'lack of faith'.[10] It is not known whether Cromwell took part in this anti-clerical tirade, but the petition resulted in three parliamentary Acts, one of which enshrined in law that papal dispensations for pluralism – a priest having more than one parish – could no longer apply. Cromwell may have been a member of the committee who worked on drafts of the legislation.[11] The first blow against the Vatican's authority in England had been landed on the body of the Church. Many of the accusations and ideas discussed during those heated Commons debates were cannily retained by Cromwell for future use as ammunition in the confrontation between Church and state that was surely to come.

The political antagonism against the Church grew ever more vehement. On 29 September 1530 – Michaelmas – the King's Council indicted fifteen clerics (including eight bishops and three abbots) under the Statute of Praemunire, alleging they had supported the power of the papal legate in the realm.[12] Patently, it was nothing more or less than state blackmail, with Henry maliciously and cynically exploiting the dominant anti-clericalism amongst his MPs. There must have been lurking doubts whether the King would have been ruthless enough to press home the charges: they were not formally delivered until the following January and Cromwell assured Wolsey on 21 October: 'The prelates shall not appear in the praemunire. There is another way devised'[13] – a statement strongly suggesting that he had a close hand in the matter.

However, the Council's indictments sent the bishops and abbots scurrying for cover, and just before they were due to appear in the Court of King's Bench at Westminster[14] to answer the charge, a timely Convocation of Canterbury on 24 January 1531 generously offered Henry the colossal sum of £100,000, or £34 million in 2006 monetary terms, 'to be their good lord' and to pardon them of all offences.[15] In return, he demanded that the clergy should adopt a new style for his dignity and title. Now, not only was he 'King of England and Defender of the Faith', he was also 'protector and only supreme head of the English Church'.[16]

The clergy's humble reply dutifully referred to the King as 'Supreme Head of the church in England', but added the weasel-worded caveat 'as far as the law of God allows'.[17] Although they had tried to face down the King's demands, they ended up granting him a title that many churchmen would bitterly regret in the future. Unsurprisingly, with the cash now on the table, they promptly received their royal pardon. The King had his badly needed funds in his exchequer and had moved one step closer to a breach with Rome. In addition, some valuable lessons had been drawn from these events within Henry's government. First, it was realised just how much ready money there was sloshing around in the Church, and second, how quickly the clergy had caved in to a little political pressure. The import of these facts was not lost on many, including Cromwell and the King himself.

The new councillor had by this point penetrated the very sinews of the Tudor government, involving himself mainly in Henry's complex financial and legal affairs, although, cautiously, he maintained his own legal and commercial businesses at the same time. He was swiftly recognised as a man of influence who could be relied upon to get things done, or to provide funds to those who were temporarily financially embarrassed. Wolsey's bastard son Thomas Winter wrote a begging letter to Cromwell on 20 October 1532 placing all his hopes in his help: 'You are now . . . in that position which I and all your friends have long wished for and you have attained that dignity that you can serve them as you please. If you take care that the next courier brings me a fair sum of money, you will oblige me much. Please send me immediately £100.'[18]

Powerful people from court circles – Attorney General Sir Christopher Hales, Master of the Horse Sir Nicholas Carew and Cromwell's old friend Sir John Gage, Vice-Chamberlain of the Royal Household – were amongst those who hesitantly knocked on his door for assistance. Amid a multitude of tasks undertaken in the service of the crown, Cromwell dealt with legal appeals and adjudged the fates of prisoners brought to his notice: life or death, imprisonment or freedom.

He also superintended the royal building works at the new Palace of Westminster, and repairs at the Tower of London and to the fortifications at Calais and in Ireland,[19] even paying for 'the labour and expenses' for constructing Henry's putative tomb at Windsor.[20] In 1532 he was appointed Receiver General of the lands redirected to 'King Henry VIII's College'[21] at Oxford, because of his specialised knowledge of Wolsey's earlier foundations. It was all part of the daily round, the common task, of a talented and industrious royal bureaucrat.

Cromwell plainly saw his varied duties as sometimes very expedient. In November 1532 he wrote to the abbot of the prosperous Benedictine abbey of Bury St Edmund's in Suffolk, seeking the lease of one of its properties for himself, as it was conveniently close to the King's house at Hunsdon, in Hertfordshire: 'I am very desirous to have some house in Essex . . . and for as much as your parsonage of Harlowbury shall shortly be in your hands and letting . . . I desire and instantly pray you to let your said farm of Harlowbury to me for [a] term of sixty years for the same . . . rent . . . that has been of old time accustomed [to be] paid for the same.' Unashamedly, this unsubtle argument was added in support of him being awarded the lease: 'In doing so, you shall bind me to you and . . . [provide] your monastery such pleasure as may lie in my little power in time to come. And what shall be [in] your mind herein, I pray you to advertise me in writing by this bearer, my servant.'[22]

Here, however, Cromwell's implied bribery was unsuccessful, even though he had agreed terms with Harlowbury's current leaseholders, known to us only as 'Malery and his wife'. Another rather more intimidating letter from him protesting at the abbot's retention of masons and carpenters in Suffolk who were needed at the King's works at Westminster and the Tower had perhaps offended monkish dignity.[23]

Henry shrewdly realised that Cromwell's greatest immediate value to the crown lay in his manipulation of parliamentary affairs. His skills in drafting new laws and browbeating intractable legislators had become vital in achieving a lengthening agenda of controversial business in the Commons, as was his ability to select suitably malleable candidates to fill by-election vacancies. By June 1531, it was widely acknowledged that 'one master Cromwell penned certain matters in the Parliament house which no man gainsaid'.[24] This recognition was fully confirmed in October that year when the King issued 'instructions unto his trusty councillor Thomas Cromwell to be declared . . . to his learned counsel and [without delay] to be put in execution this [parliamentary] term of St Michael'.[25]

The measures to be tackled covered a very wide raft of issues, ranging from the administratively banal – importation of bow-staves at

Southampton and 'diligent process' against the King's debtors – to brand-new ordinances. Two of the listed bills were passed – the first covering customs dues on wines imported via the Netherlands and the second regulating the work of the commissioners of sewers.[26] But two items of proposed legislation also failed to see the light of day: a bill of 'Augmentation of Treason' encouraging loyal informers against traitors and another governing the distribution of bishops' incomes.

A year later, in 1532, Cromwell began to amass a considerable collection of royal offices and appointments, most of which he grimly hung on to throughout his eight more years in power despite advancement in other areas of the King's service. At the New Year, he presented Henry with a 'ring with a ruby' and a 'box with the images of the children of the French king, Francis I'.[27] His sovereign gave him a small gift of a goblet, merely listed amongst those presented to other gentlemen of the court.

Now came more signs of Henry's grace and goodwill. Cromwell's first post was Mastership of the King's Jewels, granted on 14 April, at a salary of £50 a year, in succession to the London goldsmith Robert Amadas, who had died.[28] Hard on the heels of this appointment came the clerkship of the Hanaper of Chancery on 16 July. The name of this strange-sounding post comes from the Old English word 'hanap',[29] a wicker basket (the picnic hamper has the same etymological origin) in which writs and other legal documents were collected. The Clerk of the Hanaper was paid fees by suitors to ensure that their grants, charters and patents were properly impressed with the Great Seal to prove their legality, and these fees were additional to an annual salary of between £30 and £60. Cromwell apparently did not draw the 1s. 6d per day due to him for special expenses, probably because the work was done by the under-clerk.[30] Some transactions were specifically excluded from fees: the King's warrant in September 1532 ordering Cromwell to deliver to Anne Boleyn the patent creating her Marquis of Pembroke in her own right stipulated that it should be sealed 'without taking any fine for us or to our use for the seals'.[31]

These appointments were made as rewards for Cromwell's skilful stage-management of parliamentary antipathy towards the clergy. The

Commons' 'Supplication Against the Ordinaries',[32] a petition of March 1532 drawn up mainly against bishops, was probably compiled and written behind the scenes by Cromwell some time before the issue came up for debate. The complaints of 1529 were now repeated with new protests arising out of MPs' disquiet over the increasing number of heresy trials.[33] The contemporary chronicler Edward Hall wrote: 'For the ordinaries would send for men and lay accusations [against] them of heresy and say they were accused and lay articles to them but no accuser should be brought forth, which the Commons [found] very dreadful and grievous – for the party so cited must either abjure or be burned, for purgation he might make none.'[34]

Cromwell had directed the chorus in this latest assault on church authority on behalf of his master, but echoing Simon Fish's thoughts, was also pursuing his own grand vision of 'one body politic' within England.[35] On 15 May 1532, the Church's Convocation finally agreed that they should not assemble without a royal writ and no new ecclesiastical (or canon) law could be enacted without the King's full assent. Finally, all existing church laws would be examined by a thirty-two-strong committee, half of them laymen, under royal auspices. The following day, Sir Thomas More resigned as Lord Chancellor, surrendering the Great Seal of England in a white leather pouch, supposedly on grounds of ill health. In reality, as many suspected, his departure was a matter of conscience.

In 1533, Cromwell laid down a key piece of legislation as a foundation stone of the English Reformation. The Statute in Restraint of Appeals[36] prohibited any kind of appeal to the Pope under pain of praemunire and made Henry the ultimate legal authority on religious matters in England and Wales. Cromwell's preamble to the Act robustly declared: 'This realm of England is an empire . . . governed by one supreme head and king, having the dignity and royal estate of the imperial crown of the same, to whom a body politic, compact of all sort and degrees of people divided in terms and by names of spirituality and temporality, be bounden and owe next to God a natural and humble obedience.' An 'empire', the 'imperial crown' – these ringing, grandiose words fashioned the autocrat's own political and emergent religious manifesto. They also bestowed upon Henry everything he sought: exalted stature, additional grandeur to the throne of England and his perceived rightful place on the European political stage. Most importantly of all, the Act made it a crime to acknowledge papal authority over his realm.

Away from the noisy cockpit of religion and politics, Cromwell was still the man to consult if you were experiencing any kind of problem with the King's administration. Stephen Gardiner, Henry's principal secretary, was appointed Bishop of Winchester in succession to Wolsey in 1531 and was to become one of Cromwell's greatest and most devious enemies in the years ahead. In June 1532, he complained to Cromwell about having to pay too much to the King for his new diocese:

> Truth it is, I would be glad to pay nothing . . . Wherefore now all is in your hands. The delay of my end depends only upon you. In concluding, I pray you remember that I receive less of the bishopric of Winchester by £1,300 a year than Bishop Fox did and owe twice as much as he was worth when he died, if his inventory was true.
>
> I pray you good master Cromwell, determine you the end for my part, as shall be agreeable with the king's pleasure, in such ways as I should not seem to huck [haggle or bargain] or stike [delay] to pay my duty.[37]

> YOUR LOVING AND ASSURED FRIEND
>
> STEPHEN WINTON [WINCHESTER]

Within two months, Gardiner again sought Cromwell's help, and his latest appeal indicated that the lawyer's duties had now extended into diplomatic affairs: 'I send to you herewith . . . the treaty with France and a commission signed, ready to be sealed. To the doing whereof, you must necessarily help or it shall, I fear me, be undone. I pray you also to send to Dr Oliver or Dr Oliver to be with the king on Sunday to [act] as notaries at the taking of the oath.'[38] Moreover, Cromwell had attended Henry's fifteen glittering and flamboyant days of meetings with his French counterpart Francis I in Boulogne in October 1532 and had earned high praise from both monarchs.[39] It was one of the very few occasions when Cromwell left the shores of England after entering royal service: he much preferred to remain always at the heart of power.

Meanwhile, time was running out to finally resolve Henry's 'Great Matter'.

Anne Boleyn, who had accompanied the King to France amongst his two thousand-strong entourage, found herself pregnant some time in the middle of January 1533 after finally yielding to her royal lover's efforts to bed her the previous month. Doubtlessly delighted at the prospect of fatherhood again, Henry could no longer tolerate diplomatic procrastination over his divorce, or dally further in achieving his personal desires. He secretly married Anne on 25 January in the high chamber over the Holbein Gate in his new Palace of Westminster, the ceremony probably conducted by one of his chaplains, Rowland Lee.

The King had irrevocably turned his back on the Pope and the rest of Christendom and now looked to Cromwell to construct the legal means to break with Rome and allow his divorce solely on the authority of his Church in England.

A new champion had arrived to defend Henry: Thomas Cranmer, still only an archdeacon,[40] was nominated to the see of Canterbury, left vacant by the death of William Warham the previous August. His selection might, in part, be laid at Cromwell's door: he was fully aware that Cranmer had long supported the notion of the divorce being decided under English jurisdiction.[41] This information had probably been passed on to Henry when the names for a new primate were being considered. Clement VII in Rome innocently – perhaps naively – approved the choice and issued the necessary nine papal bulls on 21–2 February 1533, allowing the consecration of Cranmer as primate of England to go ahead on 30 March in St Stephen's Chapel, Westminster.

The new archbishop wasted no time in raising the question of the divorce and wrote to Henry on 11 April from his palace at Lambeth across the Thames from Westminster: 'It may please . . . your most excellent majesty . . . to license me, according to my office and duty to proceed to the examination, final determination and judgment in the said great cause touching your highness.'[42] Henry naturally agreed, licensing Cranmer

> to proceed . . . not doubting but that you will have God and the justice of
> the said cause only before your eyes and not to regard any earthly or

worldly affection therein. For assuredly, the thing which we most covet in this world is so to proceed, in all our acts and doings, as may be most acceptable to the pleasure of Almighty God, our Creator, and to the wealth, honour of us, our succession and posterity.[43]

The King also seized this opportunity to underline the new reality of religious authority in England. So there could be no doubts, he told Cranmer that the office of Archbishop of Canterbury and its powers existed 'only by the sufferances of us and our progenitors' and 'you be, *under us, by God's calling and ours* [emphasis mine], the most principal minister of our spiritual jurisdiction within this our realm'.[44]

Cromwell had meanwhile been busy drafting two new uncompromising parliamentary bills: the first established special meetings of the clerical Convocation to sit in judgment, without appeal, on the King's twenty-four years of marriage to Catherine of Aragon. There were no scruples about prejudging its deliberations or decision. The royal union was now considered 'definitely, clearly and absolutely invalid'. The second bill freed Henry to marry again.

With the cold clarity of a lawyer's mind, Cromwell had carefully considered every detail, every ramification: Queen Catherine was now to be styled 'the Princess' and the succession to the throne of England would henceforth be based solely on any offspring of Henry and Anne Boleyn. Princess Mary, the only surviving progeny from the marriage with Catherine, was effectively declared illegitimate. At the last moment, the bills were dropped, but were replaced by the Act of Appeals,[45] which effectively prevented Catherine from taking her case to Rome. Nonetheless, on 5 April, the Convocation of Canterbury, meeting at St Paul's Cathedral in London, decided with some difficulty that Henry's first marriage was impeded by divine law and that any decisions by the Pope could not, would not, alter that stark fact. Twenty-five brave clerics voted against that decision, including Bishop John Fisher, who was promptly arrested for his defiance.[46]

An ecclesiastical court was established on 10 May at Dunstable in Bedfordshire, close to where Catherine had been exiled and well away from any raucous protests by her supporters amongst the London mob.

Inevitably she refused to appear before this tribunal, presided over by Cranmer, and was promptly declared 'contumacious' – wilfully disobedient to the court's powers and jurisdiction. On 23 May 1533, the King's proctor, John Tregonwell, quickly dashed off a dispatch to Cromwell, announcing that the inescapable divorce had finally been granted:

> This shall advertise you that my Lord of Canterbury this day at ten of the clock before noon, has given a sentence in this great cause, whereby he has declared the matrimony to be against the laws of God and [has] therefore divorced the king's highness from the noble lady Catherine.
>
> My lord of Canterbury has used himself in this matter very honourably. And to say the truth, every man (sent hither by the king's grace) has handled himself with as much diligence . . . in this as any men might have done.
>
> We trust that a sentence shall be given for the king's second contract of matrimony before the feast of Pentecost.[47]

Cranmer himself wrote to Henry that day with the news 'that I have given sentence in your grace's great and weighty cause' and asking what his pleasure was regarding his marriage to Anne, 'for the time of [her] coronation is so instant and so near at hand, that the matter requires good expedition'.[48] The court decided that the marriage between Henry and Catherine of Aragon was and always had been unlawful; they should certainly no longer cohabit as man and wife and both were now free to marry again. One of them, of course, already had.

Five days later, Cranmer at Lambeth confirmed Henry's marriage with Anne Boleyn: the coronation, arranged for Whit Sunday, 1 June 1533, could go ahead. She was six months pregnant and despite her opulent flowing robes, her condition was very obvious. She left her state apartments in the Tower of London at ten o'clock

> in a [horse-drawn] open litter, so that all might see her . . . [preceded] by the cavalry, all in very fine order and richly bedecked. Then came the gentlemen of rank and then all the ladies and gentlemen on horseback and in [carriages] very brave.
>
> The queen was dressed in a robe of crimson brocade covered with

precious stones and round her neck she wore a string of pearls larger than chick-peas and a jewel of diamonds of great value.

On her head she bore a wreath in the fashion of a crown of immense worth and in her hand she carried some flowers.

As she progressed through the London streets, en route to Westminster, she 'kept turning her face from one side to the other, [but] there were not, I think, ten people who greeted her with "God save you!" as they used to when the sainted Queen [Catherine] passed by', reported a not entirely impartial eyewitness.[49] When her procession reached Westminster Hall, the waiting Henry took her into his arms and enquired how she liked the look of London. She answered: 'I liked the city well enough but I saw a great many caps on heads and heard but few tongues.'

Undaunted by the obvious dislike shown by the common people of London, Anne went into Westminster Abbey for her coronation, accompanied by thirteen mitred abbots. Sir Thomas More did not attend and his absence was noticed.

Eustace Chapuys reported triumphantly that the 'sad and dismal' Londoners turned the five days of celebration into an event more like a funeral.[50]

What of Catherine, now an unwilling and resentful 'Princess Dowager'? She had been packed off to Ampthill in Bedfordshire with a dramatically reduced household and on 3 July was visited by a deputation from Henry's Council, tasked to win acknowledgement of her new status. Cogent and compelling arguments had been prepared in advance to persuade her to forgo the title of queen.[51] The visitors found her lying on a bed in her privy chamber 'because she had pricked her foot with a pin, so that she might not well stand . . . and [was] also sore annoyed with a cough'. As soon as they began reading out a document describing her new life without Henry, she angrily interrupted, maintaining stoutly that she remained the queen and 'the king's true wife'. Her defiance continued unabated.

It was declared to her that it neither stood with the law of God, nor man, nor with the king's honour, to have two queens named within this realm and that indeed he had but one lawful wife, to the which he was now married and caused to be crowned . . .

59

The king did not a little marvel that she would disobey his commandment, not only by herself but also cause . . . his subjects to do the same.

She said in that she would rather disobey him than God and her own conscience, [or] damn her own soul.[52]

When Cromwell was told of this difficult, rather staccato conversation, he must have smiled wanly. He dryly commented that nature had done Catherine a disservice by not making her a man – as in her bravery she could have surpassed all the heroes of history.[53] Such a display of emotion was rare in him.

Henry was not nearly so sympathetic: spitefully, he ordered that Catherine should be moved again, to less salubrious accommodation at Buckden Towers in Cambridgeshire, with a further thinned-down household.

Meanwhile, in Rome, a hesitant and uncertain Pope was at last galvanised into some semblance of action. On Friday, 11 July, Clement VII finally condemned both Henry's separation from Catherine and his bigamous marriage to Anne. In a secret consistory court hearing, he gave the English king until September to restore his legal wife to the royal bed under threat of excommunication.[54] When Norfolk, on some wearisome diplomatic business in Lyons in France, heard the news, he almost fainted at the shock.

Henry, made of sterner stuff, contemptuously rejected the papal commandments. He was buoyed up by a certainty that very soon all his irksome fears about a lack of a lawful male successor would be put behind him and the Tudor dynasty would at last be secure.

But all the confident predictions by physicians and astrologers of a male heir to the throne of England came to naught.

Queen Anne was delivered safely of a girl child at about three o'clock in the afternoon of 7 September 1533 in her room at the palace at Greenwich, hung about with tapestries portraying the legend of St Ursula and her 11,000 virgins. The sex of the child was a disagreeable surprise for everyone, particularly for the royal couple, but Henry managed to put on a brave face. Embarrassingly, a pre-written circular letter addressed from the Queen to Lord Cobham, her chamberlain, had originally announced the birth of a prince. The letter 's' had to be added to the word to correctly report the sex of the child.[55] The three-day-old princess was named Elizabeth when she was christened in the Church of the Friars Observant at Greenwich.

The new Queen's unpopularity was unlikely to be improved by the birth of a girl and many saw this as God's heavy judgement upon Henry. Catherine posed little threat as long as she remained sequestered from the outside world, but the clergy's opposition to the King's policies was beginning to pose real problems.

Chief amongst these was Elizabeth Barton, the so-called 'Holy Maid of Kent'. She was born in 1506 and had been a serving girl to the family of Thomas Cobb at Aldington in that county.[56] About 1525 she became ill, perhaps suffering from epilepsy. Certainly, she fell into trances and astonished the villagers when, as she writhed helplessly in the filth and animal droppings on the ground, a loud voice cried out 'with marvellous holiness in rebuke of sin and vice'. People said these pious words had been uttered by an angel. With such claims, the Church naturally became involved, and Edward Bocking, a learned monk of Christchurch Priory, Canterbury, investigated her case. He was convinced she had experienced genuine religious ecstasy and arranged her entry into the Benedictine nunnery of St Sepulchre in Canterbury, where she lived very modestly.[57]

By the end of 1526 she had been proudly paraded before Archbishop Warham, Bishop Fisher and Sir Thomas More. Cardinal Wolsey had interviewed her in 1528, when she warned him of his impending downfall.

Such incidents were not unknown in superstitious sixteenth-century England: Ipswich had its own Holy Maid around the same time and there was another at Leominster in Herefordshire who was unfortunately exposed as an impostor.

Later, Elizabeth Barton became an unwitting pawn of those opposed to Henry's divorce, his supremacy over the Church and the growth in influence of the evangelical reformers. Egged on by her cleric supporters, she claimed that an angel had appeared and commanded her to tell Henry – 'that infidel prince of England' – that he ought now to mend his ways. He should 'take none of the Pope's right or patrimony from him . . . [and] destroy all these new folks of opinion and their new learning'. Furthermore, 'if he married and took Anne to wife, the vengeance of God should plague him' and he would die a 'villain's death'.[58] She even claimed that a letter, written in Heaven by Mary Magdalene in letters of gold, was unimpeachable evidence of the veracity of her predictions.

All this was reported to Cromwell, who had her and her accomplices[59] first watched, then arrested and thrown into the Tower of London for interrogation. Sir Christopher Hole, who had detained four men in Canterbury on Cromwell's instructions, was shocked and horrified at this grievous affront to monks. He begged him 'to send home the religious men as soon as you can' if no hard evidence could be found against them.[60] A vexed Cromwell took a much wider view, for to him Elizabeth's prophecies had a dangerous political dimension. 'If credence should be given to every such lewd person as would affirm himself to have revelations from God, what readier way were there to subvert all commonwealths and good order in the world?' he asked.[61] His investigation also demonstrated that Elizabeth had maintained seditious contacts with followers of the discarded Catherine. He seized 700 copies of *The Nun's Book*, which had just been printed, and had them burnt, along with all the writings about her he could find. This was a very overt example of Tudor political censorship and symptomatic of Cromwell's fears about the power of the printing press over popular susceptibilities.[62]

On his orders, she and five priests and monks were charged with high treason in November 1533. Fisher and More were also accused of 'misprison' of treason – improperly failing to disclose to the authorities the Holy Maid's own treachery. To Henry, she was now no mere gibbering religious fanatic: Elizabeth had conversations with the feisty Gertrude, Marchioness of Exeter, the second wife of Henry Courtenay, who was a grandson of Edward IV and thus a dormant but nonetheless possibly dangerous claimant to the throne. The matter was taking on ever more sinister overtones.

On 23 November, the mystic and some of her fellow prisoners were pushed onto a scaffold at Paul's Cross, outside St Paul's Cathedral, to be harangued by John Salcot, alias Capon, the abbot of the Benedictine abbey of Hyde, just outside the northern gates of Winchester in Hampshire.[63] He denounced her as a vain whore who had been stupidly misled by her confessor Bocking, and whipped the watching crowd up into an eager cacophony of ridicule and derision.[64] The propaganda content of her planned public humiliation smacked of Thomas Cromwell's eloquent prose. Salcot also disseminated salacious rumours of sexual improprieties between Elizabeth and her priests.

Cromwell meanwhile gathered evidence from Thomas Goldwell, prior of Christchurch Priory, and his monks, who were keen to distance themselves from both the 'Holy Maid' and Bocking. The confessor was, the monks wrote in a letter to the King,

> so heinous, so grievous and so displeasant to your majesty that we dare not open our lips to make any prayers or supplications to your highness for him, yet if it might please your highness of your most gracious benignity and natural goodness to extend your super-abundant grace upon him, he should have a thousand times more cause to laud, magnify, observe, love, and pray for your grace.
>
> Whose temerity, furious zeal and malicious blind affection, went about to . . . let, stop, impede and slander your grace's marriage and lawful matrimony which you now enjoy to God's pleasure.[65]

A special commission appointed by Cromwell examined her and she broke down under their relentless questioning, confessing that 'all that she said was feigned of her own imagination, only to satisfy the minds of them which resorted to her and to obtain worldly praise'. Cranmer called them 'mischievous . . . visions' containing 'much perilous sedition and also treason'.[66]

Briefly, Cromwell was in something of a quandary about how to deal with her. His 'remembrances' or notes to himself record: 'To know what the king will have done with the nun and her accomplices.' There were frustrating problems caused by the fact that she had merely spoken treacherous words, rather than committed treasonable acts. This made the chances of a successful prosecution under the law less than certain. Cromwell instead turned to Parliament to secure the deaths of his hapless prisoners. Elizabeth Barton and five others[67] were attainted for high treason when a bill was introduced into the House of Lords on 21 February 1534. It received the royal assent a month later[68] and they were hanged at Tyburn on 20 April. On the scaffold, the 'Holy Maid' dutifully declared:

> I am the cause not only of my own death, which most justly I have richly deserved, but of the death of all those persons who are going to suffer with me. Alas! I was a poor wench without learning, but the praises of the priests about me turned my brain, and I thought I might say anything that came into my head. I, being puffed up with their praises, fell into a certain pride and foolish fantasy with myself . . . Now I cry to God and implore the king's pardon.[69]

Her last words had probably been written for her. She was allowed to hang until she was dead, but the others had their heads struck off. These were set on London Bridge and the four main gates of the city. They had become the first true victims of the Reformation in England.

On 27 February, Cromwell had tried to persuade Fisher to seek the King's pardon for his crime of misprison, having previously employed 'heavy words and terrible threats'[70] about which the Bishop had complained. Cromwell told him:

> If you had . . . tried out the truth of her and of her revelations, you would have taken another way . . . You would not have been contented with the vain voices of the people making bruits [rumours] of her trances and disfigurations, but like a wise, discreet and circumspect prelate, you would have examined such sad and credible persons as were present at her trances . . .
>
> Surely my lord, if the matter comes to trial, your own confession . . . besides the witnesses which are against you, will be sufficient to condemn you.
>
> [If] you beseech the king's grace . . . to be your gracious lord and to remit unto you your negligence, oversight and offence committed against his highness . . . I dare undertake that his highness shall benignly accept you into his gracious favour, all matters of displeasures past before this time forgotten and forgiven.[71]

Fisher, old and sick, remained unbowed, but escaped with a fine of £300. The charge against Sir Thomas More was dropped after he disowned the nun as a 'lewd . . . and wicked woman' and 'that silly nun'. He wrote to Cromwell: 'My poor heart is pierced at the idea that his majesty should think me guilty. I confess I did believe that nun to be inspired but I put away far from me every thought of treason.'[72]

Inconvenient and politically incorrect prophecies appeared to occupy much of Cromwell's time that season. A Warwickshire priest, Ralph Wendon, predicted that 'a queen should be burned at Smithfield' and vehemently hoped it might be that 'whore and harlot Queen Anne'.[73] Mrs Amadas, widow of Cromwell's predecessor as Master of Henry's Jewel House, prophesied that the King, 'cursed with God's own mouth', would be banished from his realm, which, before midsummer 1534, would be conquered by a Scots army.[74] She claimed that there was a mysterious monk, living on an island, who would summon the Commons and Lords to the Tower of London to sit as 'the Parliament of Peace'. The distraught widow also alleged that the King had plied her with gifts to 'make her a whore' and that there had been attempts to lure her to Sir William Compton's house, where Henry planned to seduce her.[75] Poor Mrs Amadas – she was clearly completely mad.

Cromwell was still introducing a steady stream of new legislation, some directly related to the supremacy, the rest to slightly less pressing matters. Amongst this latter group was the Buggery Act of 1533,[76] the first penal law against homosexuals in England and Wales. Existing measures against heterosexual sex offences punished only rape and adultery. The new Act decreed death by hanging for anyone guilty of 'the detestable and abominable vice of buggery [anal sex] committed with mankind or beast'.[77]

The reasons why this particular piece of law-making was deemed necessary by Cromwell remain unclear, unless it was intended as yet another weapon against the clergy, specifically, perhaps, to reduce the jurisdiction of the ecclesiastical courts. Aside from this, Cromwell frequently took an unforgiving moralistic stance against immorality of any kind – although he probably supported mistresses himself – and the entry of this legislation onto the statute book may reflect a new biblical fundamentalism in his thinking. For example, in 1536, one of his henchmen visited the archdeaconry of Coventry, Stafford and Derby and found, to his horror, that 'Most of the knights and gentlemen live so incontinently, having concubines and their children openly in their houses and putting away their wives, that the country is offended and takes evil example [from] them.' The miscreants were ordered to take back their wives and expel their mistresses, or else appear before Cromwell in London to 'show cause why they should not be compelled' to do so.[78]

More pertinent was the Act of Supremacy,[79] declaring that Henry, 'his heirs and successors, kings of this realm . . . [was/were] the only Supreme Head in earth of the Church of England called *Anglicana Ecclesia* and shall have and enjoy . . . all honours, dignities . . . immunities, profits and commodities to the said dignity'. All references to the Pope, now only the 'Bishop of Rome', were to be erased from the prayer books in every church.

There was much muttering and rumbling in the country about the King's business, a lot of it stirred up by the clergy. James Harrison, the parson of Leigh, Lancashire, was incensed in July 1533 when he heard about the proclamation of Anne as queen: 'I will none for queen but Queen Catherine! Who the devil made Nan Boleyn, that whore, queen?'[80] William ap Lli, a Welsh priest, in the same month 'wished to have the king upon a mountain in North Wales called the Withvay, otherwise called Snowdon . . . He would souse [beat] the king about the ears until he had his head soft enough.'[81] The Colchester monk Dan John Frances claimed in January 1534 that the King and his Council were 'all heretics, whereas before they were but schismatics'.[82] He added graphically that when Henry had gone to Boulogne to meet Francis I, 'the Queen's grace followed his arse as the dog follows his master's arse'.[83]

Unsurprisingly, therefore, the Act of Succession, speedily enacted in March 1534, demanded personal commitment to the breach with Rome, if commanded, from every subject within the realm aged over fourteen. The preamble summed up the new reality of governance in the realm:

The Bishop of Rome . . . contrary to the great and inviolable grants of jurisdictions given by God immediately to emperors, kings and princes in succession to their heirs, has presumed in times past to invest who should please them to inherit in other men's kingdoms and dominions, which thing, we your most humble subjects both spiritual and temporal do most abhor and detest.

The continuance and sufferance whereof, deeply considered and pondered, were too dangerous to be suffered any longer within this realm and too much contrary to the unity, peace and tranquillity of the same, being greatly reproachable and dishonourable to the whole realm.[84]

All might now have to take an oath declaring their sacred belief that the marriage between Henry and Anne was lawful. At the same time they would also have to swear their allegiance to Princess Elizabeth (and any other children of the marriage) as rightful and lawful successors to the throne. There was no room now for neutrality in Henry's England: you were either for the King, or against him.

The words of the oath were drawn up by Lord Chancellor Audley and the Dukes of Norfolk and Suffolk. They were quite simple and direct:

You swear to bear faith, truth and obedience alone to the king's body and to his heirs of his most dear and entirely beloved lawful wife Queen Anne, begotten and to be begotten. Further to the heirs of our said sovereign lord according to the limitation in the statute made for surety of succession in the crown of this realm and not to any other within this realm, nor foreign authority or potentate . . .

And that to your cunning, wit and uttermost of your power, without guile, fraud or any undue means, you shall observe, keep, maintain and defend the said Act of Succession . . . against all manner of persons of what estate, dignity, degree or condition [who]soever they be . . . And in no way attempt, nor to your power suffer to be done or attempted . . . anything, privily or apartly, to the let, hindrance, damage or derogation thereof . . . by any manner of means . . . or pretence.

So help you God and all saints and the holy evangelists.[85]

It was treason for anyone to oppose the succession, by writing or any action, and misprison to speak against it.

And Cromwell now extended the legal definition of treason. His

Treasons Act,[86] passed the same year, dragged a wide-sweeping range of activities into the realm of treachery against monarch and state. It was now high treason to:

- 'maliciously wish, will or desire by words or writing, or by crafty images invent, practise or attempt bodily harm' to the king, queen or their heirs apparent.
- deprive them of their dignity, title, name or of their royal estates.
- 'slanderously or maliciously to publish and pronounce by express writing or words that the king our sovereign lord is a heretic, schismatic, tyrant, infidel or usurper'.

For good measure, he threw in a new crime of 'rebelliously' detaining or delaying any of the King's ships, ammunition or artillery.[87]

By an unkind stroke of fate, on 23 March 1534, in Rome – after seven impossible years of painful deliberation, negotiation, wrangling, recriminations and diplomatic impasse – Pope Clement VII finally awarded judgment to Catherine, ruling that her marriage to Henry was entirely valid under God's law. Unfortunately, he had missed the English boat, which had sailed on without him.

Back in London events were moving fast. On 13 April, senior members of the clergy, amongst them Bishop Fisher, were summoned to Lambeth Palace to take the Oath of Succession. Sir Thomas More was also called there from his home across the Thames at Chelsea. He was happy to swear the Oath of Succession, but would not sign any document that contained the preamble to the Act, which covered the supremacy. As Cromwell told Cranmer: 'If [Fisher and More] be sworn to the succession and not to the preamble, it is to be thought that it might be taken not only as a confirmation of the Bishop of Rome's authority but also as a reprobation of the king's second marriage. No such things should be brought into the heads of the people.' Therefore, the King demanded that both should take the full oath: 'His grace specially trusts that you will in no way attempt to move [persuade] him to the contrary. That manner of swearing, if it should be suffered, might be an utter destruction to his whole cause and also to the effect of the law.'[88]

There was no escape. Four days later, More was arrested on charges of misprison, taken by river to the Tower and lodged in the Bell Tower, next door to the rooms of the lieutenant of the fortress. Sir Richard Southwell, who had escorted him, advised him to send home the chain of gold that he wore around his neck. More refused, saying, 'No sir, that I will not, for if I were taken in the field with my enemies, as I am a knight, I wish they should fare somewhat the better for me.'[89]

Fisher, who also refused to take the oath, joined him behind the curtain walls of the Tower. Both were detained at the King's pleasure. Cromwell also arrested four Carthusian monks, the secular priest John Haile and Richard Reynolds, a monk from the Bridgettine house at Syon, Middlesex, all for refusing to take the Oath of Succession.

But elsewhere, by July 1534, a total of 7342 people in England and Wales had sworn the oath.[90]

Faithful servants should always receive their just rewards. For Cromwell, a grateful sovereign continued to bestow upon him appointments and grants of lands. On 12 April 1533, he had been appointed Chancellor of the Exchequer, in connection with his duties in dealing with the royal finances. Later that year he was given the sinecure positions of Recorder of Bristol and Steward of Westminster Abbey.

Now came his crowning moment: Henry's chief secretary, Bishop Gardiner, was in disgrace for opposing the Act of Supremacy and had been banished from court. Cromwell was chosen to formally succeed him some time around 15 April 1534 and swiftly turned the job into that of the King's Chief Minister and head of national security.

In his podgy hands, he now tightly held all the reins of England's government.

CHAPTER FOUR

A Bloody Season

By the Mass . . . it is perilous striving with princes.
And therefore I would wish you somewhat to incline to
the king's pleasure. By God's Body, Master More,
Indignatio principis mors est – *the anger of the*
prince means death.

THOMAS HOWARD, DUKE OF NORFOLK, TO SIR THOMAS MORE, 1534[1]

Henry was never a king who could endure any opposition. Bishop Fisher and Sir Thomas More were now both safely incarcerated in the Tower of London, their resistance to the Oath of Succession and the Act of Supremacy effectively neutralised. That was not enough for the King. Cromwell's new treason legislation had made 'malicious denial' of the royal title an inescapable capital offence. For Henry the issue was simple and clear cut: if you had new powers, why not use them to destroy your enemies once and for all?

The trigger for his vengeance was an inopportune decision by the new sixty-six-year-old Pope Paul III, who was elected to succeed Clement VII on 12 October 1534. On 20 May 1535, he created Fisher a cardinal priest of St Vitalis, presumably in the hope that this would improve his treatment in England.[2]

The Pope and his advisers did not understand Henry. It was like showing a red hat to a bull.

The King flew into a mighty rage and forbade Fisher's cardinal's hat to be sent to England. He declared bitingly that he would 'send [Fisher's] head afterwards to Rome for the cardinal's hat'.[3]

Sir Gregory Casalis, Henry VIII's agent at the Vatican, reported to Cromwell on 29 May regarding the reaction to his official protests at the Pope's decision:

> I went to all the friendly cardinals and remonstrated with them for offending the king and [his] kingdom in this way, for the Bishop of Rochester was sticking to his opinion against the king from vainglory for which cause he was in prison . . .
>
> I expressed the greatest indignation, so that the whole city talked of it and the Pope sent for me. I spoke even more strongly to his Holiness, telling him that he had never made a graver mistake. He tried to show that he had acted with good intent.

Casalis strongly advised the pontiff not to send the red hat without hearing from England first. Paul III, for his part, begged him to use all means to explain and excuse the act to Henry.[4]

The diplomatic ripples spread ever wider across the European pond. Ridolfo Pio, Bishop of Faenza and the papal nuncio in France, appealed to the French King in early June for his help in freeing Fisher from prison. Francis I was less than optimistic at his chances:

> He doubted his success for he feared this hat would cause [Fisher] much injury . . . The King of England was the hardest friend to bear in the world; at one time unstable and at another . . . obstinate and proud, so it was almost impossible to deal with him.
>
> Sometimes, said Francis, he almost treats me like a subject . . . He is the strangest man in the world and I fear I can do no good with him, but I must put up with him, as it is no time to lose friends.[5]

Fisher, elderly and sick, was thus left to his dire fate.

Cromwell, meanwhile, was busy accumulating evidence to provide a veneer of legality for Fisher's destruction. One account claims that one of Cromwell's servants tricked the Bishop into making an outright denial of the supremacy after being promised that nothing he said would subsequently be used against him during his arraignment.[6] So much for the lawyer's phrase 'without prejudice' that covers pre-trial conversations. Cromwell certainly led a delegation from the King's Council to see Fisher in the Tower and to question him on his attitude to the supremacy. After the Bishop again refused to take the oath, Cromwell read out the provisions of the Treasons Act, so the prelate could be in no doubt as to the consequences. The iron jaws of his legal trap had snapped tight on the frail Bishop.

The executioner in London had a busy, blood-soaked schedule that early summer.

On 29 April 1535, three Carthusian priors and two priests appeared before the Court of King's Bench at Westminster for their blatant denial of the supremacy.[7] Cromwell had led their interrogations at his official residence of the Master of the Rolls. John Houghton, prior of the London Charterhouse, and Robert Lawrence and Augustine Webster, priors of Beauvale in Nottinghamshire and the Isle of Axholme in Lincolnshire respectively, appeared with Dr Richard Reynolds, a monk of the Bridgettine house at Syon, on the banks of the Thames in Middlesex, John Hale, the vicar of nearby Isleworth, and Robert Feron or Fern of Teddington.

Syon was at that time a hotbed of treasonable gossip. A 'fellow of Bristol' had several conversations concerning the King's marriage 'and other behaviours of his bodily lust'. Reynolds recounted a conversation with the porter, who claimed that 'our sovereign lord had a sort [a company][8] of maidens over one of his chambers at Farnham [Castle, Surrey] while he was with the old lord [Bishop] of Winchester'. Thomas Moody, priest, had corresponded with Feron about the rumour that 'the king's grace had meddled with the queen's [Anne's] mother'. A layman predicted that the Pope would be in England before midsummer.[9] Hale, moreover, told Feron graphically that the King's life was

> more foul and more stinking than a sow, wallowing and defiling herself in any filthy place. For however great he is, he is fully given to his foul pleasure of the flesh . . . And look how many matrons be in the court or given to marriage, these almost all he has violated, so often neglecting his duty to his wife and offending the sacrament of matrimony.

> And now he has taken to his wife of fornication this matron Anne, not only to the highest shame and undoing of himself but also of all this realm.[10]

It was an open-and-shut case against them. All were found guilty of treason and sentenced to the traitor's death of hanging, drawing and quartering. But Feron was later pardoned, officially 'on account of his youth' but more probably because he had turned king's evidence.

The sentences were carried out on 4 May at Tyburn, the site of today's Marble Arch. None of the victims had been degraded from their order and were pointedly executed while still wearing their monks' habits and priestly vestments. They were dragged on hurdles from the Tower to the killing place and there were hanged until half-dead, then cut down, castrated and their vital organs ripped from their bodies and burnt. Finally, the corpses were beheaded and quartered. The scaffold was like a gigantic gory butcher's block. Pio, the papal nuncio in France, was horrified: 'Their heads and feet were displayed on the public gates [of the city]. One piece [was displayed] at the gate of the Charterhouse monastery to terrify the monks . . . The whole city is displeased as they were of exemplary and holy life.'[11]

There was more judicial slaughter to come. Another three monks from the London Charterhouse – Humphrey Middlemore, William Exemere and Sebastian Newdigate – were accused of denying the supremacy at Stepney on 25 May 1535.

Cromwell was amongst the judges at a special commission of oyer and terminer[12] for Middlesex, sitting at Westminster, to try the three Carthusian monks and Fisher on 11 and 17 June.[13] The monks were swiftly found guilty and sentenced to death. For thirteen days they were shackled by chains around their necks and arms in Newgate Jail, cruelly forcing them to remain standing.[14] They were executed at Tyburn on 19 June. Fisher, humiliatingly described as a 'clerk, otherwise late Bishop of Rochester', was alleged to have openly declared on 7 May that 'our sovereign lord is not Supreme Head in Earth of the Church of England'.[15] He too was sentenced to die as a traitor, but the sentence was reduced to beheading.

Three days later, on 22 June, Fisher was carried out of the chamber in the Tower in a chair, as he was too weak to walk after his months of imprisonment. The four sheriff's officers who had lugged him up the slope to Tower Hill were going to assist him up the steps to the scaffold but he shrugged them off: 'Nay, masters, now let me alone. You shall see me going to my death well enough myself without help.'

After his gown was removed, many in the crowd 'marvelled to see [any man] bearing life to be so far consumed, for he seemed a lean carcass; the flesh clean wasted away . . . As one might say, death in a man's shape and using a man's voice.'[16]

Fisher lay prone on the straw of the scaffold, his neck 'on a little block . . . Then came quickly the executioner and with a sharp and heavy axe cut asunder his neck and so severed his head.' The crowd were astonished 'to see so much blood come out of so old, lean, slender, weak and sickly a body'.[17]

Fisher's corpse was left under guard for nine hours, and that evening the executioner and some soldiers dug a grave 'hard against the wall' on the north side of the churchyard of nearby All Hallows, Barking, in Upper Thames Street. 'Without any reverence, they vilely threw his . . . dead body, all naked, flat upon his belly, without any winding sheet or accustomed funeral ceremonies and . . . following herein the command of the king, buried it very contemptuously.' His head was parboiled and set up high over London Bridge, alongside those of the Carthusian monks who had been executed before him. But even after two weeks, it 'looked very fresh and lively as though it had been alive, looking upon the people coming into London, which many of the people took for a miracle . . . and notifying the world of the blessed bishop's innocence and holiness.'[18] The chronicler Edward Hall said Fisher's face 'was observed to become fresher and more comely day by day and that such was the concourse of people who assembled to look at it, that almost neither cart nor horse could pass'.[19]

The day after Fisher's execution, Henry attended a pageant that celebrated the royal supremacy and his triumph over the clergy. The court was then at Windsor, and the King reportedly walked ten miles at two o'clock in the morning, carrying a two-handed sword, to the village where the spectacle, probably organised by Cromwell's agents, was to be staged on the eve of St John the Baptist's Nativity. 'He [Henry] got into a house where he could see everything. He was so pleased at seeing himself cutting off the heads of the clergy that in order to laugh at his ease and encourage the people, he discovered [revealed] himself. He sent to tell his lady [Anne] that she ought to see the representation of it repeated on the eve of St Peter.'[20]

It was now Sir Thomas More's turn to face Henry's justice. Cromwell had visited him at the Tower at the end of April to inform him that the King now desired his opinion about the succession and his supremacy over the Church. More replied that he had 'discharged his mind of all such matters and would neither dispute the King's titles nor the Pope's but is and will be the King's true, faithful subject'. Cromwell said this answer would not satisfy Henry – 'a prince not of rigour but of mercy and pity'. Although the former Lord Chancellor was now condemned to perpetual imprisonment, 'he was not discharged of his obedience and allegiance to the king'. More insisted he was the King's faithful subject:

> He did no one any harm, said no harm and thought no harm – but wished every one good. If this was not enough to keep a man alive, he longed not to live. He was dying already and since he came here, he had been [several] times in such a case [state] that he thought he would die within the hour; but was never sorry for it, but rather sorry when the pang passed. There-fore, his poor body was at the king's pleasure and he wished that his death could do him good.[21]

On 3 June, Cromwell, together with Archbishop Cranmer, saw More again at the Tower. Again he refused to take the oath. Exasperated, Cromwell told him he liked him 'worse than the last time, for then he pitied him. But now he thought he meant not well.'[22]

More came up for trial at Westminster Hall on 1 July. The main witness was Solicitor General Sir Richard Riche, who had gone to the Tower on 12 June with two of Cromwell's men, Sir Richard Southwell and Thomas Palmer, to collect More's books. Riche described his conversation with More:

You know that our lord and king is constituted supreme head on earth of the Church of England and why ought not you, Master More, affirm and accept him so . . .

To which More, persevering in his treasons, answered that . . . a king can be made by Parliament and deprived by Parliament; to which Act every subject being at the Parliament may give his assent but as to the primacy, a subject cannot be bound because he cannot give his consent to that in Parliament.[23]

More maintained the witness had lied: 'In good faith Master Riche, I am more sorry for your perjury than for my peril.'[24] After being condemned for treason, he abandoned his sophisticated legal arguments and relied instead on his eloquence: 'Since I am condemned (and God knows how), I will speak freely for the discharge of my conscience what I think of this law.

'For the seven years I have studied the matter, I have not read any approved order of the Church that a temporal lord could or ought to be head of the spirituality.'

Lord Chancellor Sir Thomas Audley, genuinely surprised at More's words, asked: 'What! You wish to be considered wiser or of better conscience than all the bishops and nobles of this realm?'

More replied: 'My lord, for one bishop of your opinion, I have 100 saints of mine and for one Parliament of yours, and God knows what kind, I have all the General Councils for 1,000 years and for one kingdom, I have France and all the kingdoms of Christendom.'

Norfolk, another of his judges, interrupted and declared that More's malice was now patently clear. The condemned man snapped back:

Noble sir, not any malice or obstinacy causes me to say this but the just necessity of the cause constrains me for the discharge of my conscience and satisfaction of my soul.

I say further that your Statute is ill-made because you have sworn never to do anything against the church, which through all Christendom is one and undivided and you have no authority, without the common consent of all Christians, to make a law or Act of Parliament, or council against the honour of Christendom.

I know well that the reason why you have condemned me is because I have never been willing to consent to the king's second marriage but I hope in the divine goodness and mercy, that as St Paul and St Stephen (which he persecuted), are now friends in Paradise, so we, though differing in this world, shall be united in perfect harmony in the other.

I pray God to protect the king and give him good counsel.[25]

More was brought out of the Tower at around nine o'clock on the morning of 6 July 1535. The scaffold on Tower Hill was 'ill-constructed, weak and ready to fall' and the prisoner joked with Edward Walsingham, the Lieutenant of the Tower, 'I pray you Mr Lieutenant, see me safe up, and for my coming down, let me shift for myself.' He told the executioner: 'I am sorry my neck is very short. Strike not awry for saving of your honesty.' He added: 'I pray you let me lay my beard over the block, least you should cut it.'[26] Thus, with another quip, his life was ended with one blow of the axe.

His head was also set up on a pike on London Bridge, replacing Fisher's, which was then thrown into the river. The Bishop's body was exhumed from All Hallows' churchyard and buried with More's in the Chapel of St Peter ad Vincula in the Tower, near the vestry door.

In Rome, Paul III wrote to Francis I that Henry 'had exceeded his ancestors in wickedness'. He was compelled by the 'unanimous solicitation of the cardinals to declare Henry deprived of his kingdom and his royal dignity'. The Pope sought help from the French King, 'his most dear son, having always been accustomed to have recourse to his predecessors in the [Church's] oppression, [and] earnestly implore him . . . to be ready to execute justice on Henry . . . remembering the great armies [with] which your forefathers revenged her injuries'.[27]

Cromwell expressed surprise at the Pope's indignation at the deaths of Fisher and More. He told Casalis, the English agent at the Vatican: 'They were openly tried and convicted of high treason. Their punishment was much milder than the laws prescribe and many have, from their example, returned to their loyalty. Anyone of sound judgement may see how precipitately the Pope and the Roman court have taken offence at this.' He dextrously wielded the airbrush of propaganda: 'These men alone [opposed the law of the land] pretending that they were entirely given up to the contemplation of divine things and endeavoured to refute and evade these laws by fallacious arguments. Let not the Pope be offended if the king acts in accordance with his own right and that of his kingdom.'[28]

The Spanish ambassador in London, Eustace Chapuys, reported on 11 July that John Stokesley, Bishop of London, 'who never preached a sermon in his life, on account of his stammering and bad speaking, preached this morning in [St Paul's] Cathedral by the King's order.' Cromwell was present to ensure the correct words were stuttered out: 'The whole of the sermon was to invalidate the king's first marriage and to deny the authority of the Pope and those who favoured it – even those who have suffered death in its defence. The other bishops must do the same or it will cost them their benefices and their lives.'[29]

But despite the propaganda, despite the preaching, the imperious and demanding Queen Anne remained as unpopular as ever throughout the realm.

Many of the clergy continued to be obdurate and unbending about the marriage and the supremacy. The vicar of Rye in East Sussex had a little book, Ekius's *Enchiridion*, which argued against the King being the head of the Church, and a friar at Blackfriars in London earnestly desired to see the head of every supporter of the new learning upon a stake and Henry to die a 'violent and shameful death' and also 'that mischievous whore the queen to be burnt'.[30]

Others got into trouble for less violent language. Poor old Dr Carsley, a canon residentiary of Wells Cathedral in Somerset, mentioned 'Lady Catherine the Queen' when leading the prayers one Sunday in February 1535. This crime was merely 'a slip of the tongue' and when the Bishop reproved him, he expressed his sorrow, saying he thought not 'much of the lady Catherine and meant only Queen Anne for I know no more queens but her'. Cromwell was told: 'He is a good man, not much under eighty and it was evidently said unawares.'[31]

Margaret Chancellor, alias Ellis, a spinster of Bradfield in Suffolk, was interrogated by local justices after she called the Queen 'a goggle-eyed whore' and blessed Catherine 'as the righteous queen – and she trusted to see her queen again'. Now wholly penitent, she explained she had been drunk and that 'an evil spirit' had caused her to utter those treasonable words.[32]

George Taylor, of Newport Pagnell in Buckinghamshire, claimed in February 1535 that 'the king is but a knave and lives in adultery and is a heretic and lives not after the laws of God'. Furthermore, he was not bound 'by the king's crown and if I had it here, I would play football with it'. Again, his outburst was put down to drunkenness, but nevertheless Sir Francis Bryan advocated indicting him as a traitor. He told Cromwell that 'due execution of justice in this case will be a very great example and the safeguard of many'.[33]

Continuing disapproval of Anne Boleyn was not confined to bucolic alehouse rantings and the resentful clergy. In the sumptuous surroundings of the court, Henry Percy, Sixth Earl of Northumberland, spoke bitterly of Anne's 'arrogance and malice', reporting that she had used 'such shameful words to the Duke of Norfolk as one would not address to a dog, so that he was compelled to quit the royal chamber. In his indignation . . . he uttered reproaches against [her] of which the least was to call her *le grande putain* [the great whore].'[34]

Chapuys told Charles V in May 1535 that the Queen – he scornfully called her Henry's concubine – was 'more haughty than ever and ventures to tell the king that he is more bound to her than man can be to woman, for she extricated him from a sin'. Reports also circulated in government circles in Spain that Henry was growing 'weary and tired' of her.[35]

Early the following month she clashed angrily with her ally Cromwell and threatened to cut his head off his shoulders. But he seemed curiously untroubled by her tantrum and explained to Chapuys, 'I trust so much in my master that I fancy she cannot do me any harm.' The ambassador had his doubts, however, as he needed Cromwell as his own window into the court's intrigues and machinations. He reported: 'I could not but wish him a more gracious mistress and one more grateful for the inestimable services he has done the king.' He 'begged and entreated' Cromwell 'to guard against her attacks more effectively than the cardinal [Wolsey] had done, which I hoped his dexterity and prudence will be able to accomplish'. He pondered privately whether Cromwell had invented the Queen's tirade

> in order to enhance his merchandise [standing with him]. All I can say is that everyone considers him Anne's right hand. Indeed, I hear from a reliable source that night and day, the lady [is] working to bring about the Duke of Norfolk's disgrace with the king. Whether it be owing to his having spoken too freely about her or [that] Cromwell wishes to bring down the aristocracy of this kingdom, I cannot say.[36]

But the root cause of the Queen's frequent bouts of fury was undoubtedly Catherine of Aragon, who threw a dark shadow of menace across her life at court. Cromwell's crony Thomas Bedyll told him in October 1534 that the household servants of the 'Princess Dowager' still persisted in calling her queen.[37] Thus Catherine and her daughter Mary, now aged eighteen, were a constant irritant to Anne, and the Spanish ambassador feared that her nagging would coerce Henry into treating them cruelly. 'To which the concubine will urge him with all her power . . . saying it was a shame to him and all the realm that they were not punished as traitors, according to the statues.'[38] Dr Pedro Ortiz, the imperial envoy based in Rome, recounted Anne's bitter feelings towards her stepdaughter Mary: 'She is my death and I am hers, so I will take care that she will not laugh at me after my death.'[39]

Chapuys also reported that the Queen 'constantly speaks of them as rebels, deserving death and Cromwell would willingly say what Caiaphas did', referring to the Jewish High Priest who urged that Christ should be put to death.[40] Moreover, Anne 'had suborned a person to say that he had [received] a revelation from God that she could not conceive while the two ladies were alive'.[41] Here lay the crux of the tensions afflicting England's King and Queen.

Anne no longer lived up to her personal motto: 'The Most Happy'. After probably suffering a miscarriage in July 1534, she was so desperate to become pregnant again – it was her principal role as queen, after all – that in her despair and frustration she spoke slightingly of Henry's lacklustre performance in bed where, she said, he had neither skill nor virility.[42] Attacking Henry's over-inflated ego was tantamount to suicide within his whispering, rumour-ridden court and these unwise indiscretions were to count against her in the future. But eventually, in October 1535, she conceived another child.

Catherine meanwhile lived in continual dread that she and her daughter would be called upon, under Cromwell's new statutes, formally to abjure their titles of queen and princess and recognise, by oath, the legal validity of Henry's marriage with Anne. Possibly because of her stress and fear, Mary fell seriously ill in February 1535 and Catherine pleaded with Chapuys to ask the King to send his daughter to her, so she could 'treat her with my own hands . . . There is no need of any other persons but myself to nurse her . . . I will put her into my own bed where I sleep and will watch her when needful.'[43]

But Henry feared that bringing the two women together would make them a rallying point for opposition to his marriage and his supremacy over the Church. In March 1535, with unusual frankness, he told Chapuys that he 'would take good care not to send [Mary] thither, for the queen, being so haughty in spirit, she might by favour of the princess, raise a number of men and make war as boldly as did Queen Isabella, her mother'. The King bluntly sent Mary word via her governess that 'he had no worse enemy in the world than her and that she was the cause of mischief . . . The king declared publicly that her conduct was calculated to encourage conspiracy against him.'[44]

The Spanish envoy was convinced there was a conspiracy to kill Mary, or at least so badly neglect her that she succumbed to her illness. In April he told his imperial master Charles V of a sinister conversation he had with Cromwell about the princess. The Minister 'several times told me that it was the princess who created the difficulty and troubled matters and that if it pleased God . . . He did not dare to say more, but it was quite clear what he wished.'[45]

On another occasion, he 'was not ashamed to throw out hints that it would be a comfort if the two ladies could be got rid of'. There was other circumstantial evidence to support these suggestions of his malice, which was also keenly felt by the King. Henry bragged that he would now fulfil some old prophecies about himself: at the beginning of his reign he was as gentle as a lamb 'and at the end, worse than a lion and that he would despatch those who were in the Tower and some that were not there as well'.[46] The threat was unspoken but nonetheless the King's meaning was crystal clear: if all else failed, he was willing to execute his first wife and their daughter to neutralise the danger they posed to his crown.

In October 1535, Catherine wrote to Pope Paul III urging him to have special consideration for England and warning the pontiff that 'if a remedy be not applied with all speed, there will be no end to the loss of souls or to the making of martyrs'. She was writing plainly to fully discharge her conscience 'as one who expects death, along with my daughter'.[47]

The Pope, rather limply, could only call for prayers from the faithful in Spain for Catherine and Mary, on St John's Day – 24 June 1536. He generously offered seven years and seven Lents of pardon to all those who said three paternosters 'in memory of Christ's death, when the bell rings at 3 p.m.' on that day. Ortiz in Rome believed Paul's intention was that 'all these prayers shall be offered for the queen and princess and the saints who are fighting for the faith in England'.[48] No doubt Catherine found comfort in the promise of all those devout prayers by so many of the Catholic faithful.

But by the end of the year, she was dying and Cromwell was told of her impending end that Christmas.

After New Year 1536, Chapuys hastened to Kimbolton Castle, Huntingdonshire,[49] where Catherine was now confined: 'On my arrival she called me at once, that it might not be supposed her sickness was feigned and also because there was a friend of Cromwell's who the king had sent to accompany me, or rather to spy.' The envoy spent four days at her bedside and departed, comforted that she seemed a little better.

It was her last brave rally before her death. On 9 January, Cromwell sent Chapuys a message announcing that Catherine had died two days before at two o'clock in the afternoon, having heard the news himself that morning from Sir Edward Chamberlain and Sir Edmund Bedingfield of her household.[50] She was just over fifty years old. Chapuys told her nephew Charles V:

The queen's illness began about five weeks ago . . . and the attack was renewed on the morrow of Christmas Day. It was a pain in the stomach, so violent that she could retain no food.

I asked her physician several times if there was any suspicion of poison. He said he was afraid it was so, for after she had drunk some Welsh beer she had been worse and that it must have been a slow and subtle poison for he could not discover evidences of simple and pure poison.

On opening her, indications will be seen.[51]

Cromwell played a dangerous game of disinformation to distract Chapuys and defuse any talk of Catherine's supposed murder. He told him of rumours received from France, which had 'originated from Spaniards . . . that the late queen was poisoned. This Cromwell could not tell me without some visible change of colour and countenance.'[52]

News of Catherine's death delighted the Queen and her faction at court. Anne, showing 'great joy', gave the messenger a 'handsome present'. Her father, the Earl of Wiltshire, commented that it was a pity Mary 'did not keep company with her [mother]'. Henry, when told, exclaimed: 'God be praised that we are free from all suspicion of war.' But Chapuys maintained that Anne, in the privacy of her chamber afterwards, 'cried and lamented, fearing she herself might be brought to the same end'.[53] The ambassador wrote that the next day, a Sunday, Henry was clad in celebratory yellow 'from top to toe, except for the white feather he had in his bonnet' and the

Little Bastard [two-year-old Princess Elizabeth] was conducted to Mass with trumpets and other great triumphs.

After dinner, the king entered the room in which the ladies danced and there did several things like one transported with joy.

At last he sent for his Little Bastard, and carrying her in his arms, he showed her first to one and then another.[54]

Cromwell was charged with the delicate matter of arranging a funeral for a discarded queen. Sadler reported to him that the King had decided there would be no elaborate funeral hearse[55] with candles and tapers in St

Paul's Cathedral to mark her passing and had told the French ambassador that he was not paying for any mourning clothes.[56] The obsequies should befit someone of royal status but not be too expensive. Cromwell's detailed plan for her burial in Peterborough Cathedral survives.[57] It styles her: 'The right excellent and noble Princess and Lady Catherine, daughter to the right high and mighty Prince Ferdinand, late King of Castille and late wife to the noble and excellent Prince Arthur, brother to our sovereign lord King Henry VIII.' Even in death, her status had to be politically correct. On her tomb, the arms of Wales[58] were quartered with those of Spain. Her marriage to Henry had been thoroughly expunged from history.

Catherine's belongings, stored in Baynard's Castle in London, were carefully catalogued by Sir Edward Baynton in February. Of them, two ivory chessboards and pieces, a set of red and white ivory chessmen and a desk covered with black velvet were appropriated by Henry himself. A case of wooden trenchers (plates), a coffer covered with crimson velvet and two working stools of ivory were selected by Queen Anne for her personal use.[59]

On 24 January 1536, the eve of the Conversion of St Paul, Henry took a starring role in a joust at the royal tilting yard at the palace at Greenwich. It may have been a sport full of chivalry, romance and dash, but it was also recklessly dangerous for a king without a lawful male heir to his throne. He met with a terrible accident: 'The king, mounted on a great horse to run at the lists, both fell so heavily that everyone thought it a miracle he was not killed, but he sustained no injury.'[60]

That was the official version of events. His injuries were, in reality, far more serious and were caused by his armoured charger falling on him, crushing him beneath. Later he was reported to have been laid low 'for two hours without speech', possibly through severe concussion or, worse still, bruising of the cerebral cortex.[61] Cromwell, however, reported 'that the king is merry and in perfect health', but in his words one can smell the sixteenth-century spin of a devious minister.

Five days later Anne miscarried of a heavy male fetus aged about three and a half months, after Norfolk, her uncle, told her of the King's accident. She put the loss of the child down to shock at the news.[62] Henry was less than sympathetic. He told her bluntly that 'he would have no more boys by her'.[63] He departed her bedside with 'ill grace', snapping: 'When you are up, I will come to speak to you.'

He was tiring of his sharp-tongued, jealous queen, always conscious of her status, always ready to feel affronted. During the previous three months he had barely exchanged words with her on ten occasions. The King was now forty-four and beginning to feel his age. His chances of siring an heir with his current wife looked increasingly remote. Chapuys, although armed only with second-hand court tittle-tattle, reported gleefully that Henry had told a courtier

> in great secrecy and as a confession, that he had been seduced and forced into this second marriage by means of sortileges [sorcery or witchcraft] and charms and that owing to that, he would hold it as nullified. God, he said, had well shown his displeasure at it by denying him male children.
>
> He therefore considered he could take a third wife which he said he wished much to do.[64]

This was becoming a familiar royal refrain. Coldly, calculatingly, Henry now reasoned that it was time to move on. He had already identified Anne's successor: one of her own ladies, twenty-six-year-old Jane Seymour, whose eldest brother Edward was one of Henry's esquires of the body. He had rid himself of one unwanted wife. Now that he was supreme head of the Church in England, why not again?

Henry naturally turned to Cromwell to remove this unwanted tartar.

Only too conscious of Wolsey's fate when he had failed the King in a similar situation, the Minister decided guile and cunning needed to be applied to the problem, as he knew she would not go quietly. Anne was already aware of the whispering campaign being mounted against her at court and was now openly on bad terms with Cromwell. Attack was the best form of defence. On 2 April, her almoner John Skip audaciously delivered a sermon on the text 'Which among you accuses me of sin?', taken from St John, chapter eight. He attacked Cromwell, comparing him with the Old Testament character of Haman, the scheming councillor of the Persian King Ahasuerus (also known as Xerxes), who ended up being hanged on the very gallows he had built for Mordecai, the protector of Queen Esther.[65] Skip was roundly rebuked for interfering in matters of state.

At Easter, Cromwell willingly gave up his rooms at Greenwich Palace for Jane Seymour's use. Dour Cromwell was playing the unfamiliar role of procurer, or, more generously, Cupid. His apartment was conveniently located, as Henry could visit her at all times 'by certain galleries without being perceived'.

Ironically, the text for Skip's sermon came from the New Testament parable of the woman taken in adultery and this may have inspired the Minister with the idea to investigate or, more accurately, invent accusations of faithlessness against the embattled Queen. On 24 April, a special commission headed by Cromwell and Norfolk (by now definitely no friend of his niece) was set up to find damning faults in the Queen's character and behaviour.

It was all too easy. Mark Smeaton, a groom of the privy chamber and a musician and dancer who was probably a covert homosexual, was lured from Greenwich and tortured, probably by Cromwell, into a stammering confession that he had become Anne's lover. There were always a number of youthful courtiers around the Queen, fluttering like moths about a bright flame. Now their wings were burnt for dancing too close to the King's private life. Five were accused of enjoying carnal knowledge of the Queen at Hampton Court, Westminster and at the palace at Eltham,[66] as well as with plotting Henry's death. With a spiteful, perverted twist, one of them was her own brother, George, Viscount Rochford, accused of incest in an unsubtle attempt by Cromwell to further blacken Anne's name. They all denied the accusations, except the naive Smeaton, who doubtless had been promised his life in exchange for his damning testimony.[67] Another, Thomas Wyatt, was questioned and then released.

Anne was arrested at Greenwich on 2 May and taken to the Tower of London. She was received by its constable, Sir William Kingston, who had previously escorted Wolsey to London. He described her arrival to Cromwell:

> She said to me: 'Mr Kingston, shall I go into a dungeon?'
> 'No madam, you shall go into your lodging that you lay in at your coronation.'

'It is good to me,' she said [and added], 'Jesu, have mercy upon me,' and knelt down, weeping a [great] pace and in the same sorrow fell into a great laughing, and she has done [so] many times since.

And then she desired me to move the king's highness that she [ought] to have the sacrament in the closet by her chamber, that she might [pray] for mercy. 'For I am as clear from the company of man as I am clear from you and am the king's true wedded wife.'[68]

Archbishop Cranmer, seemingly innocent of the murky world of Cromwell's conspiracy against the Queen, felt it necessary to write to Henry to comfort him in his distress:

I am in such a perplexity that my mind is clearly amazed – for I never had better opinion in [a] woman than I had in her, which makes me think she should not be culpable.

And again, I think your highness would not have gone so far except that she had surely been culpable . . .

If she proved culpable, there is not one that loves God and his Gospel that will ever favour her but must hate her above all other; and the more they favour the Gospel, the more they will hate her.[69]

Cromwell, always keen to explore every avenue of enquiry and to tie up loose ends, contacted Henry Percy, Sixth Earl of Northumberland, about his liaison with the youthful Anne Boleyn before the King had ardently lumbered onto the scene and stopped the affair. Northumberland wrote to him on 13 May, solemnly declaring that there had been no pre-contract of marriage with Anne, thus inconveniently removing a handy legal trick that could have been used to invalidate the royal marriage.[70] Cromwell then set in motion alternative arrangements for a speedy divorce before she met her death.

Four of the men accused of adultery with her – William Brereton, Sir Henry Norris, Sir Francis Weston and the hapless Smeaton – appeared on trial at Westminster Hall on 12 May. Cromwell's promises to Smeaton that his life would be spared had, of course, proved completely worthless, like most of his pledges given in such circumstances. Inevitably, they were all found guilty.

Anne and her brother were tried in the Tower of London on 15 May, watched by two thousand curious people crowded into the King's Hall, on the second floor of the White Tower. Cromwell's evidence against George Boleyn was thin, but dramatic. The Minister relied on the testimony of George's wife Jane, Lady Rochford, to secure his charge of incest between brother and sister. But she could only produce vague innuendoes – which did not even amount to circumstantial evidence. There was 'undue familiarity' between the siblings, she said; George was 'always in his sister's room'. Would Cromwell's case against his prime victims stumble and fall at the first fence?

Then he produced his trump card. Lady Rochford discreetly wrote down the Queen's incautious words about Henry's lack of manly prowess in bed and handed the paper over to the twenty-six peers who sat as judges. She had written: *'Que le Roy n'estait habile en cas de soi copuler avec femme, et qu'il n'avait ni vertu ni puissance'* – 'The King was not skilful when copulating with a woman and he had not virtue or power.' Cromwell's veiled implication was not difficult to discern: if Anne could not have a son by the King, she would look elsewhere to beget a child and pass it off as an heir. The Queen was finished. So was her brother.

Henry Percy, Anne's youthful lover so many years before, was now one of her judges. He suddenly quit the court, pleading sickness.

Norfolk, with crocodile tears in his eyes, sentenced his niece: 'Because you have offended our sovereign the king's grace, in committing treason against his person and here attainted of the same, the law of the realm is this: that you shall be burnt here within the Tower of London on the Green, else to have your head smitten off as the king's pleasure shall be further known.'[71]

Rochford was beheaded on Tower Hill on 17 May with the four other scapegoats of Cromwell's conspiracy. The same day at Lambeth, Archbishop Cranmer issued a decree nullifying the Queen's marriage to Henry.

Cromwell boasted openly of his part in Anne's downfall. He told Chapuys that he had been

> authorised and commissioned by the king to prosecute and bring to an end the mistress's trial, to do which he had taken considerable trouble. He . . .

had taken, planned and brought about the whole affair. One of the things which had mostly raised his suspicions and induced him to inquire into her case was certain prognostications made in Flanders of a conspiracy against the king's life by people, it was said, nearest to his royal person.[72]

He was a little shamefaced about his earlier role in facilitating the Boleyn marriage. 'Cromwell began to excuse himself for having promoted the king's marriage. True it was, he said, that seeing the king so much bent upon it and so determined, he [Cromwell] had paved the way towards it.'[73]

Kingston meanwhile carefully reported on Anne's behaviour to the Minister in a series of letters. Henry had decided she should be beheaded in the French manner, and a French executioner from St Omer, in the Pale of Calais, was specially brought over and paid £24 to do the grisly job with a two-handed Flemish sword. Early on the morning of Friday 19 May, the day of her execution, she discussed how she would die. She told Kingston:

> 'I hear say I shall not die before noon and I am very sorry therefore, for I thought to be dead by this time and past my pain.' I told her it should be no pain as it was so subtle. And then she said: 'I heard say the executioner was very good and I have a little neck' . . . [She] put her hand about it, laughing heartily.
>
> I have sent many men and also women executed and they have been in great sorrow and to my knowledge this lady has much joy and pleasure in death.[74]

A scaffold with five steps had been built on the greensward within the Tower. Kingston had removed all strangers from the precincts of the fortress on Cromwell's orders and had locked the gates the previous night. A small group of the King's councillors was gathered that morning, with Cromwell standing prominently in the front row to savour his triumph at her downfall.

Her head was cut off with one blow. The headsman had earned his fee.

The Queen's body was unceremoniously dumped into a long elm

chest, normally used to hold arrows, and carried off to be buried in the Tower's Chapel of St Peter ad Vincula in an unmarked grave.[75]

A Frenchman reported to Cromwell that the wax tapers about Catherine's tomb at Peterborough 'had been lighted of their own accord' the day before Anne was beheaded.[76]

On 20 May, Jane Seymour was brought to the Palace of Westminster by barge from Greenwich. Ten days later she married Henry in a secret ceremony in the Queen's Closet at Westminster.

CHAPTER FIVE

Shaking the Throne

*To remember all the jewels of all the monasteries
in England and specially the cross of emeralds at
St Paul's.*

CROMWELL'S 'REMEMBRANCES', EARLY APRIL 1535[1]

Cromwell's influence and power now pervaded almost every dark corner
of Henry's administration. Only the Church and religious doctrine still
remained officially free of his autocratic meddling – but these soon fell
prey to his domination. On 1 January 1535, the King granted him the
extravagant titles of Vicar-General and Visitor-General of the Monasteries, thereby giving Cromwell authority and precedence even over the
Archbishops of Canterbury and York, let alone the entire bench of
bishops.

In October that year, Cromwell set up his own ecclesiastical court
to issue licences to approve preachers and probates for wills and to
hear petitions for divorce. More significantly, it had the power to install
bishops or dismiss a monastic prior.[2] The Word of God had now taken on
a political dimension, as it required governmental approval in many of its
manifestations.

Cromwell was also particularly interested in the wealth of the
Church, having seen how convenient it was to appropriate monastic
property for other purposes when he had worked for Wolsey a decade
before. There seems little reason to doubt the widespread belief of the

time that it was Cromwell who suggested the suppression of the monasteries to the King, as a means of both finally severing any links with Rome and augmenting the contents of his exchequer. Henry had a ready ear: two years before, he had warned Chapuys of his determination 'to reunite to the crown the goods which churchmen held of it . . . and that he was required to do this by the oath he had taken at his coronation'. One can almost hear the canny lawyer's own words repeated.[3]

First, with typical bureaucratic thoroughness, Cromwell needed to assess exactly how much this amounted to. He accordingly dispatched agents both to monasteries and secular churches to survey all their property holdings and income. It was an ambitious project. The result of this huge clerical exercise, conducted throughout 1535, was the twenty-two volumes of the *Valor Ecclesiasticus*[4] – the largest survey of property since the Norman government's Domesday Book in the eleventh century – which listed and assessed the value of the Church in England, sometimes down to the last cow and pig. Although much was left out of the final reckoning, Cromwell now knew that the property of the religious houses was worth at least £200,000, or more than £72 million at 2006 prices. On top of that was the value of the buildings themselves and their precious possessions such as gold and silver chalices, crosiers and candlesticks.

On 21 January, Henry, as supreme head of the Church, issued him a commission for a general visitation of the churches, monasteries and clergy in England and Wales, with power, as Vicar-General, to appoint deputies for the work.[5] Cromwell's commissioners were tasked to investigate their 'condition, both spiritual and temporal . . . and the lives and morals of the abbots, removing and punishing those [with whom] they find fault'. Amongst the issues they were especially instructed to explore were those that concerned any new increase in the value of lands each monastery possessed and, very specifically, 'the behaviour of the nuns and how often they confess'. The commissioners also had injunctions to find 'relics and feigned miracles for increase of lucre' from naive pilgrims and were told they should encourage monks to leave each house.[6]

Their hidden agenda was to seek out and uncover excesses and loose and wanton behaviour, which could be used as ammunition by Cromwell in his planned attack on the realm's monastic wealth. To ensure there would be no unwanted hindrance from the church authorities, he decreed that no bishop should visit any monastery while the King's commission was in progress.

For this mission he recruited a ragtag band of lawyers and priests who had been in government service: Thomas Legh,[7] John ap Rice and, latterly, Dr Richard Layton.[8] In modern Whitehall parlance, they were all 'sound' men as far as the Minister was concerned. Legh had taken part in the Dunstable divorce proceedings against Catherine of Aragon and had interrogated one of Bishop Fisher's servants in an attempt to gather evidence against the prelate. The Welshman ap Rice, a notary public, had been in Cromwell's service since 1532: his loyalty was certain-sure. Layton had questioned both Fisher and Sir Thomas More in the Tower and had suggested a visitation of the diocese of York to root out 'frantic fantasies and ceremonies' there. He boastfully told Cromwell: 'You will never know what I can do until you try me.' The offer was irresistible.

The visitors soon discovered the salacious material they were earnestly seeking. No doubt a large degree of embellishment also went on: 'Ask and it shall be given: seek and you shall find.' In the next century, Thomas Fuller was contemptuous about the visitors' doubtful characters: 'They were men who well understood the message they went on and would not come back without a satisfactory answer to him that sent them, knowing themselves were likely to be no losers thereby.'[9] Cromwell must have been thoroughly entertained by their spicy, sensational reports when they arrived in his normally dry-as-dust administrative postbag.

At the Benedictine abbey at Cerne Abbas in Dorset, Abbot Thomas Corton had nine accusations levelled against him, including that he kept his mistresses 'in the cellars, especially one named Joan Postell or Bakers' and 'for wasting the goods of the monastery on his concubines and natural children and giving the former great gifts on their marriages'. Corton was also alleged to have sired a number of bastards including a son 'called Harry whom he begat on Alice Roberts to the great slander of our religion' at Thomas Parker's house in Cerne. His sexual appetites were plainly unrelenting and insatiable: 'He openly solicits honest women in the town and elsewhere to have his will of them.' At least he was gentleman enough to feed them, as it was reported: 'His concubines sit at table with him.' The forbidden, lusty needs of his fellow monks did not go forgotten either. 'He allows women to stay with the brethren from noon to evensong,' but the feminine attractions did not distract them from 'playing at dice and cards all night'.[10] When one of the monks remonstrated about all this wicked sinfulness around him, he was speedily exiled to a sister house in Monmouth, where he was 'very ill handled'.

Layton was scathing about the human frailties of Richard Jenyn, prior of the inappropriately named Augustinian house at Maiden Bradley in Wiltshire, where

> The holy father has but six children and but one daughter married, yet of the goodness of the monastery, [is] shortly to marry [off] the rest.
>
> His sons be tall men waiting upon him and he thanks God [he] never meddled with married women but [always] with maidens, the fairest [that] could be gotten and always married them [off] right well.
>
> The Pope, considering his fragility, gave him licence to keep a whore and [he] has good writing . . . to discharge his conscience.[11]

At the rich Cluniac priory of St Pancras outside Lewes in East Sussex, Layton claimed he found not only rampant homosexuality amongst some of the inmates, but also a treasonous sermon preached by the sub-prior, who mockingly referred to 'the authority of God the Father Almighty, the authority of the king and the authority of Master Thomas Cromwell'. Layton reported: 'I have called [the prior] heinous traitor with the worst words I could deliver, he all the time kneeling upon his knees making intercession to me not to utter to you the principal for his undoing.'[12]

Layton visited the Premonstratensian abbey at Langdon in Kent, 3 miles (4.83 km) from Canterbury, going alone to the lodgings of the abbot, William Sayer. He hammered on his door for a 'good space', but neither 'sound nor sign of life appeared, saving the abbot's little dog that within his door fast locked, bayed and barked'. This was all too much for the impatient commissioner: 'I found a short pole-axe standing behind the door and with it dashed the abbot's door in pieces [and went] about the house with the pole-axe, for the abbot is a dangerous, desperate knave. Finally the abbot's whore, alias his gentlewoman, bestirred her stumps.'

She took to her heels and fled the abbey, but 'the tender damsel' was grabbed by Layton's companion, John Bartelot (who was one of Cromwell's servants) and was incarcerated in the cage at Dover for eight days. Her clothes were triumphantly found in the abbot's coffer. Layton reported to his master in London: 'I brought holy father abbot to Canterbury and there in Christchurch [Priory] I will leave him in prison.'[13] Layton was consumed with righteous indignation. The abbot

passes all that ever I knew in profound bawdy: the drunkest knave living. All his canons [are] as he is, not one spark of virtue amongst them: arrant bawdy knaves every one. The abbot caused his chaplain to take a whore; brought her up into his own chamber, took one of the featherbeds off his own bed and made his chaplain's bed in the inner chamber and there caused him to go to bed with his whore . . .

To rehearse you the whole story [would take] too long and [be] abominable to hear. The house is in utter decay and will shortly fall down.[14]

At the Gilbertine house of nuns and canons at Chicksands in Bedfordshire, the diligent Layton, who clearly enjoyed his work, was barred entry by the defiant nuns. Two, however, he discovered were pregnant, one by the sub-prior, the other by a serving man. 'The two prioresses would not confess this, neither the parties nor none of the nuns but one old beldame[15] . . . They were bound by their religion never to confess the secret faults done amongst them, but only to their own visitor.'

He went on to the Augustinian canonesses at Harrold, also in Bedfordshire, where there were 'four or five nuns with the prioress, [and] one of them had two fair children'.[16]

Layton moved north to the College and Hospital of St Mary Newark in Leicester, which held £300 in their treasure house. 'The abbot is an honest man and does very well but he has here the most obstinate and factious canons that ever I knew. This morning I will object against diverse of them [for] sodomy and adultery and thus descend to particulars which I have learned of others.'[17]

Thomas Legh, meanwhile, was in Cambridgeshire, and had visited a Benedictine nunnery at Swaffham Bulbeck, where the prioress, Joan Spylman, had given the local vicarage, worth £30 a year, to a friar 'whom they say she loves well'. Legh told Cromwell: 'To make you laugh, we send you a letter supposed to be sent to her by the friar in the name of a woman, although anyone may perceive it comes from a lover.'[18]

The visitations were clearly open to any amount of abuse and extortion. John Bartelot, Cromwell's nimble servant who caught the abbot's mistress at Langdon, found Edmund Streatham, the prior of the Crossed Friars in London, 'in bed with his whore, both naked, about eleven of the clock in the forenoon upon a Friday' in Lent. The prior fell down on his knees and begged Bartelot and his five companions not to report him and 'freely' gave them £30 as the price of their silence, of which Bartelot received £7. The prior promised more money 'by a certain day' but did not pay, and Bartelot cheekily had him arrested for non-payment. The abbot then reported him to Lord Chancellor Sir Thomas Audley, saying that Bartelot had 'committed a heinous robbery' and was 'worthy to be hanged' and seeking repayment of his £30. Plucky prior – he knew the best way to deal with blackmailers. Bartelot begged Cromwell to intercede on his behalf, for he had spoken the whole truth.[19]

There is little doubt that the English and Welsh monasteries needed some measure of reform, as there was clearly corruption and immorality within some of the houses. More significantly, many were now in a state of dilapidation. Endowing them had gone out of fashion: no new monasteries were established in the three decades before Henry VIII's accession in 1509 and the smart money instead went into seats of learning or almshouses. But Cromwell's visitors swiftly gathered sometimes very dubious findings – from only a third of the eight-hundred-odd religious houses – which were to form the bedrock on which he would build his legislation for their dissolution.

There were other pressing decisions to be made about several houses that had become annoying thorns in Cromwell's side. It seemed highly important to him that the inmates of the Charterhouse in London and the Bridgettine house at Syon in Middlesex should fully conform to the supremacy because of their popularly perceived eminence as sanctuaries of piety and honour in an increasingly venal world.

The Charterhouse was a particular target: John Houghton, the prior, had been executed on 4 May 1535; three others died on 19 June, all for refusing to acknowledge the King's authority over the Church.[20] Sebastian Newdigate, one of the second group, had been a page at court and a gentleman of the privy chamber but had quit royal service when the issue of divorce had first been raised.

It was critical to win over the Carthusians' hearts and minds, as foreign reaction to the execution of their brethren had been especially violent.[21] At the end of April 1535, Cromwell was told by his servant John Whalley that the monks were 'exceedingly superstitious, ceremonious and pharisaical and wonderfully addicted to their old mumpsimus'.[22] He urged that a succession of approved preachers be sent into the Charterhouse to convert them 'and if this does not answer, call them before the whole nobility, temporal and spiritual, and sentence them according to law'.[23]

One of the monks, John Darley, had been at the bedside of a 'very old man . . . of our religion' called Father Raby when he lay dying the previous year. Darley had asked him: 'Good Father Raby, if the dead may come to the quick, I beseech you to come to me.' The dead monk duly appeared to him at five o'clock on the afternoon of 24 June at the entrance to his cell, and asked him: 'Why do you not follow our father [Prior Houghton], for he is a martyr in Heaven next to angels.' The following Saturday the ghost reappeared, now 'with a long white beard and a white staff in his hand', terrifying Darley. The apparition spoke of his regret at not being a martyr in life, 'for my lord of Rochester and our father was next unto angels in heaven' and added: 'The angels of peace did lament and mourn without measure.' The ghost then vanished again.[24]

Faced with such dangerously seditious reports, Cromwell dispatched another of his servants, Jaspar Fylolle, to talk to the recalcitrant Carthusians and, more prosaically, to calculate the finances of the house. In September 1535, he discovered its annual revenue was £642 0s. 4½d, but the outgoings were £658 7s. 4d. Worse still, costs were rising. 'Wheat has risen four shillings in every quarter and malt twenty pence . . . and commonly, all other victuals rise therewith.' The charitable brothers also liked to have 'plenty of bread and ale and fish [to give] to strangers . . . at the buttery door . . . and to vagabonds at the gate, which cannot be. It seems [very] necessary to diminish either their number or dainty fare and also the superfluous delivery of bread and ale.' He warned it was the time of year 'when provision was wont to be made of ling[25] . . . and of other salt store and also of their winter vestures [to] their bodies and to their beds and for fuel to their cells'.

Fylolle also reported that a lay brother from the sister Charterhouse at Axholme had been 'secretly received in the cloister, [with] the great sickness and died in four days. One of the lay brothers who tended him is now sick of the same.' Finally, he attached a roll-call of the London Carthusians, noting down his belief about each one's loyalty to either sovereign or God: on the 'first line before every man's name that has confessed himself to be the king's true man, there is set a "g" for good and before the other, a "b" for bad'.[26]

A month later, Fylolle made another plea for immediate action:

If the king and you wish this Charterhouse to stand without a prior, as now, the number of the cloister monks and lay brethren should be diminished at least by those who will not acknowledge the king as their supreme head under God.

It is no wonder that many of these monks have offended God and the king by their foul errors, for I have found in the prior's and proctor's cells three or four foreign printed books [full] of as foul heresies and errors as may be.[27]

Cromwell's patience snapped. In October 1535, he issued an order appointing 'five or six governors' of the Charterhouse – 'temporal men, learned, wise and trusty of whom two or three shall be together every meal and lodge there every night'. He laid down nine other instructions, including the stark ultimatum that the 'governors should assemble the monks, servants and officers, show them that the king has pardoned their previous heresies and treasons, but if they again offend, they shall die without mercy'.

He also planned to divide the Carthusians and so conquer their will. Each would be examined separately 'as to their opinions and exhort them to the truth'. Those who remained obstinate and refused to discard their old religious doctrines would be immediately jailed. 'Those that will be reformed must be separated from the others and gently handled to cause them to utter the secret mischiefs amongst them.'[28] The monks would be completely isolated 'for a season and let no man speak to them but by the governors' licence'. All except the sick had to attend three or four sermons a week 'preached by discreet, well-learned men', no doubt approved by Cromwell.[29]

However, Henry was not satisfied with the arrangements. On 27 September 1536, on his way in to supper with the Queen, he waylaid Ralph Sadler and asked him pointedly: 'Howbeit the Charterhouse in London is not ordered as I would have it?' Working himself up into a temper, the King complained that he had ordered Cromwell 'long ago' to expel the Carthusians who 'had been so long obstinate'.

His Minister was slow to act because he feared further adverse reaction overseas. In May 1537, the King's Council threatened to suppress the house out of hand, but still, ten inmates – three priests, a deacon and six lay brothers – refused to swear the Oath of Supremacy. They were carted off to Newgate Prison on 18 May 1537 and held there, chained to posts like their brethren before them. Nine died of starvation and ill-treatment.[30] The survivors surrendered the house on 10 June 1537[31] and the 'House of Salutation of the Mother of God', as it was officially called, was finally suppressed on 15 November 1538, to be used briefly as a store for the King's tents and hunting equipment, with the altars utilised as gaming tables by workmen.[32]

The other house that regularly featured in Cromwell's 'remembrances' was Syon, where he had been Chief Steward some time after 1524.[33] Syon was famous for its preaching and learning: it had a renowned library with at least 1400 volumes, but the invention of printing enabled it to reach a much wider audience with its devotional literature.[34] The most prolific of the community's authors was Richard Whitford, who wrote six books on monastic or spiritual life between 1514 and 1541 under the beguiling nom de plume 'the Wretch of Syon'. The power and influence of their printing press may have been another of Cromwell's worries. Amongst its nuns, however, were many daughters of the noble and courtly families, so he had to tread warily.

In July 1535, Thomas Bedyll had reported Agnes Jordan, the abbess, and the sisters agreeable 'in everything', but there were two who might have to be expelled.[35] In December, the prurient Layton was at Syon. He discovered one brother had convinced a blacksmith 'to have made a key for the door, to have in the night time received in wenches for him, specially a wife of Uxbridge now dwelling not far from old Lady Derby'. He also 'persuaded a nun, to whom he was confessor, *ad libidinem corporum perimplendam* [and completely filled with lust for her body] . . . making her believe that when so ever and as oft as they should meddle together, if she were immediately after confessed by him . . . she should be clear forgiven by God.' An iron bar in a window between the huge twin naves of the church, which separated the nuns from the monks, had also been pulled out and 'by that means was many nights in the church talking with her at the said grating of the nuns' choir'.[36]

Cromwell was not interested in these nocturnal shenanigans at Syon. He sought religious rather than moral conformity for political reasons and sent down a swarm of reformist preachers, as well as trying eloquent or even threatening argument himself. Despite the reputation of the house, and the noble connections of the sisters, there could be no exceptions allowed. Opposition continued, however, and Bedyll wearily commented in December: 'I have had much business with this house since your departing hence and as for the brethren, they stand [as] stiff in their obstinacy as you left them.' One lay brother, Thomas Brownell, was imprisoned at Newgate and this may have been a salutary lesson to the community.[37] In September 1536, Cromwell attended the election of John Copinger as Confessor-General, who had earlier conformed after a tortuous conversion by the stuttering Bishop of London, and sent books to Syon to keep them steadfast. Copinger wrote to Cromwell on 23 September:

Please . . . accept our hearty thanks with the promise of our perpetual prayers for you and yours for your high charity which we cannot recompense.

We have put [the books] in certain public places for the comfort of the convent with your lordship's name as donor. The work which you last sent is read among us for a lecture at dinner.[38]

This all smacks of the insidious 're-educational techniques' used by twentieth-century totalitarian regimes against their political prisoners. At Syon, so famous for its pious learning and devotional library, it seems incongruous that books should have been deployed against the inmates to correct their thinking and beliefs.[39]

While he attempted to bring these famous monastic foundations firmly into line, Cromwell was still anxious to sequester the wealth of the smaller houses. The parliamentary Bill for the Dissolution of the Lesser Monasteries was brought into the House of Commons early in March 1536 and the lurid, shocking details of some of the excesses Cromwell's agents had discovered were bandied about the horrified chamber during the debates. The Act was inevitably passed, yielding all religious houses with an annual income of £200 or less to Henry, his heirs and successors for ever. The colourful language of its preamble, redolent of a bureaucrat's horror at wasted assets, has all the hallmarks of being penned by Cromwell himself:

> Manifest sins, vicious, carnal, and abominable living, is daily used and committed amongst the little and small abbeys, priories and other religious houses . . . where the congregation is under twelve persons. Whereby the governors of such religious houses and their convent[40] spoil, destroy, consume and utterly waste, as well as their churches, monasteries, priories, principal houses, farms, granges, lands, tenements and hereditaments, as the ornaments of their churches and their goods and chattels to the high displeasure of Almighty God, slander of good religion and to the great infamy of the king's highness and the realm if redress should not be had.[41]

The Court of Augmentations was established on 24 April 1536 to control this legal pillage and Solicitor General Sir Richard Riche – as we have seen, a man entirely innocent of scruples or honesty – was appointed its Chancellor.[42] Cromwell issued a letter to his new commissioners for dissolution, ordering the heads of the monastic houses to cooperate or 'you will answer to the contrary at your extreme peril'. The circular also contained an inducement: obedience in surrendering the property would make an abbot or prior 'worthy to be otherwise advanced and in the mean season to deal the more liberally with you in the assignment of a convenient stipend for your honest sustentation'.[43] They were to be paid pensions in return for their collaboration: the easier the dissolution, the greater their cash handout.

As soon as news of the legislation authorising the suppressions spread amongst England's devout nobility and gentry, Cromwell was inundated with appeals from those anxious to get their hands on monastic property. Greed spread like a contagion. Lord Lisle in Calais was one of those early off the mark, beseeching Cromwell 'to help me to some old abbey in my old days'. The Duke of Norfolk – anxious not to appear too grasping, but 'where others speak, I must speak' – particularly coveted the houses at Bungay and Woodbridge in Suffolk. Sir Thomas Eliot, whilst admitting his 'natural shamefacedness', fervently hoped that his well-known friendship with the executed Sir Thomas More would not prevent him from receiving 'a convenient portion' of the suppressed lands, for which he promised Cromwell hard cash – 'the first year's fruits with my assured and faithful heart and service'.[44] One of the new Queen's sisters, Lady Elizabeth Ughtred, was not very discerning, merely seeking 'one of those abbeys' – clearly, anywhere would do.[45]

Conversely, others hoped their local abbeys would be spared Cromwell's hand of sequestration. Thomas, Lord Delawarr, wrote to him, pleading the case of Boxgrove Priory in West Sussex. It was 'very near to my own poor house, where I am founder and there lies many of my ancestors and also my wife's mother . . . and I had made a poor chapel to be buried in'. With unfortunate timing, his glorious chantry chapel, carved in Caen stone in the choir of the priory, had just been completed. He suggested: 'Whereof it might stand with the king's grace's pleasure, for the poor service I have done his highness to forbear the suppressing of the same or to translate it into a college.' Delawarr knew who would be making the decision and told Cromwell: 'I beseech you that I may have your lawful favour, goodwill and help . . . And surely sir, I shall recompense your goodness, kindness and pain herein.'[46]

Here, then, was more income for Cromwell: bribes from those who desired grants of monastic property; bribes from the abbots, priors and prioresses who wanted their houses to remain. For example, Edward Calthorpe offered him £100 'for the pains that your mastership shall take therein', as well as his eternal friendship, in order to buy the priory of Ingham, Norfolk.[47] On the other side of the coin, Nicholas Austen, the abbot of the Cistercian house at Rewley, near Oxford, discovered that his abbey was to be given to one of Cromwell's servants called Archard. In September 1536, he wrote to Cromwell: 'I submit myself fully and wholly to your mastership, as all my refuge, help and succour is in you, glad of my voluntary mind to be bound in obligation of £100 to be paid to your mastership, so that our house may be saved, although it be converted into . . . a college.'[48] It was suppressed the following year.

Sometimes it was not cash, but bribes paid in kind. John Welles, abbot of the Benedictine monastery of Croyland, Lincolnshire, sent Cromwell 'part of our fen fish, right meekly beseeching your lordship favourably to accept the same fish and to be [a] good and favourable lord to me and my poor house . . . I with my brethren shall daily pray to our Lord God for the long continuance of your good lordship in health.'[49] Doubtless Cromwell was grateful for both the fish and the prayers.[50]

The process of dissolution was simple and brutal. Cromwell's commissioners visited a monastic house, called together the community and announced their fate. Its property deeds were collected together, its great seal seized and the movable valuables – the gold and silver sacred vessels and the vestments – inventoried. The lead on the roof was measured and the bells counted as the first stages in the recycling of the monastic buildings. A second visit checked the accounts and accepted the surrender. The tombs within the church were sometimes removed by the deceaseds' families to places of safety. Others were destroyed for the price of their stone and metal and still more appropriated for re-use elsewhere by some who sought status on the cheap.[51] Some buildings were demolished; others merely had their roofs removed to render them unfit for future worship. Monasteries were also sold and converted into private homes for the gentry enriched by the redistribution of their lands.

A total of 376 smaller houses were dissolved and eighty spared from suppression over the next few years. The value of the spoils to the King may have amounted to around £68 million at 2006 prices, with income from the monastic property and lands totalling about £20 million a year. Much of the land was shared out at generous knock-down prices – sometimes even given as free gifts – in a cynical effort to buy the nobility's loyalty and bind them tighter to the fortunes of the Tudor dynasty. Henry's attempts to keep them sweet cost him dear: his excheq-uer benefited only by an average of £37,000 a year from this dissolution – an indication of just how widespread was the redistribution of wealth, planned or illicit. Thomas Wriothesley, one of Cromwell's creatures, had drawn up plans to spend £6600 a year from the monastic wealth on hospitals, and £3300 per annum on new roads to provide work for the poor and jobless. Neither scheme was implemented. Earlier royal promises of social spending came to naught.

There was another, far more direct human cost. Chapuys protested in July 1536 that it was a 'lamentable thing to see a legion of monks and nuns who have been chased from their monasteries wandering hither and thither, seeking means to live. Several honest men have told me what with monks, nuns and persons dependent on the monasteries suppressed, there were over 20,000 who knew not how to live.' The ambassador had no doubts that one day God would hear their complaints and avenge them.[52]

Cromwell had his own plans for the poor and destitute. His Beggars Act, passed in 1536,[53] ordered a parish or municipality to assume full responsibility for the 'impotent poor'. These were now restricted to their home towns and villages and prevented from wandering the countryside in search of food or money. Those capable of labour would be given work and their children taught a trade. The 'sturdy vagabonds and valiant beggars' who refused to work were to be whipped 'until their bodies were bloody'. Alms were to be raised voluntarily in each parish to support the 'lame, feeble, sick and diseased people'. It was not only the first attempt at an official welfare policy but also marked the beginnings of the civil parish as a unit of local government in England and Wales.

Henry was so delighted at the privatisation of religious houses that he heaped more offices and honours on Cromwell's willing head. Not only had his Minister organised and prosecuted the seizure of the monasteries' wealth and sorted out a new law dealing with the annoyance of beggars, he had also pushed through Parliament a second Act of Succession, declaring Henry's two previous marriages null and void and entailing the crown on Jane Seymour's male children. With commendable foresight, Cromwell included a clause that would grant the throne next to male children by any future wife.[54]

On 1 July 1536, he was appointed Keeper of the Privy Seal, with fees of twenty shillings a day paid from the customs dues of Poole, Bristol, London, Plymouth and Fowey. On 9 July, he was created Baron Cromwell of Oakham. Nine days later, he was made Vicar-General and Vice-regent of the King in matters spiritual. On the same day, Cromwell was knighted.

These appointments were not the only gains to come Cromwell's way. He reserved for himself the choice priories and abbeys of Michelham in East Sussex, St Osyth in Essex, Alcester in Warwickshire, Great Yarmouth in Norfolk, and Launde in Leicestershire, and bestowed on his nephew Richard the abbeys at Ramsay and Sawtry in Cambridgeshire, Neath in South Wales and the nunneries at Hinchinbroke, Cambridgeshire, and St Helen's in the City of London.[55]

But some monastic houses would not surrender quietly.

The commissioners found the Augustinians at Hexham Priory in Northumberland a difficult nut to crack in September 1536. Three miles (4.83 km) from the house 'they were credibly informed that the religious persons had prepared themselves with guns and artillery meet for war, with people in the same house and to defend and keep the same with force'.

Cromwell's henchmen must have taken a few deep breaths to steady their nerves. Two of the four, Lionel Gray and Robert Collingwood, rode on alone into the town of Hexham and towards the monastery. They saw:

Many persons assembled with bills, halberds and other defenceable weapons, ready standing in the street, like men ready to defend a town of war.

And in their passing in the street, the common bell of the town was rung . . . and the great bell in the monastery was likewise rung, whereby the people forcibly assembled towards the monastery when the said Lionel and Robert found the gates and doors fast shut.

One of the canons, called the Master of Ovingham, appeared on the leads of the roof with many others, all in armour and carrying bows and arrows. He told the commissioners: 'We be twenty brethren . . . and we shall die ere that you shall have the house.'

Five or six more monks, with swords strapped to their waists, appeared on the tower and the roof. Around the nervous commissioners gathered 'many people, both men with weapons and many women'. The officials shouted up: 'Advise you well and speak with your brethren and show to them this our request and declaration of the king's gracious writings and then give us answer finally.'

Eventually the sub-prior, in his monkish robes, produced a document which turned out, rather embarrassingly, to be Henry's confirmation of the priory's charter. He told the commissioners: 'We think it not the king's honour to give forth one seal contrary to another and before our lands, goods or house be taken from us, we shall all die. That is our full answer.'

The commissioners retired in disarray. Hexham held out by force of arms for two weeks but finally surrendered and was suppressed in March 1537.[56]

Similar resistance was met at Norton Priory in Cheshire a few weeks later, in October 1536. Commissioners Combes and Bolles had expelled the abbot and monks and were busy packing up all the jewels at the monastery when their work was interrupted by the return of the abbot.

This time, he had two or three hundred men with him.

The commissioners, in fear for their lives, barricaded themselves in the tower and sent a desperate plea for help to Sir Piers Dutton, Sheriff of the County of Cheshire. He reported to Sir Thomas Audley, the Lord Chancellor:

> The letter came to me about nine of the clock in the night upon Sunday last and about two of the clock in the same night I came hither with such of my [friends] and tenants as I had near about me.
>
> I found diverse fires made there . . . and the abbot had cause[d] an ox and other victuals to be killed and prepared for his company.
>
> I . . . came suddenly upon them, so that the company there fled . . . and I took the abbot and three of his canons and brought them to the king's castle of Halton and there committed them . . . to be kept as the king's rebellious [subjects] on pain of £1,000.
>
> Afterwards I saw the commissioners with their stuff conveyed thence.[57]

These appeared to be nothing more than little local difficulties. Much worse was to follow.

In September 1536, Cromwell took a long-awaited three-week break from his heavy workload for a holiday in Northampton. He returned to his official duties on 23 September at Windsor Castle. As he quietly dealt with his papers and correspondence on the morning of Monday, 2 October, a dangerous rebellion broke out 182 miles (293 km) to the north, at the prosperous market town of Louth in Lincolnshire.

It was caused by the rumours rife throughout Lincolnshire that Cromwell was now about to seize the possessions of parish churches. The cellarer Henry Thornbeck had heard talk at a market near Sleaford that 'church jewels should be taken and after, that all cattle unmarked should be confiscated and christenings and burials taxed'. Thomas Mawre, a Benedictine monk from Bardney Abbey, had seen a 'tall serving man' in Louth church the previous day 'who said openly that a silver dish with which they went about to beg for their church was more meet for the king than for them'. He was suspected to be a servant of Cromwell's and one of the congregation 'fashioned to draw his dagger, saying that Louth . . . should make the king and his master such a breakfast as he never had'. The chorister Thomas Foster told his friends during the church procession: 'Go we to follow the crosses, for . . . if they be taken from us we be like to follow them no more.'[58]

The next morning, Dr John Frankish, Registrar of John Longland, the Bishop of Lincoln, was due in Louth, probably to collect clerical taxes. The townspeople believed he was there to confiscate their church goods and a group of eighty or a hundred locked themselves into St James's to guard them. When Frankish arrived in the town, he was mobbed, his account books taken away from him and burnt at the market cross.

A priest called William Morland, formerly a monk from the dissolved Cistercian Abbey of St Mary at Louth Park, was watching and Frankish begged him: 'For the Passion of Christ, priest, if you can, save my life!' Morland helped him escape from the town and forty of the crowd, some armed, went off to the nunnery at Legbourne, 1.5 miles (2.4 km) away, to capture the commissioners charged with its dissolution. En route, they met and violently seized another of Cromwell's servants called John Bellow, who was ignominiously stuck in the stocks at Louth. Commissioners John Millicent, William Gleyn and John Brown were also detained. Millicent, who was Cromwell's receiver, was put in the stocks with Bellow. Henry Sanderson and Robert Hudson demanded that they should be hanged, and the former helpfully offered some timber for a gallows.[59]

Happily, they were spared[60] as the leaders of the crowd were more intent on the plans for the Louth rioters to journey en masse the next day the 20 miles (35 km) north-west to Caistor, where the collectors of the subsidy tax were due the next morning. The priests amongst them promised they would ring their bells to summon their parishioners for a rendezvous with the Louth protestors at Orford, midway between the two towns.

Next day, the collectors prudently withdrew outside the town to Caistor Hill, but a number were captured and Nicholas, the servant of one of the local gentry, Lord Burgh, was beaten to death as his master escaped on horseback. The captives were taken back into Caistor and John Porman told them the Lincolnshire men demanded an end to the monastic suppressions and further taxes and that Cromwell should be delivered up to them, together with a number of bishops including their own Bishop Longland and Archbishop Cranmer.[61] That night, the collectors were forced to write a letter to the King:

> The cause of their assembly was, as they affirmed to us, that the common voice and fame was that all the jewels and goods of the church of the country should be taken from them and brought to your grace's council and also that your said loving and faithful subjects should be put off new enhancements and other importunate charges, which they were not able to bear by reason of extreme poverty.
>
> Humbly beseeching your grace to be good and gracious both to them and to us to send us your gracious letters of general pardon or else we be in such danger that we will never like to see your grace nor our own houses [again].[62]

The Lincolnshire uprising rapidly spread to Horncastle, Market Rasen, Kirton Soke and north to the shores of the Humber, where beacons of rebellion burnt on the Wednesday night. John, Lord Hussey, former chamberlain to Princess Mary, wrote to Robert Sutton, Mayor of Lincoln, and Sheriff Vincent Grantham with news of what had turned into an insurrection:

> I heard at nine o'clock this morning . . . that there is a company of false rebellious knaves risen in Lindsey. I command you to see the city surely kept, so that no such evil disposed rebellious persons can pass through it and to be ready with such company as you can make to suppress them.
>
> Take up bows and arrows in the bowyers' and fletchers' hands at a reasonable price . . . and handle the matter secretly.[63]

Cromwell heard the news from the same source. Hussey told him on 4 October: 'There is a company of light persons risen in the further side of Lindsey,' and the next day warned that 'the country is becoming more and more rebellious. They are today coming towards Lincoln but not in such great numbers, I believe, as it is [rumoured]. I have called my countrymen and most . . . say they will be glad to defend me but I shall not trust them to fight against the rebels.'[64]

Cromwell also received two letters from Sir Marmaduke Constable, further south at Stilton, Cambridgeshire, one containing the oath the rebels swore on joining the uprising: 'You shall swear to be true to Almighty God, to Christ's Catholic Church, to our sovereign lord the king and unto the commons of this realm, so help you God and Holydam[65] and by this book.' Sir Marmaduke also disclosed that the rebels demanded to keep their holy days; that suppressed monasteries should be reinstated; and that 'they be no more taxed'. Cromwell must have blinked when he read their last requirement: 'They would also fain have you.'[66]

John Rayne, the Chancellor of the Diocese of Lincoln, had presided over a consistory court at Bolingbroke the previous Saturday, but then had fallen ill and stayed in a chantry priest's house to recover. The Horncastle rebels found him there and he was brought into a field, to be greeted by screams of 'Kill him, kill him!' from the crowd, many of whom were priests. One of the rebels, Brian Stanes, later testified: 'William Hutchinson and William Balderstene of Horncastle pulled him violently off his horse, kneeling upon his knees and slew him with their staves and being dead, the priests crying continually "Kill him!" this respondent also struck the chancellor upon the arm with a staff.'[67] His clothes were ripped off him and these and his purse were distributed 'to the poor men among the rebels'. Another man was also killed: Thomas Wulcie, who is known to have been in royal service, was pointed out by William Leach and accused of being a spy. He was hanged from a convenient nearby tree.[68] Was his swift and brutal death caused by his name sounding like that of the fallen cardinal?

Local gentry were now joining the rebels. At Horncastle, they declared that if they 'prospered in their journey' they intended to kill 'the lord Cromwell, four or five bishops . . . and the Chancellor of the Augmentations [Riche]' – the 'devisers of taking church goods and pulling down churches'. The commons asked them: 'If you had them, would that mend the matter?' And the gentlemen said, 'Yes, for these be the doers of all mischief.'[69]

The rebels, now numbering at least ten thousand men, entered Lincoln on Friday, 6 October to a warm welcome from the county town's inhabitants. They celebrated their arrival by wrecking the Bishop of Lincoln's palace and seizing the field artillery stored in the city.

Meanwhile, at Windsor, there were indications that Cromwell had underestimated, if not totally misjudged, the scale of the revolt. Pre-occupied by the volume of state business that had built up during his vacation, he plainly believed that some kind of minor police action would be sufficient to quell what he considered to be merely small-scale disturbances. Circular letters, signed with the stamp 'Henricus Rex', were immediately drawn up for distribution to loyal local gentry: 'As a number of evil disposed persons have assembled in Lincolnshire, robbing our subjects and putting them in danger, you are in all haste to set a sure stay in the parts about you and advance to the place where you hear the said persons haunt, joining with other faithful subjects to repress them and from time to time you shall apprehend such as you think fit . . .' There seems little recognition in these words that Henry's administration was faced with a burgeoning popular revolt and that civil war now loomed. Cromwell resorted to black propaganda as another weapon against the insurgents and began drafting more royal letters:

> Forasmuch as the king, understanding of a traitorous assembly in Lincolnshire, intending the destruction of his person and the robbing and murdering of his true subjects and the deflowering and ravishing of their wives and daughters, has, for the subduing of their most traitorous and malicious attempts and purpose [ordered the gentry] with all haste . . . [to] advance to the place where . . . the said persons haunt, joining with other faithful subjects, to suppress them.[70]

Then, suddenly, the hard truth seemed to dawn, doubtless born out of incandescent royal fury over any opposition to the crown and its policies. Henry's reply to the lay subsidy commissioners, still held by the commons of Lincolnshire, was carefully corrected in Cromwell's writing and smacks of a firm grip now being taken. There is no sympathy for his officials' plight, only anger at this affront to Henry's imperial dignity: 'We take it as great unkindness that our common and inferior subjects rise against us without any ground . . . As to the taking away of the goods of the parish churches, it was never intended. Yet, if it had been, true subjects would not have treated with us, their prince, in such violence . . . but would have humbly sued for their purpose.' The King also firmly denied that any further taxation was planned. Then came the sting within the royal message:

This assembly is so heinous that unless you can persuade them for the safety as well of your lives as theirs to disperse, and send 100 of the ringleaders with halters around their necks to our lieutenant, to do with them as shall be thought best, and thus prevent the fury of the great puissance which we have already sent against them, we see no way to save them.

The letter ends with blatant threats:

We have already sent out the Duke of Suffolk, our lieutenant, the Earls of Shrewsbury, Rutland and Huntingdon, Lord Darcy, with Yorkshire, the Lord [High] Admiral [Sir William Fitzwilliam] and diverse other nobles with 100,000 men, horse and foot, in harness [armour], with munitions and artillery, which they cannot resist.

We have also appointed another great army to invade their countries as soon as they come out of them and to burn, spoil and destroy their goods, wives and children with all extremity, to the fearful example of all lewd subjects.[71]

This was all bluff and bluster. It may have assuaged Henry's notorious temper but the threats bore no relation to the feeble strength of his forces on the ground. Charles Brandon, Duke of Suffolk, only arrived at Huntingdon with a small advance party on 9 October, with 'neither ordnance nor artillery nor men enough to do anything; such men as are gathered here have neither harness nor weapons'.[72]

Cromwell was no general. Given his reputation in the country, he probably knew that if he were to lead the King's army, he probably faced assassination by his own hastily recruited soldiers. To his chagrin, the King summoned Thomas Howard, Third Duke of Norfolk, to command the royal forces of retribution as 'high marshal'. Chapuys reported: 'The Bishop of Carlisle . . . [said] he never saw the duke so happy as he was today . . . thinking it will be the ruin of his rival Cromwell, to whom the blame of everything is attached and whose head the rebels demand.'[73] The Minister shrewdly perceived that Norfolk would seize any military glory on the field of battle against these yokels as a means to boost his influence in court and to hasten the downfall of the upstart Cromwell.

Nil desperandum! The threat of Norfolk could wait. His first priority was to ensure that the rebellion was crushed.

The King put on a brave face, but in reality feared for his crown, as 'Cromwell's nephew said today in secret to an honest man'. Richard Cromwell had been busy: he had gone to the Tower of London's arsenals and obtained a 'great quantity of arrows and other implements of war' and dispatched men to the North, including the eighty carpenters and masons commandeered as they worked on his uncle's house at Austin Friars.

On 8 October, Richard reported from Ware in Hertfordshire, north of London, where he had a hundred horsemen, with forty handguns, at nearby Waltham:

> I intend soon after midnight to repair . . . to Huntingdon and gather such company as I can. Today on my journey I met with one Hall, who was taken prisoner by the traitors in Lincolnshire and sworn as their captain but . . . escaped. He reckons them at 40,000 or 50,000 and that they increase by 500 or 600 a day. Five or six hundred handguns are required and some of the small [artillery] pieces in this Tower, for many of them are good archers. I bought harness for a hundred men at London, because it is so scant here.[74]

His uncle meanwhile was sending out frantic letters to the nobility and gentry of the Home Counties and southern England, mobilising troops and ordering contingents to concentrate at Ampthill, Bedfordshire. This was a convenient base for an advance to the north, but close enough to defend Windsor if the rebels marched south. Cromwell himself was paying for a hundred men. Other forces were instructed to maintain security in their own counties while more were hastily formed into units to guard the King and Queen.

Suddenly, the Lincolnshire rebels melted away.

As Henry's hastily assembled forces pressed nearer, the rebels, at last fearful of his terrible vengeance against them, deserted Lincoln and went home, their tails between their legs. Richard Cromwell, relishing his new life as a soldier, was sorry that his chances of battlefield glory had vanished: 'I lament nothing so much as that they fly thus, as we hoped to have used them as they deserved,' he robustly told his uncle.[75] Letters scrapping the Ampthill muster were sent out on 15 October, although twenty thousand troops had already encamped there,[76] and the ordnance was returned to London.

This was another damning miscalculation by Cromwell.

Three days before the 'stand down' order was issued, there were reports that the insurrection had spread to Yorkshire and rumours that 'certain horse-loads of bow staves and bows have been sent for to York to be carried into Lancashire'.[77] Confirmation of the new rebellion came late on 15 October. Thomas Wriothesley told Cromwell: 'A post has arrived from Lord Darcy declaring the greater part of Yorkshire to be up and the whole country to favour their opinions – the same that were reported in Lincolnshire. This matter hangs yet like a fever, one day good, another bad.'[78] The Yorkshire men had risen, too late, in support of their brothers in Lincolnshire. The issues were the same and rumour and unrest had been rampant for some weeks. At the town of Dent, a royal official called William Breyar had been attacked and the local blacksmith told him: 'Thy master is a thief for he pulls down all our churches in the country.' Others said: 'It is not the king's deed, but the deed of Cromwell, and if we had him here, we would crum him and crum him as he was never so crummed.'[79] Breyar fled for his life.

But the Yorkshire insurrection posed a far more serious threat to Henry's crown because it was more widespread and certainly better led. Cromwell also knew well that if it was not put down successfully, he would pay with his head. He was now busy finding cash to pay the hastily re-assembled troops and was having 'great trouble . . . in getting £10,000 together'. He resorted to the simple expedient of melting down plate from Henry's jewel house to turn into coin.[80] Norfolk whined continually about his lack of money to pay his men: 'All complain they cannot live on eight pence a day.'

Edward Lee, Archbishop of York, took shelter in Pontefract Castle together with a group of local nobles headed by Thomas, Lord Darcy. On 15 October, they appealed for help to George Talbot, Earl of Shrewsbury, commander of a six-thousand-strong contingent of the King's army at Nottingham: 'Today we hear there meet before York above 20,000 men . . . They increase in every parish, the cross goes before them.

'I, Darcy, have twice written to the king of the weakness of the castle but have got no answer and without speedy succour, we are in extreme danger.'[81] Two days later, the Sheriff of Yorkshire, Sir Brian Hastings, informed Shrewsbury that the rebels now numbered forty thousand and had been 'received into York with procession' the previous Monday.

Worse still, the rebellion was spreading west into Lancashire, Westmorland and Cumberland. On 19 October, Henry diverted the troops of Edward Stanley, Third Earl of Derby, to put down

an insurrection attempted about the abbey of Sawley in Lancashire, where the abbot and monks have been restored by the traitors.

We now desire you immediately to repress it, to apprehend the captains and either have them immediately executed as traitors or sent up to us. We leave it, however, to your discretion to go elsewhere in case of greater emergency. You are to take the said abbot and monks forth [with] with violence and have them hanged without delay in their monks' apparel.[82]

Events were looking bleak for the King. His northern capital of York had been taken and the major seaport of Hull capitulated on 19 October after five days of siege by six thousand rebels. The next morning, Darcy surrendered Pontefract Castle and was persuaded to join the King's enemies. They saw themselves as a 'Pilgrimage of Grace' and marched devoutly behind banners embroidered with the Five Wounds of Christ on the Holy Cross, below the sacred monogram 'IHS'[83] and the image of a chalice.

The leader, or captain, of the Yorkshire rebels was Robert Aske, a one-eyed lawyer in his early thirties who had previously been a servant to Henry Percy, Sixth Earl of Northumberland.[84] He now presided over the castle and town of Pontefract. Two days later, a messenger from Shrewsbury, Thomas Mylner, *Lancaster Herald*, arrived with a proclamation from Henry. He was taken to the hall of the fortress and, while reading out the King's words, was taken to Aske in a nearby chamber. The rebel leader looked 'as [if] he had been a great prince, with great rigour and like a tyrant'. Aske told him:

This proclamation shall not be read at the market cross nor amongst my people who are all in accordance with our articles, determined to see a reformation or die.

I asked him what his articles were, and he said one was to go with his company to London on pilgrimage to the king to have all vile blood put from his council and noble blood set up again; to have the faith of Christ and God's laws kept and restitution done for wrongs done to the Church.

The herald fell on his knees and asked to read out the King's words. This request was again refused and he was given two crowns for his pains and safe conduct out of the town.

Norfolk was meanwhile hastening north, complaining to Henry from Newark that he had 'not slept two hours these two nights and must take some rest'. At Tuxford, the old campaigner moaned about 'the scantiest supper I had for many years'.

He soon had more to complain about. Norfolk had been forced to parley with the Yorkshire rebels rather than destroy them in battle 'to avoid an effusion of blood'. Heavy rain had made the roads almost impassable for royalist artillery and the King's armies, scattered across the Midlands, were too weak to guarantee victory on the battlefield. Norfolk was incensed at the hand dealt him by fate: 'Now, forced to appoint with the rebels, my heart is near broken.'

He was also fearful of Henry's reaction and told the King's Council in London: 'It is not fear which made us appoint with the enemy but the cold weather and the want of room to house more than a third of the army and no wood to make fires; hunger both for men and horses of such sort I think never Englishman saw. Pestilence in the town is fervent and where I and my son lay, at a friar's, ten or twelve houses were infected within a butt's length.'[85]

The King's forces in Lincolnshire were now rounding up the dejected rebels there and interrogating them. John Williams told Cromwell that nowhere had he seen 'such a sight of asses, so unlike gentlemen as the most part of them be'. They were 'men void of fashion' and when it came to questioning, 'if they know more of this rebellion than they pretend, the dull wits will not hide it'.[86]

A general pardon was now offered to the Yorkshire insurgents, as well as a conference at Doncaster in December to air their grievances. The rebels, lulled by Norfolk's weasel promises, again dispersed.

In early January 1537, the embers of rebellion burst into flame again in Yorkshire, sparked by rumours that the King was reinforcing Hull and Scarborough both as refuges for the local gentry and bases from which to subdue the county.[87] The leaders were John Hallam, who had taken a prominent role in the Pilgrimage of Grace, and renegade spendthrift Sir Francis Bigod, a long-term debtor labouring under Cromwell's high interest rates.[88] This forlorn hope was launched in the unfounded belief that parts of Yorkshire and Durham were about to rise again in revolt. Hallam failed to seize Hull, while Bigod's men were attacked at Beverley and sixty-two taken prisoner.

Henry threw away the promises of mercy and benignity made to the Yorkshire rebels. This was one insurrection too many; now he wanted blood.

The ringleaders and many of those caught up in the troubles were quickly arrested. On 22 February, Norfolk was urged on by the King to be merciless in his justice: 'You must cause such dreadful execution upon a good number of the inhabitants, hanging them on trees, quartering them and setting their heads and quarters in every town as shall be a fearful warning.'[89] He joyfully imposed martial law in some areas of north-west England, executing as he progressed from county to county. At Carlisle he admitted that if he had proceeded by normal process of law, 'not a fifth of them would have suffered . . . because [of the] affection and pity of neighbours' who would have sat as juries.[90]

Cromwell drove Norfolk on to even greater cruelty, taunting him that he was soft in the suppression of the abbeys and lenient in his punishment of traitors. 'Neither here, nor elsewhere, will I be reputed Papist or a favourer of naughty religious persons,' Norfolk retorted, adding that he had been warned 'to take heed of what he ate or drank in religious houses' for fear of poison.

A total of 216 were executed for their part in the rebellions that shook Henry's throne. Of them, forty-four came from monasteries: the abbots of Jervaulx, Fountains, Barlings, Sawley and Rievaulx, the prior of

Bridlington and thirty-eight other monks. Even Thomas Mylner, the luckless *Lancaster Herald*, was tried and executed for bending his knee to Robert Aske at Pontefract.[91] Lord Darcy, under questioning in London, told Cromwell bitterly: 'It is you that are the very original and chief cause of all this rebellion and mischief. I trust that . . . though you would procure all the noblemen's heads within the realm to be struck off, yet shall there be one head remain[ing] that shall strike off your head.'[92]

So Cromwell lived on to fight another day. He bragged to Sir Thomas Wyatt in July 1537: 'The realm . . . [goes] from good quiet and peace, daily to better and better. The traitors have been executed: the Lord Darcy at Tower Hill; the Lord Hussey at Lincoln. Aske [was] hanged upon [above] the dungeon of the castle at York. The rest were executed at Tyburn. So, that, as far as we can perceive, all the cankered hearts are weeded away.'[93]

CHAPTER SIX

In a Glass Darkly

No lord or gentleman in England bears love or favour
to my Lord Privy Seal because he is a great taker
of money. He will speak, solicit or do for no man,
but all for money.

GEORGE PAULET, 1538[1]

Paintings of Cromwell, preserved in London's National Portrait Gallery and mainly by the court painter Hans Holbein the Younger,[2] show a man growing progressively more corpulent as the years pass. The impact of good food, wine and the sedentary hours spent poring over voluminous paperwork were beginning to tell.[3]

But even when you look closely at these images, there are remarkably few clues to the true character of this man of mystery. His hooded grey eyes mask any suggestion of emotion below that low, beetling forehead, as they stare, sphinx-like. Clearly absorbed in deep thought, he seems oblivious of the searching gaze of the artist.

The most famous portrait,[4] probably painted sometime in 1533–4, shows him dressed soberly in heavy black, fur-edged robes, sitting on a wooden-panelled settle, with rich dark-blue damask covering the wall behind him. He resembles very much a successful merchant, trading in staple commodities, and the aura of prosperity is emphasised by the large ring on one of his chubby fingers. On the narrow table in front of him, covered with a Turkish carpet, lies a closed clasped book, probably concerned with some devotional subject. There is also a soft leather bag, plainly containing his personal seal, a feathered quill pen and a pair of scissors with which to trim it. The sitter's identity and status are disclosed by the tiny pinched writing on the piece of paper lying on top of a small pile of parchments on the table: 'To Master Cromwell, trusty and well-beloved master of our jewel house.' As we have seen, he was appointed to this post on 14 April 1532, for the first year jointly with Sir John Williams, and held it amongst a host of other offices, both major and minor, until his death. This portrait, therefore, is likely to have been a gift from a grateful sovereign, well contented with a servant entrusted with guarding what was always closest to Henry's heart: his wealth.

As befits a man who revealed little about himself – certainly rarely his inner thoughts – his portrait itself is something of an enigma. The inclusion of the job title suggests strongly it must have been painted early on in Cromwell's service to the crown, yet the legend scroll at the top clearly proclaims him 'Earl of Essex' – a dignity not awarded him until the dark days of 1540, and thus added later.

Like many self-made successful men, Cromwell liked to surround himself with the trappings of affluence as a lasting expression of his increasing wealth. A ritual distribution of bread, meat and drink to two hundred poor Londoners twice daily at the gates of his main residence emphasised his deep pockets and his continual ability to handout largesse.[5] His chief concern, if not obsession, was the accumulation of property, which he constantly improved and extended, frequently at several sites simultaneously. Money was never an issue in these grandiose building projects. He saw them merely as another means to underline his growing importance in the politics and governance of England.

In 1536, he jotted down approvingly all the 'things done by the king's highness since I came to his service' – the purchase of St James in the Fields and the building of 'a magnificent and goodly house' there; the creation of a park around it and the demolition of old tenements to make way for the new gardens, tennis courts and cockfighting pits of the Palace of Westminster.[6] Cromwell was now to follow his master's lead in his own ambitious acquisitions of property.

His first home of any stature was in Stepney, located outside the eastern walls of the City of London, which he leased from 1524 but probably handed on to his nephew Richard some time before 1535.[7] An inventory of its contents in June 1527 provides a tantalising glimpse of his lifestyle and possessions before his salad days of service to the crown. The house boasted three bedchambers, a hall, buttery, new and old parlours, kitchen, larder and various ancillary rooms. His total of thirty-one pieces of plate included a gilt goblet with silver-gilt salt cellar; a silver-gilt ale pot and three masers, or drinking bowls, in the same precious metal. Significantly, perhaps, Cromwell may at that time have been suffering a temporary embarrassing period of straitened finances: the inventory includes notes of six gilt dishes with covers, two gilt flagons, a salt cellar and a sergeant-at-arms's ceremonial mace, all in pledge at the pawn-broker's. Cromwell's extensive wardrobe of clothes, in the new chamber, included a dark tawny gown faced with damask and an old nightgown faced with fox to keep him warm during the cold nights as he lay on his mattress on the 'truss bed, [surrounded] with curtains of red and green say [serge], with gilt bells'. He possessed twelve doublets, including five in black satin and two in crimson, twelve pairs of gloves and nine pairs of black hose. In that room, one can imagine him sitting before his polished-steel mirror, combing his hair with one of the bone combs from the box of four listed in the household contents. There were also four 'writing stands', one with five pewter inkwells. In the corner stood a 'carved and gilt altar' tablet, depicting the 'Nativity of Our Lord' with two brass pricket candlesticks on either side, symbolising his own private religious devotion. Some would believe it ironic that in later years Cromwell was to preside over the iconoclastic destruction of religious images during the state-sponsored attack on what was suddenly perceived as idolatry.

He had already amassed considerable quantities of jewellery, valued in the inventory at £64 11s. – or £22,500 in 2006 cash equivalents. These included three 'on my master's finger: a gold ring with a table diamond, a gold ring with a rock ruby' and another 'with a turquoise like a heart', possibly a gift from his wife. These jewels also included two items with devotional significance: a 'gold Agnus Dei [the image of the Lamb of God carrying a cross or a flag] graven with Our Lady and St George' and a gold brooch 'with an image of Mary Magdalene'. The last part of this list of jewellery is in Cromwell's own hand and details nine objects, all unvalued, including 'a diamond triangle set in gold, at the goldsmith's' and 'eight pearls on a string'. Were these his latest acquisitions, or were they pledges – collateral – against loans he was arranging at his notoriously high interest rates?

The hall was decorated with hangings of red- and green-bordered serge, and amongst the furnishings were six verdure[8] cushions embroidered with a red rose; a wooden table on trestles; six gilt foot stools; and three 'little gilt chairs for women'. There was also a canvas panel depicting Cardinal Wolsey's arms in gilt, prominently and loyally displayed. For special occasions, Cromwell dined off a twelve-piece dinner service in pewter.

Elsewhere in the house were two *mappae mundi* – maps of the known world – painted on canvas,[9] perhaps a throwback to his previous travels in Europe or his involvement in Wolsey's interests overseas.

The Minister's efficient steward later demolished two 'old and small tenements' in Throgmorton Street in order to build a new 'very large and spacious' house just south of the Augustinian priory of Austin Friars, in Broad Street Ward, in the north-west area of the City of London. The hall of the Drapers' Company now occupies the site[10] but then it was a fashionable residential part of the capital, with wealthy Italian merchants living in dwellings within the monastic close, and the home of Spanish ambassador, Eustace Chapuys, was located near the church.[11]

The house was erected on the friars' land, next to their churchyard, which Cromwell had leased for ninety-nine years from 1532 after he suborned their prior, George Brown. The prior became very much a creature of the ambitious administrator, to the extent that his Easter sermon in 1533 urged the congregation to pray for Queen Anne [Boleyn]. 'Astonished and scandalised', they walked out of the church in angry protest at his dutiful appeal.[12] He was suitably rewarded for his services to Cromwell by being chosen as one of the commissioners appointed to inspect the friaries in England in April the following year.[13] Cromwell plainly used a range of underhand methods to pressure the unworldly friars into agreeing to his every requirement for his new home.

In 1534, an anonymous informant – doubtless one of the friars, motivated by a well-placed, generous bribe – claimed in a badly written and misspelled letter that masses at the priory were being rushed or neglected, whilst the brothers spent much of their time drinking in the beer house in bad company. Monastic rules were no more kept there 'than in hell among devils' and the authority of the new prior, Thomas Hamond, was insufficient to maintain any discipline. In addition, the cloister and doors were so unguarded that 'the Lombards dwelling within the gate take their pleasure in conveying off their harlots'.[14] Even now, one smells the rank stench of blackmail deployed remorselessly by Cromwell.

This extortion, coupled with Austin Friars' continued debts of up to £300 (or £104,000 in today's money) must have rendered Hamond malleable and compliant with any demands forced upon him. The priory, with an annual income of £57, was finally surrendered in 1538 by Hamond and his twelve remaining brethren.[15]

Cromwell desired a mansion fully commensurate with his growing prestige and status, with attractive gardens in which he could stroll and enjoy some privacy. The major portion of the building work was finished probably some time late in 1536, but he was dissatisfied with the size of the remaining plot of land. The Tudor antiquary and topographer of London John Stow, writing six decades later, describes Cromwell's innovative solution to this problem: 'He caused the pales[16] of the gardens adjoining to the north part, [suddenly] to be taken down. Twenty-two feet [6.71 m] to be measured forth right into the north of every man's ground, a line there to be drawn, a trench to be cast, a foundation laid and a high brick wall to be built.'

Worse was to come:

> My father had a garden there and a [rented] house standing close to his south pale. This house they loosed from the ground and bore upon rollers into my father's garden, twenty-two feet [6.71 m].
> Ere my father heard thereof, no warning was given him, nor other

answer, when he spoke to the surveyors of that work, but that their master, Sir Thomas, commanded them so to do.

No one dared to argue with Cromwell and, to heap further helpings of resentment upon his anger, Stow's father still had to pay his whole rent of 6s. 8d that year for the property, of which only half now remained to him. Stow ruefully adds: 'Thus much of my own knowledge I have thought good to note: that the sudden rising of some men causes them to forget themselves.'[17]

Austin Friars remained Cromwell's preferred London home because of its convenient location between the royal palaces at Westminster and Greenwich and its proximity to the Tower of London. The house was constantly being extended and improved, right up to the end of 1539. He also acquired other properties: a farm at Canonbury, in the parish of Islington, north of London, and, briefly, the manor house at Hackney,[18] where lands formerly owned by the Knights of St John of Jerusalem were conveyed to Henry's use by Henry Percy, Sixth Earl of Northumberland, in 1535 and formally granted to Cromwell on 24 September that year.[19]

The residence closest to his heart was probably the manor of Wimbledon, comprising lands in the north Surrey parishes of Wimbledon, Putney, Mortlake, Roehampton, East Sheen and parts of Barnes and Wandsworth.[20] This area was the old stomping ground of his troubled youth and it must have given him great pleasure to become lord of the manor there. He augmented these property holdings with the lease of the manor of Allfarthing in Wandsworth in 1534, when Henry granted it to him for a term of sixty years, and the purchase of the nearby manor of Dunsford from Charles Brandon, First Duke of Suffolk, for £403 6s. 8d in 1539.[21]

During the early years of his government service, Cromwell routinely had more than two hundred 'or greater number' of retainers dependent upon him, all clad in a grey livery, the gentlemen in velvet and the yeomen wearing long tunics with 'their skirts large enough for their friends to sit upon them'.[22] In June 1537, he paid out £60 for 'diverse servants' green coats' and £53 5s. 10d for yellow velvet for the liveries of fifty-two gentlemen in July 1538.[23] He also employed a chaplain called Thomas Rose.[24]

After the death of his wife Elizabeth some time around 1529, he lacked a formal hostess for his lavish entertaining, but he clearly enjoyed the company of women. When he stayed with that rough old soldier Norfolk in 1537, the Duke joked that if he 'lust not to dally with my wife' he could find him 'a young woman with pretty proper tetins [breasts]' for his entertainment.[25]

Cromwell welcomed the great and good to his luxurious homes, surrounded by the unmistakable symbols of his wealth. Chapuys, who often dined with him at Austin Friars, said Cromwell 'lived splendidly and is very liberal both of money and fair words and remarkably fond of pomp and ostentation in his household and in building'.[26] He now had ample funds with which to indulge in luxuries; for example, eating off solid-silver plates.[27] The lawyer John Oliver recalled the 'dinners and suppers, where I indeed did hear such communications which were the very cause of the beginning of my conversion' to the truth of the Gospel. Thomas Starkey, one of the King's chaplains, enjoyed at these meals conversations 'of God, of nature and of other politic and worldly things'.[28]

Cromwell's accounts for 1537–9 fortunately survive and provide a detailed and revealing insight into his everyday life at the height of his power.[29] Away from the grim business of state, there were times when Cromwell must have allowed his inscrutable mask to slip, when he adopted almost a playful, frivolous air. One such moment is suggested by the accountant's payment of £15 in February 1537 to his henchman Wriothesley, who had acted as an intermediary with Princess Mary 'because my Lord was her valentine'. Was this bashful, coy 'suitor' the same ubiquitous autocrat, the vengeful grim reaper of the Pilgrimage of Grace, the scheming architect of the barbarous executions of those who defied the King's supremacy?

The Cromwell of his leisure hours seemed fond of gambling – particularly playing at dice, when substantial sums sometimes changed hands, although there is a payment of a mere £1 for lost wagers during a game of bowls. He was consistently unlucky, his total gambling losses for these three years amounting to at least £150, or more than £50,000 at 2006 monetary values. Most of the debts were incurred at cards and dice, played with courtiers or officials such as Walter Cromer (Henry's Scottish physician), Sir William Paulet (Comptroller of the Royal Household), or Sir Richard Riche (the avaricious Chancellor of the Court of Augmentations). With the latter's proven track record of dishonesty,[30] one finds it very difficult not to suspect cheating on his part. Other gambling cronies included the Lord Mayor of London in 1538, the haberdasher William Forman (when the stakes at dice were lower, as Cromwell's debts were only twenty shillings, calculated in groats or four-penny coins) and the distressingly named Bastard Falconbridge.[31]

Cash was also probably paid out copiously to the King, who was an inveterate gambler, for the interminable games played during those long evenings at Greenwich and Westminster. Henry may have been the winner of the £11 12s. 6d owed by the Lord Privy Seal for playing dice at Mayfield, East Sussex, during the stately royal progress in southern England in August 1538. Doubtless the old ogre derived considerable spiteful pleasure from taking money from Cromwell, and it is tempting to assign the £18 13s. 4d handed out by the Minister 'at diverse times in one night' in September 1537 to an expensive losing streak during a hard gambling session with the monarch.

One particular payment stands out above all the others because of the amount: the £2,553 (or £946,000 in modern values) paid to Anthony Denny, Henry's trusted privy chamber 'fixer', 'for the king's use' on 1 November 1538. This was no gambling debt. The circumstances strongly suggest it may have been a loan and, indeed, it was fully repaid – but without interest – twenty-eight days later. A sycophantic Cromwell regularly gave presents to his royal master. In June 1539, the herald Gilbert Dethicke, *Norroy King of Arms*, was paid nineteen shillings for providing a 'collar of velvet for the strange beast my lord gave the king'. Would that we knew what species of beast this was.

Cromwell's main forms of enjoyment were music and plays. There are a number of disbursements to actors and musicians such as the 6s. 8d for Princess Elizabeth's minstrels in June 1537, and the 7s. 6d paid to 'the king's flutes' the following month. Christmas that year must have been a jolly time, with Cromwell paying out a total of £2 10s. for three performances by separate troupes of thespians. There is no obvious sign of his own company of players, who perhaps were too busy touring the realm, staging the Minister's insidious propaganda dramas, to appear before him. He also spent money on his own household's music-making, such as the £13 6s. 8d paid to 'Mark Antonio for supplying certain shawms and other instruments' in April 1537, and to 'Weston, £2 10s. for a lute'[32] in January of the following year.

The accounts record sixteen shillings spent on, amongst other purchases, a velvet purse for Will Somers, Henry's famously witty court jester. This may have been in return for a performance at Austin Friars by the little hump-backed man and his acrobatic monkey, although as Somers was the only man who had both Henry's ear and friendship in the King's later tetchy years, there may have been a devious element of bribery on the Minister's part to this influential member of the royal household.[33] Cromwell probably considered his own establishment incomplete without his own jester, or fool, on the payroll and, accordingly, in November 1538 William Lambard was sent across the English Channel to Calais to escort back Anthony 'the fool'. He claimed modest travelling expenses of five shillings. The next month, there is a payment of 34s. 6d for 'bells for Anthony's coat', which conjures up images of noisy, flamboyant comedy to distract the Lord Privy Seal from the wearisome burdens of affairs of state. Perhaps loud guffaws creased those tight-lipped bovine features as Anthony faithfully turned somersaults or cracked a merry quip to amuse his normally taciturn master. He must have been successful in his efforts to entertain: he was still employed the following year, since Lawrence the hosier received 22s. 6d for making stockings for the jester, by warrant of the steward Thacker. Around the same time, Cromwell paid out 10s. to 'Mr Reynold's servant for bringing a cage of canary birds' to one of his houses.

The Minister's duties clearly included sometimes arranging, at his own expense, the sumptuous court masques or elaborate musical dramas so beloved of Tudor monarchs. Entries for February 1538 record one, perhaps two, such productions then staged at the court. Christopher the milliner was paid £10 17s. 11d 'for the stuff of the masque of King

Arthur's knights' and an extra £3 for 'his labour and the workmen', who probably shifted the scenery about. There is an additional 21s. 2d for his 'trimming' or embroidering the costume of 'Divine Providence when she played before the king'. Obviously this was a masque with a moral, although the action may have included some comic episodes involving hobby horses (wooden toy horses), which were made and painted for £33 17s. 6d. The same month, there was a payment of £5 10s. 5d to one Heywood who may have been the impresario of this masque, or possibly of a second, separate drama. Bargemen who ferried 'Heywood's masque to the court and home again' on the Thames were paid 16s. 8d for their pains. Robin Dromey and his colleagues received twenty shillings 'for waiting two nights the same time my Lord made the king a masque' and the Italian engineer Giovanni Portinari received £25 11s. 5d for other 'charges of the masque', most likely construction work associated with the grandiose temporary structures used as scenery or theatrical props. Surprisingly, the supposedly dour Cromwell took part in these elaborate charades: in January 1537, £13 6s. 8d was paid to the tailor Farleon for making the costume for 'my Lord's part of the masque'. It must have been a sumptuous outfit and we can only conjecture as to what type of role he played.

Cromwell also enjoyed hunting and there are innumerable entries concerning falcons and hawks, greyhounds, spaniels and new arrows for his crossbows.

The accounts also provide a picture of the food consumed at the Lord Privy Seal's dining tables, much of it gifts from a multitude anxious to please him in their attempts to curry favour. Amongst the oxen, mutton, stags, pheasants, partridges, curlews, capons, quail, geese, gulls, swans, hens and rabbits sent to Cromwell, or bought by his steward, appear some rather more exotic fare such as marzipan and oranges, ginger and nutmegs, the latter expensive luxuries at the time. The fruit and vegetables included cherries, apples, quinces, gooseberries, beans and artichokes, the last apparently an especial favourite, which came from the royal gardens at Hampton Court. Amongst the different fish and shellfish were cod, ling, oysters, cockles (these from Sir William Fitzwilliam, the Lord High Admiral) and the two porpoises delivered in June 1537 and

May the following year. Some of the food came from the royal kitchens, such as the tart sent by 'Downer of the Pastry' in December 1537, but there were also regular suppliers, such as the hearty 'Mrs Bigges', whose servant was always tipped two shillings for bringing her 'tripe and puddings'. Cromwell also paid the substantial sum of £400 to 'Mr Hill, serjeant' of the King's cellar, 'in full payment of a bargain' on 20 June 1537. Was this disposal of royal wines an entirely innocent 'rebalancing' of Henry's cellar, or was the Minister engaged in a little private trading?[34]

Overall, the cost of the Lord Privy Seal's various households increased from around £90 a month in 1537 to between £300 and £400 in 1538–9, as more properties were added and new retainers hired.

Cromwell maintained his love of jewellery. He clearly had an account with the goldsmith Cornelius Hayes, paying him '£20 on a reckoning' now and then, but his most expensive acquisition was of a diamond and a ruby from a jeweller called Jenyns in November 1537, which cost him £2,000, or a breathtaking £741,000 at today's values, a sure indication of just how much wealth he had amassed by that time. This 'great ruby' may have been the gem set in a ring by 'John of Antwerp' who the following month charged Cromwell fifteen shillings for the work and twenty-nine shillings for the gold in the ring. This was the first of many such commissions for the Dutch-born jeweller, amongst them the £19 7s. paid for making a gold cup and cover weighing fifty-three ounces (1,502 g), which was the Minister's New Year gift to Henry in 1539. It was taken straight to the safety of his secret jewel house. These presents were costly items and their value was closely monitored by a discerning royal eye. John Hussey, the London agent for Viscount Lisle, Deputy of Calais, described the ritual of gift-giving in January 1538: 'The king stood leaning against the cupboard [in the presence chamber], receiving all things and Mr Tuke[35] at the end of the same cupboard, penning [listing] all things that were presented. Behind his grace stood Mr Kingston[36] and Sir John Russell and beside his grace stood the Earl of Hertford and my Lord Privy Seal.'[37]

At least in 1534 and 1539, Cromwell could find some comfort that his was the largest gift (by weight of silver gilt and value) of any given in return by the King, and this was a certain-sure mark of continuing royal favour.[38] In the latter year, as well as dispensing the usual gifts to the royal family, Cromwell also distributed his own New Year largesse, mainly in the form of money, to members of the royal household: £36 to the gentlemen of Henry's privy chamber, and £4 10s. to the King's four gentlemen ushers. Those who brought him their own gifts received £104 16s. in return. It always paid to keep happy those close to the King.

Payments for medical services enable us to build a picture of Cromwell's health, which seemed generally good during 1537–9. Earlier, in March 1535, he had suffered from a 'rheum, which caused a swelling in his cheek and eye'.[39] This laid him low and on 17 April the King visited his loyal Minister at his house at Austin Friars to enquire after his health. Cromwell did not return to his duties until 1 May.[40] A surgeon named Forest received five shillings in February 1537, and in November the Minister required treatment from John Barnes, 'doctor of physic', who was paid '20 crowns of the sun', or £4 13s. 4d, for his services. Later that month, Forest was recalled to administer more treatment, generally painful during the Tudor period, and paid ten shillings for inflicting that pain. He was back again in mid-April 1538, and at the beginning of the following month there were two payments to Dr Cromer (one at St James), but whether these were for professional consultation or, more prosaically, gambling debts, we can only guess. In July, Philip the apothecary received £1 13s. 11d 'for necessaries for my lord' and in January 1539 Cromwell may have hurt his leg, as two foot stools were purchased 'to set my lord's leg on' at a cost of twelve pence. He is known to have walked with a rolling, awkward gait, with one leg possibly slightly longer than the other, and this treatment may have been connected.[41] Being overweight could not have helped.

On 26 August 1537, Cromwell was proudly installed as a Knight of the Most Noble Order of the Garter[42] at St George's Chapel, Windsor, and his accounts include his payments made on that glittering occasion. The next day, Richard Cromwell, on his behalf, proffered a handsome tip of £25 to 'the vergers, deans, sextons and other officers there . . . and to the king's servants that waited upon my lord at his installation'. Christopher Barker, *Garter King of Arms* was paid ten marks (£6 13s. 4d) for

Cromwell's robes, plus another five for his trouble in organising the ceremony.

There is no doubt that the Lord Privy Seal was a generous tipper – money can be a great lubricator for the wheels of government – but, in all fairness, he could also be generous in handing out alms to the needy poor. His accounts are littered with details of his donations out of his own purse, or made on his behalf by one of his retainers, all documented as carefully as if they were tax-deductible. For example:

> *20 July 1537*: Given to two poor men at Windsor, sixteen pence. Three poor women, twelve pence.
>
> *21 August 1537*: Two poor men and a maid at my lord Scorpe's park,[43] 2s. 8d.
>
> *12 September 1537*: the poor at St James, two pence each.
>
> *30 April 1538*: twelve poor women at Putney, four shillings.
>
> *28 June 1538*: a poor man of Ipswich, fifteen shillings.
>
> *24 February 1539*: Stephen Foxe, given 'to them that beg for the poor folk at Paul's Gate', 6s. 8d.
>
> *4 April 1539*: Thomas Broke, which he gave in alms in prisons about London, £6 1s. 8d.

An anonymous early eighteenth-century writer, a great champion for Cromwell, described a possibly apocryphal incident in which the Lord Privy Seal, riding in his coach with Archbishop Cranmer in Cheapside, London, recognised an old woman in the street as they passed by. She came from Hounslow, Middlesex, and he suddenly recalled that he owed her forty shillings from years before. 'He immediately ordered one of his servants to conduct her to his palace and when he returned from court, he did not only pay his debt but settled an annual pension of £4 on her and a new suit of clothes every year, as long as she lived.'[44]

From the same source comes another story of Cromwell's generosity, but this may not be wholly apocryphal as it is known to have been circulating in London in 1609. The Florentine banker Francisco Frescobaldi, who employed Cromwell in his youth in Italy, had now fallen on hard times and had come to London to recover the huge sum of 15,000 Italian ducats, more than £2,600, owed to him by obdurate English merchants.

Again, there was a chance meeting in the street, and the Minister, then on his way to the court at Westminster, immediately jumped off his horse and 'affectionately embraced him . . . scarcely refraining from tears'. They met later, probably at Austin Friars, when 'the Lord High Admiral and other lords that were with him' were astonished at the warm welcome provided to the Italian. 'My lords,' said Cromwell, 'marvel not that I am so glad to see this man, but for his means, I have attained to this dignity.' Flinging open a strongbox, this 'most assured friend' gave Frescobaldi cash for his clothes and lodgings, and then handed over four weighty money bags containing 1,600 ducats. Other kinds of practical assistance were also made available. He demanded 'an exact account of the names of his debtors and places of their abode which he gave to one of his attendants, charging them diligently to find them out and to require payment of those debts within fifteen days or to abide the hazard of his displeasure'.[45]

Needless to add, the debts were speedily repaid.

Cromwell had other debts to worry about – those of his stolid and wastrel son, Gregory. Cash handouts from an incorrigibly indulgent father totalled more than £420, or £156,000 in 2006 terms, during 1537–8, although these outlays began to tail off after twenty-year-old Gregory's advantageous marriage on 3 August 1537, at Mortlake, to Elizabeth, widow of Sir Anthony Ughtred, sister of Queen Jane Seymour. Gregory had been keen to marry the daughter of Sir Thomas Nevill of Merewith in Kent and made 'various offers' to her father. But Cromwell had other plans for his son. Sir Thomas wrote to him on 10 March 1535: 'I am comforted in my disappointment by your choice of another husband who has many virtues.' She married one of Cromwell's henchmen, Sir Richard Southwell.[46] The Seymours gave Gregory £50 for spending money on the occasion of his marriage, and doubtless subsequently the Seymour family also became a soft touch. Then there were his expenses, again picked up by a considerate Cromwell, such as:

> 7 January 1537: For two caps, with gold trimming, £9.
> 19 January 1537: Mr Gregory at his going to Mr Williams, in his purse
> £6 15s. and for his costs, £2.

7 May 1537: Henry Dawes, for things bought for Mr Gregory, £1 16s. 6d.

1 June 1537: Albert the milliner, for a cape of velvet trimmed with gold and silver for Mr Gregory, £9 10s. 2d. A sword and a dagger for Mr Gregory, £1 11s.

18 June 1537: Mr Gregory, £2 5s. and also for three shirts for him, £3.

23 December 1538: Fletcher, for Mr Gregory, £1 17s. 10d. The cape for Mr Gregory, £4 0s. 10½d.

7 January 1539: Mr Gregory's shoemaker's bill, £4 8s. 8d.

11 January 1539: The saddler, for Mr Gregory's horse harness, £11 12s.

13 January 1539: Farleon, the tailor, for making Mr Gregory's apparel, £3 8s. 6½d.

Were there angry words between father and son over all this expenditure? Probably not, as the frequency of such payments surely confirms that Gregory was the apple of his father's eye and, moreover, the Minister would have been keen to make obvious the Cromwell dynastic wealth.

Where did he get his riches from?

Thomas Polsted, his receiver, reported income totalling £4,011 17s. 4¼d, or nearly £1,500,000 in today's money, in the twelve months beginning Michaelmas (29 September) 1534.[4/] During the same period, Cromwell spent £3,290 13s., of which nearly £1,200 was on household and construction expenditure. It is interesting to compare his costs with the £3,840 incurred by Anne Boleyn at exactly the same time. There was not much difference between Queen and Minister in terms of their spending.

Cromwell's revenue came from three sources: income from his lands; fees from his offices of the crown; and a healthy level of annuities – pensions paid by those interested in maintaining his goodwill. Revenues from lands and rents totalled more than £400 and formed the smallest contribution during this period. Cromwell by now was accumulating an assortment of lucrative government posts and sinecures, all paying annual fees. His Mastership of the Rolls carried a salary of £284 1s. 6d a year, but this salary does not include the tun of wine (252 UK gallons, or 1,146 litres) munificently supplied by John, Lord Hussey, the Butler of England, or the 12 yards of broadcloth given annually by the

Order of St John of Jerusalem. Cromwell also picked up £65 10s. as Chancellor of the Exchequer; £75 as Master of the King's Jewel House; £58 6s. 0½d as Clerk of the Hanaper; and £20 as High Steward of the Queen's Lands. He also received a share of the profits of the Privy Signet, which that year yielded £94 0s. 8½d. Minor positions produced another £32. Prominent amongst those paying annuities were the heads of a number of religious houses: history was to prove their investments unwise.

The following year, covering the period 29 September 1535 to 21 July 1536, Cromwell's income almost doubled to total £7,965 19s. 11d,[48] principally from the proceeds of property speculation and the increased value of his annuities – amongst them £20 from Stephen Gardiner, Bishop of Winchester. But the Minister's expenses also jumped to £7,871 9s. 7¾d, reflecting the substantial construction work in which he was engaged. With the dissolution of the monasteries, more annuities, payments for offices in his gift and income from an informal usury business, Cromwell's revenues went up to £12,548 in 1537, or £4,650,000 at 2006 prices, and stayed roughly around this level for the next two years. Admittedly, some of this income was made up of repayments of capital sums loaned out, but the fact remains that apart from the King and probably the Duke of Norfolk, he must have ranked as the richest man in all England.

There is no doubt that he was dipping his venal fingers into the royal money pot as it received the proceeds of the privatisation of the monasteries. His accounts record a number of sales of silver and gold that look suspiciously like spoil from dissolved priories. On 9 October 1538, 'Gadbury the goldsmith' handed over £18 19s. 4d to Cromwell – probably the Lord Privy Seal's share of the plate bought from the late prior of Lenton Abbey, Nottinghamshire.[49] Martin Bowes was another purchaser of precious items, paying £44 5s. 4d on 11 October 1539 for 'the silver bought of my lord', and again, on 16 November the same year, 'for 144½ ozs of gold, at 33s. the oz', totalling £247 11s. 'Trapes the goldsmith' also made staged payments to the Minister amounting to £1,348 15s. 2d in early 1539, most likely for monastic gold items and jewellery sold to him. Indeed, a receipt survives for the £69 paid by the Dean of Hertford 'for jewels sold to

Trapes the younger'. On Cromwell's behalf, his steward Thacker also sold 'ingots of gold and silver' for £97 16s. 11d on 21 October 1539, probably once sacred vessels, subsequently melted down for the value of their metal. Other deals more overtly capitalised on monastic loot:

> 21 *January 1539*: William Lawrence, for stuff of Our Lady Chapel in Ipswich sold by him: £21 19s. 7d.
>
> 1 *December 1539*: chalice, parcel of the stuff of Our Lady of Ipswich.

In addition, Cromwell had been granted the wealthy monastery of St Pancras in Lewes, and its demolition, the subsequent sale of its goods and the recycling of its building materials raised a first instalment of £467 0s. 13½d for him in May 1539, and a second, totalling £229 18s. 5d, was sent on by Thomas Bishop in July. Another payment of £726 3s. 6d on 22 December that year was for the lead that had been stripped off its huge roof and the scrap-metal value of its bells.

Together with his habitual duplicity and ruthless manipulation of those around him, it is Cromwell's reputation as a rapacious loan shark and taker of bribes that seems so distasteful to twenty-first-century palates. He continued to lend money at exorbitant rates even after his appointment to senior government posts. The accounts for 1537–9 are full of repayments of money borrowed from him, some made by the noblest in the realm and some involving large sums of money, such Sir William Fitzwilliam, Earl of Southampton, Lord High Admiral and Treasurer of the Royal Household, who repaid a loan of £100 in November 1537; and Lord Bowrough, who repaid the £25 'my lord lent him' in April 1538, and a further £200 that June. Henry Percy, Sixth Earl of Northumberland, who died in 1537, was also deeply in debt to Cromwell, and he received £62 from Henry Lord Clifford (who bought the Earl's gold chain off him in November that year) and £28 17s. 10d in final payment of Northumberland's debts the following month. Sir Thomas Arundel, High Bailiff of Salisbury, repaid the £100 'lent him upon a bill of his hand [an IOU]' in February 1538. Andrew, Lord Windsor, wrote piteously to Cromwell in July 1535, enclosing a list of his creditors and begging 'that money will be provided for them, for they make much calling for it daily'.[50]

These grandees who had fallen on hard times were all victims of vanity: their unsuppressed urge to spend money on gaudy clothes and fine possessions to advertise their status and nobility. Penury was the harsh penalty of keeping up with the noble Joneses. Forced to go cap in hand to Cromwell, no wonder they hated and despised the Minister. Other, smaller fry also became his debtors, such as the Bishop of Hertford's executors, who borrowed £100 merely to decently bury the prelate, or, in the same year, the £80 lent to some merchants so they could recover their impounded ship. The repayment of a £10 loan by Richard Bream in December 1537 demonstrates that Cromwell charged him 15 per cent interest, although happily Sir Edward Seymour, the Earl of Hertford, paid only 2.5 per cent on a £100 loan in May 1538 – doubtless a preferential 'family' rate because of Gregory's marriage to his sister.

Recently, eloquent claims have been made that Cromwell might have been far less corrupt than his popular image suggested.[51] Certainly, bribery was regarded as almost a norm in Tudor administrations and the odd gift of a side of venison or some pheasants would not be construed by society then as wholly immoral.[52] Our loyal Minister, however, went far beyond all that and plumbed new depths of venality. The state papers are littered with supplicants promising him ample reward if he granted them this office, or the lands of that monastery. Take just two examples from April 1535. Sir Richard Riche, himself no angel of purity, wrote to Cromwell on 3 April begging him to remember him when the Mastership of the King's Liveries came to be appointed 'and I will give you £40 and pray for you, as ever I have done'.[53] Then there is the case of Elizabeth, Lady Burgh, who probably did not have to bribe Cromwell but readily declared her willingness to have done so. After her husband's death, she faced the embarrassment of her children being declared bastards by the Act of Parliament[54] procured by her father-in-law Thomas, Lord Burgh, who was plainly worried about where his estate would end up. She told Cromwell on 27 April: 'I am informed by Mr Treasurer [Southampton] how much I have been bound to your goodness in my late business, which I regret I am unable to recompense but I trust you will take the will for the deed.'[55]

The Minister's accounts reveal numerous unexplained receipts of various sums of money handed over by him to his receiver personally. Here is a strange coincidence: they normally appear to have been made after his attendance at court. Did he really carry around so much loose cash? Or was he collecting it? Then there are entries, beginning in 1538, which have similarly sinister connotations: the receipts of various sums contained in purses, 'in a white paper' and, most tellingly of all, perhaps, hidden in gloves, mostly received by Cromwell himself:

14 March 1538: in a red leather purse, £20.

22 March 1538: in a glove, £40.

16 August 1538: at Arundel's [house] in a glove, 100 marks [£67].

8 November 1538: in a purse of white leather, £30.

9 December 1538: by Little Robyn [one of Cromwell's retainers] in a glove, £20.

29 December 1538: in a crimson satin purse, £100.

7 January 1539: in a handkerchief, £20.

27 February 1539: my lord, out of his purse, £20, also in a crimson satin purse, 100 marks.

22 June 1539: in a handkerchief, £10.

29 October 1539: in a crimson satin purse, £20, of which there was a counterfeit royal.

30 November 1539: in a white paper, £20.

Why the subterfuge? Why was the money hidden in gloves? The most suggestive evidence of his dishonesty may be the money mentioned in the entries for December 1539. Here there is the £20 'which was in a glove under a cushion in the gallery window'; the £10 'under the cushion in the middle window'; and the £150 contained in white and red purses hidden in the same place. It must be nice to have so much cash that you can afford to leave it lying around.

Then there are more blatant payments. Richard Sampson, Bishop of Chichester, told Chapuys in October 1536 of a French attempt to bribe Cromwell: 'Had indeed the French been left to themselves they would have got Master Cromwell into the nets . . . Only a few days ago, they tried hard to gain him over to the cause by offering him, in

King Francis' name, an annual pension of 2,000 ducats besides certain valuable presents. Whatever they do in that respect, they will not succeed.'

By the following February, the perfidious French clearly had suc ceeded. His Imperial Majesty himself, Charles V, reported that Henry had granted permission for Cromwell 'to accept the gift (a good sum of money) and the pension upon which the councillor, who hitherto befriended us, has suddenly turned round and is working in favour of France'.[56]

Yes, in truth, Cromwell was as guilty of corruption as sin itself.

CHAPTER SEVEN

A Merry Widower Thwarted

You shall receive the king's letters with a commission to treat with those princes for his grace's part. Use all dexterity, for the king was never more willing to forget the past and make a perfect reconciliation and do all things to the Emperor's honour. If the Emperor will esteem his grace as he pretends . . . all will proceed to God's glory and the quiet of Christendom.

CROMWELL TO SIR THOMAS WYATT, ENGLISH AMBASSADOR TO CHARLES V, LONDON, 25 DECEMBER 1537[1]

At two o'clock on the morning of Friday 12 October 1537, Henry's elusive dream of a lawful male successor for his uncertain Tudor dynasty was at long last transformed into happy reality. His third queen, Jane Seymour, was delivered of a healthy boy after spending more than thirty hours in the agony of labour in her newly decorated apartments at Hampton Court. The King's joy and relief at this resolution of his greatest political and personal problem must have been unbounded.

The birth came on the eve of the feast of St Edward the Confessor, that most English of all Heaven's community of saints. Henry's loyal subjects wisely and willingly shared their sovereign's elation at the arrival of his son. Six hours after the baby's first raucous cries of life, a triumphant *Te Deum* was sung in every church in the City of London and all the bells rang out joyously to celebrate the arrival of a male heir to the throne of troubled England. Charles Wriothesley, *Windsor Herald*, reported: 'At nine of the clock, there was assembled at [St] Paul's [Cathedral] all the orders of friars, monks, canons, priests, clerks about London, standing all about Paul's in rich copes, with the best crosses and candlesticks of every parish church in London.' Solemn Masses were sung in the echoing Gothic cathedral, attended by a number of clerical and court dignitaries including Cromwell himself, who doubtless lustily joined in the anthems and responses in gratitude for the huge burden of uncertainty now lifted from his own shoulders by that tiny, weak child. Typically, his satisfaction was not only derived from purely patriotic motives: a few months earlier, his twenty-four-year-old son Gregory had married Elizabeth, the widowed sister of the Queen. With the birth of a healthy prince, the house of Seymour's star had attained the zenith of royal favour and Cromwell must have quietly congratulated himself on having backed the right noble horse. Around him, the jubilation continued:

> Then the king's waites[2] and the waites of London played with the shawms[3] and after that a great peal of guns were shot at the Tower of London, all which . . . was done to give laud and praise to God for joy of our prince.
>
> The same night, at five of the clock, there were [bon]fires made in every street and lane, people sitting at them banqueting with fruits and wine; the shawms and waites playing in Cheapside and hogsheads of wine set in [many] places in the City for poor people to drink as long as they [wished] . . .
>
> Also there was shot at the Tower that night above two thousand guns and all the bells ringing in every parish church until ten . . .[4]

Amid all this noisy rejoicing, correct protocol had to be rigorously followed. With typical Tudor bureaucratic efficiency, a circular letter, written in advance and now sealed in the margin by the Queen's signet,[5] was quickly dispatched to the great and good of the realm, announcing pointedly that 'Jane the queen had been brought in childbed of a Prince conceived in Lawful Matrimony between my lord, the King's Majesty, and us'.[6] That night, Cromwell, still toiling at his paperwork at St James's Palace 'beside Westminster', penned a letter to Sir Thomas Wyatt, the English ambassador to Charles V, instructing him to inform the Imperial Emperor of 'the good news . . . of the queen's grace's deliverance of a goodly prince'.[7]

Margaret, the Dowager Marchioness of Dorset, who was virtually quarantined in Croydon, Surrey, 11 miles (18.3 km) south of London, because of an outbreak of the plague there,[8] hastened to send her congratulations to Henry, having heard 'the most joyful news and glad tidings that came to England this many years'. For this, 'We, all your grace's poor subjects, are most bound to give thanks to almighty God that it has pleased Him, of His great mercy, so as to remember your grace with a prince,' she added piously.[9] Hugh Latimer, Bishop of Worcester, was carried away to ludicrous heights by his enthusiasm. He told Cromwell: 'Here is no less joy and rejoicing in these parts for the birth of our prince, whom we hungered for so long, than there was . . . at the birth of St John the Baptist. God give us all grace to yield due thanks to our Lord God, God of England.' The good Bishop suddenly seemed to realise that his politically correct euphoria teetered on the fulsome, as he swiftly added: 'What a great fool am I! Devotion shows many times but little discretion.'[10] But shrewdly, he had made his loyal point.

Court officials immediately began preparations for the prince's extravagant christening. On the day of his birth, a mandate was issued at Westminster instructing the Mayor and Sheriffs of London to publish a proclamation sternly forbidding access to Hampton Court on Monday, 15 October (the day appointed for the ceremony) without the personal permission of the King, 'on account of the plague'. Retinues of the invited nobles and prelates were also strictly limited, for fear of infection from them.[11]

Before Cromwell hurried off to the christening, he had one particularly important piece of business to transact: the arrest of an old adversary, Sir George Throgmorton[12] (or Throckmorton) of Coughton, Warwickshire, an MP and a staunch opponent of Henry's divorce from Catherine of Aragon. Four years earlier, he had fomented resistance to the King's ambitions and marital plans during seditious meetings at the aptly named Queen's Head Tavern in Cripplegate, in the City of London. At the time, Cromwell had warned him to 'live at home, serve God and meddle little'.[13] But he had not heeded the ominous advice and was constantly in trouble.

Throgmorton was now sent to the Tower and closely questioned. He wrote to the King, frankly recounting his past sins: how in 1533 he had discussed with Sir Thomas Dingley why the Restraint of Appeals (to Rome) Act had been passed 'so lightly' – and he had thought this unsurprising as 'few would displease my Lord Privy Seal'.

Henry had sent for him, he recalled, after he had spoken against the Act and he had seen that the King's conscience was troubled about marrying his brother's wife: 'I told your grace I feared if you did marry Queen Anne you [would] have meddled both with the mother and sister. And his grace said: "Never with the mother." And [Cromwell] standing by, said: "Nor with the sister either – and therefore put that out of your mind."'

The Minister demanded he write down other communications he might have had about the King and Queen during those meetings at the Queen's Head, but hopelessly, haplessly, he confessed he found that 'very hard to do'.[14] Henry, triumphant at the birth of a son, must have wondered at the ironic timing of the re-emergence of these old causes célèbres. He probably saw Throgmorton as merely the unwelcome residue of an unhappy past.

After this thoroughly satisfying arrest,[15] Cromwell rode on to Hampton Court for the christening in the Chapel Royal. The ceremony began at midnight and, despite Henry's injunctions on invitees, was attended by nearly 130 lords, gentlemen and clergy, as well as 270 other guests, all crowding into the recently refurbished blue and gold-leafed fan-vaulted chapel of the palace. The King had chosen the Christian name of Edward after his maternal great-grandfather Edward IV and to mark the baby's propitious day of birth, the eve of the Feast of St Edward. At the moment of naming, torches of expensive virgin wax were lit simultaneously by the congregation and then the chief herald, *Garter King of Arms*, loudly proclaimed the prince's name and new titles – Duke of Cornwall and Earl of Chester.[16]

The child was then returned, amid a strident clarion call of trumpets, to his mother's privy chamber, where Henry and his queen awaited him. Jane, cosily wrapped in a mantle of crimson velvet trimmed with ermine fur, was propped up in bed, weakly reclining on four plump cushions of scarlet-and-gold damask. The King triumphantly took the baby up in his arms, blessed him loudly in the name of God, the Blessed Virgin Mary and St George, and burst into tears of joy, watched approvingly by the noble sycophants around him, politely sipping hippocras[17] and nibbling biscuits. With the child then safely tucked up in his 'rocking chamber' in the north range of the palace's Chapel Court, the royal christening party continued until almost dawn.

Three days later, the Queen fell ill.

Her condition rapidly worsened and at eight o'clock in the morning on 24 October, her chamberlain Thomas Manners, Earl of Rutland, together with Robert Aldridge, Bishop of Carlisle, and the King's doctors, John Chambre, William Butts and George Owen,[18] wrote to Cromwell, reporting that the previous afternoon, Jane had 'a natural lax [a loosening of the bowels] by reason she began somewhat to lighten and [appeared] to mend'. Her recovery continued until the evening but then she suffered a sudden relapse. 'All this night, she has been very sick . . . Her confessor has been with her grace this morning . . . and even now is preparing to minister . . . the Sacrament of Extreme Unction' – the Last Rites of the Catholic Church.[19]

The bulletins from Hampton Court to Cromwell in London began to flow thick and fast, with news of every development as the Queen fought for her young life. Sir John Russell, now Comptroller of the Royal Household, told the Minister that Henry had planned to leave for nearby Esher that morning for a day's hunting, but

> because the queen was very sick this night and this day, he tarried. But tomorrow, God willing, he intends to be there. If she mends, he will go, and if she [does not] he told me . . . he could not find in his heart to tarry.
>
> I assure you she has been in great danger [last] night and this day, but thanks be to God, she is somewhat amended. If she scape [survives] this night, the physicians be in good hope that she is past all danger.[20]

But both Russell and Henry's doctors were overly optimistic, as the Queen was now sinking fast. Twelve hours on, Norfolk dashed off a brief, urgent note to the Lord Privy Seal, still at Westminster:

> My good lord. I pray you to be here tomorrow early to comfort our good master, for as for our mistress, there is no likelihood of her life – the more pity – and I fear she shall not be alive at the time you shall read this.
>
> At eight at night, with the hand of [your] sorrowful friend.
>
> T. NORFOLK.[21]

She died just before midnight that night, aged twenty-eight.

Cromwell later blamed her illness on the 'faults of them that were about her' who had allowed her to eat the wrong kinds of food, 'as her fantasy in sickness called for', or suffered her to catch cold.[22] In truth, she probably died from a puerperal fever and septicaemia, caused by an infection contracted during her exhausting confinement.

Her death must have been an unpleasant shock for Cromwell, who knew only too well that Henry, after a decent period of mourning, would require a new consort, and finding her would be his unenviable task. At least with the birth of the prince, the Seymours would remain in royal favour, so his efforts to ally the Cromwells to them through marriage would not have been wasted.

The King immediately departed Hampton Court for Westminster, seeking 'a solitary place to see to his sorrows'.[23] Henry was genuinely mortified at the loss of his 'entirely beloved' wife, although at the beginning of November he was reported to be 'in good health and as merry as a widower may be'.[24] The King wrote to Francis I of France: 'I have so cordially received the congratulations which . . . you have [sent] me for the son which it has pleased God to give me . . . Notwithstanding, Divine Providence has mingled my joy with the bitterness of the death of her who brought me this happiness.'[25]

While Norfolk, as Earl Marshal, arranged Jane's state funeral, Cromwell was compiling the official audit of the Queen's possessions and assets. An eighteen-page book listed her jewels, pomanders and girdles, some now gifts to her friends, family and household.[26] A two-page document, signed by Cromwell, detailed those owing money to her estate. A *valor*[27] of lands in Hertfordshire, Berkshire, Surrey and Hampshire, 'lately [a] parcel of Queen Jane's jointure and dowry and now reserved into the king's highness' own hands', was also drawn up, estimating them to be worth £938 6s. 3d,[28] or £350,000 at 2006 prices.

Cromwell had other things on his mind. Although the young prince was in good health and thriving – he 'sucketh like a child of his puissance',[29] he reported enthusiastically – that young life was a slender, uncertain thread from which to suspend the future of the Tudors in those days of virulent epidemics. There was also the ever-present threat of assassination. The Minister was only too aware that what was required, for the absolute security of the realm, was a 'spare heir' – another healthy baby prince – and to achieve that lawfully, Henry would have to take another wife.

The daughter of one of the turbulent noble houses of England was not a comfortable option, as Cromwell feared such a wife would swiftly become the focal point for a new bout of jealousies and inevitable conspiracies within the court – which might well threaten his own position. A French match seemed diplomatically advantageous, which would help neutralise a threatening alliance between the two European superpowers, France and Spain.

At the end of October, with Jane scarcely cold in her coffin and still unburied, Cromwell informed Lord William Howard, then in France, and Bishop Stephen Gardiner, now ambassador to the court of Francis I, that his sovereign was 'little disposed to marry again' but some of his Council had urged him to undertake once more 'the extreme adventure' of matrimony, purely for the sake of his realm. 'So his tender zeal for his subjects has already overcome his grace's disposition and has framed his mind, both to be indifferent to the thing and to the election of any person from any part that, with deliberation, shall be thought meet.' He added ponderously: 'We live in hope that his grace will couple himself to our comforts.'[30]

There were two girls in France who might be suitable candidates as brides, wrote the Lord Privy Seal. Firstly, 'the French king's daughter [Marguerite],[31] said to be not the meetest, and Madame de Longueville

[Marie de Guise],[32] of whose qualities you are to inquire and whom they say the King of Scots doth desire . . .' Lord William should not return without discreetly ascertaining how the Scottish king 'stands in his suit and what the conditions and qualities of both persons be'. His enquiries, Cromwell emphasised, must be kept absolutely secret.[33]

Norfolk, taking time off from the complex organisation of a queen's funeral,[34] scheduled for 12 November at St George's Chapel, Windsor, had another critical matter to settle with Henry: his personal share of the wealth and lands of the priory of St Pancras at Lewes, in Sussex, about to be surrendered to the crown.[35] One may well consider Norfolk to have been brutish, grasping and bovinely insensitive to dare to raise such an issue when Henry (at the best of times possessing an uncertain temper) had just been bereaved. Sadly, he was all that and more. On 4 November, he wrote to Cromwell, who also had his sights fixed firmly on the rich pickings of the Cluniac monastery, to report his conversation with the King at Hampton Court the previous day.

> Thanks for your venison. By your letter, you [wanted to] know how I sped [fared] with the king yesterday.
>
> First (peradventure [perhaps] not wisely, yet plainly), I exhorted him to accept God's pleasure in taking the queen, and comfort himself with the treasure sent to him and this realm (namely the prince) and advised him to provide for a new wife.
>
> After that, I thanked him for being content to give us Lewes, if we might conclude the bargain, rehearsing of your service to him, as I told you in your garden, and saying I was content you should have two parts.

Henry distractedly replied: 'As you showed unto me' – a vital indication, Norfolk believed, that the sorrowful King thought the priory's property was 'well bestowed'.[36] Here, the Duke and Cromwell were both avariciously pursuing the ripest plum in all the dissolutions of the religious houses, even though, only the previous month, Henry had granted the Lord Privy Seal the suppressed Augustinian priory of Michelham, also in Sussex, with a handsome annual income of £171 4s. 4½d, or £64,000 in today's money.

Although Norfolk was his opportunist ally and intended fellow

beneficiary for the wealth of Lewes,[37] Cromwell was privately maintaining a regular and friendly correspondence with the Duke's wronged
forty-year-old wife Elizabeth, whom Norfolk had brutally discarded in
favour of his blowsy mistress, Bess Holland. On 24 October, Elizabeth
wrote to the Lord Privy Seal, complaining that although she had been
married to Norfolk for twenty-five years and had provided him with five
children, 'because I would not suffer the bawd[s] and harlots that bound
me to be still in the house, they pinnacled [manacled] me and sat on my
breast till I spat blood, all for speaking against the woman in the court,
Bessie Holland'. Bitterly, she recounted how four years before, Norfolk
'came riding all night and locked me up in a chamber, took away all my
jewels and apparel and left me but £50 a quarter to keep twenty persons
in a hard country'.[38] Just over two weeks later, the feisty Duchess wrote
again to Cromwell, sending a seasonal gift of partridges, appealing for
his aid in persuading Henry and Norfolk to improve her bleak living
conditions at Redbourne in Hertfordshire:

> Without your aid I shall never get it. I have so many enemies – Bessie
> Holland in the court, for chief, and the bawd and the harlots at
> Kenninghall [Norfolk's seat near Norwich] and the men, Southwell one,
> and Rouse, another . . . They rule my lord as they wish . . .
>
> I have been from my lord four years come Easter . . . and will never
> return to him. I have written to him that I will do more for gentleness than
> for all their extreme handling, seeing I was his choosing, and not he mine.

So much for loveless arranged marriages. Her humiliation still rankled,
as fresh as if her hurts had occurred the previous day. It was the stuff of
real scandal, but any notion of conscience or honour seemed to wash off
arrogant Norfolk's back. After he had thrown her out, the Duke had sent
two of his chaplains to cajole Elizabeth into agreeing to divorce him, in
return for her jewels, clothes and 'much of his plate and household stuff.
I rebuked his priests and next day, he wrote it with his own hand. But
though my children be unnat[ural] to me, I still love them. I will never
trust my husband – he can speak fair to his enemy as to his friend.'[39]

This was not, by any means, the only tricky family dispute that
Cromwell was routinely involved in, although no doubt he was storing

up the salacious details for use against Norfolk on a rainy day in the future. On 12 November, before rushing off to Windsor to personally escort Louis de Perreau, Sieur de Castillon, the newly arrived French ambassador to London, at the Queen's funeral, he dashed off a sharply worded letter to John Babington, the feckless executor of his mother's will, about his careless administration of her estate:

> Your brother, Thomas, son and heir of her late father Sir Anthony
> Babington, agreed to an award . . . that Dame Katherine, your late mother,
> should have the manor place of Kingston, Nottinghamshire, with certain
> lands there during her life and for a year after her decease, paying nothing
> for it, although your brother might have £10 a year rent for it. I hear
> you . . . have during the said year after her decease, committed so great a
> waste in the same manor that £100 would not restore it.
>
> You and your brother shall each take two honest and indifferent
> [impartial] gentlemen to view the waste and take such order thereupon
> that your brother may have no cause to complain to me or the king's
> Council.[40]

Elizabeth, the distraught wife of Sir Marmaduke Constable Junior, a member of the Yorkshire family, also appealed for Cromwell's assistance as her husband refused to maintain her. She offered him income from various leases as an inducement for his help:

> I have not had a penny from my husband for two years and a half and none
> of my own kin will help me with a penny, nor [a] penny's worth this twelve
> month. Oh good my lord! How should I live? Beg, I cannot, loth and
> ashamed I am to be a harlot.
>
> If your lordship will get me my whole jointure of 100 marks [£67],[41] I
> will freely give you the first farm [lease payment] that is at Candlemas,
> 50 marks; if I have but half my jointure, I freely give you both Candlemas
> and Lammas; the farm of them both is but 50 marks.[42]

Then there was the bizarre case of Elizabeth, wife of Sir Thomas Borough, who prematurely gave birth to a son and 'was in great danger of losing it after her great travail', she told Cromwell in early November. Lady Borough spent her confinement with a relative of her husband, who wrote to him after the child was born 'that he might have no cause of jealousy against her, seeing that the child, by the proportions of his body, was born long before the time'. The distressed lady's husband was now claiming it was not his child and '[made] himself absent from her'. She therefore humbly begged Cromwell's mediation.

Worse was to come. Hard on the heels of that pleading letter came another on 13 November, piteously complaining that her husband 'always [lay] in wait to put her to shame'. She remained a 'comfortless prisoner' and now her father-in-law, Lord Borough, had complained about her to the King's Council, declaring that her child was not his son's. She added: 'Nothing but the power of God has preserved his life and I beg [that Cromwell] will prevent him being disinherited.'[43] It was not to be. Eventually, in 1542, her father-in-law procured a private Act of Parliament declaring her children bastards.[44]

Aside from his arbitration in family disputes and taking an unlikely hand in Tudor marriage guidance, Cromwell routinely had to handle a mountain of paperwork and the annoying administrative problems that daily afflicted any busy minister of the crown. Take the case of John Thompson, the Surveyor of the King's Works at Dover, who was supervising, rather inefficiently, the construction of an expensive new harbour there to 'control the narrow seas' of the English Channel, as well as repairing the defences of Dover Castle. In July 1537, he had admitted that the 'king's money was not so well spent as might be' and in October that his labourers were owed two months' wages. This had clearly led to some harsh words from Cromwell during a fraught meeting at his house, at Mortlake in Surrey, when Thompson gave a written undertaking to 'do better service this winter than had been done all summer'. On 18 November, however, the project manager was in trouble again. He was in renewed fear of his master's wrath over unexpected bills found 'in a dark place' in the great hall of the former religious house, the Maison Dieu, at Dover, 'by William Worm of Sandwich, who is blind of one eye and cannot see well with the other. [These bills] conspire to put me out of the king's favour.'

Thompson, panic-stricken at this new evidence of his financial mismanagement, had rushed off to London but had met one of Cromwell's servants at Canterbury, who prudently advised him to 'send a letter for my excuse' rather than turning up in person to face the hard consequences. Piteously, he complained that since he began work on the harbour, he had 'once been poisoned, which has been in his body this quarter of a year past, and is now descended into his legs. As Cromwell's servants, Anthony Auchar and John Anthony, can show, there are certain persons who conspire to put him out of the king's favour.'[45]

Despite this pressing issue of cost overruns and embarrassing delays in an important strategic project, Cromwell's most urgent concern remained that of quickly finding a new wife for Henry, who continued to wear mourning even though he detested the sight of black, which reminded him of death.[46] With the King's bulk growing daily and his health declining, time and his medical condition were against any chances of further royal procreation.

John Hutton, the Governor of the Merchant Adventurers in Antwerp and the English agent based in Flanders, was one of those ordered to send the Lord Privy Seal any information about likely brides, despite his rather pathetic protestations that he had 'little experience amongst ladies'. In early December 1537, Hutton reported that there was a fourteen-year-old daughter of the Lord of Brederode (in the modern Netherlands) 'waiting upon the queen [Mary, dowager of Hungary] . . . [and] of goodly stature, virtuous, sad and womanly; her beauty is competent. Her mother has departed this life.' Her uncle, Erarde de la Marck, the Cardinal of Liège, would provide her with a good 'dote' – an ample dowry – 'to have her bestowed [married off] well'.

Then, mused Hutton, there was the widow of John, Count of Egmont, who was often at court. 'She is over forty – but does not look it.' There was also Christina, the sixteen-year-old second daughter of the deposed Christian II of Denmark and widow of Francisco Sforza, Duke of Milan, 'who is reported a good personage and of excellent beauty'. She was then also living at the court of Mary of Hungary in the Netherlands.

The indecorous business was taking on all the hallmarks of a cattle market, and Hutton was clearly finding it an issue too hot to handle – a far cry from his comfortable, clear-cut world of commerce. He pleaded uneasily that he had written 'the truth as nigh as I can learn but I leave further judgement to others'. Almost as an afterthought, the agent added: 'The Duke of Cleves has a daughter, but there is no great praise either of her person or beauty.'[47]

Hutton, now in Brussels, sent across another report about the Duchess of Milan on 9 December.

> She is . . . very high of stature. She is higher than the regent, a goodly personage of body and of competent beauty, of favour excellent, soft of speech and gentle in countenance. She wears mourning apparel after the manner of Italy. The common saying . . . here is that she is both widow and maid. One of the council here suggests that the king should marry her and the Duke of Ravestein the lady [Princess] Mary.[48] She resembles one Mrs [Madge] Shelton that used to wait on Queen Anne.[49]

He also told Thomas Wriothesley, one of the Clerks of the Signet, that there was none who could be compared to Christina for 'beauty of person and birth . . . She is not so pure white as the late Queen [Jane] whose soul God pardon, but she has a singular good countenance, and when she chances to smile, there appears two [dimples] in her cheeks and one in her chin which becomes her right excellently well.'[50] Hutton was clearly captivated by the teenager's charms, for all his self-deprecating talk of inexperience with women.

More powerful figures on the European stage were now taking an interest in Cromwell's discreet soundings on a future bride for his royal master. His Most Christian Majesty Francis I of France wrote to his London ambassador Castillon on 11 December, acknowledging that he had 'taken in good part the overtures of marriage made by the Lord Privy Seal'. Indeed, he would think it a great honour if Henry would take a French girl as his new wife but: 'There is no lady who is not at his command except Madame de Longueville whose marriage with the King of Scots has been arranged.'

But not far beneath the diplomatic pleasantries lay the familiar French fist of steel. Francis instructed his envoy to try to 'ascertain what terms are desired for a treaty in connection with this marriage, both for offence and defence on either side. Since England desires the amity of

France, it should be established firmly with a clear knowledge of what one is to do for the other.'[51]

Just over two months after Jane's death, Henry, no doubt encouraged by Cromwell, could just descry the distant sound of wedding bells. He became incongruously ardent, like a star-struck boy. Castillon reported to Francis on 30 December that the English King was 'so amorous of Madame de Longueville [Marie de Guise] that he cannot refrain' from considering her as a wife. 'I assured him that the marriage between the King of Scots and her had already been sworn . . . but that no lady in France would be denied him.' Would you, the French ambassador enquired, 'marry another man's wife?' Given Henry's experience of marriage, it was a cheekily indiscreet question, but it did not dampen the King's mounting enthusiasm. Henry would not be diverted or dissuaded and audaciously sought that the betrothal to the King of Scots be broken off, promising 'he would do twice as much for [Francis]' as his nephew, this 'beggarly and idiotic' Scottish king:

> I [Castillon] asked who caused him to be more inclined to her than to
> others and he said [Sir John] Wallop [former ambassador to France] was so
> loud in her praises.
>
> Moreover, he was big in person and had need of a big wife, that your
> [Francis's] daughter was too young for him and as to [Marie] de Vendôme,
> he would not take the King of Scots' leavings.[52]

The next day, Castillon wrote again to the French King with some startling news. Cromwell had sent Sir Peter Mewtas as an agent into France, who had learned that Marie de Guise had never consented to the marriage to James V of Scotland.[53] She was ready to obey Francis in everything, but she had never specially promised to marry the King of Scotland and Francis could grant her to Henry.

Castillon strongly advised that Bishop Gardiner, the resident English ambassador in France, be clearly notified 'that the marriage was concluded and sworn . . . so that no more be said upon the subject, for the King of England would have given half his kingdom to have married her'.[54] So the voluptuous charms of Marie de Guise were to be denied the English King. This *belle femme de France* needed little discouragement:

Henry's marital reputation was notorious within the courts of Europe. Marie dryly commented that she might be a big woman, but she only had a little neck.[55]

Francis hurriedly sent her off to Scotland, where she married James V in early June 1538. Henry told Castillon petulantly: 'Well, if that is so, I am receiving offers from many quarters.' Not only had his amorous advances been spurned, but the 'Auld Alliance' between Scotland and France had been further cemented, much to his chagrin.

Thus thwarted, Henry turned to the Hapsburgs. Reports about Christina, the young widow of the Duke of Milan, had intrigued him – particularly her love of his own favourite pastimes, hunting and playing cards. The Spanish Emperor sent Don Diego Hurtado de Mendoza to London to discuss the possible match. He and the imperial ambassador Eustace Chapuys were guests of honour at a sumptuous banquet at Hampton Court.[56] Hutton meanwhile was still keeping a close eye on Christina in Brussels. He informed Cromwell on 21 February 1538: 'She speaks French and seems to be of few words. In her speaking, she lisps, which does nothing to misbecome her.' In July, he reported her conversation with one of her attendants who had been in England, but Hutton did not know

> whether it was by commission of the Duchess or for his private business
> . . . She demanded of him how he liked England [and he] answered
> that he thought he had seen another Italy. Then she demanded if he had
> seen the king which he affirmed to have done, declaring his grace's good
> and prosperous health, with as much lauding [praise of] his majesty's
> benignity, comeliness, aboundans [wealth] and bountifulness as might
> be.
>
> Unto which she answered that many times she heard much praise
> of the king's grace but now she was fully satisfied it was true.[57]

Christina appeared to have been hooked by Henry's dubious charms. Anxious to seal the match, Cromwell sent Thomas Wriothesley to Brussels to meet the widowed Duchess. He reported to an anxious Henry back in London that she had 'a very good woman's face and [was] competently fair but very well favoured' although unfashionably, her skin was a 'little brown'. With permission, he had asked her whether she would consider marrying Henry. She had a wise head on her shoulders, for all her tender years: 'As for my inclination, what should I say? You know I am at the Emperor's commandment.' The Englishman cried out: 'Oh madam, how happy shall you be if it be your chance to be matched with my master!'

Wriothesley told her persuasively that his royal master was 'the most gentle gentleman that lives; his nature so benign and pleasant that I think till this day, no man has heard many angry words pass his mouth'. Did the sixteen-year-old believe this outrageous canard? Wriothesley quickly pressed on: Henry, he said, was 'one of the most puissant and mighty princes of Christendom. If you saw him, you would [talk of] his virtue, gentleness, wisdom, experience, goodliness of person; all . . . gifts and qualities meet to be in a prince.' The young Duchess looked him straight in the eye. Wriothesley told Henry afterwards: 'She smiled again and I think could have laughed . . . had not her gravity forbidden it and restrained it with much pain. She heard me well and like one (I thought) that was tickled.' Finally, she said 'she knew your majesty was a noble and good prince'.[58] Cromwell's man was another clearly enchanted with the young widow.

But before the canny Henry went any further, he wanted a portrait of her to study, if not to gloat over. One of the gentlemen of his privy chamber, Philip Hoby, was sent secretly to Brussels to meet her, together with Henry's talented court artist, Hans Holbein the Younger. The painter dashed off a sketch of her in just three hours on 12 March 1538, and was back in London six days later with it under his arm, to show his king. Henry was captivated by the modest, coy image of the teenager and commissioned Holbein to paint him an enchanting full-length portrait of her in oils, shown wearing mourning dress.[59] In his heart and in his mind, she rapidly changed into a comely, compliant bride and he swaggeringly boasted that after their wedding, there would follow 'our younger sons', ennobled with the ancient dukedoms of York, Gloucester and Somerset.[60] Moreover, proposed Henry, his daughter Princess Mary could marry Don Luis, the brother of the Portuguese King, in a double wedding, thereby ensuring England's participation in any future peace treaty with France.

But for anyone, even a king with imperial pretensions, the path of true love can be rocky. There remained the delicate issue of 'affinity' – too close a blood relationship between man and wife, banned, then as now, by canon law. Christina was niece to the Emperor Charles V, and thus great-niece to Henry's discarded first wife, Catherine of Aragon. Not only was there affinity in such a match, but clerical pedants could claim, with some justice, that it was really a double affinity because of the earlier marriage between Catherine and Henry's elder brother Arthur. Traditionally, such inconvenient impediments to royal nuptials could be removed by papal decree, as had happened in 1518 when Manuel I of Portugal had married Eleanor of Hapsburg, the niece of his first two wives, Isabella and Maria of Aragon, themselves sisters. However, for Henry, such an intervention by Rome would have been complete political and personal anathema. London's alternative and brazen offer of his services as supreme head of the Church of England on Earth was equally unacceptable to the Spanish.

But the French were not to be outdone. Other nubile Gallic ladies were offered up, as was Francis's younger son, the nineteen-year-old Henri, as a husband for Princess Mary. The new candidate brides again came from the Guise clan. Marie had two younger sisters, Louise and Renée, the former – remarkably, as she was at the French court – rumoured to remain a virgin. Castillon, who by now understood how to handle the English King, urged Henry uncouthly: 'Take her! She is a maid, so you will have the advantage of being able to shape the passage to your measure.' Henry burst into bawdy guffaws of laughter, slapped the envoy laddishly on the back and walked devoutly into his morning mass.[61]

Two more cousins of Francis were potentially available for the English King's rheumy eyes to cast over: Marie de Vendôme and Anne of Lorraine. However, Marie had announced her intention to become a nun, but as far as the pragmatic French were concerned, this was not necessarily an obstacle to her joining Henry in his royal marriage bed. Annede Montmorency, the blunt Constable of France, was 'sure the king of England, who considers himself Pope in his own kingdom, would choose her in preference to all others'.[62] Rules were there to be broken where diplomacy was concerned.

Once more Henry dispatched Hoby and Holbein to inspect the prospective brides, and to faithfully portray them in drawings so that the King could examine their ample charms at his leisure. They discovered Louise staying in Le Havre, on the north-west French coast, in June, and returned home with two drawings of her, even though she had taken to her bed with a fever – hardly flattering to a lady's self-esteem. Their breathless European merry-go-round continued in August when the pair were sent on a mission to seek out Renée in Joinville on the River Marne, but they missed her, and Holbein was sent on to the town of Nancy, in north-east France, to draw Francis's cousin, Anne of Lorraine. As the French had produced another painting of Louise de Guise and Marie de Vendôme, Henry was now assembling his own portrait gallery of European wannabe queens of England.

As Cromwell doubtless frequently pointed out to him, there were some diplomatic imperatives that required a decision on whether to favour a French or imperial bride. But it was difficult for the King to make up his mind, faced with all these drawings, and in the back of his mind there were nagging doubts about just how much flattery, or artist's licence, had gone into the young faces that stared blankly back at him off the paper or canvas. Doubtless the Latin phrase *caveat emptor* – 'let the buyer beware' – was in the forefront of his mind. His innovative solution was as daring as it was direct: the French should arrange a beauty parade of sorts within a marquee pitched, impartially, on the border between France and Calais, so he could inspect them personally and evaluate the attractions of each girl. Perhaps seven or eight young ladies could be assembled to make his trip worthwhile? To bumptious, bluff King Hal, there was no question of impropriety in this simple request, as the French Queen, Eleanore of Austria, could chaperone the maidens to ensure there was no chance of any hanky-panky amongst the guy ropes.

Monsieur le Roi was outraged at Henry's suggestion and instructed his envoy in London in August to primly tell his brother England: 'It is not the custom of France to send damsels of noble and princely families to be passed in review as if they were hackneys [horses] for sale.'[63]

Predictably, Henry was by no means abashed by such a show of moral rectitude. He pressed his demand to scrutinise the would-be brides, insisting: 'By God! I trust no one but myself. The thing touches me too near. I wish to see them and know them some time before deciding.' Castillon, in turn, knew the value of a joke to turn aside royal wrath. He neatly punctured the English King's pomposity by embarrassing him: 'Then maybe your grace would like to mount them one after the other and keep the one you find the best broken in. Is that the way the knights of the Round Table treated women in times past?'[64] His mocking taunt hit home. Henry 'laughed and blushed at the same time and recognised that the way he had taken was a little discourteous', the ambassador reported later. 'After rubbing his nose a little, he answered: "Yes, but since the king [Francis I] my brother has already so great amity with the [Spanish] emperor, what amity should I have with him? I ask because I am resolved not to marry again, unless the emperor or the king prefer my friendship to that which they have together." '

Henry was growing impatient and his hopes and dreams of a new bride were fading rapidly. Even Christina now had doubts about the ageing English King as a suitable husband, likely fuelled by his notorious reputation. Her advisers talked openly of the rumours of the sinister demise of Henry's previous wives: 'Her great-aunt was poisoned; that the second wife was put to death and the third lost for lack of keeping her childbed.' After all the diplomatic effort, in the end she turned him down. With the wisdom of a lady far more experienced than her years would suggest, she reportedly declared that if she had two heads, just one would be at Henry's disposal.[65]

The sands of diplomacy had also run their course. On 17 June 1538, Francis and Charles met in Nice and through the mediation of Pope Paul III signed a ten-year truce, raising the unwelcome spectre of a powerful Catholic alliance against Henry and England, both now dangerously isolated.

Cromwell turned to the Lutheran princely states for new allies and perhaps even a new bride. Another unlikely double marriage was tentatively suggested: Henry to Anne, the twenty-two-year-old sister of Duke William, heir to a newly formed group of duchies on the Lower Rhine.

William, in turn, would marry Princess Mary, Catherine of Aragon's daughter. On paper, neither alliance nor bride looked too encouraging after the lost opportunities with mighty France and Spain. But it was all Cromwell had left up his sleeve.

CHAPTER EIGHT

Reformation and Retribution

I have pulled down the image of Our Lady at Caversham, where unto was great pilgrimage. The image is plated over with silver and I have put it into a chest fast locked and nailed up and by the next barge that comes from Reading to London, it shall be brought to your lordship.

DR JOHN LONDON TO CROMWELL, AFTER SUPPRESSING THE CHAPEL AT CAVERSHAM, BERKSHIRE, SEPTEMBER 1538[1]

Aside from the difficult foreign adventures in seeking a blushing bride for Great Harry of England, Cromwell was still fully occupied with formulating and imposing religious reform and converting monastic assets into hard cash. In the pre-Reformation religion, many monasteries gleaned considerable revenues from their guardianship of precious holy relics. Devout pilgrims visited these numerous and sometimes obscure objects of reverence in the confident expectation that a response to an anxious prayer, a generous oblation, could cure their hopeless medical conditions, resolve a tiresome everyday problem or provide some other miraculous assistance.

For example, St Petronilla was reputed to cure fevers; St Clare, those unfortunates afflicted with sore eyes; and St Genow, the painful gout. St Appollania's ubiquitous molars relieved sufferers from toothache.[2] Other saints could be called upon to help with specific, targeted powers. An intercession by St Anthony of Padua assisted those exasperated people who had lost a possession and St Leonard helpfully opened jail doors and caused prisoners' fetters to suddenly fall away. Some saints were also designated patrons of particular trades or professions: St Gertrude looked after the interests of rat-catchers; St Honoratus, those of bakers; St Nicholas, mariners; and St Crispin, shoemakers. The volume of daily supplication from the faithful must have deafened Heaven's community of saints.

For the religious houses, this meant in practice that the holier their relics – or the more of them they possessed – the greater the stream of pilgrims visiting their abbey, bringing in their purses a welcome and steady income. In the face of competition from a hundred other monasteries, each with its own compellingly powerful sacred relics, it was a pious activity all too easily open to abuse by an ambitious or astute abbot or prior. For a few with a keen eye for God's business, the temptation to exploit the old adage that 'a fool and his money are soon parted' must have been impossible to resist. And so it proved down the centuries.

It is not too difficult to view with a jaundiced if not cynical eye, for example, the extravagant claims made by the Benedictine abbey at Bury, Suffolk, for their odd assortment of relics: the coals that toasted St Laurence alive; the nail parings of St Edmund; the penknife and boots that belonged to St Thomas Becket; and 'other relics for rain . . . [and] for avoiding of weeds growing in corn'.[3]

Today, we would recognise the culture of relics as pure and simple marketing. But for Cromwell and the Protestant reformers, the issue was very clear-cut: these bits of dusty old bone and graven images were merely superstitious hokum and sinful idolatry, to be ruthlessly swept away in the virtuous act of cleansing Henry's Church. There was also, of course, the valuable bonus of the 'great riches' stripped from the shrines, which rapidly accumulated in the King's secret treasury in the Tower of London, an imperative that must always have been at the forefront of Cromwell's mind.[4]

The fragment of the True Cross, upon which Christ was crucified, kept at the Benedictine priory at Bromholme, Norfolk, was proudly proclaimed to have brought thirty-nine dead men back to life and cured the sight of nineteen blind pilgrims. Commissioner Thomas Legh told Cromwell that at Chertsey Abbey in Surrey the monks had the arm bone of St Blaise 'through which they give wine in cases of illness' and an image of St Faith, before which they placed candles on behalf of the sick. They 'hold that if the candle remains lighted till it is consumed, the sick person will recover, but if it goes out he will die'.[5] One fears how draughty the abbey was.

A cell of St Dogmael's Abbey, 1 mile (1.61 km) west of Cardigan in Dyfed, Wales, boasted a figure of Our Lady bearing a taper, said to have been found miraculously in the nearby River Teifi, the candle burning brightly in its hand.[6] William Barlow, the energetic Bishop of St David's, visited the abbey in March 1538 and branded it a 'devilish delusion'. He interrogated the prior, Thomas Hore, who claimed he had been innocently deceived by the taper, and the Bishop, huffing and puffing over such heinous superstition, issued injunctions that the prior and local vicar should

> declare to the people the abominable idolatry and deceitful juggling of their predecessors there, in worshipping and causing to be worshipped a piece of old rotten timber, putting the people in belief the same to be a holy relic and a taper which had burned away without consuming or waste.
>
> The prior and vicar shall do away [with] or cause to be done away [with] all manner of clothes, figured wax, delusions of miracles, shrouds and other enticements of the ignorant people to pilgrimage and idolatry.[7]

Barlow also confiscated relics he found at the religious house at St David's, which included two heads of silver plate enclosing two rotten skulls stuffed with putrefied cloths, two arm bones and a worm-eaten book covered with silver plate.

The state's assault on relics began in those religious houses exempted from the dissolution of the smaller monasteries from 1536. The images of St Anne at Buxton in Derbyshire and St Modwen at Burton upon Trent in Staffordshire stood in niches over local holy wells and were believed to possess healing qualities. Both statues were sent to Cromwell's London home at Austin Friars, as was the image of Our Lady of Ipswich in July

1538 from the shrine located just outside the Suffolk town's west gate. His steward Thomas Thacker, in a series of letters, described their safe arrival in disappointed tones, like a pawnbroker valuing new but mediocre stock: 'I have received . . . the image of Our Lady of Ipswich which I have bestowed [put] into your wardrobe of beds till your lordship's pleasure be known. There is nothing about her but two half shoes of silver and four stones of crystal set in silver.'[8]

Later, he reported receiving the two images from the Midlands:

> The image of St Anne of Buxton and also the image of St Modwen of Burton, with her red hair and her staff which women labouring of child in those parts were very desirous to have with them to lean upon and walk with and had great confidence in the staff.
>
> [These] two images I have bestowed by Our Lady of Ipswich. There came nothing with them but the bare images.[9]

But a few days later, Thacker took delivery from Ipswich of 'Our Lady's coat with two gorgets[10] of gold to put about her neck and an image of Our Lady of gold in a tabernacle of silver and gilt, with the feather in the top of gold and a little relic of gold and crystal with Our Lady's milk in it, as they say'.[11]

There were other valuable items in the same consignment of loot, this time from the dockside church of St Peter's, Ipswich – a silver-gilt cross with figures of the Virgin Mary and St John; a silver pax;[12] a silver-gilt chalice; a gilt censer; and two silver cruets.[13] What happened to these precious sacred objects remains a matter of conjecture – probably they were appropriated by Cromwell himself and turned into ready cash. He certainly ordered the images to be burnt at Chelsea.

In February 1538, a representation of the Crucifixion of Christ – the famous 'Rood of Grace' – at the Cistercian abbey of Boxley, near Maidstone in Kent, was jubilantly exposed as a fraud. It had long been the object of virtuous pilgrimage, as the figure's eyes rolled, the lips moved and it could nod and shake its head, hands and feet. This regular performance, undertaken strangely only when money was donated to the abbey, was believed by the faithful to be a recurrent and wondrous miracle. In reality, that miracle was more one of medieval engineering:

the monks caused the movements of Christ's effigy simply by secretly tugging on a system of wires, levers and pulleys. Cromwell's long-time friend Geoffrey Chambers jubilantly reported to the Lord Privy Seal that on plucking down the images he had found 'certain engines and old wire [and] rotten sticks, in the back of the same that did cause the eyes . . . to move and stare in the head, like . . . a lively thing and also the nether lip likewise to move as though it should speak'. The abbot 'with other [of] the old monks' naturally denied any knowledge of the automaton, but were sent to London to be questioned by Cromwell, even though the abbot pleaded piteously that he was 'sore sick'. Chambers took the contraption to Maidstone market and demonstrated its workings 'to all the people there present to see the false, crafty and subtle handling thereof, to the dishonour of God and illusion of the people'.[14] It was then taken to Westminster and shown triumphantly to Henry, who plainly could not decide whether to celebrate the fraud's exposure or lament at the deception inflicted upon his faithful subjects.[15] On 12 February, the Rood made positively its last performance at Paul's Cross, outside the great London cathedral, when John Hilsey, Bishop of Rochester, happily smashed it into a hundred pieces. The destruction revealed the figure to be made of 'paper and clouts [patches of cloth] from the legs upward; each leg and arm were of timber and so the people had been deluded and caused to do great idolatry by the said image of long continuance to the derogation of God's honour and great blasphemy of the name of God'.[16] The huge crowd of people that witnessed the Rood's destruction now laughed at 'that which they adored but an hour before'.[17] The 'rude people and boys' then joyfully hurled the remains of the automaton onto a bonfire.

Then there was the notorious case of the 'Blood of Hailes', which, wonder of wonders, liquefied only when penitents handed over their donations to its Cistercian guardians. It was held at the thirteenth-century Hailes Abbey, near Winchcombe, Gloucestershire, contained in a tiny glass phial and proudly held to be the sacred blood of Jesus, after being guaranteed authentic by the Patriarch of Jerusalem. The relic was obtained from the Count of Flanders in 1267 and given to the abbey three years later by Edward, Duke of Cornwall. A new apse at the east end of the abbey church had been specially built behind the high altar for the new shrine. Six years earlier Hugh Latimer, Bishop of Worcester, when vicar of West Kington, Wiltshire, complained: 'I live within half a mile of the Fosse Way[18] and you would wonder to see how they come by flocks out of the West Country to many images . . . but chiefly to the Blood of Hailes.'

The Abbot of Hailes, Stephen Whalley, had now cannily discerned which way the wind was blowing and hastened to distance himself from the relic's reputed miracles. In September 1538, he sought permission from the Lord Privy Seal to destroy the shrine, offering a generous bribe for his agreement:

> That feigned relic called the Blood . . . stands yet in the place still . . . so that I am afraid lest it should minister to any weak person, looking there . . . to abuse his conscience.
>
> Therefore I do beseech you to be a good lord to me . . . to give me licence that I may put it down, every stick and stone, so that no manner of token or remembrance of that feigned relic shall remain.
>
> Touching the value of the silver and gold therein, I think it is not worth £40, scant £30 by estimation . . .
>
> Beseeching you . . . to accept this poor token, a strange piece of gold.[19]

The abbot's perceptive change of heart was timely, although his gift was regarded as wholly inadequate. Whalley subsequently had to hand over an extra £140, his mitre and best cross and 'a thing or two' to the Minister, who knew a thing or two about monastic wealth and was experienced in squeezing a defenceless victim in a tight spot.[20] Latimer meanwhile worked diligently to reveal the relic to be a fraud. He wrote to Cromwell on 29 October: 'We have been . . . sifting the blood all this forenoon. It was wonderfully closely and craftily enclosed and stopped up and cleaved fast to the bottom of the glass . . . Verily, it seems to be an unctuous gum. It has a certain . . . moisture and though it seems like blood while it is in the glass, yet when any parcel of the same is taken out, it turns to a yellow colour.'[21]

The phial was taken to London and on 24 November, Bishop Hilsey, that earnest debunker of miracles, waved it contemptuously before his astonished congregation at Paul's Cross and loudly denied it was the Saviour's blood. No, it was not even duck's blood, as a former abbot had allegedly admitted to his concubine.[22] Its contents were simply 'honey clarified and coloured with saffron and lying like a gum, as evidently had been proved and tested before the king and his council'. Would you have tasted it to find out its true ingredients? The Bishop duly handed the phial around to allow 'every man to behold' the fraud.[23]

So the state attacks on idolatry and superstition continued. In September 1538, John London seized the 'spearhead that pierced our Saviour's side upon the Cross' during his suppression of a chapel at Caversham, Berkshire, apparently brought there by an angel with one wing. During his suppressions in and around Reading, he also discovered a dagger allegedly used to kill King Henry VI and 'the knife that killed St Edward', but failed to confiscate 'the piece of holy halter [with which] Judas was hanged'. London reported to Cromwell: 'I have required my lord abbot [of Reading] the relics of his house which he showed me with goodwill. I have taken an inventory of them and have locked them up behind their high altar and have the key in my keeping and they be always ready at your lordship's commandment.'[24]

A vindication of the religious changes being enforced in England, written by Cromwell's privy seal clerk Thomas Derby in 1539, dismissed scornfully such 'feigned' relics 'as the blood of Christ [which] was but a piece of red silk enclosed in a thick glass; instead of the milk of Our Lady, a piece of chalk . . . [and] more of the Holy Cross than three carts can carry'.[25]

The destruction of the shrines must have come as an enormous emotional shock to the faithful of England. Much of what they had believed in – and relied upon – was suddenly and literally swept away. Many supposed, more in hope than reason, that the obliteration of all that they held most dear must only be a temporary aberration in government policy. Thomas Cowley, alias Rochester, the traditionalist vicar of Ticehurst in rural East Sussex, steadfastly continued to urge his parishioners to venerate the images. During a sermon, he held up a groat – a coin worth four pennies, or £6.20 in 2006 money – bearing Henry's head on the reverse and demanded of his congregation:

Dare you spit upon this face? You dare not do it. But you will spit upon the image [and so] spit upon God.

Hold you there, hold for a while! For . . . within four years, we shall have it as it was again.

Therefore do as you have done. Offer up a candle to St Loys [Eliguis or Eloi] for your horse and to St Anthony for your cattle.[26]

In Shropshire, the vicar of Highley defiantly regilded the statue of the Virgin Mary in his church (to which 'much offerings was made in the past') because his flock firmly believed it had cured a woman of her blindness when she touched it.[27] He was betrayed to Cromwell by John Harford, a loyal yeoman of the crown.

In January 1540, a 'poor woman' from Wells-next-the-Sea in Norfolk was still claiming miracles were being performed by the statue of Our Lady of Walsingham[28] two years after Cromwell had burnt it in London. She suffered for her rash claims – but only through humiliation and discomfort, rather than anything more penal or painful. The Minister was told that she was sat in the stocks

in the morning and about nine of the clock when the market was fullest of people, with a paper set about her head written . . . with these words: 'a reporter of false tales'. [She] was sat in a cart and so carried about the market and other streets in the town, staying in diverse places where most people assembled, young people and boys of the town casting snowballs at her.

This done and executed, [she] was brought to the stocks again and there sat until the market ended. This was her penance, for I knew no law otherwise to punish her but by discretion; trusting it will be a warning to other light persons . . . but the said image is not yet out of their heads.[29]

Cromwell, always having an eye for the main chance, decided to use an image as a vehicle for his propaganda.

John Forrest, a Friar Observant[30] and Doctor of Divinity, had been interrogated in April 1538 at Lambeth by Cranmer over his 'most abominable heresies and blasphemy' against both God and England. These included his beliefs that the Holy Catholic Church was the Church of

Rome; that Englishmen should believe in the Pope's pardon for the remission of sins; and that priests could reduce the time spent in the pain of Purgatory for truly penitent and contrite sinners. Moreover, although he had sworn the oath confirming Henry's supremacy over the Church in England, he secretly claimed this had been taken 'by his outward man, but his inward man never consented'.[31]

His treasonous stance would have come as no surprise: he had been confessor to Catherine of Aragon and had been in and out of prison on several occasions for his creed. Forrest was now repeatedly given the chance to disown his beliefs and to repent, 'but standing yet stiff and proud, refused to do [so]' and rejected any penance 'maliciously by the instigation of the devil'.

After a career of such intransigence, there could only be one outcome for his obstinacy.

On 22 May 1538, he was tied to a sheep hurdle and dragged by horse through the stinking streets from London's Newgate Prison to Smithfield to be burnt for heresy.

Ten thousand citizens awaited his terrible death, summoned to watch by special proclamation. A wooden stand had been constructed for privileged spectators alongside the gate of the Church of St Bartholomew the Great: amongst them were the Dukes of Norfolk and Suffolk, the Earls of Sussex and Hertford, members of the King's Council, and the Lord Mayor of London, Sir Richard Gresham and his aldermen. Near the railed-off double gallows, a pulpit had been erected from which Bishop Latimer could harangue the prisoner, who was seated on a facing platform.

The choice of preacher had been Cromwell's and Latimer, a popular orator, was the obvious man for the job. He was curiously jocular in his acceptance of the task. He wrote on 17 May:

> If it be your pleasure . . . that I shall play the fool after my customary manner when Forrest shall suffer, I would wish that my stage [pulpit] stood near to Forrest for I would endeavour myself to content the people, that . . . I might also convert Forrest, God so helping, or rather working. Wherefore I would that he should hear what I say . . . If he would yet, with

heart, return to his abjuration, I would wish his pardon, such is my foolishness.[32]

On the day, in a tiresome three-hour sermon, the Bishop tediously described Forrest's errors and 'with many and godly exhortations moved him to repent ... but he would neither hear nor speak'. Latimer demanded in what state he would die and Forrest

> openly declared ... with a loud voice ... that if an angel should come down from heaven and show him any other thing than that he had believed all his lifetime, he would not believe him and that if his body should be cut, joint after joint, or member after member, burnt, hanged, or what[ever] pain might be done to his body – he would never turn from [adherence to] his old sect.

These were brave words from a man faced with the imminence of a horrible, lingering death and doubtless goaded by the smug, self-righteous oration he was forced to hear. What is more, Forrest defiantly told Latimer, the Bishop would never have dared to deliver such a sermon seven years before without endangering his own life. But times had changed and the tide of religious reform in England was ebbing back and forth. Forrest was now stranded high and dry and any hopes of an eleventh-hour reprieve had rapidly disappeared.

Cromwell had decided ruthlessly to make a special example of him to maximise the opportunity for showy propaganda and, equally importantly, to create a lasting deterrent to others.

Ellis Price, one of Cromwell's ubiquitous religious visitors, had the previous month confiscated a giant wooden image from the early sixteenth-century church at Llandderfel, Merionethshire. The crudely carved and painted statue was of St Derfel, a seventh-century warrior-turned-hermit who later became abbot of a monastery on the tiny holy island of Bardsey, or Yns Enlli, 2 miles (3 km) off the Llŷn Peninsula in North Wales.[33] It portrayed the Celtic saint as a larger-than-life-sized man in armour, carrying a small spear and a shield, with an iron casket hanging by a ribbon around its neck. The Welsh venerated the figure and prayed to it, bringing with them offerings of pigs, oxen, horses and

EARL OF ESSEX.

Thomas Cromwell, 1533–4, after Hans Holbein the Younger. His corpulence increased, as the years of good food and wine and the sedentary hours spent pouring over voluminous paperwork began to tell.

A contemporary view of the opening of Parliament at Blackfriars on 15 April 1523.
On Henry VIII's right is Thomas Wolsey, Archbishop of York, indicated by his
Cardinal's hat. At upper left, Sir Thomas More, Speaker of the Commons with 13 more
MPs behind him. Is Cromwell one of them? He was returned to this Parliament,
representing an unnamed constituency – his first step on the ladder to fortune.
From *The Wriothesley Garter Book*, purchased by Queen Victoria.

Henry VIII, by Hans Holbein the Younger. A propaganda portrait painted *c.* 1534–6, showing Henry in all his imperial splendour. In reality, in the words of one of Cromwell's victims, Sir Edward Nevill, the King was 'a beast and worse than a beast'.

Cardinal Thomas Wolsey, by an unknown artist, c. 1520. His letters to Cromwell after his fall from power make pitiful reading.

Thomas More, after Holbein. He warned Cromwell always to tell the king what he ought to do, 'but never what he is able to do . . . For if a lion knew his own strength [it would be] hard for any man to rule him.'

Catherine of Aragon, c. 1525. Cromwell believed that nature had done the discarded queen a disservice by not making her a man; in her bravery, she could have 'surpassed all the heroes of history'.

Jane Seymour, who provided Henry with his longed-for legal male heir.

Anne Boleyn, by an unknown artist, painted 1533–6. Henry's second queen was brought down by Cromwell's trumped-up charges of incest.

Anne Boleyn's last letter to Henry VIII, 'from my dolefull prison in the Tower', 6 May 1536, and signed: 'Your most loyal and ever faithfull wife Anne Bullen'. It was found with the papers of Thomas Cromwell after his arrest.

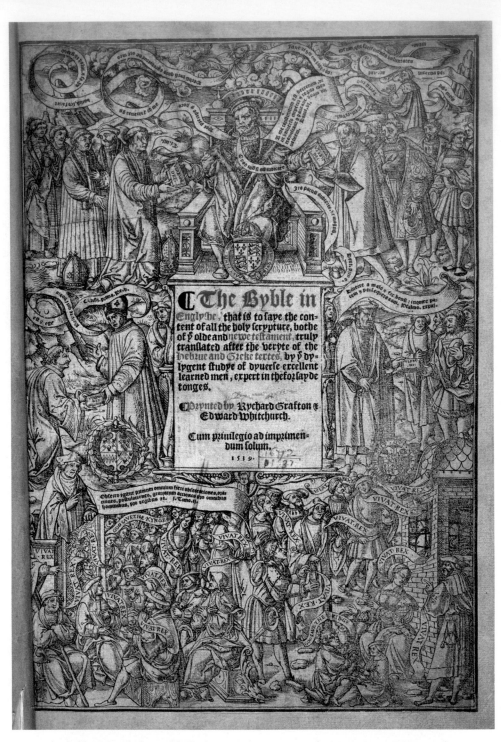

The Byble in Englyshe, published in London in 1539, showing Henry VIII amidst a
rejoicing population and Cromwell and Archbishop Thomas Cranmer distributing
copies of the Bible. This title page design was used in subsequent editions in
1540 and 1541.

Anne of Cleves, 1539. Cromwell negotiated Henry's marriage and alliance with Cleves but when the King met her face-to-face, he was less than enamoured with her charms. He told Cromwell before the wedding: 'My lord, if it were not to satisfy the world, and my realm, I would not do that I must do this day for no earthly thing.' She became the catalyst for his downfall.

Thomas Howard, 3rd Duke of Norfolk, c. 1539–40, by Holbein. Norfolk stage-managed Cromwell's arrest at a Privy Council meeting on Saturday 10 June 1540.

Stephen Gardiner, by an unknown artist: Cromwell's jealous and implacable opponent in numerous conspiracies at Henry's court.

Cardinal Reginald Pole, by an unknown artist after 1556. His open letter to Henry in May 1536 – *Pro Unitate Ecclesiae* – sent the King into an apoplectic rage. Bishop Tunstall warned him of 'the discomfort it will be to . . . your mother . . . to see you swerve away from your prince . . . and also your brother.' Cromwell arrested them.

Portrait of an unknown lady, probably Catherine Howard, c. 1540. A conspiracy by Norfolk and Gardiner used the teenager as bait to trap Henry into a new marriage.

hard cash.[34] It was a very lucrative business for the local church, with almost constant revenues pouring into its coffers. Price had reported:

> There were five or six hundred pilgrimages . . . that offered to the said image the fifth day of this present month of April.[35] The innocent people have been sore allured and enticed to worship the image . . . [and] there is a common saying that whoever offers anything to the image, he [will] have power to fetch him or them that so offers out of hell when they be damned.[36]

It is hardly surprising that Cromwell's man had been offered a hefty bribe of £40, or £15,000 in 2006 values, by the distraught parish not to take the wooden statue to London. But he had refused all blandishments and sent it on to the capital on the Lord Privy Seal's instructions.[37]

The Welsh also had a superstition that the image, called Darvell Gadarn,[38] would set a forest alight. This was to be Cromwell's little joke. With a macabre sense of humour, he was about to prove the prophecy true. Deliberately, the execution was organised as pure theatre.

Latimer told the onlookers: 'Oh, what errors has [the Pope] introduced into the church! And in order that you may the better understand this, you shall presently see one of his idolatrous images, by which the people in Wales have long since been deceived.' Right on cue, the image was carried into Smithfield's huge open space by eight men, to a great shout from the pressed mass of spectators. Three executioners, laughing and joking, made a clumsy charade of preventing its escape, throwing ropes around it 'like a criminal condemned to death'.

Cromwell, directing the proceedings like a ghoulish master of ceremonies, turned to Latimer: 'My lord bishop, I think you strive in vain with this stubborn one. It would be better to burn him.' He ordered the waiting soldiers: 'Take him off at once.'[39]

Forrest was led to the scaffold and brutally hoisted up in the air, suspended by chains around his waist and under his arms. Below his dangling and kicking feet, they started building the fire that would destroy him.

As the three executioners manoeuvred the wooden image into place on the pyre, Forrest jokingly warned them: 'Brethren, I pray you do not drop it on me, for my hour is not yet come,' and, turning to the Bishop, added: 'All the treasures of the world, Latimer, will not make me move from my will, but I much desire to speak with one of the gentlemen here.' Norfolk, watching in the stand, stood up to talk to him, but Cromwell immediately silenced him: 'My lord duke, take your seat again. If he wants to say anything, let him say it out [loud] so that we can all hear.' Forrest merely responded: 'Gentlemen, with this body of mine, deal as you wish.'[40]

Faggots of tinder-dry wood were piled on the image and the fire lit with flaming torches. As the crackling flames rose and scorched Forrest's feet, he drew them up, shrinking from the heat. He beat his blackened breast with his right hand and offered up prayers in Latin: '*Domine miserere mei*' – 'God have mercy upon me.'

The friar, swinging in the thick smoke from the blaze, caught hold of the ladder set against the gallows and, as a later (rather partisan) chronicler put it, 'would not let go, but so unpatiently took his death that no man that ever put his trust in God never so unquietly nor so ungodly ended his life'.[41]

Forrest took almost two hours to die, finally yielding up his soul when the flames reached his chest. His supporters claimed that a dove 'as white as snow' hovered over the place of execution for some time as the fire died down.

After it was finally out, Cromwell arranged for a placard to be nailed to the scaffold with this doggerel verse painted on it 'in great letters':

> David Darvell Gadarn,
> As say the Welshmen,
>> Fetched outlaws out of Hell.
> Now he is come with spear and shield
> In harness to burn in Smithfield,
>> For in Wales he may not dwell.
> And Forrest the friar,
> That obstinate liar,
>> That wilfully shall be dead,

> In his contumacy
> The Gospel does deny,
>> The king to be Supreme Head.[42]

Cromwell's propaganda had an immediate effect. Some time after midnight that night, the Holy Rood – the figure of Christ crucified, flanked by the Virgin Mary and St John – standing atop the chancel screen in one of London's churches, St Margaret Pattens,[43] on the corner of Eastcheap, was smashed to pieces 'by certain lewd persons, Flemings and Englishmen and some persons of the said parish'.[44] The old religion was being slowly but surely swept away.

Cromwell, meanwhile, was also concerned with more personal and lucrative matters. In February 1538, Henry granted Lewes Priory and its possessions to his Minister, with the Duke of Norfolk receiving his share of the proceeds in the valuable properties at Castleacre in Norfolk and a total of 126 manors and lordships, together with the rectories and advowsons[45] of twenty-nine parishes in the same county. Cromwell was anxious to speedily destroy the Cluniac priory and provide a new, grand house at Lewes for the enjoyment of his son Gregory, worthy of his family's status. He recruited the Italian engineer Giovanni Portinari,[46] who earlier had built scenery for Henry's masques, to take charge of the demolition operations. The huge priory church, which had a nave 150 ft (45.72 m) long, was one of the great Romanesque churches of Western Europe and its destruction remains an incomparable architectural loss to English culture.

Progress was reported on 20 March, Portinari having previously described how they had sapped under the church walls to bring them crashing down, employing the same methods by which castles were undermined in siege warfare:

> I told your lordship of a vault on the right side of the high altar that was borne up with four great pillars, having about it five chapels, which be compassed in with the walls seventy steps of length, that is 200 feet. All this is down on Thursday and Friday last.
>
> Now we are plucking down an higher vault, borne up by four thick and gross pillars, thirteen feet from side to side, about in circumference forty-five feet. This shall [go] down for our second work . . .

We have brought from London seventeen persons; three carpenters; two smiths; two plumbers; and one that keeps the furnace [to melt the lead taken off the roof] . . . Ten of them hewed the walls about, among the which were three carpenters [who] made props to underset [the walls] where the others cut away, [while] the others broke and cut the walls. These men exercised [worked] much better than the men we find here in the country.

Wherefore we must both have more men and other things also that we have need of . . .

On Tuesday, they began to cast the lead and it shall be done with such diligence and saving as may be so that . . . your lordship shall be much satisfied with that we do.[47]

Many of the monastic buildings were swept away; others kept for agricultural purposes. One structure, the Prior's House, was preserved and converted into a suitable dwelling for Gregory Cromwell, called 'Lord's Place'. The following month, Cromwell's son went to see it: 'Concerning the house and the situation of the same, it does undoubtedly right much please and content me and my wife, and is . . . so commodious that she thinks herself to be here right settled.'

The local gentry had enthusiastically, sycophantically welcomed the son and heir of the Lord Privy Seal to his new home and 'both with their presences and their presents, right friendly entertained me and [greeted] me to these parts'.[48]

Back in London, Cromwell was always worried about safeguarding the Tudor grip on the throne of England, if only because his own flag was nailed so very firmly to Henry's mast. He always feared that the remaining Plantagenet families were uncomfortably close to the royal line and consequently posed a constant threat to the ageing king and his young heir. These survivors of the White Rose Yorkist faction of the bitter civil wars of the previous century – the Nevills, the Courtenays and the Poles – walked a narrow, dangerous path between life and death, especially since their overt support of Catherine of Aragon over the royal divorce. Henry himself now declared his own intention to finally pluck the White Rose, even though some were his blood relatives.[49]

The Poles were already suspect because of the treasonable activities of Reginald Pole, a son of Margaret, Countess of Salisbury, the daughter of George, Duke of Clarence, and niece of Edward IV. Pole had studied in Padua, Italy, and had returned to England in 1527, where he met Cromwell, at that time serving in Wolsey's household. Their conversation then was a harbinger of the personal strife between them that was to follow. Cromwell told Pole, in an obvious reference to the required divorce from Catherine of Aragon, that princes were not bound by the same code of morals as mere ordinary subjects. Pole later claimed that Cromwell handed him a copy of Niccolò Machiavelli's controversial book *Il Principe*, which discussed how princes could govern Renaissance states, and told him, dismissively, to read and inwardly digest its contents.[50]

The lesson was wasted. In May 1536, Pole, back in Italy, wrote a book in the form of an open letter to Henry entitled *Pro Unitate Ecclesiae*, which included an eloquent and stinging attack on the King's supremacy over the English Church. Even conservative Bishop Cuthbert Tunstall of Durham told Pole that the book 'made me heavy in my heart, seeing the vehemence and eagerness of it all through'.[51] With a nervous eye on Henry's certain vengeance, one piece of information made Tunstall 'cold in heart . . . when you wrote of two quires which be not in your hands to repress . . . Burn them for your own honour and that of your noble house.' Tunstall bluntly warned Pole 'of the discomfort it will be to my lady, your mother, to see you swerve away from your Prince and also to my lord your brother'.

Henry was predictably apoplectic with rage and Pole's family horrified. The Countess of Salisbury told her son, in a letter clearly dictated to her, probably by one of Cromwell's clerks: 'I send you God's blessing and mine though my trust to have comfort in you is turned to sorrow. Alas that I, for your folly, should receive from my sovereign lord such [a] message as I have late done . . . [and] to see you in his grace's indignation.'[52] His father had the uncomfortable experience of an angry King reading out choice extracts from the book, 'that it made my poor heart so to lament that if I had lost mother, wife and children, it could no more have done . . . It is incredible to me that by reason of a brief sent to you by the bishop of Rome, you should be resident with him this winter. If you take that way, then farewell, all my hope.'[53]

Henry apparently calmed down enough to disingenuously invite Pole to England to discuss the letter. Cromwell, anxious to avoid reconciliation between them, wrote to Pole 'to stir him the more vehemently'[54] and he prudently declined to come, fearing a charge of treason against him.

Then came the rebellious Pilgrimage of Grace. Pole was created a cardinal on 22 December 1536 and the following March papal legate to England. Paul III made no bones about the reasons behind the appointment. Pole was instructed to exhort, persuade, cajole Henry to return to the true faith. 'It may be that the enemy of mankind [Satan] has such a hold upon the king that he will not . . . be brought to reason except by force of arms. It is better that he and his adherents should perish than be the cause of perdition to so many.'[55] The new Cardinal was sent to France to rouse support for the rebels in England. Henry immediately demanded his extradition as a traitor but his French brother sovereign, Francis I, trapped between antagonising the English King or the Pope, only ordered Pole out of his dominions. The Cardinal sought refuge in the Low Countries but was stopped at the frontier and forced to return to Rome after abjectly failing in his mission.

He was lucky to escape with his life. A remorselessly vengeful Henry planned to kidnap Pole and bring him back to England to pay for his treachery with his head. 'For as much as we would be very glad to have the said Pole by some means trussed up and conveyed to Calais, we desire and pray you to consult and devise between you thereupon,' he told his ambassadors in France, Gardiner and Sir Francis Bryan. The latter, Henry added pointedly, should 'secretly appoint some fellows for the purpose'.[56]

But Cromwell had already launched an operation to snatch or assassinate Pole. Sir Thomas Palmer, Knight-Porter of Calais, wrote to him on 6 May 1537 reporting that he would leave the next day for Flanders, on pretence of buying a horse there, and arrange for half a dozen accomplices to meet him along the coast at Gravelines.[57] He was clearly watching Pole's movements, ready to strike, for he told Lord Lisle ten days later from Tournai that 'the man you want . . . does not come out of his lodging, nor intends not, as [far as] I can learn, for I take the French king too much to be his friend, which I trust he will repent at length'.[58] Pole himself told a Welshman at Liège that not only Palmer but four others had been sent into the Low Countries to destroy him.[59] Pole informed Pope Paul III that if he remained in that city, 'the King of England will make still greater efforts to take [me]' and the English had offered the astronomical reward of 100,000 crowns in gold – worth more than £8 million in 2006 values – for him 'alive or dead'.[60]

He escaped Henry's clutches and Cromwell sought, but failed, to subvert Pole's servant Michael Throgmorton into spying on the cardinal. In September 1537, Cromwell wrote a bitter, vituperative five-page letter to Throgmorton. He did not mince his words:

> I thought the singular goodness of the king's highness showed to you and the great and singular clemency showed to that detestable traitor, your master, in promising him not only forgiveness . . . of his most shameful . . . conspiracy against his honour, might have brought him from his so sturdy malice, blindness and perversity, or else encouraged you to be . . . a true and faithful subject.
>
> I might have better judged that so dishonest a master could have even such a servant as you are.
>
> No, no, loyalty and treason dwell seldom together; you could not have been a spy for the king so long without showing it.

Cromwell continued:

> You and your master have both well declared how little fear of God rests in you, which, led by vain promises of promotion, work treason against your natural prince and country, to serve an enemy of God, an enemy of all honesty, an enemy of right religion, a defender of iniquity, of pride, a merchant and occupier of all deceit and of twenty things that no honest man's pen can well touch, much less utter and put forth.

So much for Pope Paul III. The Minister then swept back to attacking Throgmorton's character: 'You have bleared my eyes once – your credit shall nevermore serve you so far to deceive me a second time . . . [You] now stick to a rebel, follow a traitor who mortally hates your sovereign lord, love him whom God cannot but hate; what folly it is to excuse such mad lewdness!'

Cromwell then turned his steely attention to Pole and his words took on an ominously threatening tone:

> Now if those who made him thus mad can also persuade him to print his detestable book, where one lie leaps in every line in another's neck, he shall be as bounden to them for their wise counsel as his family shall be to him for his wise dealings. God, I doubt not, will send him little joy thereof as his friends and his kinsfolk are like to take profit of it.
>
> Pity is that the folly of one brain-sick Pole, or to say better, of one witless fool, should be the ruin of so great a family.

As for the cardinal himself, he might marvel that 'no way is found to take away the author of such treachery. Surely, when an answer shall be made to this heady malice, I think there shall be very few, but they will think as I do, that he has, as he deserves, if he be brought to a most shameful death.'

Cromwell added:

> There may be ways found enough in Italy to rid [ourselves of] a traitorous subject. Let him not think, but where justice can take place by process of law at home, sometimes she may be forced to seek new means abroad.
>
> I must, I think, do what I can to see you condignly punished. God send you both to fare as you deserve, that is either shortly to come to your allegiance, or else to a shameful death.[61]

The Lord Privy Seal's vicious eloquence could only be seen as menacing for Pole's family and the other White Rose descendants, who now came under close surveillance by his agents. They were old enemies of Cromwell: Henry Courtenay, Marquis of Exeter, some time before had reportedly tried to kill him with a dagger – but his murder attempt had failed because Cromwell was prudently wearing breastplate armour beneath his doublet.[62]

On 29 August 1538, Cromwell swooped upon Sir Geoffrey Pole, the younger brother of the cardinal, and left him to sweat in the rank summer heat of the Tower of London. He was accused of writing to his traitorous sibling and having interfered with the King's orders to arrest him.[63] Cromwell looked to him to provide incriminating information about his family. He was not disappointed.

Geoffrey Pole cravenly turned king's evidence to save his own head, even though his testimony would inevitably bring down his kinsfolk. His poisonous tittle-tattle flowed thick and fast, incriminating first his eldest brother Henry, Lord Montague, who had unwisely said on 24 March 1537: 'I like well the proceedings of my brother, the Cardinal . . . but I like not the doings . . . in this realm and I trust to see a change of this world. I would [wish] that we [were] both over the sea. The world in England waxes all crooked; God's law is turned upside down, abbeys and churches overthrown. I think they will cast down parish churches.' Then, a little later, he had dreamt the King was dead, and two days afterwards traitorously said: 'The king is not dead but he will die one day suddenly, his leg will kill him and we shall have jolly stirring.'[64] Appropriately on 1 April – All Fools' Day – Montague had commented: 'Cardinal Wolsey [would have] been an honest man if he had an honest master.'[65]

In November, Cromwell believed he had enough evidence and arrested the White Rose faction in a clean sweep.[66] Pole's mother Margaret, Countess of Salisbury, Montague, Courtenay and his wife Gertrude, Marchioness of Exeter, Lord Delawarr and Sir Edward Nevill were all imprisoned. Even the young sons of Montague and Exeter were thrown into jail. A tunic or vestment bearing the Five Wounds of Christ – the emblem of the Pilgrimage of Grace rebels – was later found triumphantly amongst the Countess's household effects. Some members of the faction were undoubtedly carrying on a reckless correspondence with Chapuys, the Spanish ambassador. Others were no friends of Cromwell, such as Nevill, who fumed with frustration over the activities of the King's Council: 'God's Blood! I am made a fool amongst them, but I laugh and make merry to drive forth the time. The king keeps . . . knaves here that we dare neither look nor speak and if I were able, I would rather live any life in the world than tarry in the privy chamber.' Evidently the sentiments of a man who had sat through too many committee meetings. One of his outbursts was clearly targeted at the upstart Cromwell: 'I trust knaves shall be put down and lords reign [again] and that the world will amend one day. The king is a beast and worse than a beast.' Exeter shared his viewpoint: 'Knaves rule about the king. I trust to give them a buffet [a punch] one day.'[67] The old nobility's abhorrence and jealous envy of the Lord Privy Seal's power and position oozes from their very words and they did not have to wait long before paying a heavy price for such indiscretions.

Three days of treason trials were staged at the beginning of December. Montague was tried by his peers in Westminster Hall on 2 December 1538, on charges that he 'devised to maintain, promote and advance one [Cardinal] Reginald Pole, esquire of London, late Dean of Exeter, enemy to the king beyond the seas and to deprive the king of his throne'. Judgment: guilty. The following day, Exeter was attainted for treason at the same venue and on 4 December, Nevill, the spineless Sir Geoffrey Pole and a number of small fry caught up in Cromwell's net were all condemned to death for treason.[68] The commoners faced the full rigour of the law and were hanged, drawn and quartered at Tyburn on 9 December. Exeter, Montague and Nevill were beheaded at Tower Hill. The Countess of Salisbury was eventually attainted by Act of Parliament in June 1539 and was confined in the Tower until she was executed – more accurately, hacked to death – on Tower Green on 27 May 1541, aged sixty-seven.[69] Montague's heir Henry disappeared within the walls of that grim fortress and died some time after September 1542, while Exeter's twelve-year-old son Edward was held there until Princess Mary ascended the throne in 1553 and he was, at last, freed. The obsequious, oily Delawarr, too naive and stupid to be involved in any conspiracy, managed to win a royal pardon by granting his estates at Halnaker, near Chichester, West Sussex, to a rapacious Henry. Geoffrey Pole, who unsuccessfully attempted suicide in the Tower in a fit of remorse, was granted a full pardon on 2 January 1539 by a grateful sovereign.[70] Half-crazed by guilt, he subsequently roamed throughout Europe, finally dying in 1558.

Catholic priests and members of the nobility were not the only groups to suffer for their beliefs and actions in 1538. That November, Cromwell and Cranmer opened up a campaign against members of the burgeoning Anabaptist sect in England, who argued against 'the Real Presence' of God in the sacrament of communion. That was rank heresy in Henry's mind. Some had to die for possessing such profane beliefs.

There was enough burning motivation.

Accusations of heresy against the King continually stung his pride and overdeveloped ego. He was taking quite literally his title of 'Defender of the Faith', even though it was now a somewhat different faith in England from the one ruled over by Pope Leo X when he had granted the honour to Henry in October 1521. Henry needed a very public demonstration of his piety and religious knowledge.

It was probably the conservative Bishop Gardiner who chose John Lambert, alias John Nicholson, as the victim.

Cromwell, for his part, laid on the propaganda trial within the banqueting hall of the Palace of Westminster. He was as thorough as ever over the details and knew full well how to put on a good spectacle. Seats on tiered wooden scaffolding had been erected along the walls to allow the invited nobility and clergy to witness the King's own personal prosecution of a known heretic.

The outcome of the trial was, of course, a foregone conclusion.

Lambert, a radical evangelical, once a chaplain to the English merchant community in Antwerp and now a London schoolmaster, had already been found guilty of heresy by Cranmer in a hearing at Lambeth Palace.

On the stroke of noon on 16 November, the King, attired head to foot in white silk – symbolizing purity – strode into the crowded hall, escorted by his Yeomen of the Guard, also clad in specially made white uniforms. Henry took his seat beneath a canopy of estate, flanked on his left by his temporal peers, led by Cromwell, and on the right by Cranmer and his bishops.

Lambert was brought in and stood on a small wooden platform to face his royal accuser.

The King leant forward and asked the prisoner: 'Ho good fellow! What is your name?'[71] Lambert, possibly lulled by this apparently jovial royal greeting, started badly. He had employed an alias to escape persecution, but his stumbling explanation was quickly silenced by Henry, his 'look, cruel countenance and his brows bent into severity'. He snapped at Lambert: 'I would not trust you, having two names, although you were my brother.'

The noted preacher George Day, Provost of King's College, Cambridge, then explained helpfully that the 'assembly was not at all convened to dispute about any point of faith, but the King – being supreme head – intends openly to condemn and confute that man's heresy in all their presence'.

Henry knew the script and its inevitable finale. Piously removing his cap every time he mentioned the Name of Christ, he demanded to know whether Lambert believed that the consecrated wafer and wine truly represented the Body of God the Son. Lambert said he agreed with St Augustine 'that it is the body of Christ,' and then fatally added, 'after a certain manner'.

The King leapt upon his prevarication: 'Answer me neither out of St Augustine, nor by the authority of any other. Tell me plainly whether *you* say it is the Body of Christ. Yes – or no.'

The prisoner had no escape. 'It is not his Body. I deny it.'

Henry doubtless dramatically exploited the intakes of breath that must have echoed around the great banqueting hall at the reply, before commenting sonorously: 'Mark well – for now you shall be condemned even by Christ's own words: "This is my Body." '

For five long hours the well-prepared bishops railed against Lambert's heretical beliefs in impeccable Latin, with Gardiner rudely interrupting Cranmer's discourse as he felt the Archbishop 'argued but faintly'.[72] The 'general applause' at the end unsurprisingly gave the victory to Henry, who asked the prisoner: 'Will you live or die? You have yet a free choice.' But Lambert, unbowed by the gruelling experience, merely committed his soul to God and his body to the King's mercy.

That was never on offer. Henry shrugged his shoulders and told him: 'That being the case, you must die. I will not be a patron to heretics.'[73]

Cromwell stepped forward. In a loud voice, he pronounced the prisoner an incorrigible heretic and condemned him to die. Six days later, on 22 November, Lambert was executed at Smithfield, ironically six months to the day after the Catholic John Forrest had perished in the flames on the same site. When Lambert's thighs and legs had been burnt off to stumps, the fire sank lower and two officers lifted up his still-living body on the points of their halberds and let it fall back into the flames. As death finally came to kindly end his sufferings, he cried out: 'None but Christ! None but Christ!'[74]

Two Dutch Anabaptists, a man and a woman, quickly followed him to the stake at Smithfield on 29 November 'for heresy against the sacrament of the altar', and elsewhere, 'a goodly young man and about twenty-two years of age', was also burnt at Colchester, Essex, for the same beliefs.[75]

On 16 November 1538, the same day as Lambert's trial was staged, a royal proclamation was issued seeking to control the purchase and use of Bibles printed in English; banning clerical marriage; ordering the execution or expulsion of Anabaptists or Sacramentarians; and insisting on the strict adherence to those religious rites not abolished.[76] The first eight injunctions listed in the proclamation had been substantially annotated personally by Henry, with the text of the eighth article significantly starting off with the word 'finally'. But bizarrely, another two injunctions had been added later, no doubt by Cromwell's hand, to the original proclamation. These two interlopers attacked both false superstitions and the population's adoration of St Thomas Becket, and ordered that

> the said Thomas Becket shall not be esteemed, named, reputed, nor called a saint but 'Bishop Becket', and that his images and pictures through the whole realm shall be put down and avoided out of all churches, chapels and other places; and that from henceforth, the days used [as a] festival in his name shall not be observed; nor the service, office, antiphons, collects and prayers in his name read, but erased and put out of all the books because it is found that he died like a traitor and rebel to his Prince.

The late addition of these two extra injunctions suggests long, drawn-out arguments between the religious factions on the King's Council over the content of the proclamation. Clearly, a compromise had been hammered out at the eleventh hour.

In the case of Archbishop Thomas Becket and its uncomfortable undertones of previous ecclesiastical opposition to the monarch, Cromwell, always a master of propaganda, simply rewrote history to match his political needs of the moment. Utilising old Lollard[77] tales dating back more than a century, he wove a cunning tale that the Archbishop had not really been assassinated in Canterbury Cathedral by knights anxious to obey a royal tantrum of King Henry II (remember 'Will no one rid me of this turbulent priest?')[78] Instead, the saint died ingloriously during a common riot – according to Cromwell, that is. Like all good propaganda, the Lord Privy Seal's version of events had a mixture of truth – about Becket's character – and blatant omission to enhance its veracity.

The Archbishop had wilfully resisted his King's laws, established to correct the 'enormities of the clergy', and when one of his servants was arrested, Becket had tried to rescue him, causing an unseemly brawl or riot. Becket had then used 'opprobrious words' and grabbed one of his opponents 'by the bosom and violently shook him and plucked him in such a manner that he almost overthrew him to the pavement of the church'. Cromwell's version adds: 'And so in the throng he was slain' – a death 'which they untruly call martyrdom'.[79] Canonisation of Becket 'was made only by the Bishop of Rome because he had a champion to maintain his usurped authority and a bearer of the iniquity of the clergy'.

Why all this sudden interest in St Thomas Becket?

Three months earlier, in August, Archbishop Cranmer had sought a royal commission to be issued to examine the phial of his martyred predecessor's blood, which Cranmer suspected was merely red ochre. Then, some time around 8 September, Becket's tomb in the Trinity Chapel of Canterbury Cathedral[80] had been sacrilegiously looted for the gold, silver and jewels that sumptuously adorned it. His shrine had been constructed by Archbishop Thomas Langton and dedicated on 7 July 1220, with its decoration created by the goldsmith Walter of Colchester. It consisted of a tomb, supported on four pillars, containing an effigy of Becket in ecclesiastical vestments, surmounted by a jewel-encrusted gable covering a casket containing the holy relics. This was covered with oriental pearls, rubies, diamonds, emeralds and sapphires, mounted on plates of gold.[81]

No wonder both Henry and Cromwell saw it as a prime target for attack in September 1538. The spoils were carried off in twenty oxen carts to the jewel house in the Tower for Henry's personal use. Moreover, the saint's remains had been scattered – 'his bones, skull and all, which was there found, with a piece broken out by the wound of death, were all burnt in the same church by [order of] the lord Cromwell' according to the chronicler Raphael Holinshed.[82] The 'disgarnishing' of Becket's shrine, as the despoilment was coldly called at the time, took the Lord Privy Seal's agent Richard Pollard several days of wanton iconoclasm to complete.[83] Henry was particularly anxious to get his avaricious hands on a famous jewel 'of great lustre', a large ruby known as the 'Royal of France' that had been donated to the shrine by the French King Louis VII in 1179; Henry later proudly wore it as a ring on his thumb.[84]

An account of a visit to the magnificent monument, written only a week or so before its destruction began, is preserved in a letter written, ironically, to Cromwell from William Penison.

> Yesterday my Lady of Montreuil,[85] accompanied with her gentlewomen and the ambassador of France, arrived in this town . . . where I showed her St Thomas's shrine . . . at the which she was not little marvelled of the great riches thereof; saying [them] to be innumerable, and that if she had not seen it, all the men in the world could never [have] made her to believe it.
>
> Thus looking over and viewing more than an hour as well at the shrine as St Thomas's head, being at both set cushions to kneel, and the Prior, opening St Thomas's head, saying to her three times: 'This is St Thomas's head,' and offered her to kiss it.

Wisely, perhaps, and with an eye for hygiene far ahead of her time, she declined. She also refused to kneel, preferring to 'view the riches thereof' instead.[86]

By Cromwell's commandment, Becket's image was torn down from the high altar of the Church and Hospital of St Thomas Acon (or Acre) on the north side of Cheapside in the City of London. The stained glass in the windows of the church, which included images of his martyrdom, were also smashed 'so that there shall be no more mention be made of him ever'.[87] Government archives and legal documents were searched and Becket's name effaced by pen, or crudely sliced out with a knife. The city of Canterbury had to change its coat of arms. St Thomas Becket was being brutally erased from the pages of history – by an official diktat worthy of any modern totalitarian state.

Later that September, Thomas Wriothesley, en route for Flanders on a mission for Cromwell, encountered Stephen Gardiner, Bishop of Winchester, returning from his ambassadorship to France, on the road between Rochester and Sittingbourne in Kent, the proud prelate riding at the head of an impressive and colourful cavalcade of retainers. Wriothesley asked the Bishop's companion what Gardiner thought of 'our doings here' – a coy reference to the destruction of Becket's shrine. He was told the religious conservative 'misliked not the doing at Canterbury, but rather seemed to like it, saying that if he had been at home he would have given his counsel to the doing thereof and wished the like were done at Winchester'.[88]

Unbeknown to Gardiner, his surprising and perhaps uncharacteristic wish was about to become true. After his sacrilegious vandalism at Canterbury, Pollard, with Wriothesley and John Williams, had ridden westwards to Winchester to attack the shrine of St Swithun. This was second in popularity to that of Becket at Canterbury and from 1200 had stood in the priory's retrochoir, later flanked by the chantries of Bishops Beaufort and Waynflete.[89] They began their work at 'three o'clock this Saturday morning', the early hour selected doubtless because of fears of local opposition. Pollard and his colleagues planned to 'sweep away all the rotten bones' in case it was thought 'we came more for the treasure than for avoiding of the abomination of idolatry'.[90] Here was a man now entirely happy in his work. However, disappointment lurked inside the great Romanesque church: all the jewels on the saint's tomb were found to be merely glass and paste, but the iconoclasts had the consolation of the £1,300 worth of spoil (or £490,000 at 2006 prices) they sequestered. Pollard told Cromwell later that Saturday morning:

We have also received into our possession the cross of emeralds, the cross called Jerusalem, another cross of gold, two chalices of gold with some silver plate . . . of the vestry. The old prior made the plate of the house so thin [disposed of it] that we can diminish none of it and leave the prior anything furnished. We found the prior and all the convent very conformable.[91]

The destruction of Becket's shrine at last galvanised the Vatican into action against Henry. On 17 December 1538, Pope Paul III prepared to promulgate the bull of excommunication drawn up by his predecessor, Clement VII, five years before. It declared the English King a heretic and fully discharged his subjects from their oaths of allegiance to him. The Catholic monarchs of Spain and France were urged to unite to return England to papal authority, and Cromwell, 'that limb of Satan', was singled out personally to be cast into Hell's all-consuming fire. Plainly, the bull could not be published in England, so it was read out rather lamely at the nearest locations safe from Henry's vengeance: at Coldstream, across the border in Scotland, and across the English Channel at Boulogne and Dieppe, within the realm of His Most Christian Majesty Francis I.[92]

Papal anger was not just confined to the damning words of anathema: two days after Christmas, Cardinal Pole was dispatched secretly once more from Rome to rally Europe against Henry, that 'most cruel and abominable tyrant'.

The forces of the Catholic Church were at last being marshalled to attack England and her recalcitrant, egotistical monarch.

Both were terribly vulnerable to invasion by the European superpowers.

CHAPTER NINE

The Distant Sound of Conflict

Come, my lord of Winchester. Answer the king here,
but speak plainly and directly and shrink not, man!
Is not that which pleases the king a law?

CROMWELL TO BISHOP STEPHEN GARDINER, 1539[1]

Throughout the early months of 1539, Cromwell marshalled the defences of the realm in fearful expectation that French and Spanish troops could land on the shores of England at any time. The signing of the Treaty of Toledo by Charles V and Francis I on 12 January was another straw in the wind of impending war. Under its terms, both rulers agreed they would not conclude any alliance or diplomatic pact with Henry without first obtaining the other's full agreement. In addition, Pope Paul III also made the conservative Scottish abbot David Beaton[2] a cardinal and commissioned him to inveigle James V of Scotland into attacking England from the north. In London, all this European hurly-burly raised the spectre of a simultaneous three-pronged invasion of the realm and appeared to place it in the unenviable position of being 'but a morsel amongst choppers', as a gloomy Wriothesley graphically wrote.

Henry appealed to the nobility, warning that the Pope – that 'pestilent idol, enemy of all truth and usurpator of all princes' – was now conspiring to corrupt England's religion and strip her of all her wealth. He sought pledges that they each would supply at least forty men, preferably archers and gunners, to be available, rather optimistically, at one hour's notice.[3] Persistent rumours that the imperial and French ambassadors would both be recalled from London heightened the jittery fears of an imminent outbreak of war[4] and just before the Frenchman Castillon departed, Cromwell pointedly escorted him around the Tower of London so he could see the large stocks of armour and weaponry stored there.

To underline his less-than-subtle warnings of English military might, the Minister read out interminable lists of ordnance, munitions, warships and volunteers, all of which, he claimed, were ready for immediate mobilisation. The Lord Privy Seal later told the King that he had also allowed the ambassador to visit his own personal armoury,

> and have showed him such store of harness [armour] and weapons as I have, the which he seemed to esteem much. I told him there were other particular armouries of the lords and gentlemen of this realm, more than the number of twenty, as well or better furnished than mine was, whereat he wondered and said he thought your grace the prince best furnished thereof in Christendom.[5]

The Frenchman collected his passports and departed London the following day, naively impressed by all he had seen during Cromwell's tours: such is the value of carefully orchestrated disinformation.

This militarist hyperbole was all very well, but some substance was required to cloak the illusion of strength. Henry's realm was, in reality, largely unprepared to repel a determined and powerful invasion. To deploy the limited forces more efficiently, England and Wales were divided into eleven defensive regions. Work also began on the construction of new circular artillery forts, all protected by dry moats and providing 360° arcs of fire from their bastions – 'all-round defence', in modern military jargon. These were sited at Walmer, Sandgate and Deal in Kent, facing the narrowest section of the English Channel, and at Camber in Sussex, to guard the south-coast harbour of Rye. The forward defence of the naval base at Portsmouth was to be bolstered by building forts at Hurst Spit and Calshot, overlooking the Solent, and on the Isle of Wight. Some of the building material used was stone looted from demolished religious houses.

It would take time to complete these new defences, so, as temporary measures, Cromwell organised an army of labourers to dig barrier ditches and erect barricades at vulnerable points. Beacons were set up along the south and east coasts of England, ready to be fired in warning that enemy forces had landed. Men aged seventeen and over were liable to be conscripted into the militia and foreign ships were impounded, under pain of death if they sailed, at the ports of London and Southampton, to be commandeered for naval service if necessary. At Harwich in Essex, even women and children were pressed to work on the defences of the harbour.

The panic of war intensified when reports reached London in April of 8000 mercenaries mustering in Friesland in the Low Countries and, more worrying still, a threatening fleet of sixty-eight ships was spotted off Margate in Kent on 9 April 1539. Defence forces were swiftly mobilised at Ashford, in the same county, and at Hayling Island, near Portsmouth, but happily the alarm proved false and the ships sailed on to Spain to join the Emperor's navy in the imperial campaign against the Turks in the Mediterranean. The mercenaries ended up in the Baltic.

A new religious bulwark was also thrown up: an officially approved edition of the Bible in English, which Cromwell firmly believed would calm religious controversies and improve morality.[6] He also viewed it as an elegant and cost-effective method of constantly re-emphasising the King's supremacy over the Church of England.

Cromwell had issued injunctions to the clergy in September 1538 requiring them to formally warn their congregations at least once every three months against false works devised by men's fantasies: offering money or candles idolatrously to relics or images and reciting 'meaningless' prayers over their rosary beads. He also ordered the parishes to maintain their own registers of baptisms, deaths and marriages and to provide, before that Easter, a copy of the Bible in English 'in a convenient place in the . . . church . . . whereas your parishioners may most commodiously resort to the same and read it'.[7] The clergy 'should expressly provoke, stir and exhort every person to read the same, as that which is the very lively word of God, that every Christian man is bound to embrace, believe and follow if he look to be saved; admonishing them . . . to avoid all contention'.

Almost inevitably, the requirement to keep parish registers – today, the greatest boon to family historians and genealogists – was viewed with deep distrust, and many suspected this instruction was a wily precursor to a brand-new tax about to be imposed by Cromwell. Lewis Herbert, who returned to Gloucestershire from London just after the religious injunctions were issued, unwisely repeated rumours he had heard that no capon, goose or pig was to be eaten without a tribute being paid to the King.[8] William Hole, a blacksmith from Horsham, West Sussex, maintained in March 1539 that fifteen pence would have to be paid for every christening, wedding and burial,[9] and the month before, Sir Piers Edgecombe scribbled to Cromwell 'in haste', warning him that the men of Devon and Cornwall, 'in great fear and mistrust', believed 'that some charges, more than have been in times past, shall grow to them by this occasion of registering of these things. Wherein, if it shall please the king's majesty to put them off doubt, in my poor mind shall increase much hearty love.'[10] Cromwell was at some pains to explain that the motivation behind the registers was purely administrative: to avoid 'sundry strifes, processes and contentions rising upon age, lineal descendants, title of inheritance, legitimation of bastardy and for knowledge whether any person is our subject or no'.[11] But his bureaucratic blandishments fell on deaf ears.

Delivering those quarterly sermons must have been an irksome duty for many clergy. Robert Mawde, the angry curate of Whatcote, Warwickshire, told his congregation on 2 March 1539:

> By God's bones, I have read this out to you a hundred thousand times, and yet you will never [be] the better [for it]. And it is a matter that is as light to learn as a boy or a wench should learn a ballad or a song.
>
> And by God's flesh, there is a hundred words in these injunctions where two words would serve, for I know what it means, as well as they that made it. For lo, it comes like a rhyme, a jest or a ballad.

One can sympathise with the priest's frustration at government verbosity, but he probably went too far for his own good when he added: 'A vengeance upon him that printed these injunctions, for by God's bones, there is never one in Westminster Hall that would read this much for twenty nobles [£6 6s. 8d, or £2,500 in 2006 money].'[12]

Cromwell was hopelessly over-optimistic in believing that the English Bible would be ready to be distributed around the parishes in time for Easter 1539. Two years before, two printers – Richard Grafton and Edward Whitchurch – had brought out a new English translation. Because of the very limited capacity of English printing presses, a revised edition of this was to be produced in Paris, with a generous contribution of 600 marks (£400, or £150,000 at 2006 values) provided by Cromwell out of his own purse. Archbishop Cranmer believed each copy should be sold at 13s. 4d each, but Cromwell preferred the neat round sum of ten shillings,[13] the cost to be met equally by clergy and congregation in each parish.

However, just as the typesetting was completed, the Parisian printers were reported to the Inquisitor General of France, who promptly seized their work, and despite Cromwell's best efforts to rescue both the Bible and his own largesse, production had to be completed in London by Grafton. The title page of the so-called *Great Bible* was a woodcut portraying a munificent Henry, with Cranmer and Cromwell, surrounded by his loyal subjects patriotically crying '*Vivat Rex*' and 'God Save the King' as they received their new Bibles. Copies, however, only became widely available in November 1539.[14]

Henry, no doubt cajoled by Cromwell, meanwhile was looking overseas for friends in his hour of need. He wrote to Guidobaldo da Montefeltro, Duke of Urbino, whose territory in Italy had been seized in a papal invasion, encouraging his resistance to the Bishop of Rome – that 'enemy of God and ours' who was in league with his 'false prophets and sheep-clothed wolves'.[15] For all his immoderate rhetoric, Henry's overtures were to no avail. He then tried to recruit a potential ally in the German Protestant League of Schmalkalden, who after much prodding finally sent over a low-key delegation in April, headed by the Vice-Chancellor of Saxony, Francis Burckhardt. The English King, however, was not interested in adopting Lutheran beliefs – indeed, was intent on maintaining the old, familiar and comfortable doctrine of his Church. That Good Friday, at his Palace of Westminster, he had practised the pre-Reformation rite of devoutly creeping to the cross on his knees from the door of the Chapel Royal and had served at the altar during the mass with 'his own person, kneeling on his grace's knees'[16] – despite the pain in his legs caused by unhealed fistulas. Every Sunday Henry received 'holy bread and holy water and does daily use all other laudable cere- monies . . . In London no man upon pain of death [can] speak against them'. The King was anxious to demonstrate that he was no heretic; indeed, that he was a truer Catholic than the Pope.

Fortunately, the threat of invasion receded as it became apparent that neither Charles V nor Francis I were interested in heeding strident papal cries for military action against Henry and embarking on a costly and perilous assault on the heretics across the Channel. England was safe, for the time being, at least.

On 28 April, a new Parliament met at Westminster. Cromwell, who was too ill to attend, had nonetheless carefully scrutinised the member- ship of the House of Commons to ensure that he had solid support for the controversial legislation he intended to table for ratification during the opening session.[17] His first proposal was both audacious and unpre- cedented: that the King should be granted powers to legislate merely by proclamation, thus effectively bypassing any need for parliamentary scrutiny or approval.

Just before the Bill was presented to Parliament, Cromwell used the issue in an attempt to cut Bishop Gardiner down to size in front of Henry. The Bishop, recounting the episode eight years after, said he had been summoned to Hampton Court, where he was confronted by the proposals for the King 'to have his will and pleasure regarded [as] a law'. Gardiner 'stood still and wondered in my mind to what conclusion this should tend'. Henry saw him thinking and 'with earnest gentleness said, "Answer him [Cromwell] whether it be so or no." I would not answer my lord Cromwell, but delivered my speech to the king.' Gardiner told Henry that he had read of kings whose will was 'received of a law but . . . to make the law his will was more sure and quiet'. Henry turned his back 'and left the matter after, until the Lord Cromwell turned the cat in the pan before company, when he was angry with me, and charged me as though I had played his part'.[18]

Gardiner's opposition made Cromwell even more determined to implement the measure. The Lord Privy Seal strenuously forced the bill through its first and second readings in the House of Lords, but then even his stooges revolted at its provisions and he was forced to withdraw it for amendment. This new version was also thrown out by the Commons[19] and Cromwell was obliged to point out privately some harsh truths to his nominees. Eventually, his threats worked: the measure was passed by both Houses at the end of June as the Statute of Proclamations.[20] The legislation was now cloaked in comfortable, reassuring words:

> . . . that sudden causes and occasions many times do require speedy remedies, and that by abiding for a parliament in the meantime might happen great prejudice to ensue to the realm . . . it is therefore thought . . . more than necessary that the king's highness, with the advice of his honourable council, should make and set forth proclamations for the good and politic order and governance of his realm . . . from time to time for the defence of his regal dignity and the advancement of his commonwealth and good quiet of his people . . .
>
> Be it therefore enacted . . . that always the king, with the advice of his honourable council, or with the advice of the more part of them, may set forth . . . by authority of this Act his proclamations, under such penalties and pains and of such sort as to his highness and his said honourable council or the more part of them shall see[m] necessary and requisite; and that those same shall be obeyed, observed and kept as though they were made by act of parliament for the time in them limited.

A modern Whitehall apparatchik would dismiss concerns that parliamentary liberties were being eroded by describing this Stalinist legislation as purely 'an enabling measure' – to be used only in appropriate circumstances. Cromwell doubtless stressed that it was true (in theory, anyway) that the power of the King remained very limited, as he still could not arbitrarily condemn his subjects to death, imprisonment or even sequester their goods and chattels solely by proclamation. But the sting in the tail was that any offenders against the Act would now be summoned before the sinister Star Chamber at Westminster, and if found guilty, 'shall lose and pay such penalties, forfeitures of sums of money . . . and also suffer such imprisonment of his body as shall be expressed, mentioned and declared in any such proclamation'.[21] In truth, it was carte blanche for despotism. Today, those who operate the levers of power in the British government fondly refer to any measures that amend primary legislation by ministerial order without parliamentary debate as 'Henry VIII powers'.

As if to reinforce the image of a state taking a firm grip on its subjects' lives, Cromwell moved on to subtly change the Law of Attainder, the means whereby guilty verdicts against traitors were confirmed by Parliament and the confiscation of their property and estates agreed. He had been frustrated by the legal system's failure to deal adequately with Elizabeth Barton, the so-called 'Holy Maid of Kent', in 1534. She and her associates had had to be condemned by an Act of Attainder after the likelihood of a successful trial had collapsed because her offence had involved words only – and treason by word of mouth was not then unlawful.

Now he seized an opportunity to refine his process for punishing crimes against the state following the precedent of this expedient decision. This appeared in the frail guise of the ageing Countess of Salisbury, still miserably imprisoned after the execution of her son Henry, Lord Montague, and his allegedly treacherous accomplices some months earlier.[22] Although collectively warned by the judges of the dangers of the measure, Cromwell proposed, and Parliament meekly agreed, that Acts of Attainder could now always be used against traitors without the tiresome formality of a full trial. For someone skilled in packing Parliaments with his payrolled nominees, it was a convenient device with which to secure the condemnation of an individual when evidence was insufficient to ensure a successful prosecution in the courts, even with his carefully selected juries. The Countess was accordingly attainted on 28 June 1539. She was probably selected as the first victim because of Henry's monomania about the Yorkist threat to his dynastic succession.[23]

Ironically, Cromwell was later to painfully discover to his cost just how potent was this weapon he had blithely handed to a ruthless, absolute ruler.

The Lord Privy Seal also had very personal concerns about some aspects of the mechanics of the governance of the realm. His Act of Precedence[24] for the House of Lords added fresh importance to the role and status of the secretary to the King. Now, 'the chief secretary being of the degree of a baron of the parliament shall sit and be placed afore and above all barons . . . and if he be a bishop, that then he shall sit and be placed above all other bishops'. Moreover, the Act laid down that the Vice-regent in ecclesiastical affairs – Cromwell again – should rank above the Archbishop of Canterbury in the House of Lords. In 1539, the Minister stood low in precedence, being merely baron of the realm. By this simple measure, he leapfrogged all the other members of the upper chamber of Parliament, to the simmering anger of his fellow peers, who now felt their own positions degraded. Was this legislation simply a matter of clarifying the labyrinth of protocol, or perhaps an attempt to reflect more accurately the impact of his reorganisation of the workings of the King's government? No, more likely for the low-born Cromwell, it was an issue of enhanced personal pride, clout and status, and a further, permanent demonstration of his authority in the land to the arrogant nobility swaggering about him.

Meanwhile, propaganda now began to play a greater role in Cromwell's exercise of power and he regularly wielded an impressive array of media to shape and influence the minds of Henry's subjects: from licensed public preaching to pamphlets; from plays to proclamations; and, finally, popular polemical ballads. Even with the threat of invasion now fading, he still required a show of strength, not only as a demonstration of English resolve, intended for the benefit of ambassadors and the foreign spies undoubtedly based in the capital, but also as a domestic morale-building exercise, a stage-managed outpouring of patriotism.

But he had no standing army at his disposal to parade. Instead, he summoned the citizens of London to the King's colours to mount an inspiring display of defiance and to warn any adversary who still nurtured any thoughts of aggression of the scale of opposition they would have to confront. On Thursday, 8 May 1539, thousands of able-bodied men and youths, aged between sixteen and sixty, armed and clad in what armour they could scavenge, assembled at Mile End and Stepney, in the East End of

London. It was 'a beautiful sight to behold: for all the fields from White-chapel to Mile End and from Bethnal Green to Ratcliffe and Stepney were covered with men and weapons . . . The battalion of pikes seemed to be . . . [like] a great forest'.[25] At about seven o'clock that spring morning, the citizen soldiers began to march westwards through the narrow streets of the city in three battalions, led by their light field guns, complete 'with stone [ammunition] and powder' and followed by a band of drums and fifes. The long, straggling column eventually circled the King's park at St James's and turned back over the verdant fields to Holborn before dispersing at Newgate at four o'clock in the afternoon. An eyewitness reported:

> The battalions were thus ordered: first gunners and four great guns drawn amongst them in carts; then morris pikes;[26] then bowmen and then bill men.[27] All the chief householders . . . having coats of white damask and white satin on their harness [armour], the constables in jerkins of white satin and the aldermen riding in coats of black velvet with the cross and sword of the city[28] on their coats over their harness . . .
>
> My lord Cromwell had amongst them one thousand . . . gunners, morris pikes and bowmen, going in jerkins after the socager [armed tenants'] fashion and his gentlemen going by, to set them in array.

Cromwell's own contingent included his son Gregory and nephew Richard, mounted on 'goodly horses and well apparelled' in armour.[29] The personal cost of this martial splendour to Cromwell is reflected in the sum of £117 16s. 3d, or more than £44,000 in 2006 money, paid to one of his servants, Henry Habblethorne, who was probably involved in the organisation of the muster, most likely for all those jerkins and expensive weapons.[30] Henry, preening himself with pride, watched the warlike cavalcade pass by from his vantage point of the new gatehouse of his palace at Westminster.

> They were numbered by my Lord Chancellor[31] . . . [at] 16,500 and more. However, a man would have thought they had been above 30,000 [as] they were so long passing by. They went five men [abreast] together and began to enter the city . . . at Aldgate at nine of the clock and it was five . . .

before the end passed before the king and, ere the last battalion . . .
entered Cornhill, the first battalion were breaking home at Newgate.

Henry was elated by the parade and even more thrilled by another of
Cromwell's propaganda extravaganzas, staged on 17 June. It was not a
subtle piece of persuasion, but then it was not intended to be. Cromwell
knew full well that the citizens of London probably appreciated the
delights of a humorous entertainment rather more than a finely argued
intellectual debate. Nonetheless, his underlying message to the masses
was unequivocal.

He organised a spectacle staged by two barges on the River Thames,
both fitted with guns equipped to fire blank shots and darts, or *flèchettes*,
harmlessly made of reeds. One was crewed by men dressed flamboyantly as
the Pope and his cardinals; the other represented Henry and his government. A special platform was constructed 'over the leads' or roof of the privy
steps leading from the river to the Palace of Westminster from which Henry
and his cronies would witness the political pantomime. It was covered with
canvas and 'set with green boughs and roses properly made, so that rose
water sprinkled down from them into the Thames upon ladies and gentlemen which were in barges and boats under to see the pastime'. Whether
they found this dampening benefit to the attractions of the sham fight in
any way welcome must remain a matter of conjecture.[32] Both sides of the
river bank were crowded with expectant onlookers.

Battle then commenced.

The barges rowed energetically up and down from Westminster
Bridge to the King's Bridge[33] and

> the Pope [and his cardinals] made their defiance against England and shot
> their ordnance at one another and so had three courses up and down the
> water.
>
> At the fourth course they joined together and fought sore, but at last
> the Pope and his cardinals were overcome and all his men cast over into
> the Thames.[34]

Happily none were drowned, as those taking part had been hand-picked
for their prowess in swimming. Cromwell, with an admirable regard for

the rigours of health and safety, had also organised the King's barge to be at hand to quickly pluck the soggy vanquished out of the water. Lord! What a merry jape this was – as one eyewitness recorded, 'a goodly pastime' with much merriment for the spectators. But the all-important political message had been planted in the citizens' minds: this 'triumph' was intended, albeit crudely, to illustrate how the King would always entirely confound and abolish the power of the Pope.

This noisy charade was not the only weapon in Cromwell's pervasive propaganda campaign against the enemies of the realm. The new French ambassador Charles de Marillac, who also watched the Thames tour de force, three days afterwards reported angrily that there was no village feast or celebration anywhere in England that did not include some derogatory allusion to the Holy Father in Rome. There was clearly a widespread government initiative at work.

Drama itself was an important vehicle for Cromwell's propaganda. The notion may have come to him via his old friend Richard Morison, appointed a prebendary of Salisbury Cathedral in 1537. In a treatise addressed to Henry, obscurely entitled 'A Persuasion to the King that the Laws of the Realm should be in Latin'[35] he had suggested that plays should be specially written to declare

> lively before the people's eyes, the abomination and wickedness of the
> Bishop of Rome, monks, friars, nuns and suchlike, and to declare and open
> to them the obedience that your subjects by God's and man's laws owe
> unto your majesty. Into the common people, things sooner enter by the
> eyes than by the ears; remembering more better that [which] they see than
> they hear.[36]

This was a political manifesto that would have been immediately recognised by any of history's great propagandists, from Roman historian Titus Livy to Joseph Goebbels, the Minister for Public Enlightenment in the Third Reich. Cromwell certainly became an enthusiastic patron of staunchly Protestant playwrights such as John Bale.[37] In 1534, Bale had been dragged up before Archbishop Edward Lee at York to explain one of his more vituperative sermons, but Cromwell rescued him from any punishment.[38] He wrote a number of plays, all containing strongly royalist overtones, including *King John*, *The Tradition of Thomas Becket* and *The Three Laws*, all produced before 1536. His drama about the English King in particular appealed to Cromwell, as the Plantagenet monarch was an especial hero for Protestant reformers because of his excommunication by Rome in 1212 and his subsequent retaliatory confiscation of church property. The Minister's personal accounts, kept by Thomas Avery, include a number of disbursements to the playwright and his merry actors, such as for 8 September 1538: 'Bale and his fellows at St Stephen's beside Canterbury, for playing before my lord [Cromwell], 40 shillings', and again on 31 January 1539: 'Bale and his fellows, for playing before my lord, 30 shillings'[39] – the latter possibly a performance of *King John* staged at the home of Archbishop Cranmer himself.[40] Bale's company of actors could well be the group known as 'Lord Cromwell's Players' who performed between 1537 and 1540 at Leicester and elsewhere.[41]

Thomas Wiley, Vicar of Yoxford in Suffolk, sought Cromwell's assistance in February 1537 after he had written a play denouncing the Pope, but had encountered fierce opposition to his preaching from his brother priests and was now existing 'fatherless and forsaken'. His gripping drama consisted of a dialogue between children, who were murky metaphors for the Word of God, Christ Himself, the saints Paul and Augustine and a nun, rather obviously called 'Ignorance'. He told Cromwell that he had been called 'a great liar' after producing the allegory, which fulminated 'against the Pope's counsellors, Error, Clogger of Conscience and Incredulity'. Wiley was no mere flash in the Protestant pan of playwrights: he had also penned *A Rude Commonalty* and *The Woman on the Rock*, two more spellbinding tales, 'in the fire of faith and a purging in the true purgatory'.[42]

Morison also published topical pamphlets designed to shape and mould public opinion. His 'Invective Against the Great and Detestable Vice of Treason,' written in early 1539,[43] was a virulent attack on those whom Cromwell had lately slaughtered as traitors: the Courtenays, Nevill and Cardinal Pole himself, an 'arch-traitor . . . whom God hates, nature refuses, all men detest, yes, and beasts too would abhor if they could perceive'. England was secure, declared Morison, because of the wisdom of her 'honoured' king: 'Of all the miracles and wonders of our time, I take the change of our sovereign lord's opinion in matters concerning religion to be even the greatest.' The pamphlet was so popular amongst the Tudor predecessors of the chattering classes that it speedily went into a second edition and there was even talk, never fulfilled, of it being translated for foreign circulation.[44]

Within a month or so, Morison weighed in with a second pamphlet, 'An Exhortation to Stir all Englishmen to the Defence of their Country',[45] written with an eye to the growing threat of invasion by the Catholic continental superpowers. It was a paean of patriotism, a rallying call to the barricades, and deliberately invoked England's valiant past in passionate, ringing tones: 'We may forget the Battle of Agincourt, but they will remember and are like never to forget with how small an army . . . King Henry V vanquished that huge host of Frenchmen . . . Let us fight this one field with English hands and English hearts: perpetual quietness, rest, peace, victory, honour, wealth, all is ours.' All the familiar tricks of the adept propagandist are contained in its pages, such as utilising the adversary's mistaken contempt for English courage and military prowess, as allegedly expressed by Chapuys, the Spanish envoy. This was deployed to shame the reader and rouse up, in English hearts, a brave response to Morison's strident call to arms: 'The activity of Englishmen has been great, if historians be true, but if I may judge by my conjectures, it is nothing so now. I see neither harness [armour] nor weapons of manhood among them . . . They have been of good hearts, courageous, bold, valiant in martial feats, but those Englishmen are dead.'

No wonder he appears on Cromwell's payroll: the Lord Privy Seal's accounts record the generous payment to Morison of £20 (£7,500 at 2006 prices) 'by my lord's command' in April 1539, possibly for writing the 'Exhortation'.[46] In 1537, Morison wrote to Cromwell: 'Your lordship sees all my living in your liberality. Thanks to your bounty I have no cause to complain of fortune and, whatever may hereafter befall me, my hope is in you.'[47]

Not everyone welcomed this onslaught of government-inspired invective. John Hussey, the London agent of Lord Lisle, the religiously conservative Deputy of Calais, fell foul of Cromwell over his master's sacking of one of the town's garrison for avidly reading such government publications. Hussey and Cromwell were deep in conversation when the dismissed soldier came in sight, and the Lord Privy Seal pointed him out: 'Yonder comes a man whom my lord has put out of wages – wherein he has not done well.' The Lord Privy Seal's words were ominous and worse were to follow. Cromwell sternly counselled Hussey:

> Well, I would you advise my lord to meddle in no such light matters.
>
> For what is passed by books, or otherwise, by the king's privilege must be common [circulated] and it is lawful for every man to occupy [read] them.
>
> All such books are set out in furtherance of the king's matters, in derogation of the Pope and his laws.[48]

Another propaganda method was the nationwide promulgation of the printed statutes of the realm, which naturally included a strong element of politically correct information and exhortation. Not all of these government documents were always treated with the respect they merited. In the city of Coventry, Warwickshire, in November 1535, four late-night drunken revellers got into hot water with the mayor and aldermen over their unfortunate destruction, or more accurately defilement, of such proclamations. John Robbins, a local tailor, had earlier happily met up with old friends – the yeomen Henry Haynes of Allesby in the same county, William Apreston of Windsor and Robert Knottesford of Lutterworth – and to celebrate they had gone drinking at 'Roger's tavern'. Their evening turned into a real tavern crawl. About ten o'clock, 'overseen by drink', they had staggered on to the city's Pannier Inn and continued imbibing there until late. After such a prodigious intake of alcohol, it is not surprising that their normal inhibitions were cast aside. They all fell out of the inn and into the silent and darkened market square, where urgent and pressing calls of nature unfortunately overtook them at the market cross. After these were fully and satisfactorily answered, one of the carousers, possibly Apreston, tore down some of the proclamations nailed to the notice boards there and carelessly tossed the papers to Haynes 'and bid him wipe his tail with them'. They also ripped down 'other proclamations and acts', but the next morning, no doubt barely sober and certainly oppressed by stonking hangovers, they failed to remember what they had done with them. Their actions were technically treason under the law, but their fate sadly remains unknown.[49]

Cromwell's adroit manipulation of Parliament in the spring of 1539 marked the high-water mark of his period in power. Despite his earlier promises that the suppression of monasteries had ended, a new Act for the lucrative dissolution of the last remaining and larger, wealthy religious houses was passed in early July,[50] without protest from the abbots then sitting in Parliament, or any other opposition. The great monasteries in the North involved in the Pilgrimage of Grace had been punitively dissolved in 1537 and now the last vestiges of monastic life were to be wiped from the landscape. Fifty-seven surrendered to the crown in 1539. At Christchurch in Dorset Cromwell's commissioners found the house 'well furnished with jewels and plate, whereof some be meet for the king's majesty's use, as a little chalice, a goodly large cross, double gilt with a foot garnished with stone and pearl, two goodly basins, double gilt, having the king's arms well enamelled, a goodly great pyx for the sacrament, and there be other things of silver right honest and of good value'. They also found a tomb, already prepared in stone imported from Caen by the attainted Countess of Salisbury, mother of Cardinal Reginald Pole. 'This we have caused to be defaced and all the arms and badges to be deleted' – an official action necessary to expunge the standing of a traitor.[51]

Cromwell's despoilers were by now well versed in the methodology of dissolution. Once valuable assets like the roof lead had been recycled into 'pigs' or ingots[52] for easy transportation and the bells scrapped; the stone was sold off as building materials. Recent archaeological excavation has shown that the systematic looting of architectural features and stone was well thought out and disciplined. At the Benedictine churches at Coventry and Chester, salvaged stone was removed in wagons through the great west doors to take advantage of easy access to local highways. A large earth ramp was built up the western steps at Coventry Cathedral's priory so that carts could drive straight into the nave. The wheel ruts in the floors, by now stripped of stone slabs, demonstrate that they then reversed into the north arcade, turned around and came out laden –

thereby utilising an early one-way system.[53] The echoing, empty monastic churches must have resembled builders' yards, with material stored in piles, ready to be sorted for sale or re-use.

There were human victims, too, in this new wave of monastic obliteration. At the Benedictine house at Glastonbury, in September 1539, the commissioners searched the abbot's rooms and that night 'found in his study secretly laid [hidden] as well a written book of arguments against the divorce of his king's majesty and the lady dowager [Catherine of Aragon] . . . also diverse pardons, copies of [papal] bulls and the counterfeit life of Thomas Becket in print.'[54]

Abbot Richard Whiting was swiftly taken to the Tower of London, even though he was 'but a weak man and very sickly'.[55] They later found money and plate hidden 'in walls, vaults and other secret places' and assured Cromwell 'that the abbot and monks have embezzled and stolen as much plate and ornaments as would have sufficed to have begun a new abbey'. The abbot paid dearly for his temerity in hiding the wealth. He was taken back to Glastonbury, with Cromwell jotting down a note reminding himself 'to see that the evidence be well sorted and the indictments well drawn' at Wells in Somerset. But the outcome of the trial had already been decided: another of Cromwell's terse aides-memoires talks of 'the abbot of Glastonbury to be sent down to be tried and executed at Glastonbury'. Whiting and two monks died by hanging, drawing and quartering on Tor Hill, Glastonbury, on 15 November 1539. The abbot's head was set up over the main gate to his abbey and the quarters of his body distributed around the local market towns. The previous day, the Abbot of Reading, that 'stubborn monk' Hugh Cook, alias Faringdon, a former royal chaplain[56] who had paid Cromwell an annual bribe of just over £13, had suffered the same barbarous fate outside the gates of his monastery for denying the King's supremacy. Two priests called John Rugg and John Enyon or Onyon died with him in the Berkshire town for the same reason. On 1 December, John Bech, Abbot of Colchester, was also slaughtered[57] after maintaining that God would take vengeance on Henry 'for pulling down the religious houses' and that Fisher and More 'died like good men and it was a pity of their deaths'.[58]

Cromwell may well have provided a new source of wealth for a rapacious Henry, but he must have sensed that slowly, the King was moving away from supporting some of his religious reforms, egged on by those fundamentalists around him at court. Was it a surprise to him on 16 May 1539 that Thomas Howard, Third Duke of Norfolk, stood up in Parliament and announced that Henry desired the passing of legislation to create new tenets of religion in England 'to abolish diversity in opinions'?

These draconian measures – 'the Six Articles' or, in Protestant eyes, 'the whip with six strings' – stopped the evolutionary religious reforms dead in their tracks and strongly reflected Henry's personal obsession with orthodoxy. The British Library today retains a copy of the proposals, copiously corrected and amended in the King's own hand,[59] which indicates his considerable personal involvement. The first article, targeted chiefly at the 'Sacramentaries' and Anabaptists, laid down legally that the Body of Christ was truly present within the consecrated bread and wine during mass, the so-called 'transubstantiation' of God. The penalty for denying this was death by burning at the stake for heresy, even after a recantation. The other articles covered the continued validity of the vows of celibacy for nuns and monks, a new prohibition against the marriage of priests, the continuation of private masses 'as whereby good Christian people . . . do receive both Godly and goodly consolations and benefits' and the importance of the sacrament of confession and the administration of Holy Communion.

The new measures were probably inspired by Gardiner: certainly the harsh measures now faced by offenders bear his distinct stamp of intolerance. Penalties for transgressors were death by hanging, drawing and quartering and forfeiture of estates and goods. Anyone who tried to flee England in the teeth of the new articles would also be guilty of treason and would suffer the awful fate of traitors after capture.

Those priests already married – and there were probably around three hundred of them in England at that time[60] – had to desert their wives. Those who married after the law came into force also faced the death penalty. The notion of married priests was one of Henry's specific dislikes amongst the changes brought in by the reforming religion. Two years later, he told the French ambassador de Marillac that he was even more opposed to the clergy marrying than he was to papal supremacy. There was no doctrinal issue involved here: the King feared that if priests did marry, their benefices could be passed on to their sons and a new powerful hereditary class thereby be born in England that might one day challenge the power of the monarch.

The statute also modified and consolidated existing laws against religious deviation and dissent. Taken together, they made heresy a secular offence and closely redefined it. Any person 'by word, writing, imprinting, ciphering[61] or any other wise [ways] to publish, teach, say, affirm, declare, dispute, argue or hold contrary opinion', together with their aiders and abettors, would now 'be adjudged heretics and therefore have [to] suffer judgement, execution, pain and pains of death . . . by burning'.

The doctrinal changes so alarmed Archbishop Cranmer that he boldly sought the King's permission to speak against the legislation in Parliament. It was perhaps not merely concerns about their impact on the embryonic Church of England that moved him: Cranmer was himself married.[62] Cromwell kept his head down and took no part in the parliamentary proceedings, as he knew only too well his royal master's views. The debate raged in the House of Lords on three successive days, 19–21 May 1539, with Gardiner and his fellow orthodox bishops leading the charge for the approval of the Six Articles. Henry insisted on attending each day's debate and spoke strongly in support of the Six Articles on each occasion. 'Never [has a] Prince showed himself so wise, learned, Catholic as the king has done in this Parliament,' reported one conservative and sycophantic peer.[63] His personal intervention meant that continued opposition was nugatory. The Act duly became law on 28 June by royal assent[64] and Parliament, its work done, was prorogued.

The next morning, Henry joined Cromwell and the Dukes of Norfolk and Suffolk at a conciliatory dinner with a chastened Cranmer across the river at Lambeth Palace. After the meal, in conversation, the Lord Privy Seal supported his ally Archbishop Cranmer, favourably comparing his qualities with those of Wolsey: the Cardinal 'had lost his friends by his haughtiness and pride' but Cranmer 'gained on his enemies by his gentleness and mildness'. Norfolk sneered that at least he could speak well of Wolsey, as 'he knew him well, having been his man'. Cromwell was nettled by the sly remark and snapped back that yes, he had worked for Wolsey, 'yet he never liked his manners'. Furthermore, he 'was never so far in love with Wolsey as to have waited on him to Rome, as he thought Norfolk would have done', adding that if the Cardinal had become Pope, Norfolk would have been his Lord Admiral. The Duke retorted 'with a deep oath' that Cromwell had lied.[65]

Norfolk's recent amity with the Minister ended in that one brief angry exchange and Cromwell had created an implacable and jealous enemy.

The evangelical bishops were placed in great difficulty by the Six Articles. There was wild talk that Latimer, Bishop of Worcester, had been caught in disguise at Gravesend in Kent, illegally trying to flee England for the safety of the Lutheran states in Germany. The rumour was untrue, but Latimer and his fellow reformer Bishop Nicholas Shaxton of Salisbury resigned their bishoprics within the week and were placed under house arrest in London.

Cranmer sent his wife back to Germany – a case, plainly, of out of sight, out of mind. At the end of the month, he presided uncomfortably at the trial of a local priest in Croydon, Surrey, accused of fornication with a woman with whom he had cohabited for three years. Although the lady confessed to enjoying the delights of illicit sex with the priest after the Act came into force, they demonstrated that they were unmarried. Cranmer, doubtless relieved at the legal loophole, sentenced them to imprisonment for fornication rather than imposing the death penalty for married priests, as prescribed under the Act.[66]

The new law triggered large-scale arrests of dissidents over the coming months. But it was not used as a licence for wholesale slaughter, as many Protestants feared, probably because of Cromwell's efforts to protect potential victims, such as arranging for their flight overseas. Five hundred who had been detained were freed by Henry in a general pardon of 'all heresies, treasons, felonies, with many other offences committed before 1 July 1540' and of the two hundred incarcerated in the diocese of London, only three remained imprisoned. Overall, only six were burnt at the stake for transgressing the Act, again probably owing to Cromwell's influence.[67]

Cranmer, however, walked a precarious tightrope between Henry's favour and displeasure. After the Six Articles entered into law, he wrote detailed notes on his reasons for opposing the measures, backed up by citations from various learned scholars' writings and the Bible. He planned to give these fresh arguments to the King in the hopeless, perhaps vain, belief that, even now, he could persuade Henry to change his mind. His long-serving secretary Ralph Morice made a fair copy of the Archbishop's thoughts in a small notebook and departed by boat from Lambeth to deliver them to the King just downriver at his Palace of Westminster.

Some others that were with him in the wherry[68] needed to go to the Southwark side to look at a bear-baiting that was near the river, where the king was in person.

The bear broke loose into the river [with] the dogs after her. Those that were in the boat leapt out and left the poor secretary alone there.

But the bear got into the boat, with the dogs about her, and sunk it. The secretary, apprehending [that] his life was in danger, did not mind his book, which he lost in the water.

But being quickly rescued and brought to land, he began to look for his book and saw it floating in the river.

So he desired the bearward [bear-keeper] to bring it to him; who took it up but before he could restore it, put it into the hands of a priest that stood there, to see what it might contain.[69]

The bearward, employed by Princess Elizabeth's household, could not read. The priest naturally could and quickly realised that the notebook's contents disputed the Six Articles. He appreciated immediately that the writer was guilty of treason and refused to hand it back to Morice, who stupidly acknowledged it was Cranmer's book. The Archbishop's secretary then panicked and sought out Cromwell, to plead for his assistance. The next day they both went to the court at Westminster and saw the bearward trying to hand the book over to one of Cranmer's enemies. Cromwell 'took the book out of his hands, [and] threatened him severely for his presumption in meddling with a privy councillor's book'.[70] The Archbishop was safe.

Overseas, Protestants were aghast at the contents of the Six Articles. The Lutheran reformer Philip Melanchthon was enraged and disappointed and blamed Gardiner for the new measures. He wrote to Henry on 1 November 1539:

It was your bishops who were responsible . . . not you. Really wise princes are capable of reconsidering their decisions. Do not take up the cause of the Antichrist against us. Your bishops may pretend to take your part but they are in league with the Pope . . .

I blame the bishops, especially Gardiner. They are concerned about their own incomes.

No one can deny that the church has come through a period of horrible darkness, like paganism, as is still the case in Rome. Now at the end of time, God has intervened against the Antichrist [and] I thought England was leading the way. But your bishops are still plotting to retain idolatry, hence the Articles.[71]

He pleaded: 'I suggest you think again. Otherwise your bishops will tyrannise the church. Christ will judge.' John Frederic, Elector of Saxony, was amazed that Henry had been hoodwinked 'by the conspiracy and craftiness of certain bishops, in whose mind, the veneration and worshipping of Roman godliness is rooted'.[72] Their appeals fell on stony ground in London.

The Six Articles firmly put paid to any hopes of an alliance with the German League of Schmalkalden. But there were more ways of securing foreign support than religion and Cromwell returned once again to the question of Henry's new bride. Cranmer was unsure whether a politically inspired marriage would be entirely appropriate; would it not be better, he asked, for Henry to marry 'where he had his fantasy and love, for that would be most comfort for his grace'? Cromwell rejected this opinion out of hand, his mind still firmly fixed on the diplomatic imperatives.

After all the frustrated excitement over the Valois and Hapsburg candidates, he realistically saw that he was left with one suitable foreign candidate: Anne, the sister of the Duke of Cleves, or at a pinch, perhaps, her sister Amelia. Cromwell enthusiastically told the King of reports he had received that Anne of Cleves was very attractive and that 'as well for the face, as for the whole body, above all other ladies excellent'. Moreover – and here was the clincher – she excelled the Duchess of Milan 'as the golden sun excels the silver moon'.

Henry must have been startled by his Minister's unexpectedly lyrical words. He still wanted some physical confirmation of her looks, thoroughly mistrusting diplomatic enthusiasm. He was quite right to be cautious. The English envoys wanted a good look at the two Clevois princesses, but were frustrated by their discreet, heavy clothing. Under such 'monstrous habit and apparel' they complained, they had 'no sight, neither of their faces, nor of their persons'. Duke William's chancellor was horrified at the envoys' forwardness: 'Why,' he asked, his starchy susceptibilities thoroughly affronted, 'would you see them naked?' A portrait was the neatest solution, but the best local painter, Lucas Cranach the Elder, was sick and in July 1539 Hans Holbein the Younger was sent off to Düren to paint both girls, with £13 6s. 8d in his purse to buy parchment, canvas and paints.

He was back in London by the end of August and Henry seemed pleased by his portrait of Anne. Amelia was forgotten. Cromwell pressed home his advantage, and on 24 September, Duke William's emissaries arrived in England to negotiate a marriage treaty, pledging that Anne was 'free to marry as she pleased'. It is a measure of the Minister's determination to finally settle the issue that the treaty was quickly signed, on 6 October.

Cromwell doubtless heaved a huge sigh of relief that the matter of a new wife had at last been settled.

Henry, enchanted at the prospect of a new young occupant of his bed, ordered preparations for a sumptuous wedding, worthy of a king who had adopted the ringing title 'majesty'. A 126-strong household was appointed for the new queen, including six ladies-in-waiting, one of them Lady Elizabeth Clinton, better known as Bessie Blount, Henry's cheerful former mistress.

CHAPTER TEN

The Royal Neck in the Yoke

My Lord, if it were not to satisfy the world, and my realm, I would not do that I must do this day for no earthly thing.

HENRY VIII TO THOMAS CROMWELL BEFORE HIS MARRIAGE TO ANNE OF CLEVES, GREENWICH PALACE, 6 JANUARY 1540[1]

Anne of Cleves arrived at Calais from Düsseldorf, via Antwerp, at about seven o'clock on the morning of 11 December 1539, at the head of a glittering retinue comprising 263 attendants with 228 horses. Her arrival at the English-held town[2] was as grand and imposing as any entrance of the Queen of Sheba. Henry's queen-to-be was formally met by Sir William Fitzwilliam, Earl of Southampton, and Lord William Howard, 1 mile (1.61 km) outside the walls of Calais, accompanied by thirty gentlemen of Henry's household. As befits the Lord High Admiral of England, Southampton wore a gold whistle 'set with stones of great value' around his neck as a badge of office.[3] The English entourage was escorted by 400 nobles, knights and yeomen, gorgeously attired in new coats of crimson satin damask and blue velvet. These showy followers included Gregory Cromwell,[4] basking in the reflected glory of his in-laws the Seymours, whose contingent was led by Edward, Earl of Hertford, recently appointed commander of the defences of Calais and Guisnes. Gregory's father was back in England, preoccupied with state business.

The winding mounted procession finally arrived at the Lantern Gate of Calais. Waiting to greet it were cheering lines of gaudily dressed merchants and the guards of honour provided by the soldiers of the garrison. The mayor, puffed up with civic pride, stepped forward to humbly present Anne with a generous gift of 100 marks (£67 or £26,000 at 2006 prices) to which the merchants of the Staple of Calais added 'a hundred sovereigns of gold [£100 or £35,000 in modern terms] in a rich purse' as their own loyal offering.[5] Then there was a brief pause to listen to the martial music provided by the thirteen trumpeters given to Anne by the Duke of Saxony. There was also 'one that plays upon two things as drums made of a strange fashion'. These were kettle drums, a novelty at which the English spectators marvelled. After all the tootling and drumming ended, the party viewed two of Henry's warships moored in the harbour just outside the town walls. The *Lion* and the *Sweepstake*[6] were to lead the large flotilla escorting his new bride to England and Anne happily 'much commended' these carracks.[7] Both vessels were festooned with 100 banners and streamers of silk and gold, and the decks were crammed with 200 cheering master gunners and mariners. Southampton reported to Henry that night: 'Your grace's ships were well furnished with men standing in the tops [of the masts], the shrouds [rigging], on the yard-arms and their shot of ordnance therein [was] marvellously well ordered.'[8]

What Southampton did not tell the King, who was happily celebrating Christmas at Greenwich, was that the thunderous salutes fired in welcome by the ships' 150 guns created a pall of smoke so thick 'that one of [Anne's] train could not see another'. It was not an auspicious beginning and the Earl hurried his regal guest into a sustaining and costly banquet and then on to the Tudor testosterone delights of a joust, 'where were places prepared and trimmed [decorated] for her grace to stand and also for her ladies and gentlemen and others'. Poor Anne – first deafened by the fusillades of guns, then choked by the smoke of gunpowder and finally confronted by the noisy and boastful gallants of the Calais garrison valiantly trying to unhorse each other or beat their brains out while fighting on foot. The jousts, however, were 'well handled', Southampton told Henry.

Moreover, Anne had probably never seen the sea before and certainly had never sailed on a ship. The prospect of the 25-mile (40 km) voyage to England, then, even in good weather, must have been truly intimidating for a lady from a small landlocked German state. Aside from the daunting dangers of crossing the English Channel, she and her ladies feared that the sea air and the spray might damage her complexion.[9] If all this were not bad enough, strong winds postponed Anne's departure from Calais. Southampton, well aware of Henry's impatience to see his new wife and his malevolent temper when thwarted, hastened unctuously to explain the delay: 'I doubt not but that your majesty of your gracious goodness and high wisdom will consider that neither the wind nor the sea will be ordered at man's will and that more, than men may do, cannot be done.' Even God's deputy on Earth could not control the waves with a flourish of his imperious arm.

So to occupy the time until the weather cleared, Anne of Cleves learnt to play card games, in the knowledge that this (and gambling) was a favourite evening occupation of her ageing husband-to-be. Southampton taught her *cent*, later called piquet,[10] and he remarked that 'she played as pleasantly and with as good grace and countenance as ever in my life I saw any noble woman', despite her lack of English. She also wanted to find out about Henry's dining etiquette – 'the manner and fashion of Englishmen sitting at their meat'.[11] Southampton, in his dispatches to Henry, studiously tried to avoid mentioning the future queen's appearance or nature, other than adding, almost as an afterthought, 'On my faith, her manner, usage and semblance which she has showed us all, was such as none mightier be more commendable nor more like a princess.'

On 19 December, Gregory Cromwell, still in the town, reported that the weather was still 'too bad to cross, though a passenger or two has been compelled to attempt it. A Hollander hulk has been lost near Boulogne; certain packs of Spanish wool and some white soap [were] cast ashore in the English dominions and therefore reserved to the Lord Admiral's use.'[12] It must have been a trying and tedious time for everyone involved, while the high winds and rain continued to buffet Anne's lodgings in Calais, called 'The Checker'.

Two of England's most experienced shipmasters, William Gonson and Sir William Spert, had been posted on the Calais coast to watch the weather. At last they were able to report that the gales had finally abated and, on an icy 27 December, Anne and her entourage embarked for the passage to Deal. They departed on the noon tide, escorted by fifty gaily decorated ships, and landed safely on English soil at five o'clock that evening. The bride and her party were met by Charles Brandon, Duke of Suffolk, and after a brief respite at the newly built artillery blockhouse at Deal (doubtless to warm up and for her ladies to anxiously inspect her complexion), she was escorted to Dover Castle to continue her recovery from the voyage.

Further north in Kent, frantic construction work at the Abbey of St Augustine, outside the western walls of Canterbury,[13] had been finished just in time for Anne's arrival. The abbot's former lodgings had been transformed into an opulent royal palace, with a new range of buildings added to the south side of the inner court. The conversion had been under way, night and day, since 5 October, and included new decorative heraldry showing Henry's royal arms and Anne's badge of the white swan. Charcoal had to be ordered as fuel for brazier fires to fully dry out the plasterwork on the ceilings and walls.[14] On 29 December, eight days after the last workmen had hastened off the site, the bride slept in the comfortable new apartments for just one night. One hopes the smell of fresh paint did not bother her.

Two days later, the stately bridal train reached the bishop's palace in Rochester and would spend the New Year there, before the final leg of Anne's journey to Greenwich, where Henry was scheduled to joyously welcome her on 3 January 1540.

That was the plan. Henry, however, still at his Palace of Placentia at Greenwich,[15] grew steadily more impatient to see her in the flesh and impetuously decided on a far more gallant course of action. Throwing aside any notion of royal protocol tediously laid down by Cromwell, he impulsively gathered together five of his favourite gentlemen of the privy chamber and, incognito, galloped off to Rochester, he and his cronies wearing disguises of garish multicoloured cloaks. Their breakneck journey was a daring, romantic gesture and the very stuff of chivalry. Riding through the frozen Kent countryside, the icy wind full in his face, the years seemed to roll back for the King and Henry could even believe he was a passionate young lover once again.

His new bride meanwhile was torpidly passing the hours with her own ladies, chatting in the guttural Low German that the English had found so nasal and unattractive during those interminable stormy days of waiting in Calais. On the afternoon of New Year's Day, she sat at the window of her lodgings, listlessly watching a bear being cruelly baited by dogs down in the courtyard below. Amid the cheers and cries of the watching crowd and the furious barking and growling of the hounds, she was startled by the appearance in her chambers of a breathless and sweating Sir Anthony Browne, the Master of the King's Horse, fresh from his pell-mell journey from Greenwich.

Suddenly, romance flew out of the window.

The courtier, after making a low bow, stared at his new queen. His hard look, he said afterwards, left him 'never more dismayed in all his life, lamenting in his heart . . . to see the lady so far and unlike that [which] was reported'.[16]

Unfortunately, he had no time to prepare his royal master for the coming shock, as Henry was hard on his heels. The King, with two companions, burst into the room amid much merriment.

Anne must have wondered who this forty-eight-year-old man-mountain was. Shyly, she continued to be seemingly absorbed by the bear's sufferings below.

Henry's first sight of his bride left him 'marvellously astonished and abashed'.[17]

Where was the stunning beauty of Holbein's portrait? Where was the blushing, sensual princess of Cromwell's promises?

She looked much older than her twenty-four years. Her complexion was solemn and sallow, her nose bulbous and her face disfigured by smallpox scars. She looked bored and, what was worse, dull and frump-ish. Her German ladies-in-waiting were even less eye-catching and even more unfashionably attired than their unexciting mistress.

Sir Anthony immediately saw 'discontentment' sweep across his king's plump features and sensed his instant 'disliking of her person'.[18] Henry's desire drained away like water running out of a bathtub, his contrived love evaporating in the warmth of the chamber. He exchanged barely twenty polite, stilted words with his future bride, sulkily grabbed his New Year's gift of a richly garnished partlet of sable skins, chosen for Anne to wear around her neck, and stalked grumpily out of her room.[19]

He left behind a sorely perplexed German princess, possibly wondering whether what she had just witnessed was some bizarre ritual of English royal courtship. The next morning, Henry's gift was sent round to Anne with as 'cold and single a message as might be'.

Henry's hurried return to Greenwich was not nearly as pleasurable as the outward journey. 'Sore troubled', he consulted his friend, Sir John Russell: 'How like you this woman? Do you think her so fair and of such beauty as has been reported to me? I pray you tell me the truth.'

It was a tough question for any courtier. Diffidently, Sir John said he did not believe her quite as fair as he had expected and commented that she had 'a brown complexion'. The King cried out: 'Alas! Whom should men trust? I promise you I see no such thing in her as has been showed me of her and [I] am ashamed that men have praised her as they have done.' Ominously, Henry growled as an afterthought: 'I like her not.'[20]

One can only speculate at the scale and clamour of the regal tirade that would have assailed Cromwell's ears on Henry's return to his palace at Greenwich on 2 January. The Tudors' rages were notorious and his anger may have been expressed physically. George Paulet, one of the royal commissioners in Ireland, when gossiping about Cromwell in June 1538, related how 'The king [calls him a knave] twice a week and sometimes knocks him well about the pate [head] and yet when he has been well pummelled about the head and shaken up, as it were a dog, he would come out into the great chamber, shaking of the bush [hair] with as merry a countenance as though he might rule all the roost.'[21] Perhaps the hapless Minister had his ears boxed by his enraged sovereign on this occasion. Certainly, Henry was in a tight spot and could quite easily have lashed out. He may have been disappointed, discontented and dismayed by the first sight of his new queen, but the reality was, thanks to Cromwell, that the marriage had vital diplomatic benefits for his realm. Time was also against him to resolve the problem: the wedding was planned for 6 January – Twelfth Night, traditionally a time for unbridled merriment at his court. Jollity would be a sparse commodity in the corridors of the Palace of Placentia that year.

Anne of Cleves and her followers finally arrived, behind schedule, at Shooters Hill, Blackheath, south-east of London, on Saturday, 3 January. A large pavilion 'of rich cloth of gold' had been pitched at the centre of a small town of tents, 'in which were made fires and perfumes for her and such ladies as were appointed to receive her'.[22] Bushes and fir trees had been specially cleared to make a brand-new roadway leading up to the palace's park gate. Crowds were already massing on this 3-mile-long (4.83 km) open space: merchants from Venice, Genoa, Florence, Spain and Germany on one side; those of London, together with the mayor and city aldermen, on the other. The Lord Privy Seal had carefully stage-managed the event; all the foreigners, save the Germans, had agreed to be dressed in velvet riding tunics and red caps with white feathers. More than three thousand attended, and Cromwell, the master of ceremonies, 'himself looked more like a post-runner than anything else, running up and down with his staff in his hand'.[23]

Around noon, Henry appeared, resplendent in a coat of purple velvet 'somewhat like a frock' with great buttons of diamonds, rubies and pearls, worn under a jacket of cloth of gold.[24] Attended by a hundred horsemen, including the Dukes of Norfolk and Suffolk and the Archbishop of Canterbury and other bishops, he trotted sedately down Shooters Hill towards the tented encampment. Anne alighted from her carved and gilded coach and warmed herself in the pavilion. She emerged, to be helped up onto a 'fair and beautiful horse, richly trapped', and rode forth towards her bridegroom.

Normally, Henry loved such showy pageantry. Today, he had no taste for such frippery but knew he had to present a brave face to the crowds of onlookers. He swept off his cap and 'with most loving countenance and princely behaviour, saluted, welcomed and embraced her, to the great rejoicing of the beholders . . . She, with most amiable aspect and womanly behaviour, received him with many apt words and thanks.'[25] Henry then talked with her 'a small while' – no doubt a *very* small while, considering his unbending distaste for her and her inability to speak English – before, hand in hand, they rode in stately fashion to the palace amid strident clarion calls by the trumpeters and rolling flourishes from Anne's kettle-drummers, mounted on horseback.

Afterwards, inside the palace, Cromwell was still experiencing a torrid time as his master's rage continued unabated. Like some spoilt child, disappointed by not receiving the Christmas present it asked for, the King railed continuously about his bride's unfortunate appearance and demanded that his Minister quickly find a way to stop the imminent marriage.

It was all too late.

Events overseas dictated that the marriage, with all its diplomatic ramifications, must go ahead. Charles V had arrived in Paris, en route to the Netherlands to put down a rebellion in Ghent. He was warmly greeted as an old friend by Francis I and lodged in the Louvre for eight days of feasting and entertainment. A new military coalition between the great continental powers of Europe against England, backed by the Pope, now seemed almost inevitable. Cromwell no doubt pointed out the dangers of an England totally isolated: an alliance with Cleves was better than no European ally at all.

So, for all his trouble to find a fitting bride to become the mother of his 'spare heir', Henry was now entrapped into marrying a woman whom he allegedly (and history has unkindly) labelled the 'Flanders Mare'. He plainly (and vociferously) believed this tribulation of a marriage was all Cromwell's fault. The Minister had personally advanced her as a candidate queen. He had praised her beauty. He had urged an alliance with Cleves against Spain. Cromwell alone was responsible.

The King had a long memory for grudges and an insatiable appetite for vengeance.

Resentful and 'nothing pleasantly disposed', Henry complained to his Minister, just before the unwanted nuptials, about the 'state of princes . . . in marriage'. They suffered more than the poor, he maintained, since 'princes take as is brought to them by others, and poor men be commonly at their own choice and liberty'. Piteously, he asked Cromwell: 'Is there no other remedy [than] that I must . . . against my will, put my neck in the yoke?'[26] But in his heart, the King already knew the answer.

At eight o'clock on the morning of Tuesday, 6 January, the wedding took place between Henry VIII, by the grace of God King of England, France and Lord of Ireland, Defender of the Faith and of the Church of England on Earth the Supreme Head, and Princess Anne of Cleves in the first-floor Queen's Closet, overlooking the chapel in the Palace of Placentia.[27]

She wore her fair hair long, as unmarried women did during that period, and a 'rich gold coronet of [gem]stones and pearls' set with branches of the herb rosemary, a symbol of both love and fidelity. Her gown was of cloth of silver, embroidered with 'great oriental pearls' and jewels, 'made after the Dutch fashion'.

Anne, 'with most demure countenance and sad behaviour',[28] curtsied low three times as she confronted Henry in the gallery on the way to the closet. He presented a majestic, if sulky, figure dressed in a black-fur-trimmed gown of cloth of gold, decorated with flowers of silver, worn beneath a cloak of crimson satin sewn with large diamonds.

Thomas Cranmer, Archbishop of Canterbury, dutifully married the unhappy couple, the bride being given away by the Count of Overstein. The memories of an earlier wedding, to his beloved Jane Seymour, in the same room could hardly have cheered the King. Anne's wedding ring was engraved with her motto – 'God send me well to keep'. She would certainly need some divine intervention to make this marriage blissful.

The couple then went hand in hand to the King's Closet to hear mass together, before being refreshed by draughts of celebratory spiced hippocras and wine and going in to dine together. Afterwards there were further banquets and masques to entertain if not to distract Henry's mind from what was expected of him later.

Almost inevitably, the wedding night was an embarrassing physical disaster. Anne was able to employ the skills she learnt in Calais by playing cards with the King before they both retired. The traditional public bedding ceremony at the start of royal marriages was coldly dispensed with and eventually, the couple scrambled up onto a specially made great bed, bearing the initials 'H' and 'A'. Its headboard was carved with erotic figures of cherubs, one clearly pregnant.[29] Now beneath these symbols of lust and fecundity, Anne had to endure the fumbling, groping and grunting attentions of her obese bridegroom.

Henry was characteristically brutal in his displeasure when he met Cromwell the following morning: 'I have felt her belly and her breast and thereby, as I can judge, she should be no maid, which struck me so to the heart when I felt them, that I had neither will nor courage to proceed further in other matters. I left her as good a maid as I found her.'[30]

After four nights of grudgingly dutiful husbandly effort, the King still had not consummated the marriage. Moreover, he patently did not intend to, even though he continued to sleep with his wife every night, or at least every alternate night. During such visits, he apparently did not even shed his voluminous tent-like nightshirt. In sixteenth-century royal marriages of convenience, little was confidential and Henry felt free to discuss his most intimate marital problems with his confidants amongst the gentlemen of the privy chamber, chiefly Sir Thomas Heneage, who anyway looked after his very private and personal needs as Groom of the Stool. The courtier later testified: 'In so often that his Grace went to bed with her, he ever grudged and said plainly he mistrusted her to be no maid, by reason of the looseness of her breast and other tokens. Further-more, he could have no appetite with her to do as a man should do with his wife, for such displeasant airs as he felt with her.'[31]

Anne tried hard to look alluring. On the Sunday following the wed-ding, a grand tournament of jousting was staged at Greenwich and she appeared at it dressed 'in the English manner, with a French hood [a pedimental headdress] which became her exceeding well'.[32] A con-temporary chronicler loyally reported that she 'so set forth her beauty and good visage that every creature rejoiced to behold her'.[33] All except Henry: her stylish dress did nothing to change his cold feelings towards her.

The Queen's forthright English ladies-in-waiting became impatient at the delay in her conceiving. Jane, Lady Rochford, believed that direct-ness was the only remedy and one day told her: 'I think your grace is still a maid.' After an embarrassed silence, Anne replied, naively: 'How can I be a maid . . . and sleep every night with the king?' and described her innocent bedtime ritual: 'When he comes to bed, he kisses me and takes me by the hand and bids me, "Goodnight sweetheart," and in the morning, kisses me and bids me, "Farewell darling." Is this not enough?' Lady Eleanor Rutland told her pointedly: 'Madam, there must be more than this, or it will be long ere we have a Duke of York, which this realm most desires.'

The Queen was sorely puzzled. What more could possibly be expected of her? Her mother was the Duchess Maria, a strait-laced and strict Catholic who had told her nothing of such things. Lady Rutland suggested delicately that she should have a little chat with kindly 'Mother Lowe' who looked after the welfare, moral and physical, of her German maids, Gertrude and Katherine. Anne was shocked, if not wholly scandalised: 'Marry, fie, fie, for shame, God forbid,' she cried, and said of her relations (or rather lack of them) with her husband: 'No, I am contented with this, for I know no more.'[34] With a heaving, corpulent and flatulent spouse twenty-three years her senior, perhaps we should not blame her for not wanting to explore further the pleasures of love.

One of Henry's favourite court physicians, Dr John Chambre, advised him not to 'enforce himself' for fear of causing an 'inconvenient debility' of his sexual virility.[35] The King willingly obeyed this sage medical advice, indeed stopped sleeping with his Queen altogether after four months. Enough was more than enough, as far as Henry was concerned.

It seemed an intractable problem. Was the obstacle to the King's passion perhaps the rank odour of poor Anne's body – her 'displeasant airs' – possibly caused by the effects of her hearty diet? Was it merely the King's continuing repugnance towards her appearance? Or was Henry playing a devious, cunning game: already secretly planning a quick annulment of his fourth marriage on the grounds of non-consummation? Despite that overarching gamecock ego, he must have been painfully conscious of both his advancing years and rapidly declining health – which would soon diminish his physical ability to sire further sons. Perhaps with a cynical eye on encouraging future candidates for a new bride, the King was very anxious to quash prurient rumours that he was already impotent. He told another of his physicians, Dr William Butts, that he had experienced '*duas pollutiones nocturnas in somno*' (two nocturnal ejaculations) and firmly believed 'himself able to do the act with others – but not with her'.[36] These breathtakingly personal statements were deliberately disseminated around the royal household, not only to silence the sniggering, smutty gossip amongst some of the courtiers, but also in the hope that they would be heard by foreign ambassadors and so protect Henry's chances of another marriage with a foreign princess.

Meanwhile, Anne occupied her time by playing cards and dice with her ladies and embroidering cushion covers – one thing she did excel at was needlework. She also developed a love for music and created her own troupe of musicians, including members of the Jewish family of Bassano, found for her by Cromwell in Venice and housed in part of the dissolved London Charterhouse. They introduced with them, that spring, a new instrument to England called the violin. A number of her countrymen – Master Schulenberg, her cook, and Englebert, her footman – remained members of her household, so at least she could retain some vestiges of her own culture. Anne also had a pet parrot to help while away the hours of servile boredom. But soon the English noblemen and gentlemen who had been attracted to her court in hopes of generous patronage began to drift away, as word spread of the King's displeasure with his latest queen.

He showed it in petty or vindictive ways. Plans for her coronation at Westminster Abbey on 2 February were abruptly abandoned. On 4 February 1540, Henry brought his new wife to Westminster, not by the traditional glittering procession winding through the decorated streets of the City of London, but by barge, along the Thames. The convoy from Greenwich, escorted by the boats of twelve livery companies of London, was led by a gilded barge, decorated with banners, conveying the King and his closest nobles, followed by his yeomen guard in another boat. Anne, with her household, followed in their own vessels. As the procession rowed up the river, ships fired salutes and as they passed the Tower of London – 'there was shot above a thousand chambers of ordnance which made a noise like thunder'.[37] The royal party finally landed at Westminster and entered the palace.

Henry had given up all pretence of married life with his queen. He began looking around for some other feminine comforts to ease his distress and satisfy his yearning for love.

CHAPTER ELEVEN

No Armour Against Fate

Master Cromwell: If you follow my poor advice, you shall, in your counsel giving [to] his grace, ever tell him what he ought to do, but never what he is able to do. So shall you show yourself a true faithful servant and a right worthy councillor. For if a lion knew his own strength, [it would be] hard for any man to rule him.

ADVICE TO CROMWELL FROM SIR THOMAS MORE, MAY 1532[1]

On 17 April 1540, a grateful sovereign granted Cromwell the earldom of Essex and added yet another prestigious position to his already glittering CV – that of Lord Great Chamberlain of England.[2] The Lord Privy Seal had now collected the second of the six traditional great offices of state.[3]

On the following day, a Sunday, in a ceremony at the Palace of Westminster, Cromwell was formally created an earl and presented with a patent for the title, bearing a heavy yellow wax seal, by the Chamberlain of the Royal Household, William, Lord Sandes. The King then limped grumpily off to dinner in the Queen's chamber and the dukes and earls retired separately to their own meal in the council room. There, the herald Christopher Barker, *Garter King of Arms*, proclaimed, in ringing tones, Cromwell's latest impressive style of address: 'Earl of Essex, Vice-regent and High Chamberlain of England, Keeper of the Privy Seal,

Chancellor of the Exchequer and Justice of the Forest beyond the Trent.'
The new Earl promptly dipped into his purse, tipped Barker £10 and
liberally paid the price of his gown, especially bought for the occasion.[4]

To those many courtiers who were hostile to Cromwell, Henry's
unexpected generosity seemed to be a warning signal that he still enjoyed
royal protection and patronage. Although a few days earlier he had
handed over the duties of secretary jointly to his long-standing protégés
Thomas Wriothesley and Ralph Sadler,[5] there was no visible or actual
diminution of his authority in the land,[6] merely a downgrading of
the administrative role of secretary because of the Lord Privy Seal's
impending new prominence.[7]

But the King's Minister was aware that the religiously conservative
faction at court and the old established nobility, with their simmering,
vengeful spite, were both resolved to bring him down. Cromwell had
suspected for some time that his own disgrace would come suddenly, just
as surely as it had for his former master Thomas Wolsey, more than a
decade before. Two years previously, Cromwell had quietly gathered
together his domestic servants and described to them 'what a slippery
state he stood [in] and required them to look diligently and circumspectly
into their order and actions, lest, through their default, any occasion
[trouble] might arise against them'. To each of his boy choristers, he gave
£20 apiece and sent them home to their parents, safely out of harm's
way.[8] No doubt he also prudently transferred some of his wealth to his
immediate family to prevent their complete penury after his fall and the
inevitable forfeiture, to the crown, of all his property.

For Cromwell, the taste of this latest success must have savoured
even sweeter after surviving the previous months of conspiracy and
uncertainty. It was the longed-for apogee of his power and status and
seemed finally to confound his enemies' attempts to bring him down.
John Uvedale, Secretary of the Council of the North, unctuously wrote to
him 'rejoicing at the great honour to which the king' had called Cromwell.[9] Doubtless there were more flattering letters from others who had
discovered that the fickle wind of royal favour was still blowing strongly
in his direction. However, there were some, yet more cynical, at court,
who pointed to Henry's lavish gifts to Anne Boleyn just before she was

arrested and claimed that this latest preferment was a harbinger of Cromwell's own imminent ruin.[10]

Cromwell's new noble title had been conveniently left vacant by the death of sixty-eight-year-old Henry Bourchier, the ebullient Second Earl of Essex, who had snapped his neck when he was thrown to the ground while recklessly riding a young, inexperienced horse at Broxbourne in Hertfordshire, on Friday, 12 March. The office of Lord Great Chamberlain had been held since December 1526 by John de Vere, Fifteenth Earl of Oxford, who had also died, aged around fifty, a week after Bourchier, at his manor in Essex.[11]

In reality, the King's munificence did hammer another kind of nail into his Minister's coffin, but this was not through some Byzantine stratagem on the part of a cunning Henry. By choosing a title to bestow on Cromwell that had been created around 1139 and enjoyed, down the centuries, by some of England's greatest noble families such as the de Mandevilles and the de Bohuns, the King had (possibly unconsciously) caused the nobility's poisoned cup of hatred and intolerance of Cromwell to finally overflow. Almost to a man, they heartily detested him both for his lowly birth and his firm, apparently unshakeable grip on power and patronage in the realm. These new preferments had rubbed salt into their raw, gaping wounds of hurt pride and injured status and it was now only a matter of time before they would move to destroy him.

But the final instrument of his demise was to be in the forlorn shape of Henry's fourth wife, the pockmarked and sadly malodorous Anne of Cleves.

Norfolk and Gardiner, the leaders of the religious conservatives at court, had already set a subtle honey-trap for Henry and, by association, Cromwell. In March 1540, the Bishop staged a magnificent dinner at his sprawling fourteenth-century Gothic palace in Southwark, on the banks of the River Thames, directly south of the City of London. Henry had graciously accepted an invitation to attend. As he watched the dancers pirouette in the multicoloured light thrown down by the stained glass in the thirteen-foot-diameter (3.96 m) rose window of Gardiner's banqueting hall,[12] he suddenly noticed a pretty eighteen-year-old auburn-haired girl, stylishly dressed in the French fashion, giggling and laughing amongst the strutting young courtiers. He was immediately attracted by her youth, vivacity and beauty. Something surprising stirred deep within his vastly increased bulk: the first flowering of an unexpected love, coming late in life.

The encounter was probably no mere accident. That flighty, wanton girl was Catherine Howard, daughter of the recently deceased Lord Edmund Howard,[13] and yet another niece of the Duke of Norfolk.[14] She had first come to court in December 1539 as a maid of honour to the now unwanted foreign queen, Anne of Cleves. Today, she would be regarded as rather unfashionably plump and certainly something of a bimbo, as she was vain and rather scatterbrained. Her task, set by the conniving, Svengali-like Norfolk and Bishop Stephen Gardiner, was to act as sensual bait for the unhappy, resentful and frustrated Henry. Whether knowingly or not, she performed her role perfectly.

Like all successful plans, theirs was brilliant in its simplicity: if Cromwell failed to rid Henry of his unloved and spurned wife, he would, no doubt, quickly fall victim to the thwarted King's rage. But if he succeeded in sending Anne of Cleves packing, Henry would be free to marry the giddy Catherine. With her as a malleable and naively compliant queen, their power and influence would increase mightily at court and probably enable them to topple Cromwell from his pinnacle of authority. In such a favourable climate and with such a doting monarch, they might also be able to halt the inexorable contagion of religious reform infecting the realm and even, they whispered in the dark corridors of the palaces of Westminster and Greenwich, establish a rapprochement with Rome. It may have been pimping, plain and simple, but the plan could hardly fail: Gardiner and Norfolk knew their sovereign and his proclivity for a pretty face all too well. As soon as he clapped eyes on Catherine Howard amongst that swirling, glittering throng at Winchester House, 'he did cast a fancy to her', and to the ageing, adoring monarch, she swiftly became a 'blushing rose without a thorn'.[15]

Truly, there is no fool like an old fool, especially when he is an absolute monarch, with nothing to comfort him during the dark evenings save only his vivid memories of a glorious, chivalrous past and gambling over a hand or two of cards with his male cronies.

For Henry, it was always a case of what the King wanted, the King quickly got. By Easter, during the following month, Henry was shamelessly showering expensive jewellery upon Catherine and other valuable gifts on her sycophantic family whilst poor Anne of Cleves watched helplessly from the marriage sidelines. Ralph Morice, Cranmer's secretary, remarked that the 'king's affection was so marvellously set upon that gentlewoman as it was never known that he had the like to any woman'.[16]

His mounting obsession with Catherine only served to pour fuel onto the already fiercely burning flames of discontent over his marriage to the 'Flanders Mare'. Cromwell once again felt the dark, dank shadow of the Tower fall upon him. Thomas Wriothesley, one of the new secretaries to the Council, said he was 'right sorry that his majesty should be so troubled' by the problem of how to rid himself of his queen. He urged Cromwell – 'for God's sake' – to quickly devise some plan to achieve this and grimly predicted that if Henry 'remained in this grief and trouble they should all one day smart for it'. Cromwell could only shrug his shoulders hopelessly and answer: 'Yes! . . . How?'[17] On top of this intractable and dangerous problem, Gardiner, his tenacious and eloquent arch-opponent, already had the ear of the King. The Minister now sensed his enemies closing in on him as they circled for the kill.

At the end of March, Wriothesley, perhaps innocently hoping to defuse the mounting animosity between Cromwell and Gardiner, arranged a private dinner for them to discuss their differences. It must have been an interesting encounter between two mighty intellects: on the one hand, the devious, scheming and odious prelate; on the other, the Machiavellian panjandrum. After four hours of talking, they 'concluded that . . . there be truth and honesty in them [and] not only all displeasure be forgotten but also in their hearts be now perfect friends and likewise . . . Wriothesley and the said bishop'.[18]

Cromwell knew that for all his fulsome protestations of friendship, Gardiner would remain at the very vortex of all the underhand attempts to bring him down. He had to strengthen his defences and, if possible, launch a pre-emptive strike at the conspirators ranged against him.

His first weapon was Henry's vanity and love of showy displays of glory. Cromwell had been instrumental in setting up a new and glamorous bodyguard for Henry and was now finalising their organisation and terms and conditions of employment. The fifty 'Spears' or 'Gentlemen Pensioners' had made their first appearance, armed with poleaxes,[19] at Greenwich during the official ceremonies welcoming Anne of Cleves to England in January that year. They were deliberately mustered from the younger sons of the nobility and the ranks of the senior gentry[20] and were a conscious replication of the 200 *Gentilhommes du Bec de Corbin* who had protected the French kings since the fifteenth century. Four of the Spears were identified as 'my Lord Privy Seal's men', and these included a black sheep amongst them – 'John Portinary', probably the Italian military engineer whom Cromwell had employed to demolish Lewes Priory so ruthlessly and efficiently in March 1538. The new corps must have presented a dazzling image in their uniform of velvet and cloth of gold with silver ornaments and heavy gold chains around their necks. But this new appendage to the royal household was more than mere empty, glittering show, pandering to the King's well-known egotistical love of pomp and pageant. In the aftermath of the dangerous Pilgrimage of Grace rebellions, Henry needed additional personal security from a military force that he could rely on for absolute loyalty. Indeed, each Pensioner swore an oath to be a 'true and faithful subject and servant to our sovereign lord King Henry the Eight and to his heirs . . . and diligently and truly give my attendance . . . and I shall be retained to no man . . . of what degree or condition, [who]soever he be, by oath, livery badge, promise or otherwise, but only to his grace'.[21]

Henry's mistrust of religious reform was probably the most potentially dangerous weapon being deployed against Cromwell by his enemies at court. On 29 February, the third Sunday in Lent, Robert Barnes, a headstrong former Augustinian friar and friend of Cromwell,[22] preached a vitriolic sermon against Gardiner at Paul's Cross, the open-air pulpit alongside the great cathedral.[23] He told his congregation that if he and the Bishop of Winchester were 'both in Rome, he knew that great sums of money would not save his life', but Gardiner would have no such fear as 'a small entreatance [pleading] would serve [him]'.[24] Moreover, he mockingly referred to the Bishop as a 'gardener setting ill plants in a garden'[25]

– a pun guaranteed to nettle the humourless Bishop of Winchester. Gardiner unsurprisingly took great offence and forced Barnes to seek his pardon. The Bishop's only response, when 'being twice desired by him [Barnes] to give some sign that he forgave him, [was to] lift up his finger'.

Contrition, however sincere, was not enough for the prelate and he complained to the King about Barnes, who was promptly summoned to Hampton Court to explain himself. His fellow evangelicals William Jerome, the vicar of Stepney in East London, and Thomas Garret, who had narrowly escaped execution for heresy in Oxford in 1532,[26] were also called to the palace. Both had also recently delivered inflammatory sermons attacking orthodox religious doctrine. Barnes humbly apologised to the King, but Henry ignored him and limped to the small altar standing against the wall of his privy chamber, devoutly genuflected to the crucifix and told him piously: 'Submit not to me. I am a mortal man, but yonder is the Maker of us all – the author of truth.'[27] He 'sharply reprimanded' them and ordered all three to make public recantations of their beliefs during special sermons at St Mary's Church Spitalfields, north of the city, at the end of March. Sir John Wallop told Arthur Plantagenet, Lord Lisle, the devoutly Catholic Lord Deputy of Calais, that they had recanted 'from their lewd opinions, and be plain, his highness is of such sort that I think all Christendom shall shortly say "the King of England is the only perfect of good faith", God save him'.[28]

But even this was not enough for Gardiner. Despite his subsequent denials, it seems clear that he was behind their arrest and imprisonment in the Tower by the King's commandment on the following Saturday. There, all too conscious of the fate of heretics, they renounced their earlier recantations, preferring to die steadfast in their faith. For the Bishop of Winchester, their downfall registered a palpable hit on the position and authority of Cromwell, who was uncomfortably associated with some of the miscreants. It also rekindled the King's anger over liturgical change and fuelled his growing intolerance of unorthodoxy and heresy within his own church in England.[29]

The French ambassador de Marillac reported on 10 April that now Cromwell and Cranmer 'do not know where they are'. He predicted that within a few days, there will be seen in this country a great change in many things; which this king begins to make in his Ministers, recalling those he had rejected and degrading those he has raised.

Cromwell is tottering; for all those recalled, who were dismissed by his means, reserve [not] *une bonne pensée* [one good thought] for him – among others, the bishops of Winchester, Durham and Bath, men of great learning and experience, who are now summoned to the Privy Council.

The envoy had heard 'on good authority' that Cuthbert Tunstall, Bishop of Durham, 'a person of great esteem with the learned', would soon replace Cromwell as Vicar-General and that John Clerk, Bishop of Bath and Wells, would become Keeper of the Privy Seal:[30] 'In any case, the name of Vicar-General will not remain to [Cromwell] as even his own people assert. If he remains in his former credit and authority, it will only be because he is very assiduous in affairs, although rough in his management of them, and that he does nothing without first consulting the king.'[31]

The next day, a Sunday, a triumphant Gardiner preached himself at Paul's Cross, but his words sparked an angry fight between 'three or four serving men' amongst those listening in the churchyard and his sermon was disrupted.[32]

Another front in this war of religious ideas had opened up in Calais, where many religious reformers had fled after the Six Articles became law in June 1539. Both Cranmer and Cromwell had turned a conveniently blind eye to their vocal presence there: another case of out of sight, out of mind. But Lisle, the Lord Deputy of the English town and fortress, had been plotting against Cromwell for months. He had recently complained to Sir Anthony Browne, Master of the King's Horse, that Cromwell's inaction against religious reformers had made his job enforcing the Six Articles virtually impossible in Calais. Only too conscious of the Minister's power, he ended his letter: 'I beseech you, keep this matter close, for if it should come to my Lord Privy Seal's knowledge or ear, I [would be] half undone.'[33] Unbeknown to him, his words had a prophetic edge.

After Norfolk had gleefully reported Lisle's concerns to London, Cromwell was forced in early April to appoint a six-man commission, under Robert Radcliffe, Earl of Sussex, to investigate the activities of the 'Sacramentaries' in Calais. With great speed, they began their inquiries and on 5 April wrote to Henry about the 'great division about religion' in the town. They discovered not only a nest of heretics, including one William Kennedy, who said 'there were twenty more of his opinion in the town', but other disquieting information such as the fact that Sir George Carew, Lieutenant of the town of Rysebank within the English Pale, had been eating flesh during Lent, as had Thomas Brooke, one of the two Members of Parliament for Calais, the latter with 'none other excuse but that he has great pain with the colic and would neither have mass, matins nor evensong'.[34]

Three days later, the King replied to the commissioners, marvelling 'that no more persons were convicted [by] you. It appears you intend to banish four persons named in your letters, one of them Brooke, who seems to have used himself very arrogantly before you.' Henry urged them to impose heavy-handed justice: Brooke had been imprisoned in the Tower the previous year for his opposition to the Six Articles, but had saved his life by recanting and performing a public penance by carrying the heretic's bundle of wood faggots in a humiliating parade through the London streets. The King chillingly pointed out how much more the 'execution of one or two should confer to the redubbing [resolution] of these matters than the banishment of many. Thinking how this contempt and eating flesh of . . . Brooke will extend to . . . as grievous an offence as a relapse into his former heresies, we wish, if you find further matter upon our new Statute [the Six Articles] to condemn him . . . either as a traitor or heretic . . . then immediately cause him to be executed.'

As for Sir George Carew: 'We reserve the determination of his case to ourselves. If you think him a man of so evil a sort . . . and that all the depositions against him are substantial, send him over [to London] under guard, together with a copy of the evidence against him.'[35]

Then the witch-hunt against the heretics fell pell-mell into an unexpected hole, which pulled it up short. The investigators discovered that Gregory Botolph, who had been Lisle's chaplain, had not only joined the traitorous Cardinal Pole in Rome, but had devised a ludicrously unworkable plan to betray Calais into his hands. Botolph had now arrived at the Crown Inn in Gravelines and was secretly exchanging letters with Clement Philpot, a parish priest inside Calais. Moreover, the commission revealed that Lisle had granted a passport to his chaplain.

If you even dared to utter the name 'Pole', Henry's suspicions and deep mistrust would immediately surface and become rampant. He quickly wrote to his commissioners on 17 April, cunningly instructing them to 'devise among you a letter from Philpot to the priest Gregory, giving him some hope of a benefice to be obtained . . . in those parts and requiring his immediate repair thither for that purpose. Get Philpot to write it in his own hand and send it to the priest.'[36]

Furthermore, he summoned Lisle to London, appointing the Earl of Sussex to remain in charge of Calais in his absence. Philpot duly wrote the required letter to Botolph, offering him the parish of Arderne, within the Pale of Calais, valued at £20 a year, and suggesting a meeting there 'where is a good fellow that serves the cure and has stable and hay for your horse. Bread and drink shall you find, cheese and eggs, but no other cares,' he added reassuringly.[37] Botolph eluded the King's ambush and Richard Pate, the English ambassador in Ghent, was forced to invent a tale of sacrilegious theft from a church as an excuse for the Netherlanders to arrest him. But they refused to extradite the errant chaplain.

Back in London, it was high time Cromwell seized the initiative on the thorny religious issue. He had now recovered from a short bout of sickness. On the first day of the new session of Parliament, 12 April, Cromwell, speaking in the King's name, told the lords temporal and spiritual and the assembled commons of the importance of a 'firm union' on religious issues amongst Henry's subjects. He knew that

> there were many incendiaries and much cockle grown up with the wheat. The rashness and licentiousness of some, and the inveterate superstition of others in the ancient corruptions had [caused] great dissent, to the sad regret of all good Christians.
>
> Some were called papists, other[s] heretics; which bitterness of spirit seemed the stranger, since now the Holy Scriptures, by the king's great care of his people, were now in all their hands in a language they understood.

But these were grossly perverted by both sides who studied rather to
justify their passions out of them than to direct their belief by them.

He had come there with a clear message to deliver from Henry, beset by
the constant wrangling of the religious factions at court: 'The king leans
neither to the right nor to the left hand, neither to the one nor the other
party, but set[s] the pure and sincere doctrine of the Christian faith before
his eyes.'[38]

Cromwell stressed that his royal master was anxious to see 'decent'
religious ceremonies continued in the cathedrals and parish churches
'and the true use of them taught, by which all abuses might be cut off and
disputes about the exposition of the Scriptures cease'. Moreover, Henry
was firmly 'resolved to punish severely all transgressors . . . [who]soever
they were' and was piously determined 'that Christ, the gospel of Christ
and the truth shall have the victory'. The Lord Privy Seal therefore asked
the Lords to set up 'commissions of bishops'[39] to investigate and correct
abuses and to 'enforce respect for the Church' – but this was merely a
piece of empty political flummery on Cromwell's part, as he had little
interest in burning those heretics who denied the presence of Christ
at communion, or hanging married priests for their wanton trans-
gressions.[40] Such prosecutions were the thin edge of the wedge and
would be seized upon by the conservatives as nails in the coffin of
Cromwell's reforms of the Church. Now, cannily, he was simply providing visible evidence that he was acting to promote observance of his
King's well-known and steadfast conservatism towards the old liturgy.

He had successfully won a trick, unexpectedly playing the religious
card, but unbeknown to him, while he was haranguing Parliament at
Westminster, Norfolk and Gardiner were down the River Thames at
Greenwich Palace, closeted with Henry, slowly pulling the drawstrings
of their conspiracy against him ever more tightly around his neck.

The Lord Privy Seal swiftly moved on to another of Henry's pre-
vailing preoccupations: the level of spending money he had in his
exchequer. Cromwell had already implemented a widespread reform of
the organisation of the royal household, which had reported a financial
deficit in 1539 and was now running perilously close to the red again,

owing to an additional number of those pensioned and more than £7,000 in extra pay,[41] partially caused by the recruitment of the Spears.[42]

On 22 April, the Lord Privy Seal returned to the House of Lords with a startling proposal: the abolition of the Knights of St John of Jerusalem in England and the personal appropriation of their substantial lands, property and wealth by the King.

It was a characteristically blatant and opportunistic bribe to secure Henry's goodwill via his purse. It had worked earlier with the lucrative dissolution of the monastic houses, and here was one remaining religious order, just ripe for the plucking.[43]

But with the Knights of St John, there could be no trumped-up accusations of carnal excesses or corruption: the Hospitallers, in their distinctive black robes blazoned with a white Maltese cross, were famed for their irreproachable lives and Christian fervour.

Cromwell picked the only tenable accusation: their denial of the royal supremacy. For him, it was an old friend, well tried and absolutely reliable. But when his proposals were laid before the Commons, they were greeted by vocal and violent hostility. Approval of an Act dissolving the order[44] finally came in early May, but only after three days of heated debate when the cronies on Cromwell's parliamentary payroll finally wore down the opposition.

He moved fast to sequester the Hospitallers' assets to provide Henry with an ample return. A now mutilated account sheet shows a total of 959½ ozs (27.2 kg) of gilt plate and 1,093½ ozs (31 kg) of parcel gilt seized from their church at St John's Clerkenwell, north of London, within days of the Act's passing onto the statute book. A total of £588 6s. 8d in ready money (£220,000 at 2006 values) was also grabbed, together with 'ornaments of the church remaining in the vestry'. Much of the booty was immediately sold off, including stocks of wine, three carts and four working horses.[45] Sir William Weston, the last Grand Prior of the order in England, shocked at the abolition of all he loved and worked for, died suddenly on the day the Act of Dissolution took effect.

The court had joyously celebrated May Day with five days of jousting against all-comers at the tiltyard at the Palace of Westminster.[46] On 2 May, Richard Cromwell, the Minister's nephew, was knighted. Open house was kept at Durham House, the former grand London palace of the Bishops of Durham, not far away on the Strand,[47] where the revellers were supplied with 'all delicious meats and drinks so plenteous . . . and such melody of minstrelsy and were served every meal with their own servants after the manner of war, their drum warning all the officers of household against [of] every meal which was done, to the great honour of this realm'.[48] The celebration ended with a sumptuous feast at Durham House, open to the citizens of London as envious spectators. It was to be the last public appearance of Anne of Cleves as queen. Henry spontaneously gave every one of the challengers in the tournament 100 marks each (just over £67) and a house to live in 'for ever' from the revenues of the Hospitallers' lands.[49] Even given the improved state of the exchequer, Cromwell must have ground his teeth in frustration at his monarch's gallant generosity, even though one of the recipients was his nephew.

Despite all the carousing at court, there was no holiday for the Minister, still intent on filling the King's purse as a means of securing his favour. On 3 May, he introduced a new taxation bill into the Lords[50] – a Subsidy of Fifteenths and Tenths – which passed into law just five days later.[51] These were both irregular taxes, normally raised only in an emergency, such as paying for the physical defence of the realm or a foreign war. But Cromwell knew full well how to manipulate the legislators into sycophantic compliance. The draft preamble to the law is a model of political obsequiousness:

The Commons, men selected to express the voice of the realm in this Parliament, seeing the benefits God has poured upon us through the opening and showing of His Word and remembering the errors we have so long slept in, through the deceits of the subtle serpent, the bishop of Rome, cannot but embrace the one and hate the other and therefore we look for the extreme prosecution and devilish hatred of the bishop of Rome.

And to show that we have banished the papacy out of our heads and desire to set forth Christ and His Gospel, we do offer and give unto your most royal majesty, toward the maintenance, propagation and setting forth and defence of the Gospel and this, the defence of our country . . .[52]

... sizeable handouts of cash from Henry's subjects. To ensure a generous contribution, Cromwell emphasised just what a grievous fiscal burden their gracious sovereign was labouring under. The introduction to the Act describes the charges the King had recently underwritten: the military repression of the rebellions in Lincolnshire and the North; maintenance of three councils (the Welsh Marches, the North and the West); the naval preparations of the previous year against 'the pretended invasion'; the fortification of the English Pale in France and two castles along the Scottish border; and, finally, the new artillery forts along the south coast from Kent to Cornwall (and the cost of arming them with ordnance). If all this was not enough, the hard-pressed exchequer also had to fork out for the 'repair of Westminster Hall and abolishing the bishop of Rome's authority'.

Never have a group of legislators been so anxious to donate their constituents' hard-earned cash to the crown. The provisions of the bill were so complex that few members of the Commons fully understood them and, pushing home his advantage, Cromwell told them that Henry would be very vexed indeed if they disloyally rejected the measures.[53] Obediently, they complied, voting for a double grant of taxation, firstly of four-fifteenths and tenths of total personal income, payable over four years, and secondly, a shilling (5 pence) in the pound levied on the value of property – double that for foreigners resident in England – payable annually for two years.[54]

One would suppose that Henry would have been more than satisfied by the unexpected and welcome income from the sequestration of the Hospitallers' property and the new taxation. It proved not to be case: always a slave to his passions, he was preoccupied with other, even weightier matters.

On 9 May, the King, fresh from the excitements and spectacle of the tourney, was still at Westminster and sent for Cromwell, ordering him to

> repair unto us for the treaty of such great and weighty matters, as
> whereupon do consist the surety of our person, the preservation of our
> honour and the tranquillity and quietness of you and all other loving and

faithful subjects, like as, at your arrival here, you shall more plainly perceive and understand. And that you fail not, as we especially trust you.[55]

The matter at hand was his unfortunate loveless marriage to Anne, and, more pertinent and immediate, the associated and now wholly inconvenient alliance with her brother, Duke William of Cleves. Under this agreement, William could invoke English military assistance if he was attacked by Emperor Charles V. Now, Spain had demanded that the Duke should surrender his province of Gelderland (part of modern Holland) – or face invasion. Henry would never dream of going to war with mighty Spain over a tinpot little German ducal state, even if it was ruled by his brother-in-law, and Cromwell was peremptorily told to get England out of this embarrassing diplomatic bind. Two days later, Cromwell wrote to the English ambassador at the imperial court with instructions to inform Charles V that the English alliance with Cleves could be scrapped if necessary.

Again feeling under threat, Cromwell lashed out. Lord Lisle, who arrived in London in May, was arrested on treason charges at ten o'clock on the night of 19 May and sent to the Tower. Although the scandal surrounding his chaplain was ostensibly the cause of his downfall, it is more likely that being an illegitimate son of Edward IV was a major factor in the arrest, as Cromwell no doubt played on Henry's latent fears of a new flowering of the White Rose in England. The Minister then turned his sights on England's bishops and their religious loyalties. He swooped on Dr Richard Sampson, Bishop of Chichester and Dean of the Chapel Royal, a former ambassador to France and, most significantly, an ally of Gardiner, amid accusations of his denying the royal supremacy and being in traitorous communication with Cardinal Pole. Sampson, although a close friend of the King, was dispatched to the Tower on 31 May, and Henry did nothing immediately to save him. Dr Nicholas Wilson, one of the King's chaplains – 'a great theologian' – was also imprisoned for 'relieving certain traitorous persons which denied the royal supremacy'.[56]

On 1 June, Ambassador de Marillac reported to Francis I of France:

The rest of the bishops are in great trouble, some for fear of being found guilty of the same deed and some for the differences they have upon some religious questions, as each party to establish what they maintain would destroy those who sustain the contrary.

For this and the affair of the prisoners, parliament is still kept sitting and one cannot say when it will end, for every day new accusations are discovered.[57]

The same day, de Marillac told Annede Montmorency, the Constable of France, that a 'trustworthy person . . . says he heard from Cromwell that there were still five bishops who ought to be treated thus, whose names, however, cannot yet be learnt unless they are those who lately shook the credit of Master Cromwell so that he was very near coming to grief'.[58] The ambassador added: 'Things are brought to such a pass that either Cromwell's party or that of the Bishop of Winchester must succumb. Although both are in great authority and favour of the king, their master, still the course of things seems to incline to Cromwell's side, as Winchester's dear friend, the said Dean of the chapel is down.'

There were also rumours, later proved unfounded, that Sir John Wallop, the ambassador to France, had fled to Rome. De Marillac reported: 'Last night a secretary to the king was sent by Cromwell to learn if I had any news of Wallop.'

Sadler wrote to the Minister about his conversation with Henry about the Bishop of Chichester. Sampson, said the secretary, had

denied the chief points laid to his charge. His majesty said little but that he liked both him and the matter the worse, perceiving by the examinations that there were witnesses sufficient to condemn him . . .

[The King was content] that [the Duke of Suffolk] should have the use of the Bishop's mule and, if the Bishop's goods were confiscated, have the mule as the king's gift.[59]

On 7 June, Sampson, still in the Tower, wrote to Cromwell denying that he sought any return to the 'old usages and traditions of the church'. Gardiner, he said, had lately wisely urged him to 'leave ceremonies to the king's ordering and not to break them without great cause'. Winchester had said the bishops were all of one opinion about the liturgy – that 'many old traditions, [such] as praying for souls [of the dead], baptising of infants . . . must be kept'. He commended himself to Henry's goodness and thanked Cromwell for 'signifying that the king is his gracious lord'.[60]

The Minister again felt safer, more secure.

But he had reckoned without the relentless spite and venom of Stephen Gardiner, the Bishop of Winchester.

Some time on Thursday, 8 June, Henry gave Lord Chancellor Audley secret instructions to draw up a parliamentary bill pronouncing that Cromwell had undermined his sovereign's objective of a religious settlement.

CHAPTER TWELVE

A Traitor's Cry for Mercy

These laws I made myself alone to please
to give me power more freely to my will,
even to my equals, hurtful [in] sundry ways
(Forced to things that most do say were ill)
upon me now as violently seize
by whom I lastly perished by my skill.

MICHAEL DRAYTON, *HISTORY OF THE LIFE AND DEATH*
OF THE LORD CROMWELL, 1609

Cromwell's arrest was as ruthless as it was sudden. Sir Anthony Wing-field, Captain of the Guard, seized Cromwell as the Privy Council met at the Palace of Westminster, soon after dinner on Saturday, 10 June 1540.

Norfolk, cock-a-hoop at the downfall of his arch-enemy, must have relished springing the trap. As the Lord Privy Seal walked into the room and sought his place at the head of the council table, he shouted: 'Cromwell! Do not sit there! That is no place for you! Traitors do not sit amongst gentlemen.'

If the Minister was shocked at the insult, he showed no sign. Calmly, he replied: 'I am not a traitor.'

Before he could utter another word, Wingfield, with six halberdiers lined up behind him, strode quickly into the room and seized his arm. Unnecessarily, the captain announced the patently obvious: 'I arrest you.'

'What for?' said Cromwell, his lawyer's mind quickly searching for the legality of the moment. 'That, you will learn elsewhere,' replied the captain laconically, and his men moved forward to escort their prisoner away.

But this was no ordinary prisoner. He demanded to speak to the King and was brusquely told that this was 'not the appropriate time'. He must have promptly realised he would never again be granted access to Henry and that, once in the Tower, he would be, to all intents and purposes, already a dead man.

Cromwell now quickly grew both angry and despairing. Red-faced, his grey eyes starting from their sockets in fury, he tore off his hat and hurled it down onto the stone floor in a hopeless gesture of frustration and surrender. Gone was his notorious mask of inscrutability, now stripped away by fear and defeat. He glared at Norfolk like a defiant, trapped animal and cried out: 'This, then, is the reward for all my services.' Turning to face the other councillors, now all on their feet, he appealed: 'On your consciences, I ask you, am I traitor?'

His words caused uproar in the crowded room. Sensing the blood of their victim, their hatred and animosity burst forth in a torrent of invective. Some answered: 'Yes!' yelling, 'Traitor, traitor,' and others joined the chant, beating out a rhythm of loathing by thumping the table with their fists. Another shouted, his bitter words rising above the hubbub: 'Let him be judged by the bloody laws that he has made. Under them, many an innocent word has become treason.'

Cromwell regained his calm amid all this wrath and the barb-like, jabbing fingers of his fellow councillors. He took a deep breath: 'I have never thought to offend, but if this is to be my treatment, I renounce all claims to pardon and only ask that the king should not make me languish long.'

If he thought his words would be placatory, he grievously under-estimated the depth of their burning hatred for him. No doubt some would have happily stabbed him in the heart then and there in the Council Chamber, but were restrained from such gratifying vengeance only by their fear of Henry's strictly enforced ordinances prohibiting any form of violence within the precincts of the royal palaces.

Wingfield, probably fearing such bloodshed, turned to take his prisoner away, but Norfolk was intent on inflicting a final, ritual humiliation of his defeated prey. 'Stop, Captain,' he snapped, 'traitors must not wear the Garter.' And he marched up to Cromwell and ripped off the gleaming Order of St George from around his neck, while Southampton, his former friend, tugged the Garter insignia from the Minister's gown. Cromwell stood shocked and speechless, pulled this way and that like a rag doll, as the nobles tore at his clothing.[1]

Finally they succeeded and stood back, panting, as the prisoner was hustled away and taken out of the palace through a small postem gate on the river bank. A waiting wherry took him downriver to the Tower of London. He left behind an exultant Norfolk, his long-time ambition to destroy Cromwell finally and satisfyingly achieved. After Wolsey, the scalp of another upstart Minister had been claimed.

Outside, in the sunshine, more than three hundred of Cromwell's retainers stood in restless ignorance at Westminster, still expecting their master's imminent departure from the Council meeting and the instructions he would then issue. Finally, they were told to go away, as the sole means of their livelihood was now being held in the Tower.[2]

A few yards away, inside the Parliament House, Lord Chancellor Audley announced the news of Cromwell's downfall to a stunned House of Lords, attended that afternoon by the two archbishops, eighteen bishops and forty-three members of the nobility.[3] The list of attendees included Gardiner and Norfolk, the latter having hurried across to enjoy their moment of triumph. The House then adjourned for the day. Only a few hours earlier, Cromwell had been sitting amongst them as a consummate master of the parliamentary process; now his power and influence had completely dissolved away.

Government meanwhile had to continue: Southampton was appointed to replace him as Lord Privy Seal.

De Marillac heard of the arrest within the hour and dashed off an urgent dispatch to his royal master in France. He clearly shared the contempt of the English nobility for Cromwell and his letter reflected his prejudice:

This might be thought a private matter and of little importance, as they have only reduced a personage to the state from which they raised him and treated him as hitherto everyone said he deserved.

Yet, considering that public affairs thereby entirely changed their course, especially as regards the innovations in religion on which Cromwell was the principal author, the news seems of such importance that it ought to be written forthwith.

A 'gentleman of the court' had come swiftly to the envoy's residence with a personal message from the King. Cromwell's downfall should not astonish de Marillac, he was told, and as the 'common, ignorant people spoke of it variously', Henry wished the French ambassador to know the precise truth. The King earnestly desired 'by all possible means to lead religion back to the way of truth', said the letter, and Henry had found Cromwell too close to the German Lutherans 'who preached such erroneous opinions'.

Some of the King's principal servants had warned him that his Minister was working against both his wishes and the law and that he had 'betrayed himself . . . and hoped to suppress the old preachers and have only the new'. The issue had been coming to a head and 'the king, with all his power, could not prevent it' – and what was more, Cromwell's own faction 'would [soon] be so strong that he would make the king descend to the new doctrines, even if he had to take arms against him'.[4] Gardiner's scheming fingerprints were all over the message, even though Henry had apparently dictated it himself.

After bidding farewell to Henry's messenger, de Marillac wrote to the Constable of France, pointing out that the fallen Minister's party, which had appeared the strongest when the Bishop of Chichester had been arrested, now 'seems quite overthrown' and there remained on his side only Thomas Cranmer, Archbishop of Canterbury, 'who dare not open his mouth'.

The normally adroit and well-informed Frenchman was quite wrong and had underestimated Cranmer's undoubted moral courage.

The next day, the Archbishop wrote to Henry pleading for his friend's life in an impassioned letter full of contradictory emotions. He expressed his amazement and grief that Cromwell should be a traitor, who had been so advanced by the King and 'cared for no man's displeasure to serve him'. This was a servant whose

> wisdom, diligence, faithfulness and experience as no prince in this realm ever had. He that was so vigilant to protect your majesty from all treasons that few could be so secretly conceived but that he had detected the same in the beginning. If the noble princes King John, Henry II and Richard II, had had such a councillor about them, I suppose that they should never have been so traitorously abandoned and overthrown as those good princes were.

These were probably unhappy allusions to make, as Henry would never have equated himself with such unpopular or unlucky earlier monarchs of England. Nonetheless, Cranmer pressed on recklessly: he had loved Cromwell

> as a friend . . . but I chiefly loved him for the love which I thought I saw him bear ever towards your grace singularly above all others. But now, if he be a traitor, I am sorry that ever I loved him or trusted him and I am very glad that his treason is discovered in time. But yet again I am very sorrowful, for whom shall your grace trust hereafter, if you might not trust him? Alas! I bewail and lament your grace's chance herein, I know not whom your grace may trust.
>
> But I pray God continually night and day to send such a councillor in his place . . . and who for all his qualities can and will serve your grace like to him and that will have so much solicitude and care to preserve [you] . . . from all dangers, as I ever thought he had.[5]

Here was a brave sideswipe at the conservative faction – Gardiner and Norfolk – who were now paramount at court and were working urgently to finally seal Cromwell's fate. But the King was, as ever, more immediately interested in other, more mundane matters – his amassment of cash.

Henry, ever rapacious, had lost no time in seizing his fallen Minister's wealth. Within two hours of Cromwell's arrest, the King dispatched Sir Thomas Cheney, the Treasurer of the Royal Household, with an escort of fifty archers, to the Minister's home at Austin Friars. A large crowd had gathered outside and watched jubilantly as £14,000 of movable assets – gold and silver-gilt plate, such as crosiers and chalices and other spoil from the monastic churches – were rapidly inventoried, placed in carts and carried off under close guard to Henry's jewel house at Westminster,[6] followed by a jeering rabble. This loot, together with Cromwell's ready cash held at the house, is estimated to have been worth £6 million at 2006 prices – far too much wealth, sneered de Marillac, for such 'a villainous, low-born upstart'.[7]

That night the good citizens of London lit bonfires in the streets to celebrate the downfall of Cromwell, who from his window in the Tower must have seen the orange and red glow of the fires flickering above the dark, ill-lit streets and heard the shouts of the mob.

Edward Hall, the contemporary chronicler, believed that many lamented Cromwell's downfall, but

> more rejoiced and specially such as had been religious men [monks] for they banqueted and triumphed that night, many wishing that day had been seven years before [but] some fearing lest he should escape . . . and could not be merry. Others who knew nothing but truth by him, both lamented him and heartily prayed for him. Of certain of the clergy, he was detestably hated . . . for he was a man . . . [who] could not abide the snuffing pride of some prelates.[8]

The plunder of Cromwell's possessions did not stop with Cheney's raid on his home. Richard Rugeley and David Vincent of the Royal Wardrobe and Beds Department, and Nicholas Bristow, Henry's clerk, were paid for stripping Cromwell's 'stuff' – how contemptuous that sounds – from his house, under the supervision of Henry's household 'fixer', the odious and thuggish John Gates, then a groom of the robes. They submitted their expenses for conveying the loot in a cavalcade of carts to the Tower, Hampton Court and Greenwich Palace, taking six days and charging twenty pence a day each, the costs charged on the vice-chamberlain's account. Ever pragmatic, Henry arranged for some of the Minister's furniture to be appropriated for Anne of Cleves' use.[9] Cromwell's Garter robes, in crimson and purple velvet, all trimmed with miniver fur, were taken to Hampton Court and delivered to the Lord Chamberlain on 10 August.[10]

Amid all this rummaging through Cromwell's possessions, letters between him and the German Lutherans – possibly planted by Norfolk's agents – had conveniently been discovered by the diligent searchers. After they had been shown to Henry, he was so exasperated about their contents that he 'could no longer bear him [Cromwell] spoken of, but rather desired to abolish all memory of him as the greatest wretch ever born in England', according to de Marillac a few days later. Cromwell had already been stripped of his ranks, titles and estates and now he was to be called merely 'Thomas Cromwell, shearman' – a brutal allusion to his humble origins. His less valuable possessions were distributed amongst his servants, who were ordered to no longer wear his livery badge.[11]

Henry's propaganda machine slipped easily into top gear. On the day of Cromwell's arrest, the King's Council wrote to the English ambassador in France, Sir John Wallop, repeating the official reason for his seizure, as described to de Marillac. They said that although Henry had put his trust in Cromwell over religious issues, he 'had . . . only of his sensual appetite, wrought clean contrary to his grace's most godly intent, secretly and indirectly advancing the one of the extremes'.[12] Copies of this cleverly spun version of events were also sent to Ireland, Calais and the Presidents of the Councils in Wales and the North.

Emperor Charles V sank to his knees and prayed to God in thanks when told of Cromwell's downfall. Francis, the French King, who reportedly shouted with joy over the arrest, told his envoy in London that Wallop had informed him

> of the taking of Mr Cromwell, news which has been to me not only agreeable, but such as, for the perfect amity I have always borne towards my good brother [Henry] I have thanked God for . . .
>
> Tell him from me that he has occasion to thank God for having let him know the faults and malversations [corrupt administration] of such an unhappy person as Cromwell, who alone has been the cause of all the suspicions conceived against not only his friends, but his best servants.
>
> He shall know how much the getting rid of this wicked and unhappy

instrument will tranquillise his kingdom, to the common welfare of Church, nobles and people.[13]

In the Tower, Cromwell was in the charge of Sir William Kingston, the Constable, who was also Comptroller of the Royal Household. The prisoner must have wryly remembered that it was Kingston who had been sent to arrest Wolsey in the Midlands more than a decade before. History was repeating itself as Henry remorselessly shed another Minister.

The conservative cabal at court was meanwhile working hard to ensure that Cromwell would leave the Tower of London only on his way to the scaffold. There remained fears that he could yet somehow slip the noose and wreak his own revenge on his enemies. Leading members of the Council, including a gloating Norfolk, questioned the Minister closely and passed on the King's instructions for him to answer the charges against him.

Cromwell penned a cleverly constructed and eloquent letter to Henry on 12 June. He was careful to avoid making any protests against the accusation of treason, as such a denial would contradict the King's own statements – and this was hardly a propitious time to further enrage Henry. He wrote:

> Prostrate at your most excellent majesty's feet, I have heard your pleasure . . . that I should write . . . such things as I thought meet concerning my most miserable state and condition, for which your most abundant goodness, benignity and licence, the Immortal God, Three and One, reward your majesty.
>
> Where I have been accused of treason, to that I say I never in all my life thought willingly to do [any] thing that might or should displease your majesty; much less to do or say that thing which of itself is so high and abominable [an] offence as God knows, who, I doubt not, shall reveal the truth to your majesty.

Henry knew his accusers well – 'God forgive them!' But Cromwell had always been concerned to protect and enhance 'your honour, person, life, prosperity, health, wealth, joy and comfort' and therefore 'God so help me in this my adversity and confound me if ever I thought the contrary'. Cromwell then tried flattery and the one thing he had achieved that would appeal to the King's inherited Tudor instincts: the accumulation of money and power.

> What labours, pains and travails I have taken according to my most bounden duty, God also knows, for if it were in my power, as it is God's to make your majesty live ever young and prosperous, God knows I would. If it had been or were in my power to make you so rich as you might enrich all men, God help me as I would do it. If it had been or were in my power to make your majesty so puissant as all the world should be compelled to obey you, Christ knows I would.

The King had been the

> most bountiful prince to me that ever was king to his subject and more like a dear father . . . than a master. Such have been your most grave and godly counsels towards me at sundry times. In that I have offended, I ask you [for] mercy. Should I now for such exceeding goodness . . . liberality and bounty, be your traitor, no, then the greatest pains would be too little for me.

He committed his soul to God, his body and goods to Henry's pleasure, to do with as he wished. As for the people of England:

> I have after my wit, power, knowledge, travailed [laboured] therein, having had no respect to persons, your majesty only except, and my duty to the same but that I have done any injustice or wrong wilfully I trust God shall be my witness and the world shall not be able to justly to accuse me and yet I have not done my duty in all things as I was bounded, wherefore I ask mercy . . . Sir, I have meddled in so many matters . . . that I am not able to answer them all.

Cromwell pressed on to the specifics of the King's complaints against him – that 'within these last fourteen days I have revealed a matter of great secrecy. I remember the matter but never revealed it.'

This secret was Henry's unfeigned dislike of his new wife, the dull Anne of Cleves, and his plans to rid himself of her that Cromwell stood accused of disclosing to Sir Richard Riche and Sir George Throgmorton, brother of Michael, personal secretary to Cardinal Pole.[14]

> After your grace had spoken to me in your chamber of the things you disliked in the queen, I told you she often desired to speak with me, but I dared not [speak with her], and you thought I might do much good by going to her and telling her my mind.
>
> Lacking opportunity, I spoke with her lord chamberlain, for which I ask your mercy, to find some means to induce her to such pleasant and honourable fashions as might have been to your grace's comfort, thinking thereby to have some faults amended to your majesty's comfort. I repeated the suggestion when the lord chamberlain and others of her council came to me at Westminster for licence [permission] for the departure of the [German] maidens [back to Cleves].
>
> This was before your grace committed the secret matter to me, which I never disclosed to any but my Lord Admiral [William Fitzwilliam, First Earl of Southampton][15] by your commandment on Sunday last in the morning, whom I found equally willing to seek a remedy for your comfort and consolation and saw by him that he did as much lament your highness' fate as ever did man and was wonderfully grieved to see your highness so troubled. Wishing greatly your comfort . . . he would spend the best blood in his belly [for that object] and if I would not do the like, yes, and willingly die for your comfort, I would I were in hell.

During his questioning by the councillors, Cromwell was also accused of hiring large numbers of retainers – deemed an offence since the Wars of the Roses, to prevent the creation of private armies in England.[16] Here he was on safer ground to make denials. He firmly rejected claims that he 'ever retained any except his household servants' – and this had been against his will. Disingenuously, perhaps, he claimed he had been so 'besought by persons who said they were his friends that he received their children and friends'. But if he had offended, he now desired pardon.

Humbly, Cromwell acknowledged himself a miserable sinner towards God and the King and loyally desired prosperity and long life for Henry and the infant Prince Edward. He ended his letter: 'Written with the most quaking hand and most sorrowful heart of your most sorrowful subject and most humble servant and prisoner, this Saturday at your [Tower] of London.'[17] Strangely, he omitted the word 'Tower' – as if he could not bring himself to write the name of his prison and the symbol of his destruction.

Henry's reaction to this passionate plea is unrecorded. He had probably seen straight through Norfolk and Gardiner's trumped-up charges of treason, but his all-consuming vanity and pride were probably more than pricked by the well-chosen accusation that Cromwell had gossiped about the intimate secrets of the royal marriage bed. His Minister had innocently (and fatally) been seeking discreet ways of fending off the alluring rival attractions of Catherine Howard by encouraging Anne of Cleves to behave more sensually towards her bored and distracted husband. He recognised she needed to learn the artful lessons of seduction. But now Henry just wanted to speedily divorce his unwanted German queen with her unpleasant nasal, guttural speech and her 'displeasant airs'. Cromwell's crime had struck too close to home and could never be forgiven or forgotten by the rampant royal ego.

There were other unconfirmed reports of Cromwell's recent behaviour that enraged the King. Sir John Wallop (an enemy of the former Lord Privy Seal) had told Henry that he had heard from various foreign sources that Cromwell intended to make himself king and that he intended to marry Princess Mary.[18]

Five days after Cromwell wrote his letter, Norfolk and Gardiner introduced a bill of attainder against him in the House of Lords.[19]

It did not mince words. Cromwell, Earl of Essex, whom the King had raised from a 'very base and low degree' and had 'enriched him with manifold gifts' had now become the 'most false and corrupt traitor, deceiver and circumventor' of all Henry's reign – as had been proved by many 'personages of great honour, worship and discretion'. The Minister 'of his own authority and office, set at liberty diverse persons convicted of misprision of high treason and others apprehended upon suspicion of treason'.

Moreover, he had 'for sums of money, granted licences for the export of money, corn, grain, beans, beer, leather, tallow, bells, metals, horses and other commodities . . . contrary to the king's proclamations' and had also appointed 'commissioners in important affairs without the king's knowledge'.

All this was merely the precursor to a veritable litany of heinous crimes. The bill, addressed to Henry, went on to claim that Cromwell, 'being a person of as poor and low degree as few be within this your realm', had publicly boasted 'that he was sure of you which is detestable and to be abhorred that any subject should speak so of his sovereign'. So much for the nobility's hatred of him. Now for Gardiner's personal vengeance:

> Being a detestable heretic, [he] has utterly disposed to set and sow common
> sedition among your true and loving subjects, has secretly set forth and
> dispersed into all shires . . . great numbers of false and erroneous books,
> many of which were printed beyond [the] seas . . . tending to the discredit
> of the blessed sacrament of the altar and other articles of religion declared
> by the king by the authority of Parliament and has caused parts of the said
> books to be translated into English . . . Although the report made by the
> translator . . . has been that the matter has been expressly against the
> sacrament of the altar, [Cromwell] has after reading the translation,
> affirmed the heresy so translated to be good.

Cromwell also 'obstinately maintained that every Christian may be a minister of the said sacrament as well as a priest'. Being Henry's vice-regent for religion 'to reform errors and direct ecclesiastical causes [Cromwell] has, without the king's knowledge, licensed heretics to preach and teach and has actually written to sheriffs in sundry shires, as if it were the king's pleasure, to set at large many false heretics'. Upon complaints made to him about such heretics, Cromwell had by his 'crafty and subtle means and inventions' defended them 'and rebuked the credible persons, their accusers'.

Then comes Norfolk and Gardiner's final damning accusation. The Attainder said that on 31 March 1539, in the parish of St Peter the Poor in London, Cromwell had 'arrogantly' defended reformist preachers like Robert Barnes, saying:

That if the king would turn from it, yet I would not turn. And if the king did turn and all his people, I would fight in the field . . . with my sword in my hand against him and all others, and held up his dagger, saying, 'Or else this dagger thrust me to the heart if I would not die in that quarrel against them all and I trust if I live one year or two, it shall not lie in the king's power to resist or let [hinder] it, if he would.'

He [affirmed] these words with a great oath, raising his right arm, adding, 'I will do so indeed.'

The last word went to Cromwell's enemies amongst the nobility:

By bribery, extortion and false promises, he obtained innumerable sums of money and treasure and being so enriched, has held the nobles of the realm in great disdain, derision and detestation . . . and being put in remembrance [by] others of his estate . . . said 'most arrogantly, willingly, maliciously and traitorously', on 31 January 1540 in the parish of St Martin's in the Fields, 'that if the lords would handle him so, he would give them such a breakfast as never was made in England and that the proudest of them should know'.

The attainder declared that he should suffer death as a heretic or traitor, at Henry's pleasure, and should forfeit all property granted or held since 31 March 1539.[20] It was passed, without dissent, on 29 June,[21] just before the House adjourned.

In another letter to Henry, Cromwell remonstrated about the bill of attainder passed against him. He had been told that

my offences being [proved] by honest and probable witnesses . . . I was by your honourable Lords of the Upper House and the worshipful and discrete communes of your Nether House, convicted and attainted.

Gracious sovereign, when I heard them, I said, as I now say, that I am a subject and born to obey laws and know that the trial of all laws only consists in honest and probable witnesses, considering that the . . . realm had heard and received them.

But then he muses: 'Albeit, laws be laws.' Although through one of Henry's mercurial changes of mind he seems to have received money from the King to provide some personal comforts in his imprisonment, Cromwell sensed that his time had expired. His main concern now was to protect his family: 'Sir, upon my knees, I most humbly beseech your gracious majesty to be [a] good and gracious lord to my poor son, the good and virtuous woman [who is] his wife and their poor children and also to my [servan]ts and this I desire of your grace for Christ's sake.'[22]

But as far as Henry was concerned, there was still some vital unfinished business in which Cromwell could still prove useful: his loveless marriage and how to end it without too much diplomatic damage. The King, as God's deputy on earth, saw no problem with having his bishops annul the union – but needed evidence to demonstrate that it had never been consummated and, more importantly, that he had never willingly consented to the marriage.

On 24 June, Anne was sent to Richmond Palace, Surrey, for 'health, open air and pleasure' as an outbreak of the plague threatened London, and the King promised reassuringly that he would join her there in two days' time. This was hardly a credible statement as anyone at court could testify: Henry's fear of the disease bordered on the obsessional and normally he would have been cravenly in the vanguard of his courtiers heading out of harm's way at the first suggestion of the plague appearing in the capital. In reality, of course, he wanted her conveniently out of the way so he could resolve the thorny issue of their marriage without any unseemly Germanic tantrums.

He also needed a veneer of legality to lay over the proceedings. For a monarch who disliked paperwork so much, there were rare times when Henry could demonstrate impressive attention to detail, as long as the circumstances were important to him. Accordingly, he sent Norfolk, Audley and Lord John Russell, the new Lord High Admiral, to see his disgraced Minister in the Tower and demand his evidence in support of the case for annulment. Henry sat down and wrote out in his own hand the five questions they would put to Cromwell about the events in his marriage, but in fact these created a template for the desired testimony from the prisoner: Henry's words merely dictated Cromwell's answers. His 'interrogatories' ended: 'Doubtless Cromwell remembers how that often, since, the king has said his nature abhorred her [Anne].'[23]

The deputation solemnly charged him as he would 'answer God at the dreadful day of judgement and also upon the extreme danger and damnation' of his soul and conscience, to write down what exactly he knew. He quickly acquiesced and scribbled down on a copy of the questions: 'All these articles be true by the death I shall die and . . . as more plainly app[ears by a] letter written with my [own hand] sent by Mr Secretary [Wriothesley unto] the king's highness.'[24]

On 30 June, Cromwell sat down to write that letter to Henry, laying out the sorry saga of Anne of Cleves, the 'very truth, as God shall save me, to the uttermost of my knowledge'.

He described Henry's romantic gallop to Rochester to meet his new bride and the preparations for the wedding at Greenwich, 'where I spoke with your grace and demanded of your majesty how you liked the lady Anne; your highness answered, [I thought] heavily and not pleasantly. "Nothing so well as she was spoken of," saying further, "that if your highness had known as much before as you then knew, she should not have come within this realm."' Henry then had added 'by way of lamentation' a short, pointed question to his Minister: 'What remedy?' Cromwell, caught off-balance, knew of none and was 'very sorry indeed' and 'so God knows I was, for I thought it a hard beginning [to the marriage]'. He faced some difficult questions the following day when the King, speaking of his bride's appearance, called out to him: 'My lord, is it not as I told you? Say what they will, she is nothing as fair as she has been reported.' Cromwell replied: 'By my faith sir, you say [the] truth,' but added, rather lamely, 'I thought she had a queenly manner.'

The Council had been summoned to find a way to stop the imminent wedding and Cromwell, with a lawyer's mind, had seized on an old pre-contract of marriage between Anne and Francis, the son of the Duke of Lorraine, mooted in 1527 when she was just twelve and he was aged ten. However, the Clevois ambassadors who accompanied her made 'light matter of it' and assured the English courtiers that the agreement had never taken effect. They offered themselves as hostages until papers 'that should put all out of doubt' were sent over to England.[25] Henry was by now building himself up into a characteristic Tudor rage. In his privy chamber, he had shouted: 'I am not well handled' – menacing words to those around him – and Cromwell was told by his sovereign that 'if it were not that she is come so far into my realm and the great preparations that my states and people have made for her, and for fear of making a ruffle in the world – that is to drive her brother into the hands of the emperor [Charles V] and the French king's hands – [I] would never have married her'.

On the day of the wedding at Greenwich Palace, Henry had told Cromwell beforehand in his presence chamber: 'My lord, if it were not to satisfy the world and my realm, I would not do that [which] I must do this day for no earthly thing.' The warnings of trouble to come were now clearly written for Cromwell.

The following morning, a Tuesday, an unwisely prurient Chief Minister had hurried to the King's privy chamber to enquire how the wedding night had gone.

> Finding your grace not so pleasant as I trusted to have done, I was so bold to ask [you] how you liked the queen? . . . Your grace soberly answered: 'As you know, I liked her before not well, but now I like her much worse. I have felt her belly and her breasts and thereby, as I can judge, she should be no maid. This struck me so to the heart when I felt them that I had neither will nor courage to proceed any further in other matters. I left her as good a maid as I found her.'

Cromwell thought the King spoke 'displeasantly which made me very sorry to heart' and Henry subsequently repeated that his heart 'could never consent to meddle with her carnally'. In the early days of the marriage, the King haplessly slept with her every night or every second night, but maintained 'that she was as good a maid, as ever her mother bore her, for anything . . . [Henry] had ministered to her'. By Lent 1540, Anne, frustrated at the prospects of a successful marriage lying in ashes around her, understandably began to 'wax stubborn and wilful . . . and [was] ever verifying that [he] never had any carnal knowledge with her'. After Easter and in Whitsun week, in the privy chamber at Greenwich, Henry 'exceedingly lamented' his fate and complained that he would 'surely never have any more children for the comfort of this realm' and assured Cromwell, 'Before God, [I] thought she was never [my] lawful wife.'

The Minister told the King then that he would do his utmost to 'comfort and deliver your grace of your afflictions and how sorry I was both to see and hear your grace, God knows'.

Cromwell ended his long letter by beseeching Henry 'most humbly to pardon this my rude writing and to consider that I, a most woeful prisoner, [am] ready to take the death, when it shall please God and your majesty'.

Up to this point, Cromwell had maintained an image of moral resolve, mingled with contrition. Then abject fear, despair and a wretched hopelessness overwhelmed him: 'Yet the frail flesh incites me continually to call to your grace for mercy and grace for my offences, and thus Christ save, preserve and keep you . . . Written at the Tower this Wednesday, the last of June with the heavy heart and trembling hand of your highness' most heavy and miserable prisoner and poor slave.' There is a long gap, almost half a page, then a pitiful *cri de cœur* scrawled right at the bottom edge of the document: 'Most gracious prince, I cry for mercy, mercy, mercy.'[26] And it was signed 'Thomas Cromwell'.

Henry commanded his secretary Ralph Sadler to read the long letter to him three times. He is reported to have been visibly affected by his disgraced Minister's words and may even have blubbered like a child. But these crocodile tears did not save Cromwell. A bill granting a general pardon by the King was introduced into the Lords on 5 July, but an exception was made for those with 'heretical opinions touching the sacrament, treason [and] murder' and some other crimes. Cromwell's name headed the list of those unfortunates not receiving the pardon.[27]

He had offered up to his sovereign his last act of loyal service. Henry now felt more confident of his own evidence to the Clerical Convocation investigating the validity of his marriage and cynically used Cromwell's plight to add weight to his own words. In his deposition, the King declared that he was speaking the absolute truth, without 'sinister affection, nor yet upon no hatred or displeasure'. Henry 'from the beginning, ever entreating with the friends of the lady Anne of Cleves . . . desired that the pre-contract . . . might first be cleared', which 'thing the king's highness so looked for that if he had known no such thing to have come with her, she should never had been conducted into England nor accepted into the realm'.[28] But after she arrived at Greenwich,

> the next day after, I think, and doubt not, but that the lord of Essex well examined can, and will, or has declared what I then said to him in that case.
>
> Not doubting, but since he is a person who knows himself condemned to die by Act of Parliament [and therefore] will not damn his soul but truly declare the truth, not only at that time spoken by me but also continually until the day of marriage – and also many times after, whereby my lack of consent, I doubt not, does or shall well appear and also lack enough of the will and power to consummate the same.

The truth, declared Henry boldly, is that 'I never for love to the woman consented to marry, nor yet if she brought maidenhead with her, took any from her by true carnal copulation.' He ended: 'This is my brief, true and perfect declaration' – and signed it 'H. R.' for *Henricus Rex*.[29]

The royal evidence was inevitably supported by his courtiers, and his chief doctor, William Butts, testified that his master was physically capable of copulating with his bride.[30]

It came as no surprise that the Clerical Convocation of two archbishops, sixteen bishops and 139 learned academics, meeting in the Chapter House of Westminster Abbey, ended Henry's fourth marriage on 9 July, following a 'lucid' opening speech by Gardiner, who had his own reasons for wanting to see the marriage ended. Their decision was confirmed by Parliament four days later.[31]

Henry's old sparring partner, the Duke of Suffolk, together with Southampton, Sir Richard Riche and Wriothesley, his secretary, travelled to Richmond Palace to officially inform Anne that not only was her marriage now over, but she was also no longer Queen of England. She listened quietly to their polite speeches as her interpreter translated them, sentence by sentence, phrase by phrase, 'without alteration of countenance'.[32] There were some reports that she fainted at the news, but if she did swoon, it may have been through a sudden and wholly rational fear that the terrible fate of Anne Boleyn now awaited her, as befitted a discarded wife of Henry VIII. She was swiftly reassured that this was not the case.

Anne wrote to Henry on 11 July, in a letter that was probably dictated to her by Wriothesley. She said that although 'this case must needs be most hard and sorrowful to me, for the great love I bear to your most noble person, yet, having more regard to God and his truth than to any worldly affection', she fully acknowledged the Convocation's decision that the

> pretended matrimony between us is void and of no effect, whereby I neither can or will repute myself . . . your grace's wife.
>
> Considering . . . your majesty's clean and pure living with me, yet it will please you to take me for one of your most humbler servants . . . and that your highness will take me for your sister for the which I most humbly thank you accordingly.[33]

She signed herself merely as 'Anne, daughter of Cleves'.

Although the annulment must have been humiliating and crushingly hurtful to her pride and femininity, beneath that impassive, stolid exterior, Anne was certainly no slow-witted fool. She had now been presented with an elegant way to escape Henry's intermittently noisome attentions and preserve what was left of her dignity. As regards her status, she would remain the premier lady in all England after any new queen taken by Henry and the two princesses, Elizabeth and Mary. She would be allowed to keep all her clothes, jewels and gold plate and a fifteen-strong household of German servants appropriate to her rank and station. She would be given extensive lands and property, some of it ironically confiscated from Cromwell, and a generous annual pension of £500, or £220,000 at 2006's monetary values, for life. All in all, the King promised she would be looked after as the price of her silence and acquiescence.

Henry was still concerned that she would suddenly change her mind and complain about his cavalier treatment of her to her brother, Duke William of Cleves. 'All shall remain uncertain upon a woman's promise,' he wrote doubtfully to Suffolk on 13 July and ordered him down to Richmond again to see 'his sister by adoption . . . and press the Lady

Anne to write to her brother' with a copy to him in English, so he would know what she said.

His fears were totally unfounded. Five days later she wrote again to the King, promising ever to remain 'your majesty's most humble sister and servant'. True to her word, she also wrote the required letter to William, saying that 'I account God pleased with [what] is done and know myself to have suffered no wrong or injury'. Anne agreed that her body was still 'preserved in an integrity which I brought into this realm' and that Henry remained 'a most kind, loving and friendly father and brother'. The King was treating her 'as honourably and with as much humanity and liberality as you, I myself, or any of our kin or allies could wish or desire' and begged him not to cause any difficulties over the settlement.[34] She had agreed to stay in England – Henry wanted her to remain firmly under his control – 'God willing, I purpose to lead my life in this realm.'

Duke William, also anxious to find a diplomatically convenient solution, was 'glad his sister fared no worse' and Henry, relieved at the lack of international repercussions, could now happily turn his full, ungainly, amorous attentions on the fragile and fragrant Catherine Howard.

It was all so neat and tidy. After the six bitter and dangerous years he had suffered to rid himself of the unwanted Catherine of Aragon in favour of Anne Boleyn, it had taken him just six days to oust Anne of Cleves from another of his loveless marriages.

Within days, Henry had more good news, this time welcome allegations that Cromwell had been lining his pockets while on legal duties. The French King told him that Cromwell had provided the judgment in a dispute over a French merchant ship seized by vessels belonging to le Sieur de Rochepot, Governor of Picardy, in 1539. The ship had been claimed as a prize and Cromwell was alleged to have financially benefited from the case, through payment of cash from the sale of the ship. On 24 July, in the last letter he ever wrote, this time to the Privy Council, Cromwell firmly denied these claims: 'That ever I had any part of that prize, or that I was promised any part thereof, my lords, assure yourselves I was not, as God shall and may help me.'[35]

On 26 July, Wriothesley moved into Cromwell's house at Austin Friars. He had switched his allegiance from his mentor and patron in May when the Council investigated his involvement in an alleged fraud over some of his properties in the city of Winchester. Can we detect the subtle whiff of another Gardiner conspiracy here: a plot to bring pressure on someone who had detailed knowledge of the Lord Privy Seal's affairs? Suddenly, in June, the inquiry was dropped and Wriothesley was now back in favour, with substantial rewards coming his way.[36]

Now Cromwell had only days to live.

There was still speculation amongst his enemies about the precise nature of his death. De Marillac believed (or hoped?) he would be dragged on a hurdle through the streets to Tyburn, and there hanged, drawn and quartered, the prescribed and terrible fate of traitors.

Norfolk, his wishful thinking shining through his words, said Cromwell's final demise would be the 'most ignominious in use in the country'. By this, he may have been referring to Henry's squalid decision to kill Cromwell at the same time as the clearly mad Walter, Lord Hungerford, who had been sentenced to death by attainder for sodomy, raping his daughter, paying magicians to predict the date of Henry's death and finally employing a chaplain who sympathised with the rebels in the Pilgrimage of Grace.[37] His appearance on the same scaffold was a deliberate attempt to publicly humiliate Cromwell even at his last hour.

Soon after dawn on the day of his execution, 28 July, Cromwell calmly called for his breakfast, which he ate quietly enough. He did not have to wait long for the dreaded rap on the door of his room from Sir William Laxton and Martin Bowes, the two Sheriffs of the City of London who had been ordered to take him to the scaffold. He now learnt that by Henry's abundant mercy and special grace, he would suffer death by simple decapitation on Tower Hill.

As he emerged into the full light of that summer's day, Cromwell must have blinked, startled at the scale of the security precautions around him. The King and his new advisers clearly feared a rescue attempt by the disgraced Minister's numerous liveried retainers within the crowd. A thousand halberdiers[38] were mustered on duty that morning, drawn up in ranks, the sun flashing on their morion helmets and the polished axe-heads of their studded and beribboned staff weapons.

On the way to the place of execution, Cromwell met the dejected and clearly deranged Hungerford, who was destined to follow him onto the scaffold that morning. He tried to comfort the hapless baron, urging the gibbering and muttering wretch to be of good heart:

> There is no cause for you to fear. If you repent and be heartily sorry for what you have done, there is for you mercy enough [from] the Lord, who for Christ's sake, will forgive you.
>
> Therefore be not dismayed and though the breakfast which we are going [to] be sharp, yet, trusting in the mercy of the Lord, we shall have a joyful dinner.[39]

His soothing words probably failed to provide any solace for Hungerford and one wonders now if they were spoken more to reinforce Cromwell's own resolve and to present a calm and courageous front to the watching bystanders. For Cromwell was determined to die with dignity. Some claimed he had been threatened with the penalty for heresy – burning at the stake – instead of death by the axe if he did not confess his crimes at his execution.[40]

He had spent many of those powerless, frustrating hours in the Tower drafting and rewriting the last words he would utter in public, if indeed the King allowed him to speak. He sought no opportunity to justify or excuse himself – nor desired any last strike at his noble enemies. With one foot in a traitor's anonymous grave, Cromwell wanted nothing more than to prevent royal retribution from being heaped on his kith and kin – particularly his son Gregory – and to demonstrate his religious piety for all to see as a means of refuting the charges of heresy against him.

As he approached, with firm, confident step, the straw-strewn wooden scaffold on the huge open space just north of the Tower of London's walls, he noticed wryly the presence of his old adversary and diplomatic sparring partner, the Spanish ambassador Eustace Chapuys, positioned on a privileged vantage point. The two men's eyes must have met, but their half-smiles of recognition were motivated by different emotions: the Spaniard's, by contempt and perhaps triumph; Cromwell's, by the certain knowledge that nothing short of divine intervention would have prevented the envoy from the pleasure of witnessing his bloody end.

He had committed his last words to memory, and after mounting the stairs to the crowded scaffold, he stepped forward to the wooden balustrade surrounding the platform and looked down at the multitude behind the serried ranks of soldiers and the forest of halberds and partisans pointing skywards.

The crowd was strangely silent. In a flat, toneless voice, Cromwell addressed them:

> Good people, I am come here to die and not to purge myself, as some may think that I will. For if I should do so, I [would be] a wretch and a miser [a miserable man].
>
> I am by the law condemned to die and thank my Lord God that has appointed me this death for my offence.
>
> For since the time that I have had years of discretion, I have lived [as] a sinner and [have] offended my Lord God, for which I ask Him heartily for forgiveness.

Cromwell paused and looked the crowd in the face. Amongst them, he must have recognised some as his gloating enemies and others as his worried servants. He hastened on: 'And it is not unknown to many of you that I have been a great traveller in the world but being of a base degree, was called to high estate.'

He sought the royal pardon in words spoken 'carelessly and coldly':[41] 'Since the time I came thereunto, I have offended my prince, for which I [also] ask him [for] hearty amnesty. I beseech you all to pray to God with me that he will forgive me. O Father, forgive me; O Son, forgive me; O Holy Ghost, forgive me; O three Persons and one God, forgive me.'

Cromwell was anxious to firmly dispel the widespread popular belief that he was a Lutheran:

And now I pray you that be here, to bear record [that] I die in the Catholic faith, not doubting any article of my faith – no, nor doubting any sacrament of the church.[42]

Many have slandered me and reported that I have been a bearer [supporter] of [those who] have maintained evil opinions, which is untrue.

But I confess that as God, by His Holy Spirit, instructs us in the truth, so the devil is ready to seduce us – and I have been seduced.

He repeated his central theme, anxious that no one should be in any doubt as to his religious beliefs and fidelity:

Bear witness that I die in the Catholic faith of the Holy Church.

I heartily desire you to pray for the king's grace [and] that he may long live with you in health and prosperity and after him, that his son, Prince Edward, that goodly imp,[43] may long reign over you.

And once again, I desire you to pray for me, that so long as life remains in this flesh, I waver nothing in my faith.[44]

These words were to be printed, under official imprimatur, and widely disseminated.

Another eyewitness reported some especial words of advice Cromwell dispensed to the courtiers he saw in the press of the crowd near the scaffold:

Gentlemen, you should all take warning from me, who was, as you know, from a poor man made by the king into a great gentleman and I, not contented with that, not with having the kingdom at my orders, presumed to a still higher state. My pride has brought its punishment.

I confess I am justly condemned and I urge you, gentlemen, study to preserve the good you possess and never let greed or pride prevail in you.

Serve your king, who is one of the best in the world, and one who knows best how to reward his vassals.

His words may have been interrupted by poor, mad Hungerford, who, almost in frenzy, called out again and again for the executioner to get his bloody business over with.

Cromwell then knelt down on the straw and made his peace with his Maker: 'O Lord, grant me that when these eyes lose their use, that the eyes of my soul may see Thee. O Lord and father, when this mouth shall lose his use that my heart may say *"O Pater, in manus tuas commendo spiritum meum"* ["Father, into your hands I commend my spirit"].'

He stood up and told those with him on the scaffold: 'Pray for the prince and for all the lords of the council and for the clergy and for the commonalty [people]. Now I [beg] you again that you will pray for me.'[45]

Taking a last long look around, Cromwell spotted his old friend Sir Thomas Wyatt the Elder[46] in the front ranks of the shifting and pressing crowd. He called out: 'Gentle Wyatt, goodbye – and pray for me.' Wyatt, imprisoned in the downfall of Anne Boleyn, immediately dissolved into tears. 'Do not weep,' Cromwell added, 'for if I were no more guilty than you were when they took you, I should not be in this pass.'

With that, he told the executioner: 'Pray, if possible, cut off the head with one blow, so that I may not suffer much.'[47] It was a faint hope. The headsman was called Gurrea, 'a ragged and butcherly wretch', and moments later he botched the execution: some claimed he was deliberately chosen because of his lack of experience. It seems likely that his axe stroke missed Cromwell's neck and bit deeply into the back of his skull; one account grimly talks of two executioners 'chopping the Lord Cromwell's neck and head for nearly half an hour'.[48]

The arrogant Henry Howard, Earl of Surrey and the son of Cromwell's arch-enemy Norfolk, sneered: 'Now is the false churl dead, so ambitious of others' [noble] blood. These new erected men would, by their wills, leave no noble man a life.' Triumphantly, he pointed to the process of attainder, the Minister's own personally devised weapon against traitors, as being the instrument of his eventual downfall: 'Now he is stricken,' he said, 'with his own staff.'[49]

Hungerford was swiftly dispatched and the two bodies carried back to the Tower to be buried in unmarked graves in the tiny Church of St Peter ad Vincula, within the walls of the fortress.[50] Irony of ironies, Cromwell's body was buried within a few feet of Anne Boleyn, the queen whose downfall he had so efficiently engineered.

The heads of the two traitors – Cromwell's badly mangled – were parboiled and set on pikestaffs above London Bridge.

The same day as Cromwell was executed, Henry married Catherine Howard in a private ceremony at Otelands Palace, near Weybridge, in Surrey. The old ogre was almost deliriously happy.

Epilogue

If we consider his coming up to such high degree as he attained, we may doubt whether there be cause to marvel at his good fortune or at his worthy and industrious demeanour.

RAPHAEL HOLINSHED, CHRONICLER[1]

After Cromwell's execution, an extraordinary propaganda war of pamphlets and broadsides broke out in London. A 'Ballad on Thomas Cromwell' was swiftly published containing sixteen doggerel verses, each with a repetition of the last line. It begins:

> Both man and child is glad to tell
> Of that false traitor Thomas Cromwell
> Now that he is set to learn to spell
> Sing troll[2] on away.

And it ends:

> God save King Henry with all his power
> And Prince Edward that goodly flower
> With all his lords of great honour
> Sing troll on away
> Sing troll on away
> Here and now rumellow,[3] troll on away.

264

Several rebuttals quickly followed, broadly sympathetic to Cromwell but careful to avoid any direct or implicit criticism of the King. One such broadside, 'A Ballad Against Malicious Slanderers', was written by Thomas Smyth, sewer[4] to Henry and possibly a member of the evangelical faction at court. This was in the form of eighteen verses beginning:

> Although Lord Cromwell a traitor was
> Yet dare I say the King of his grace
> Has forgiven him that great trespass
> To rail on dead men, thou art to blame
> Troll now into the way again for shame.
>
> In that he the law has offended
> By the law he is swiftly condemned
> This mortal life full godly he ended
> Wherefore to rail thus they are to blame.
> Troll etc.
>
> For all his offences in everything
> He asked God's mercy and grace of the King
> And of the wide world for his transgressions
> Then nor no man can say nay to the same.
> Troll etc.[5]

Henry meanwhile was demonstrating his even-handedness in punishing transgressors in religion. Two days after Cromwell's death, the three evangelicals Robert Barnes, Thomas Garret and William Jerome were brought out from the Tower to be burnt at Smithfield for heresy. Alongside them, en route to Tyburn, were three papists, Richard Featherstone, Thomas Abel and Edward Powell, who were to be hanged, drawn and quartered for their denial of the royal supremacy. As they were bumped along on the traditional wooden sheep hurdles, they argued furiously about which of them were truly facing a martyr's death.[6]

This incident personifies and encapsulates Henry's constant changes of mind in the creation and fulfilment of religious policy in the later years of his reign. How much Cromwell pushed this most single-minded of all English sovereigns can only be a matter of debate: his Minister's problem was that the King had a number of different minds at times on difficult religious issues. Henry's accusation that Cromwell was in league with the Lutherans, plotting to impose radical new Protestant doctrines in England, was either convenient propaganda for the moment or the product of the fevered brain of Stephen Gardiner. Certainly Cromwell had an interest in Lutheranism in the 1530s and some sympathy for its adherents. But there is no evidence that he denied Christ's Presence in the sacrament of communion or wanted to move further down the road of Protestantism than other evangelicals at Henry's court.

What Cromwell did achieve was to widen the access of ordinary people to their religion by providing worship in their own language, through the *Great Bible* of 1539. Although Henry was nervous about its impact and sought to restrict its readership, by 1541 parishes were being fined for failing to buy a copy. Cromwell also destroyed some of the superstitious flummery that pervaded much of the Catholic Church of the time through his attacks on images, pilgrimages and shrines.

His real attainments, however, were in government. He reformed the royal household and machinery of administration in England, laying down the foundations for today's departments of state. His loyalty to Henry was unquestionable: all his inventive measures, all his punitive actions were directed at safeguarding the Tudor dynasty. He would have heard his brutish father talk of the mayhem of the Wars of the Roses more than five decades before. Cromwell was determined that his England would never be torn apart by internecine rivalry between aristocratic power bases; he thus ensured that the nobility's loyalty was purchased by the redistribution of monastic property. The proceeds of that privatisation also spread to a new class of emerging gentry, who became stakeholders in the peace and tranquillity of a prosperous England.

Cromwell may appear authoritarian, cruel and malevolent to our modern eyes, with a cynical contempt for Parliament and justice, but his actions were always motivated by what he perceived to be the best interests of his royal master and his realm. Naturally, Cromwell's own best interests also lay in keeping the despotic Henry happy, with the benefits of ever-increasing power and the opportunity for enrichment. He was single-minded in pursuit of his policy objectives and there was no room in his heart for compassion or the quiet, still voice of conscience. No doubt Thomas Cromwell would have felt comfortable in the government of a twentieth-century totalitarian state. Many who governed those states could plead similar motivations to Cromwell's in seeking to justify their actions. In his case, he could not have sought to hide behind appeals that he was 'only following orders'. Within the limits on his authority always imposed by Henry, he was the one issuing the orders.

He enjoyed (almost) absolute power, and in fulfilment of the old dictum, he was certainly corrupt. His apologists point to the widespread practice of bribery in Tudor times, but Cromwell went far beyond that. His greed and avarice knew few bounds, except stealing from his King. His wealth and property at the end of his life surpassed that of all except the King himself and the 'old money' of the Duke of Norfolk. That eventually spelt his ruin and he became a victim of those nobles consumed with envy and hatred for a self-made man doing far better than them.

Surprisingly, Cromwell's downfall did not damage his family, perhaps in return for his meek acceptance of his guilt or even some faint, lingering gratitude deep in the King's black heart for a loyal servant's services through thick and thin.

Five months after his father's death, Gregory was ennobled himself, becoming Baron Cromwell on 18 December 1540, and in the following year was granted the house and site of the abbey at Launde in Leicestershire, together with some of his father's lands. There were other grants of property before Henry died in January 1547 and at the coronation of his son, Edward VI, Gregory was one of the forty who were knighted in celebration of the event.

Gregory's wife Elizabeth wrote obsequiously to Henry thanking him for his 'pity and gracious goodness' after the execution of her father-in-law as a traitor.

Whereas it has pleased [your majesty] of your mercy and infinite goodness, notwithstanding the heinous trespasses and most grievous offences of my father-in-law, yet graciously to extend your benign pity towards my poor husband and me, as the extreme indigence and poverty wherewith my father-in-law's most detestable offences had oppressed us, is thereby much helped and relieved.

I have of long time been right desirous . . . to render most humble thanks, as also to desire continuance of . . . your highness' most benign goodness.

Most humbly beseeching your majesty, mercifully to accept this my most obedient suit and to extend your accustomed pity and gracious goodness towards my poor husband and me who never have, nor God willing never shall, offend your majesty, but continually pray for the prosperous estate of the same long time to remain and continue.

YOUR MOST BOND WOMAN

ELIZABETH CROMWELL

Gregory was a Member of Parliament for the last decade of his life with an undistinguished performance. He died at Launde from the 'sweating sickness', like his mother, on 4 July 1551. Three days later, his widow married John Paulet, later Second Marquis of Winchester.[7]

Gregory's heir was a minor at his father's death, but later married the daughter of his stepfather. He died in December 1592.

The baronetcy continued until it was inherited by Cromwell's great-great-grandson, another Thomas, who was created Viscount Lecale in November 1624 and, twenty years later, Earl of Ardglass. It became extinct with the death of the Fourth Earl on 26 November 1687.[8]

Sir Richard, Cromwell's nephew who had changed his name from Williams in 1531, enriched himself from the dissolution. He married Frances Myrfin in 1518 and had two sons. He kept his appointment as a gentleman of Henry's privy chamber and died on 20 October 1544, aged only thirty-two. He founded the arm of the family that later produced another protector of England, Oliver Cromwell.

Of the others in this tight little human drama, Richard Sampson, Bishop of Chichester, who had been thrown into the Tower by Cromwell in the tussle for power just before his downfall, was saved by his arrest and was eventually pardoned the following August. Sir Richard Riche died in his bed in 1567 after a lifetime of narrow escapes from entirely just retribution. Stephen Gardiner was imprisoned soon after Henry's death in 1547 and remained incarcerated for much of Edward VI's reign for sedition and his failure in religious conformity. On the accession of Mary I, who returned England to Catholicism, he became Lord Chancellor. He died at the Palace of Westminster on 13 November 1555. Norfolk was condemned for treason in the dying days of Henry's reign but escaped execution when the King died. He too remained imprisoned in the Tower until Mary's reign and was another who died peacefully in his bed, in 1554. Mary burnt Cranmer as a heretic on 21 March 1556, leaving as his legacy the wonderful rolling English words and phrases of the Book of Common Prayer.

Both Sir Thomas More and Bishop Fisher were canonised by Pope Pius XI in 1935. The Carthusian priors also became saints in 1970.

Catherine Howard was beheaded on 13 February 1542 for her rampant adultery. Anne of Cleves died in 1557 and was the only one of Henry's wives to be buried in Westminster Abbey, amongst the kings and queens of England.

The last word has to go to Henry, so well served by that corpulent, black-coated Minister. Legend has it that whenever the King, an inveterate gambler, was dealt a knave at cards, he would exclaim: 'I have got Cromwell.'

And, scornfully, he told the French ambassador in May 1538 that his Minister was 'a good household manager, but not fit to meddle in the affairs of kings'. If it were humanly possible, Henry may have come to regret those dismissive words.

Once he had lost the loyal services of his most ruthless and resourceful administrator, as well as the Machiavellian architect of England's foreign policies, he began to feel uncomfortable and isolated. Henry confidently believed only he possessed the supreme skills and cunning required to rule England alone. His self-assurance swiftly dissipated. Never endowed with any patience for the minutiae of government, the King soon became tired of the burden and within less than a year, he was angrily ruing the day that Cromwell was destroyed.

In one of his increasingly frequent outbursts of tearful, vituperative rage, he complained bitterly that his subjects were 'unhappy people to govern whom he would shortly make so poor that they would not have the boldness, nor the power, to oppose him'.

Most of his privy councillors were concerned more with lining their own pockets than serving him and, moreover, 'upon light pretexts, by false accusations, they made him put to death the most faithful servant he ever had'.[9]

Cromwell would have enjoyed the unexpectedly fulsome epitaph and laughed at the discomfiture of his enemies.

Chronology

c.1485	Thomas Cromwell born, at Putney in Surrey.
1491	
28 June	Henry born at Greenwich Palace, third child of Henry VII and his wife, Elizabeth of York.
1502	
2 April	Henry's elder brother, Prince Arthur, dies at Ludlow of tuberculosis, aged fifteen. He had been married to Catherine of Aragon for five months.
1503	
28 December	Cromwell serves as a soldier with the French army when they are defeated by the Spanish at the Battle of Garigliano in Italy.
1509	
23 April	Henry proclaimed king, aged seventeen.
June	Marriage (11 June) and coronation (24 June) of Henry and Catherine of Aragon, widow of Henry's brother Arthur.
1511	
1 January	Birth of Prince Henry, son of Henry and Catherine of Aragon. The infant dies on 22 February.
c.1512	Cromwell in Antwerp, working as a secretary to English merchants based in the Low Countries.
Before 1516	Cromwell marries Elizabeth Wykes, daughter of a cloth-worker of Putney. A son, Gregory, born.
1516	
18 February	Birth of Princess Mary, daughter of Henry and Catherine of Aragon, at Greenwich Palace.
1520	Cromwell advising Cardinal Wolsey on legal matters and members of the nobility on financial issues.

1521

11 October	Pope Leo X declares Henry VIII 'Defender of the Faith'.
1523	Cromwell becomes a Member of Parliament, under Wolsey's patronage.
1524	Cromwell admitted a lawyer at Gray's Inn. Becomes Wolsey's solicitor and counsellor.

1525

4 January	Cromwell appointed to investigate five small monasteries to establish their wealth and becomes Wolsey's agent in their suppression.
1526–9	Suppression of twenty-nine 'decayed' minor monasteries and priories, to fund Cardinal Wolsey's foundation of two colleges at Oxford and Ipswich.

1527

October	Cromwell purchases the manor of Tolleshunt D'Arcy in Essex from Anthony Darcy: his accumulation of lands and property has begun.
1528 or 1529	Death of Cromwell's wife Elizabeth, probably from the 'sweating sickness'. His two daughters, Anne and Grace, die young, probably during the same epidemic.

1529

12 July	Cromwell signs his will, the main beneficiary his son Gregory. His nephew Richard Williams, alias Cromwell, great-grandfather of Oliver Cromwell, is also remembered.
9 October	Fall of Wolsey.
3 November	Cromwell becomes Member of Parliament for Taunton.
1530	Cromwell enters the service of Henry VIII as parliamentary manager and ad hoc legal adviser.
29 November	Death of Cardinal Wolsey.

1531

January	Cromwell sworn in as a junior member of the King's Council.
24 January	Clerical Convocation offers £100,000 to Henry in return for a pardon of fifteen clerics indicted under Statute of Praemunire.
1532	Cromwell appointed Receiver General and supervisor of the lands lately belonging to Wolsey's former 'Cardinal's College' at Oxford.
March	Commons passes 'Supplication Against the Ordinaries', an anti-clerical petition.

14 April	Cromwell appointed Master of the King's Jewel House (a position held jointly with Ralph Sadler from 24 April 1535, after sharing the post with Sir John Williams for one year).
16 July	Cromwell appointed Clerk of the Hanaper.
	Appointed Master of the Court of Wards.

1533

25 January	Henry secretly marries Anne Boleyn at Westminster. She is crowned queen on 1 June.
March	Act for Restraint of Appeals passed, the foundation stone for the English Reformation.
30 March	Thomas Cranmer consecrated as Archbishop of Canterbury.
12 April	Cromwell appointed Chancellor of the Exchequer.
23 May	Cranmer grants divorce between Henry and Catherine of Aragon.
8 August	Cromwell appointed Recorder of Bristol.
7 September	Birth of Princess Elizabeth at Greenwich, daughter of Henry and Anne Boleyn.
12 September	Cromwell appointed Steward of Westminster Abbey.

1534

27 February	Cromwell appointed Joint Constable of Hertford Castle and Hertingfordbury and Keeper of the Park there.
23 March	First Act of Succession passed.
c.15 April	Cromwell appointed Chief Secretary to Henry VIII.
20 April	Execution of Elizabeth Barton, the 'Holy Maid of Kent', and accomplices.
September	Cromwell appointed Joint Constable of Berkeley Castle and Keeper of Berkeley Park; Master of the Game and Keeper of Hynton Wood and Red Wood.
8 October	Cromwell appointed Master of the Rolls (until 10 July 1536).
12 October	Pope Paul III elected to succeed Clement VII.
November	Act of Supremacy passed.
3 November	Treasons Act passed.

1535

1 January	Cromwell appointed Vicar-General and Visitor-General of religious houses.
21 January	Henry commissions a general visitation of churches, monasteries and clergy of England and Wales.
4 May	Execution of three Carthusian priors, a Bridgettine priest and another priest for denying Henry's supremacy.

14 May	Cromwell appointed Steward of the Manor of the Savoy and Bailiff of Enfield, Middlesex.
	Appointed Chancellor of the University of Cambridge.
16 May	Appointed Steward and Bailiff of the Manors of Edmonton and Sayesbury, Middlesex.
20 May	Pope Paul III creates John Fisher, Bishop of Rochester, a cardinal.
19 June	Three Carthusian monks executed for denying the supremacy.
22 June	Execution of Bishop John Fisher for treason.
6 July	Execution of Sir Thomas More for treason.
	Cromwell appointed High Steward of the University of Cambridge and Visitor of the University of Cambridge.

1536

7 January	Death of Catherine of Aragon at Kimbolton.
24 January	Henry injured in jousting accident at Greenwich. Five days later, Anne Boleyn miscarries a male child when told of the accident.
March	Act for the Dissolution of Minor Monastic Houses passed, supervised by Cromwell.
24 April	Court of Augmentations set up to control dissolutions.
11 May	Cromwell appointed Prebendary of Blewbury, Diocese of Salisbury.
17 May	Anne Boleyn's brother, Viscount Rochford, executed for incest with the Queen. Cranmer issues decree nullifying the marriage between Henry and Anne.
19 May	Execution of Anne Boleyn by French swordsman.
30 May	Henry VIII marries his third wife, Jane Seymour, at Westminster.
9 June	Cromwell appointed Chief Steward of the Manor of Writtle, Essex, and Keeper of the Park.
June	Second Act of Succession passed.
1 July	Cromwell appointed Keeper of the Privy Seal, with fees of twenty shillings a day.
9 July	Created Baron Cromwell of Oakham.
18 July	Cromwell appointed Vicar-General and Viceregent of the King in Spirituals (religious issues).
	Cromwell knighted.

2 October	Start of rebellions in Lincolnshire, Yorkshire, Lancashire, Westmorland and Cumberland – 'the Pilgrimage of Grace' – suppressed by Norfolk as 'high marshal'.

1537

January	New rebellion in Yorkshire, quickly suppressed.
26 August	Cromwell installed as a Knight of the Order of the Garter, Windsor.
September	Cromwell appointed Dean of Wells Cathedral, Somerset.
12 October	Birth of Prince Edward, son of Henry and Jane Seymour, at Hampton Court.
24 October	Death of Queen Jane Seymour; search begins for a new queen for Henry.
November	Cromwell appointed Commissioner of the Peace, Yorkshire (West Riding), Cornwall, Oxfordshire and Lincolnshire (Holland), Wiltshire, Dorset, Gloucestershire, Hertfordshire and Suffolk.
3 December	Cromwell appointed Steward of the Honour of Havering-atte-Bower, Essex, and Keeper of the House, Park, South Gate, Palace, Forest and Warren and Bailiff or collector of the rent of the lordship.
21 December	Cromwell appointed Commissioner of the Peace, Kent and Westmorland.
30 December	Appointed Warden and Chief Justice of all royal forests, parks, chases and warrens north of the Trent, and Master of Deer Hunting in those forests.

1538

22 May	Execution of John Forrest for heresy at Smithfield.
September	Thomas Becket's shrine at Canterbury looted and destroyed. Cromwell issues injunctions to clergy and orders the keeping of parish registers.
2 November	Cromwell appointed Captain of the Isle of Wight, Steward, Surveyor, Receiver and Bailiff of Crown Lands, Isle of Wight, and Constable of Carisbrooke Castle, Isle of Wight.
16 November	Royal proclamation controlling purchase and use of Bibles in English.
22 November	Execution of John Lambert at Smithfield for heresy.
9 December	Exeter, Montague and Nevill executed for treason.
17 December	Pope Paul III prepares to promulgate Bull of Excommunication against Henry.

1539

4 January	Cromwell appointed Constable of Leeds Castle, Kent.
12 January	Francis I and Charles V sign the Treaty of Toledo.
8 May	Muster of London militia.
June	Statute of Proclamations passed by Parliament.
28 June	Royal Assent granted to Act Abolishing Diversity in Opinions (Statute of Six Articles) against Protestant practices.
July	Dissolution of major religious houses begins.
6 October	Agreement on marriage between Henry VIII and Anne of Cleves.
14 November	Execution of Abbot of Reading for denying the King's supremacy.
15 November	Execution of Abbot of Glastonbury for treason.
20 December	Cromwell appointed Steward of the Honour of Rayleigh, Essex, and Bailiff of Rayleigh and the Hundred of Rochford. Also appointed High Steward of Reading, Berkshire.

1540

6 January	Marriage of Henry VIII and Anne of Cleves at Greenwich Palace.
	Cromwell appointed Steward of the late monastery of Furness.
17 April	Cromwell created Earl of Essex and appointed Lord Great Chamberlain.
10 June	Cromwell arrested at Privy Council meeting at Westminster.
9 July	Marriage of Henry VIII and Anne of Cleves dissolved by Clerical Convocation.
28 July	Execution of Cromwell at Tower Hill.
	Marriage of Henry VIII and Catherine Howard at Otelands, near Weybridge, Surrey.

1547

28 January	Henry VIII dies about two o'clock in the morning at his Palace of Westminster.

Dramatis Personae

Henry Tudor (1491–1547). King of England, France and Lord of Ireland, Defender of the Faith and supreme head of the Church of England.

Catherine of Aragon (1485–1536). Henry's first queen. Youngest child of Ferdinand of Aragon and Isabella of Spain, and aunt to Charles V, the Spanish emperor. Married Henry's elder brother, Prince Arthur, on 14 November 1501 but left a widow, aged sixteen, at his death on 2 April 1502. Married Henry on 11 June 1509 and crowned queen on 24 June. Between 1510 and 1518 she bore six children, of whom only Princess Mary survived. The couple's failure to produce a living male heir led to Henry's decision to seek a divorce. Died at Kimbolton Castle, of cancer of the heart, 7 January 1536.

Anne Boleyn (?1501–36). Second wife of Henry VIII and second daughter of Sir Thomas Boleyn, later Earl of Wiltshire. Her sister Mary was Henry's mistress. Anne became pregnant by him and they secretly married on 25 January 1533. She gave birth to Princess Elizabeth on 7 September but failed to produce any male heirs. Executed 19 May 1536.

Jane Seymour (?1509–37). Henry's third queen, whom he married on 30 May 1536 at the Palace of Westminster. Died from puerperal fever and septicaemia following birth of Prince Edward at Hampton Court, 24 October 1537.

Anne of Cleves (1515–57). Henry's fourth queen. Married at Greenwich Palace, 6 January 1540. Marriage annulled by Clerical Convocation on 9 July 1540 and by Parliament on 13 July 1540. Pensioned off. Died 16 July 1557 at Chelsea. Buried in Westminster Abbey.

Catherine Howard (1522–42). Henry's fifth queen. Married 28 July 1540 at Otelands, Surrey. Beheaded at Tower Green, 13 February 1542, for treason.

Princess Mary, later Queen Mary I (1516–58). Fourth and only surviving child of Henry and his first wife, Catherine of Aragon. Proclaimed queen 19 July 1553. Reintroduced Catholicism to England. Married Philip, son of Charles V of Spain, at Winchester, 25 July 1554. Died, childless, from ovarian or stomach cancer, St James's Palace, London, 17 November 1558.

Princess Elizabeth, later Queen Elizabeth I (1533–1603). Daughter of Henry and his second wife, Anne Boleyn. Succeeded Mary as queen November 1558. Secured Protestantism as state religion. Died, unmarried, from pneumonia and dental sepsis, Richmond, 24 March 1603.

Prince Edward, later King Edward VI (1537–53). Legitimate son of Henry and Jane Seymour. Proclaimed king 31 January 1547 at the Tower of London. Died of tuberculosis, Greenwich Palace, 6 July 1553.

CANDIDATES FOR HENRY'S BRIDES

Anne of Lorraine (1522–68). Married three times, firstly to René de Châlon, Prince of Orange, in 1540, then to Renatus von Nassau-Breda, also Prince of Orange, in the same year, and finally to Philip Herzog von Croÿ-Aerschot in 1548.

Christina (1522–90). Daughter of Christian II of Denmark, widow of the Duke of Milan. Married François, Duc de Bar, 1541. Became Regent of Lorraine, 1545.

Louise de Guise (1520–42). Married Charles de Croÿ, Prince de Chimay, in 1541.

Marie de Guise (1515–60). Married Louis d'Orléans, Second Duc de Longueville, in 1534. He died in 1534. In 1538 she became the second wife of James V of Scotland (1512–42) and mother of Mary, Queen of Scots. Regent of Scotland during her daughter's absence in France, 1554.

Marguerite de Valois, Duchesse de Berry (1523–74). Daughter of Francis I of France and his first wife Claude. Married Emmanuel Philibert, Duke of Savoy, in 1559.

Marie de Vendôme (1515–38).

Renée de Guise (1522–1602). Died as abbess of St Pierre de Reims.

FOREIGN RULERS AND THEIR AMBASSADORS

Francis I, King of France (1494–1547). Crowned at Reims, 1515. Died at Château Rambouillet, 30 miles (48 km) south-west of Paris, and succeeded by son Henry II.

Francis I's ambassadors to Henry's court:
Louis de Perreau, Sieur de Castillon. Ambassador, November 1537–January 1539.
Charles de Marillac (*c*.1510–60). Ambassador, 1539–43. Later Bishop of Vannes (1550); Archbishop of Vienne (1557).

Charles V, King of Spain and Holy Roman Emperor (1500–58). Nephew of Catherine of Aragon, first wife of Henry VIII. Acceded to Spanish throne 1516. Abdicated in favour of son, Philip (husband of Mary I of England), 1556. Retreated to monastery of Yuste, dying two years later.

Charles V's ambassador to Henry's court:
Eustace Chapuys (d.1556). First embassy, 1529–38. Second embassy, 1540–5.

THE ROYAL HOUSEHOLD AND HENRY'S GOVERNMENT

Charles Brandon, First Duke of Suffolk (?1484–1545). Appointed Warden of the Scottish Marches in 1542. Commanded English army invading France in 1544. Lord Steward of the King's Household, 1541–4. Died at Guildford, Surrey, 22 August 1545. Buried in St George's Chapel, Windsor.

Sir Anthony Browne (d.1548). Master of the King's Horse, 1539–48.

Sir Thomas Cheney (?1485–1558). Appointed Warden of the Cinque Ports 1538 and Treasurer of the Royal Household from 1539. Retained office under Edward, Mary and Elizabeth.

Thomas Cranmer (1489–1556). Archbishop of Canterbury. Supervised preparation and publication of first Prayer Book, 1548. Burnt at the stake in Oxford, 21 March 1556, for repudiating his admissions of the supremacy of the Pope and the truth of Catholic doctrine.

Sir William Fitzwilliam, Earl of Southampton (d.1542). Lord High Admiral, 1536–40. Died on active service whilst commanding the vanguard of Norfolk's expedition against Scotland, 1542.

Stephen Gardiner, Bishop of Winchester (*c*.1483–1555). Secretary to Wolsey and later to Henry VIII until ?15 April 1534. Later ambassador to France. Imprisoned from 1547 during most of Edward's reign for sedition and failure in religious conformity. Appointed Lord Chancellor by Mary I on her accession in 1553. Died at Palace of Westminster, 13 November 1555.

Thomas Howard, Third Duke of Norfolk (1473–1554). Soldier, Earl Marshal and Lord High Treasurer of England. Suppressed Pilgrimage of Grace in 1536–7. Commanded English forces against the Scots, 1542. Lieutenant General of English army in France, 1544. Condemned to death for treason but saved from execution by Henry VIII's death. Imprisoned in the Tower of London until Mary's accession in 1553. Presided at trial of Northumberland, 1553.

Sir Richard Riche (?1496–1567). Speaker, House of Commons, 1536. Appointed Chancellor of the Court of Augmentations, 1536–44, overseeing revenues from dissolved monastic houses. Created Baron Riche on Edward's accession. Lord Chancellor, 1548–51. After signing the proclamation declaring Lady Jane Grey queen, he later switched sides to declare for Mary and was confirmed as a privy councillor. He was active in Essex in the prosecution of Protestants during the Counter-Reformation and was not confirmed as a privy councillor by Elizabeth on her accession.

John, Lord Russell (?1486–1555). Comptroller of the Household, 1537–9. Lord High Admiral, 1540–2. Lord Privy Seal, 1542, 1547 and 1553. Created Earl of Bedford, 1550.

Sir Ralph Sadler (1507–87). Cromwell's servant and secretary. Made a gentleman of the privy chamber in 1536 and one of the two joint principal secretaries to the King (with Wriothesley) in 1540. He was then knighted and made a member of the Privy Council. Retired from public life during Mary's reign and became jailor to Mary Queen of Scots in 1572 and 1584 after Elizabeth came to the throne.

Sir Thomas Wriothesley (1505–50). Joint principal secretary to Henry VIII, 1540. Created Baron Wriothesley, 1544. Lord Chancellor, 1544–7. Created Earl of Southampton, 1547. Deprived of office in 1547, fined £4,000 for acting illegally in his use of the Great Seal and put under house arrest at his London home. Reinstated to Privy Council in 1548. Struck off list of councillors, 1550.

THE CROMWELL FAMILY

Thomas Cromwell, Earl of Essex (?1485–1540). Lord Privy Seal and Viceregent for religious affairs. Beheaded for treason, 28 July 1540, on Tower Hill.

Elizabeth (?–?1528). Cromwell's wife, daughter of Henry Wykes, a cloth-worker of Putney. Bore Cromwell two daughters, Anne and Grace, who died young, and a son, Gregory.

Gregory Cromwell (1513–51). Created Baron Cromwell 18 December 1540. Many of his father's lands restored to him. Died of the 'sweating sickness', 4 July 1551.

Richard Williams, alias Cromwell (?1512–44). Changed his name, 1531. Knighted, 1540. Gentleman of Henry's privy chamber from 1538. Enriched himself from the dissolution of the monasteries. Ancestor of Oliver Cromwell.

THE VICTIMS

Robert Barnes (1495–1540). Protestant martyr. In 1539 he was sent to Germany to negotiate the marriage with Anne of Cleves. Preached a sermon attacking Gardiner. Burnt at stake for heresy, 30 July 1540.

William Exemere (?–1535). Monk of the London Charterhouse. Executed for denying the royal supremacy, 19 June 1535.

John Fisher (1469–1535). Bishop of Rochester. Counsellor to Catherine of Aragon in 1528 during her divorce from Henry. Refused to take Oath of Supremacy. Executed 22 June 1535.

John Forrest (1471–1538). Studied at Oxford University and became a friar in 1491, rising to become provincial of the Franciscan Friars in England. Confessor to Catherine of Aragon. Burnt for heresy, 22 May 1538.

Thomas Garret. Burnt for heresy, 30 July 1540.

John Houghton (?1488–1525). Prior of the London Charterhouse. Executed for denying the royal supremacy, 4 May 1535.

William Jerome (?–1540). Vicar of Stepney, East London. Burnt for heresy, 30 July 1540.

John Lambert, alias John Nicholson. After a show trial, burnt 22 November 1538 for denying the 'Real Presence' – the corporeal presence of Christ in the Holy Sacrament of Communion.

Robert Lawrence (?–1535). Prior of the Carthusian monastery at Beauvale, Nottinghamshire. Executed for denying the royal supremacy, 4 May 1535.

Humphrey Middlemore (?–1535). Monk of the London Charterhouse. Executed for denying the royal supremacy, 19 June 1535.

Sir Thomas More (1478–1535). Helped Henry VIII to write his book on the Seven Sacraments against Martin Luther. Chancellor of the Duchy of

Lancaster, 1525. Lord Chancellor after fall of Wolsey. Refused to take Oath of Supremacy. Executed 6 July 1535.

Sebastian Newdigate (?–1535). Former page and gentleman of the privy chamber but quit the court over the divorce issue. Executed for denying the royal supremacy, 19 June 1535.

Augustine Webster (?–1535). Prior of the Carthusian monastery at Axholme, Lincolnshire. Executed for denying the royal supremacy, 4 May 1535.

Thomas Wolsey (*c.*1473–1530) Cardinal Archbishop of York, Lord Chancellor, papal legate and Henry's Chief Minister 1515–1529. Indicted under the Statute of Praemunire, 9 October 1529, and property confiscated. Died 29 November 1530 at Leicester after being arrested for treason.

Notes

Prologue

1 Fuller, p. 231.

2 Hume, p. 98.

3 Hume, pp. 98–9.

4 Except perhaps Sir Francis Walsingham, Elizabeth I's principal secretary of state. For an account of his extraordinary life, see Robert Hutchinson, *Elizabeth's Spymaster: Francis Walsingham and the Secret War that Saved England*, London, 2006.

5 See Elton, 'Revolution', pp. 6–7. Reginald Pole (1500–58), son of Sir Richard Pole and Margaret, Countess of Salisbury, daughter of Edward IV's brother, George, Duke of Clarence. He was appointed a cardinal in 1536 and Archbishop of Canterbury on the accession of Mary I to the throne of England in 1553.

6 At the time of writing, the British government was seeking to itroduce a similar measure. The innocent-sounding Legislative and Regulatory Reform Bill would empower ministers to amend, repeal or replace legislation and reform common law. Their proposals, however, would still require limited parliamentary debates.

7 The current British government's plans for identity cards from 2008 include proposals for storing information about individuals on Whitehall databases.

8 NA SP 1/116/187. See also LPFD, vol. XII, pt i, p. 264.

9 'Decener' comes from the old French word *decanier* and describes the chief of a tithing, an administrative division of ten households.

10 NA SP 1/129/73. See also: LPFD, vol. XIII, pt i, p. 103.

11 NA SP 1/162/157.

12 John Stokes of Fulham, Middlesex, was committed to Newgate Prison for saying too openly that Cromwell should 'at the hour of his death, depart very sorry and penitent and die like a Christian man' (NA C 1/1,063/75). Edward Fland, chaplain to Dr Knolys, the vicar of Wakefield, was accused in May 1538 of

mischievously teaching his schoolboys 'seditious' and malicious songs about Cromwell (NA SP 1/132/163. See also LPFD, vol XIII, pt i, pp. 387–8). Knolys claimed, rather limply, that he had been given the words of the song by a man, aptly named 'Birkhead', who lived in Bole, Nottinghamshire, but 'who is now in London'. Sadly, their defamatory song is lost to us.

CHAPTER ONE: **The Most Hated Man in England**

1 LPFD, vol. IX, p. 289.

2 Merriman, vol. I, p. 5 and LPFD, vol. VI, pp. 311–12. Nicholas Glossop wrote to Cromwell in June 1533, sending him twelve Banbury cheeses, 'half hard and half soft and wish they were worth £20,000', soliciting his help in a legal case. 'I am almost four score years old, impotent, lame of the gout and cramp and one of my eyes is gone. My mistress, your mother, was my aunt.'

3 This information emerged during a conversation in May 1535 with Chapuys about the possibility of Catherine of Aragon, who was forty-eight at the time, ever conceiving again. The ambassador said he knew of 'some women in this very country who at fifty-four had delivered'. Far from denying the fact, Cromwell himself confessed that his own mother was fifty-two when he was born. See CSP, vol. V, pt i, p. 468.

4 The final battle of the civil war was at Stoke Field, 4 miles (6 km) from Newark, Nottinghamshire, on 16 June 1487, when 12,000-strong Tudor forces slaughtered a smaller raggle-taggle Yorkist army of 'beggarly, naked and almost unarmed Irishmen'. See Richard Brooks, *Cassell's Battlefields of Britain and Ireland*, London, 2005, pp. 270–2.

5 Phillips, p. 166. He maintains the property was conveyed to Walter as a reward for his services to Henry Tudor. As he apparently served only as a farrier in Henry Tudor's contingent at the Battle of Bosworth on 22 August 1485, this seems unlikely.

6 Merriman, vol. I, p. 3.

7 Merriman, vol. I, p. 4 and Phillips, p. 167.

8 LPFD, vol. IV, pt iii, p. 2,573.

9 Foxe, vol. V, p. 365.

10 LPFD, vol. IX, p. 289.

11 Novella 34. They contain 214 tales and were first published in 1554. Shakespeare may have drawn many of his plots, including *Romeo and Juliet*, from the *Novelles*. Bandello (1480–1562) was a Dominican priest who fled Italy after the Battle of Pavia in 1525, when the army of the Spanish Emperor Charles V defeated the French. Bandello's home in Milan was burnt and his property lost.

12 Collier, vol. II, p. 180, claims Cromwell was a sentry at the sack of Rome. This occurred, however, in 1527, when 20,000 mutinous *Landsknechts*, German Protestant mercenaries in the service of the Spanish, attacked the city. At that time, Cromwell was working for Cardinal Wolsey.

13 Cardinal Reginald Pole, *Apologia ad Carolum Quintum Casarem, Epistolarum pars I*, Brescia, 1744–57, chap. xxviii, p. 126.

14 LPFD, vol. X, p. 508.

15 LPFD, vol. IX, p. 289. Joan, the sister of his wife, married John Williamson, who later worked for Cromwell on his building projects. See LPFD, vol. IV, pt iii, p. 2,573. His brother-in-law Harry Wykes told him on 2 November 1523 that he wanted to see some of his lands in Chertsey 'on account of his necessities and because his children are not as he would have them'. See LPFD, vol. III, pt ii, p. 1,455.

16 Not Pope Julius II, as DNB2 has it – vol. 14, p. 367. Julius died on the night of 20–1 February 1513. John Foxe, in his *Acts and Monuments*, also has Julius as the Pope, as he says the incidents occurred in 1510.

17 The church tower is 272 ft (83 m) tall and is known locally as 'the Boston Stump'.

18 Probably the song which begins: *Cold's the wind and wet's the rain*
Saint Hugh be our good speed
Ill is the weather that brings no gain
Nor helps good hearts in need
Trowl the bowl, the jolly nut-brown bowl,
And here kind mate to thee
Let's sing a dirge for St Hugh's soul
And down it merrily.

From the 'Shoemaker's Holyday', recorded in 1600. See Thomas Evans, *Old Ballads, Historical and Narrative*, 4 vols., London, 1810, vol. I, no. LIV.

19 Foxe, vol. II, p. 429.

20 *Archiv für Reformationsgeschichte*, vol. LXIII, Berlin, 1967, p. 193.

21 See LPFD, vol. IV, pt ii, pp. 155–6 and vol. III, pt i, p. 377. For an account of the nunnery and the protracted legal action, see *Victoria County History of England: Hertfordshire*, vol. IV, Woodbridge, 1971, pp. 426–8. The nunnery was dissolved before 9 September 1536 and the property acquired by Anthony Denny, an up-and-coming courtier and one of Henry VIII's gentlemen of the privy chamber.

22 DNB2, vol. 14, p. 367.

23 Also in 1521, the Bakers' Guild, the second oldest livery company in London, retained Cromwell to draft appeals to Wolsey and the Lord Mayor, the draper Sir John Milborne, for sanction to reform their craft (DNB2, vol. 14, p. 368). In January 1522, William Popley of Bristol asked Cromwell to act on his behalf in a case being considered by the King's Council (LPFD, vol. III, pt ii, p. 843). Popley's letter included pleas from fellow citizens and clients of Cromwell who were frustrated at the lack of progress by their lawyer: 'Hugh Eliot . . . wonders that he has heard nothing of his writs and John Green does the same.' Nothing changes in the legal profession. Later the same month, Cromwell appeared in an action between Richard Chauffer, alderman of Calais, and Lord Mountjoy, over the will of Henry Keble, alderman of London. The case was originally to be arbitrated by the Bishop of London ('as umpire') in Calais (LPFD, vol. III, pt ii, p. 1,028) but some of the other adjudicators had not turned up and the case had been referred to London.

24 LPFD, vol. V, p. 422.

25 LPFD, vol. VII, p. 605.

26 Ellis, 'Cromwell', p. 12.

27 Cecily, the 'old lady' marchioness, wrote to Cromwell in August 1522, addressing him as her son's servant and requesting him to send quickly 'the truss bed of cloth of tissue and the feather bed with the fustians [thick twilled cotton cloth] mattress, with the counterpoint' and to deliver 'all her tents and pavilions' to her son Leonard. See BL Cotton MS Vespasian F xiii, fol. 91 and LPFD, vol. III, pt ii, p. 1,026.

28 LPFD, vol. IV, pt iii, p. 2,573.

29 Bindoff, p. 729.

30 Ibid. It was the first Parliament summoned since December 1515.

31 The speech includes his modest assertion: 'Thus have I uttered my poor and simple mind right heartily thanking you all of your benign support and how that you have [heard] so patiently my ignorance . . . ' It is quoted in full by Merriman, vol. I, pp. 30–44.

32 Cromwell has ignored the Parliament's three-week prorogation.

33 Merriman, vol. I, pp. 313–14

34 The fragment of a document containing indentures and agreements concerning the manor of Kexby is reprinted in Merriman, vol. I, p. 316.

35 In December 1526 he received a letter from Laurence Gillys there, acknowledging that a woman's name was spelt wrongly in a subpoena in his suit for debt ('her right name is Gertrude Cornelys') and sending him a barrel of white herring as a present (LPFD, vol. IV, pt ii, p. 1,197). In June, Sir John Vere reported gratefully that the dispute 'between my neighbour Edmund Horsley and Mr Kitchwick is at an end. Your sending [writing to] the former made him more pliant than either I or Sir Giles Capel could get him to be' (LPFD, vol. IV, pt ii, p. 1,434). In 1527, Philip Brain of Exeter in Devon sought his help in advancing his petition in the Star Chamber (so called because of the stars painted on the ceiling of the room. In 1487–1641, it became a separate judicial body to hear petitions for redress by members of the royal Council, acting as common-law judges) at the Palace of Westminster, concerning a curious quarrel over the legacy left by a deceased local

priest. John Reed, the feisty and avaricious abbot of the Cistercian monastery at Buckfast, Devonshire, had sent his monks over to the home of John Clegger, a local vicar, who was lying seriously ill. They bound him 'to a bier with cords and carried him to the abbey where he died in three days'. Now the abbot was refusing to hand over Clegger's goods to his brother, as he claimed they were his 'by deed of gift'. Two local dignitaries, Sir William Courtney and Sir Thomas Denis, had been commissioned by Wolsey to investigate the case but 'would do nothing for fear of the abbot' (LPFD, vol. IV, pt ii, p. 1,668). In April 1527, Cromwell received a letter from Henry Lacy in Calais, congratulating him on promotion 'through Wolsey's favour' but seeking his speedy action in a legal wrangle over the will of Robert Oxenbridge, his wife's deceased first husband. Lacy requested that Cromwell bring the case up before Wolsey in the Chancery Court, but also raised another embarrassing family problem. The bearer of his letter was his cousin Richard, 'a soldier of Calais', who brought with him a notebook detailing the immodest behaviour of Richard's wife, 'who has left him and gone to Master Stock, her daughter's husband' (LPFD, vol. IV, pt ii, pp. 1,381–2).

36 A writ that demands that lands, tenements and chattels are returned to their rightful owner and commanding a sheriff to deliver them to the plaintiff.

37 Merriman, vol. I, pp. 316–18 and LPFD, vol. IV, pt ii, p. 1,670.

38 Boleyn was created Earl of Wiltshire and Ormonde in 1529 and his son, George, then acceded to the Rochford viscountcy.

39 LPFD, vol. IV, pt ii, p. 1,477.

40 LPFD, vol. IV, pt ii, p. 1,568.

41 Ellis, 'Original Letters', 3rd series, vol. II, pp. 140–1 and Merriman, vol. I, pp. 357–8.

42 Williams, 'Cardinal', p. 59.

43 A type of satin damask.

44 A felt hat or cap, worn by doctors of divinity in the fifteenth and sixteenth centuries; probably derived from the Latin *pileus*, a conical hat.

45 'Cavendish', pp. 96–101 and 104–7.

46 Pollard, pp. 321–4.

47 Those founded or controlled by overseas abbeys – mainly in France.

48 NA E 24/23/1.

49 A cell of the Cluniac abbey of Marmoutier at Tours in France. An excavation by the North Bucks. Archaeological Society of parts of the site in October 2000 uncovered a portion of the north wall of the priory church. A robber trench from the dissolution revealed pieces of roof tiles and a single fragment of stained-glass window.

50 Knowles, pp. 59 and 61 and LPFD, vol. IV, pt ii, p. 1,129. The value of all the suppressed monasteries is given on p. 1,594.

51 Allen (1476–1534) was appointed Archbishop of Dublin in 1528 and murdered in 1534. He was the brother of Thomas Allen, Cromwell's friend and debtor.

52 'State Papers', vol. I, p. 261.

53 LPFD, vol. IV, pt ii, p. 1,695.

54 A criminal who had sought sanctuary within the precincts of a church or monastic house to avoid punishment under the law.

55 LPFD, vol. IV, pt ii, p. 3,334.

56 Ellis, 'Original Letters', 3rd series, vol. II, pp. 138–9 and LPFD, vol. IV, pt ii, p. 1,829.

57 LPFD, vol. IV, pt ii, p. 1,863.

58 Merriman, vol. I, pp. 320–1.

59 BL Cotton MS Titus B i, fol. 275. Capon complained that the singing men in the choir 'are well chosen but some of them who are very excellent say they got better wages where they came from'. One man could do not cope with maintaining the college chapel's vestry, keeping the church clean and 'ring[ing] the bells, prepar[ing] the altar lights'. He had therefore hired another man with the job title of sexton. 'There are but five priests under the sub-dean – too few to keep three Masses a day and the sub-dean cannot attend as he is required to survey the buildings.'

60 Merriman, vol. I, p. 324.

61 LPFD, vol. IV, pt ii, p. 1,855.

62 Sadler (1507–87) was made a gentleman of Henry's privy chamber around 1536 and one of the two principal secretaries in 1540. He was also knighted and appointed a member of the Privy Council. He was made Master of the Great Wardrobe in 1543 but retired from public life during Mary I's reign. He was jailor to Mary Queen of Scots in 1572.

63 Ellis, 'Original Letters', 3rd series, vol. II, p. 156.

64 The medical name is *Sudor Anglicus*, and symptoms included headaches, myalgia (muscle pain), fever, profuse sweating and dyspnoea, or laboured breathing. See G. Thwaites, M. Taviner and V. Gant, 'The English Sweating Sickness', *New England Journal of Medicine*, vol. 336 (1997), pp. 580–2. There were epidemics in 1508, 1517 and 1551, as well as in 1528. Some believe that the disease was transmitted by ticks or lice.

65 Bindoff, p. 728.

66 LPFD, vol. IV, pt ii, p. 1,898.

67 LPFD, vol. IV, pt ii, pp. 1,988–9.

68 Multi-coloured rough and heavy woollen cloth that originally came from Friesland in Holland.

69 Cromwell may have been slow in reimbursing Checking and claimed that he had not done well 'with his folks'. See LPFD, vol. IV, pt ii, p. 1,939 and pt iii, pp. 3,564 and 2,791.

70 LPFD, vol. IV, pt ii, pp. 2,090–1 and 2,134.

71 LPFD, vol. IV, pt iii, p. 2,564.

72 LPFD, vol. IV, pt ii, p. 2,125.

73 The first draft had an entry, subsequently crossed out on her death, leaving 100 marks to 'my daughter Anne . . . when she come to her lawful age or happen to be married. And £40 towards her funding until she shall be of lawful age or married.' The same applies to a bequest to 'little Grace', who would have received the same amounts had she lived.

74 Merriman, vol. I, pp. 56–63.

CHAPTER TWO: 'Make or mar'

1 'Cavendish', p. 259, fn.

2 Pollard, p. 268.

3 Vergil, bk XXVIII, p. 331.

4 Hume, p. 8.

5 The offence of serving a foreign dignitary (in this case, the Pope), thereby committing treason.

6 Henry purchased the property in 1537. Part of the palace, known as Wayneflete's Tower, named after the Bishop of Winchester who built it, remains as a private residence today.

7 LPFD, vol. IV, pt iii, pp. 2,686–7.

8 LPFD, vol. IV, pt iii, p. 2,726.

9 Cavendish (?1499–?1562) had entered Wolsey's service before 1522. After the Cardinal's death in 1530, he quit public life and retired to Suffolk to write his *Life and Death of Cardinal Wolsey*, which he probably completed in 1558. This remained in manuscript until 1641 and did not appear in its entirety until it was included in Christopher Wordsworth's *Ecclesiastical Biography, or Lives of Eminent Men Connected with the History of England*, 6 vols., London, 1810.

10 'The Little Office', or 'Hours of Our Lady', was customarily recited by the pious laity in the pre-Reformation Church in England.

11 Made painful or laborious effort.

12 A press or crowd of people.

13 'Cavendish', pp. 258–62.

14 From the Latin *counter valere*, 'be of worth against'.

15 For an assessment of this statesman and military commander, see David Potter, 'Sir John Gage, Tudor Courtier and Soldier, 1479–1556', *English Historical Review*, vol. 117 (2002), pp. 1,109–46.

16 BL Cotton MS Cleopatra E iv, fol. 178 and printed in Merriman, vol. I, pp. 67–8.

17 Paulet was responsible for the lands controlled by the diocese of Winchester during the interregnum between Wolsey's disgrace and the appointment of Stephen Gardiner in 1531.

18 Bindoff, pp. 729–30.

19 'Cavendish', p. 274.

20 Amongst the attainder's charges was the preposterous claim that Wolsey had attempted to infect the King with syphilis: 'The same lord Cardinal, knowing himself to have the foul and contagious disease of the great pox, broken out upon him in diverse places of his body, came daily to your grace [Henry, whispering] in your ear and blowing upon your most noble grace with his most perilous and infective breath to the marvellous danger of your highness, if God, of his infinite goodness, had not better provided for your highness.' An early example of black propaganda. See MacNalty, p. 161.

21 'State Papers', vol. I, p. 349.

22 'State Papers', vol. I, p. 350.

23 Daventry was dissolved on 16 February 1525 by John Allen, in the presence of Cromwell. Wolsey's fears were realised: the crown seized the revenues. See *Victoria County History of Northampton*, vol. II, London, 1906, pp. 109–14.

24 'State Papers', vol. I, pp. 351–2 and also printed in Ellis, 'Original Letters', 2nd series, Vol. II, pp. 27–8.

25 CSP, vol. IV, pt i, p. 449.

26 Pollard, p. 268.

27 Cited by Ives, p. 173. It was apparently the motto of the Burgundian Hapsburgs and Anne had the slogan removed soon after this was pointed out.

28 CSP, vol. IV, pt ii, p. 3.

29 LPFD, vol. IV, pt iii, p. 2,730.

30 A letter from Member of Parliament Reynold Littleprow of Norwich to Cromwell, dated 6 February 1530, includes the statement: 'I hear that you be the king's servant and in his favour.' See NA SP 1/65/132.

31 Henry was happy to pick up the physicians' bill. In February, Eustace Chapuys suspected it was 'a feigned illness' staged in 'the hope that the king would go and see him'. On another occasion, Chapuys reported that Wolsey had been ill for eight days and 'the doctors fear an access of madness which they say will bring on immediate death' – see CSP, vol. IV, pt i, pp. 444, 449. Wolsey's own doctor,

Augustine de Augustinis, asked Cromwell on 19 January for Butts' attendance and to procure some leeches – they had to be hungry ones – for bloodletting, insisting that 'no time should be lost'. The leeches were to be applied by another Italian, Balthasar Guersie, surgeon to Catherine of Aragon. See BL Cotton MS Titus B i, fol. 365.

32 Oedema, formerly known as dropsy, is a swelling of a body organ or tissue through the accumulation of excess fluid. It is sometimes caused by diseases of the heart or kidneys.

33 Wolsey visited the Charterhouse every day 'and in the afternoons, he would sit in contemplation with one of the ancient fathers of that house in their cells, who converted him and caused him to despise the vain glory of the world and gave him shirts of hair to wear, the which he wore diverse times after'. 'Cavendish', p. 285.

34 CSP, vol. IV, pt i, pp. 449–50.

35 His efforts included loans of £100 from Sir William Paulet, together with the Master of the Savoy Hospital and Robert Browne of Newark, who lent £124. See LPFD, vol. IV, pt iii, p. 3,078.

36 Pollard, p. 277.

37 LPFD, vol. IV, pt iii, p. 2,849.

38 'State Papers', vol. I, pp. 367–8.

39 LPFD, vol. IV, pt iii, p. 2,949. See also BL Cotton MS Appendix XLVIII, fol. 13.

40 'Cavendish', pp. 296–7.

41 'State Papers', vol. I, p. 370.

42 BL Cotton MS Appendix XLVIII, fol. 25.

43 Cited by Williams, 'Cardinal', p. 159 and Merriman, vol. I, p. 328.

44 A palace of the Archbishops of York. Cawood Castle, in the West Riding of Yorkshire, was largely demolished in 1750 but the chapel and gatehouse, built in 1526–50, survive.

45 Hall, p. 773.

46 Vergil, bk XXVII, p. 333.

47 Sylvester and Harding, p. 205.

48 'Cavendish', pp. 371–2 and p. 371, fn.

49 'Cavendish', p. 389.

50 Pollard, p. 300.

51 'Cavendish', p. 387.

52 'Wriothesley', vol. I, p. 16.

53 'Cavendish', p. 395.

54 CSP, vol. V, pt i, p. 569.

55 NA STAC 2/7.

CHAPTER THREE: **Daily Round, Common Task**

1 CSP, vol. V, pt i, p. 569.

2 Nichols, pp. 52–6.

3 Tyndale (?1491–1536) translated the New Testament from Greek into English in 1525 in Wittenberg, Germany. It was printed in Cologne.

4 See Rex, p. 866.

5 Tyndale, pp. 174–5 and 177–9 and Ridley, p. 198.

6 Strype, vol. I, bk i, p. 172 and Nichols, p. 56.

7 Tanner, p. 77. Sir Thomas More wrote a stringent reply to Fish's pamphlet in *A Supplication of Souls*, published in 1529.

8 Haas, p. 133, fn.

9 BL Cotton MS Cleopatra F ii, fol. 249.

10 Hall, p. 766.

11 The Clergy Act, 21 Henry VIII cap. 13. Hall, p. 766, suggests all the lawyers were involved in this work, which presumably included Cromwell.

12 NA KB 29/162/12. See also Scarisbrook, 'Pardon', pp. 25ff.

13 Merriman, vol. I, p. 334.

14 The court, together with the Court of Chancery, sat in Westminster Hall until 1825.

15 The last vestiges of the Statute of Praemunire, relating to the appointment of bishops and deans, were swept away only in 1965. See NA HO 304/155.

16 Scarisbrook, 'Pardon', pp. 34ff.

17 Holinshed, p. 766.

18 LPFD, vol. V, pp. 613–4. In 1535 John Clasey wrote to Cromwell about a 'secret matter'. Wolsey had asked him 'to put a young gentlewoman into the nunnery at Shaftesbury [Dorset] . . . in my name, though she was his daughter. She is now commanded to depart by your visitation and knows not whither. I beseech you to write to the abbess that she may continue there until her full age . . . She was born about Michaelmas and is about twenty-four years old'. See LPFD, vol. IX, p. 75.

19 LPFD, vol. V, pp. 117, 491, 600, 618, 732.

20 For more on this sad story of unrealised grandeur, see Hutchinson, pp. 259–73.

21 Elton, 'Revolution', pp. 88–90 and p. 88, fn.

22 Merriman, vol. I, pp. 349–50.

23 Cromwell had threatened the abbot: 'I would be loath and also very sorry [that] the king's highness should be informed of your demeanour . . . I doubt not though peradventure his highness would esteem you to be abbot of his monastery of Bury, yet he would not forget that [it] is your kind and sovereign lord who . . . might think some unkindness and presumption in you so to handle him . . .' See Merriman, vol. I, p. 351.

24 LPFD, vol. V, p. 288.

25 BL Cotton MS Titus B i, fol. 48. Reprinted in 'State Papers', vol. I, pp. 380–3.

26 Foreign Wine Act, 23 Henry VIII cap. 7 and Statute of Sewers Act, 23 Henry VIII cap. 5.

27 LPFD, vol. V, p. 329.

28 Cromwell's first inventory of the jewel house holdings is in NA E 36/85.

29 This in turn was derived from the medieval Latin *hanaperium*.

30 John Judd until 1538 and then Richard Snow.

31 NA E 163/10/19. She also received lands worth £1,000 a year to support the estate.

32 An 'ordinary' is a cleric, such as a bishop.

33 The Commons complained about: the legislative powers of the Church's Convocation; 'subtle questioning' by prelates during heresy trials; conferment of ecclesiastical offices upon young men said to be relatives of bishops; excommunication as punishment for minor offences; the expense suffered by laymen having to appear in distant ecclesiastical courts; excessive church court fees; the 'great charges' levied on parishes when clergy were instituted into them; the large number of holy days; and the secular offences committed by clerics.

34 Hall, p. 784.

35 LPFD, vol. V, pp. 343–4.

36 24 Henry VIII cap. 12.

37 Muller, 'Letters', pp. 50–1.

38 Signed at Langley, Buckinghamshire, 22 August 1532. The treaty was sworn at Windsor on 1 September. See Muller, 'Letters', p. 51.

39 Cited by Elton, 'Revolution', p. 96 and fn. For further information on this extravagant diplomatic *coup de théâtre*, see Alfred Hamy, *Entrevue de François premier avec Henry VIII à Boulogne-sur-Mer en 1532*, Paris, 1898.

40 He was appointed to the archdeaconry of Taunton. See Nichols, p. 244.

41 Wilding, p. 51.

42 'State Papers', vol. I, pp. 390–1.

43 BL Cotton MS Otho C x, fol. 159.

44 'State Papers', vol. I, pp. 392–3.

45 Statute in Restraint of Appeals, 24 Henry VIII cap. 12.

46 He was released after the coronation of Anne Boleyn.

47 Ellis, 'Original Letters', 3rd series, vol. II, p. 276. Thomas Bedyll had written regularly to Cromwell reporting progress at Dunstable. His letters are in BL Cotton MS Otho C x, fols. 164B and 166B.

48 'State Papers', vol. I, pp. 396–7. The divorce decree, in Latin, is in BL Cotton MS Titus B i, fol. 71. The twelve grounds for the divorce, also in Latin and written in Cranmer's own hand, form the ninety-one-page volume of BL Cotton Vespasian B v, and is reprinted by Burnet, vol. II, pt i, bk ii, p. xliii.

49 Hume, p. 13.

50 CSP, vol. IV, pt ii, p. 700.

51 BL Cotton MS Otho C x, fols. 168–170.

52 BL Cotton MS Otho C x, fols. 199–203B. Another copy is in BL Harleian MS 283, fol. 112B, which supplies words missing from the damaged original. This version has the words 'Princess Dowager' crossed out in ink in two places, probably by Catherine herself.

53 Cited by Paul, p. 123.

54 LPFD, vol. VI, pp. 357 and 682.

55 BL Harleian MS 283, fol. 75. It says: 'Where as it has pleased the goodness of almighty God to send to us at this time, good speed in the deliverance and bringing forth of a princes to the great joy . . . and inward comfort of my lord, us and all his good and loving subjects of this his realm.'

56 See Shagan, chapter 2, 'The Anatomy of Opposition in Early Reformation England: The Case of Elizabeth Barton, Holy Maid of Kent', pp. 61–88.

57 Her possessions were later seized by the crown under her attainder and were listed by Cromwell's officers. Henry would not have found much profit from her 'two carpets, (one cut in pieces); an old mattress, seven coarse sheets, a coverlet and a pair of blankets with two pillows and a bolster; two plates, four dishes, two saucers and a little basin; a little old diaper towel; two candlesticks; a piece of plank for a table and a little chest'. See BL Cotton MS Cleopatra E iv, fol. 84.

58 BL Cotton MS Cleopatra E iv, fol. 75.

59 Her aiders and abettors were: Bocking, Richard Dering – also a monk of Canterbury, Richard Master – priest of her home village of Aldington, Thomas Laurence – Registrar to the Archdeacon of Canterbury, Hugh Riche – friar observant, Henry Gold – Parson of Aldermary in London, and two gentlemen – Edward Thwaites and Thomas Gold. See 'Wriothesley', vol. I, p. 23, fn.

60 LPFD, vol. VI, p. 479.

61 Wright, p. 29.

62 Scarisbrook, 'Henry', p. 322 and Devereux, pp. 91ff.

63 He was consecrated Bishop of Bangor on 19 April 1534, but retained his abbey. He had written to Cromwell the previous November: 'I beseech your mastership to call to your remembrance that you devised and thought it good [that] the king's highness to give me the temporalities of the said bishopric, whereon I humbly desire you to be a man for me, if it may stand with your pleasure.' See 'State Papers', vol. I, p. 410.

64 The text of his sermon is printed in Whatmore, pp. 463ff.

65 BL Cotton MS Cleopatra E iv, fols. 79 and 81. Reprinted in Wright, pp. 19–25.

66 BL Harleian MS 6, fols. 40A and 148ff., and Ellis, 'Original Letters', 3rd series, vol. II, pp. 315–18.

67 The others were Master, Bocking, Dering, Gold (the London priest) and Risby.

68 Treason of Elizabeth Barton (Pretended Revelations) Act, 25 Henry VIII cap. 12.

69 Burnet, vol. I, bk ii, p. 115.

70 BL Cotton MS Cleopatra E vi, fol. 161.

71 BL Cotton MS Cleopatra E iv, fol. 85.

72 BL Cotton MS Cleopatra E vi, fol. 149.

73 Elton, 'Police', p. 58.

74 BL Cotton MS Cleopatra E iv, fol. 84.

75 Elton, 'Police', p. 60 and Taylor, pp. 48ff.

76 25 Henry VIII cap. 6.

77 Ironically, Lord Hungerford was the first to die under the Act in 1540, on the same scaffold as Cromwell, although the prime charge against him was treason. Nicholas Udall (1504–56), cleric, paedophilic Provost of Eton College and playwright of the first English comedy, *Ralph Roister Doister*, was the first to be charged for this crime alone in 1541. His death sentence was commuted to life imprisonment and he was released from Marshalsea Prison in Southwark before a year was out. Buggery remained a capital offence in England and Wales until 1861.

78 BL Harleian MS 604, fol. 62.

79 26 Henry VIII cap. 1.

80 Elton, 'Police', p. 278.

81 NA SP 1/77/203.

82 Schismatic – someone who is guilty of splitting a Church in two.

83 NA SP 1/82/151.

84 26 Henry VIII cap. 22. Tanner, p. 383.

85 Burnet, vol. I, bk ii, p. 111.

86 26 Henry VIII cap. 13.

87 Tanner, pp. 379 and 388–9.

88 Merriman, vol. 1, p. 381.

89 Roper, pp. 89–90.

90 Ridley, p. 237.

CHAPTER FOUR: **A Bloody Season**

1 Roper, p. 71.

2 Seven were created cardinals at the same time, five Italians and Jean du Bellay, who had been the French ambassador to London. The last named was Fisher. The Pope later disingenuously denied that he knew the Bishop was imprisoned.

3 The hat got as far as Calais. LPFD, vol. VIII, p. 345.

4 LPFD, vol. VIII, p. 291.

5 LPFD, vol. VIII, p. 320.

6 Harpsfield, pp. 232–4.

7 NA KB 8/7 pt i includes the charges against them.

8 As in Psalm 62: 3: 'Ye shall be slain all the sort of you.'

9 LPFD, vol. VIII, pp. 213–15.

10 LPFD, vol. VIII, p. 280. By European standards, Henry was not the great libertine of folklore. Aside from court flirtations, surviving accounts document extramarital affairs with just three women – Elizabeth Blount – mother of his bastard son Henry Fitzroy, later Duke of Richmond, Mary Boleyn and Margaret Shelton.

11 BL Add. MS 8,715, fol. 53.

12 A criminal court. From the French oyer, 'to hear'.

13 Their charges of high treason are detailed in NA KB 8/7 pt ii.

14 BL Harleian MS 530, fol. 54.

15 Another copy of Fisher's indictment is in BL Cotton MS Cleopatra E vi, fol. 178B.

16 Harpsfield, p. 243.

17 Harpsfield, p. 244.

18 Harpsfield, p. 246.

19 Hall, p. 212.

20 CSP, vol. V, pt i, p. 179 and LPFD, vol. VIII, p. 373. The feast day of St Peter is 29 June.

21 BL Arundel MS 152, fol. 294.

22 LPFD, vol. VIII, p. 309.

23 LPFD, vol. VIII, p. 385.

24 Harpsfield, p. 189. Riche was thought even by his contemporaries to be 'very light of tongue, a common liar, a dicer and of commendable fame'.

25 LPFD, vol. VIII, p. 395.

26 Roper, pp. 94 and 103.

27 LPFD, vol. III, pt ii, p. 437.

28 LPFD, vol. III, pt ii, p. 81.

29 LPFD, vol. III, pt ii, p. 403.

30 LPFD, vol. VIII, p. 284.

31 'State Papers', vol. I, p. 427.

32 LPFD, vol. VIII, p. 75.

33 LPFD, vol. III, pt ii, p. 114.

34 LPFD, vol. VIII, p. 1. Another translation is 'the big fuck', which is probably more accurate given Norfolk's sometimes blunt, coarse speech.

35 BL Add. MS 28,587, fol. 81.

36 CSP, vol. V, pt i, p. 484 and vol. V, pt ii, p. 81.

37 BL Cotton MS Otho C x, fol. 213.

38 LPFD, vol. VIII, p. 251.

39 LPFD, vol. IX, p. 294.

40 See the New Testament, John, 11: 50.

41 LPFD, vol. VIII, p. 169.

42 Cited by Fraser, p. 220.

43 LPFD, vol. VIII, p. 76.

44 LPFD, vol. VIII, p. 167.

45 LPFD, vol. VIII, p. 209.

46 LPFD, vol. VIII, p. 290.

47 LPFD, vol. VIII, p. 195.

48 LPFD, vol. X, p. 3.

49 It is now a co-educational boarding school.

50 BL Add. MS 28,588, fol. 149.

51 LPFD, vol. X, p. 22. No surgeon was allowed near her corpse. Eight hours after her death, her body was opened up by the chandler who embalmed her. It was found to be 'as sound as possible' except for the heart, 'which was quite black and hideous' with 'a black round body stuck to the outside' – ibid., p. 51. She probably died of cancer of the heart, as all this seems symptomatic of a secondary melanotic sarcoma. See Sir Alfred MacNalty, 'The Death of Queen Catherine of Aragon', *Nursing Mirror*, 27 December 1962, pp. 275ff.

52 CSP, vol. V, pt ii, p. 59.

53 CSP, vol. V, pt ii, p. 28.

54 LPFD, vol. X, p. 51.

55 A hearse was an elaborate temporary structure, normally covering the coffin, which was set up in the choir of a church during requiem masses.

56 Ellis, 'Original Letters', 3rd series, vol. III, pp. 8–10.

57 Her will asked that her body should be buried in a convent of the Observant Friars, that 500 Masses should be said for her soul and that some personage should go to the shrine of Our Lady of Walsingham in Norfolk and distribute twenty nobles (£6 13s. 4d) on the way on her behalf. She also desired the King to pass on to her estate 'the money due to her in times past' and that it should retain the goods in gold and silver she possessed. See BL Cotton MS Otho C x, fols. 216–216B.

58 Because of her first marriage to Arthur, Prince of Wales.

59 The inventory demonstrates Catherine's piety. It includes four needlework altar cloths, one having an image of the Virgin Mary and Child, another the arms of England and Spain. There were also thirteen tablets of ivory, one depicting the martyrdom of St Katherine, another the Virgin and St Anne, and a third, poignantly, figures of Henry and Catherine. Just as moving were the 'smocks and other things provided . . . when in childbed'. See LPFD, vol. VIII, pp. 78–9.

60 LPFD, vol. X, p. 71.

61 Bert Park, *Ailing, Aging Addicted: Studies of Compromised Leadership*, Lexington, Kentucky, 1993, p. 44.

62 'Wriothesley', vol. I, p. 33 reported that 'she took such a fright . . . that it caused her to travail [labour] and so was delivered afore her full time which was a great discomfort to all this realm'.

63 Cited by Ives, p. 344. Chapuys reported his comment as: 'I see that God will not give me male children.' CSP, vol. V, pt ii, p. 59.

64 CSP, vol. V, pt ii, p. 28.

65 Cited by Wilson, p. 388. For analysis of Skip's sermon, see Diarmaid MacCulloch, *Thomas Cranmer*, London, 1996, pp. 154–5 and Eric Ives, 'Anne

Boleyn and the Early Reformation in England', *Historical Journal*, vol. 37 (1994), pp. 395–40.

66 Eltham Palace was located in Kent but has now been swallowed up by south-east London. Henry grew up there.

67 BL Cotton MS Otho C x, fol. 209B. Sir Edward Baynton reported that 'no man will confess anything against her but only Mark [Smeaton] of any actual thing. I cannot believe that the other two be as fully culpable as ever was he.'

68 BL Cotton MS Otho C x, fols. 222–5 and reprinted in 'Cavendish', p. 451.

69 BL Cotton MS Otho C x, fol. 225.

70 BL Cotton MS Otho C x, fol. 221.

71 Bell, p. 102.

72 CSP, vol. V, pt ii, p. 137.

73 CSP, vol. V, pt ii, p. 82.

74 BL Cotton MS Otho C x, fol. 223.

75 In February 1866, by command of Queen Victoria, a small brass plaque was erected on the site of her execution, inscribed: 'Site of the ancient scaffold: on this spot Queen Anne Boleyn was beheaded on the 19th May 1536.'

76 BL Cotton MS Vitellius B xiv, fol. 220B.

CHAPTER FIVE: **Shaking the Throne**

1 LPFD, vol. VIII, p. 183.

2 See Elton, 'Police', p. 248. The register of the court, kept by William Saye, is in BL Add. MS 48,022, fols. 83–96. The contents were extracted by the Elizabethan Privy Council clerk Robert Beale. His note, dated June 1588, on fol. 83 says they were 'out of an old book which I borrowed of Mr Saye whose father was Principal Register for Ecclesiastical Causes'.

3 Scarisbrook, 'Henry', p. 337.

4 The volumes are in NA E 344/1 to E 344/21/8.

5 BL Cotton MS Cleopatra F ii, fol. 131. Another copy is in BL Add. MS 32,091, fol. 121.

6 BL Cotton MS Cleopatra E iv, fol. 21.

7 Legh (d.1545) was a cousin of Rowland Lee, Bishop of Coventry and Lichfield.

8 Layton (*c*.1498–1544) met Cromwell in the 1520s, when Layton was vicar of Stepney, north of London.

9 Fuller, p. 214.

10 LPFD, vol. III, pt ii, p. 46.

11 BL Cotton MS Cleopatra E iv, fol. 249, 24 August 1535. The abbey was first founded as a home for leprous women in 1152 and became a monastery in 1184. Jeyn was appointed rector of Shipton Moyne, Gloucestershire, after its dissolution. Printed in Wright, p. 58.

12 Cook, pp. 55–6 and Ridley, p. 255.

13 BL Cotton MS Cleopatra E iv, fol. 127.

14 Ellis, 'Original Letters', 3rd series, vol. III, pp. 164–7. The abbot resigned and was paid the relatively small pension of £7 a year.

15 An ugly old woman.

16 BL Cotton MS Cleopatra E iv, fol. 131.

17 Cook, pp. 72–4.

18 LPFD, vol. IX, p. 238. Her romantic attachment to the area continued after the dissolution of the house. In 1602, Robert Manning of Burwell, Cambridgeshire, then aged eighty, remembered that for more than a year after its surrender, she lived 'in a cave in the ground at the vicarage'. See *Victoria County History of England: Cambridge*, vol. II, London, 1948, pp. 226–9.

19 BL Cotton MS Cleopatra E iv, fol. 134B. See also Wright, p. 59.

20 There were thirty choir monks and eighteen lay brothers in Houghton's day, of whom twenty were under the age of thirty-eight when he took office.

21 Edmund Harvel in Venice said their deaths were seen as 'extreme cruelty' and 'all Venice was in great murmuring to hear it and spoke a long time of the business to my great displeasure for the defaming of our nation with the [most] vehement words they could use. They are persuaded of the dead men's great honesty and virtues . . . I promise you faithfully I never saw Italians . . . so vehement as at this thing: it seem[ed] so strange and so much against their stomach'. See BL Cotton MS Nero B vii, fol. 93.

22 Pharisaical: the strict adherence to tradition and law, from 'Pharisee', the ancient Jewish sect.
    Mumpsimus: a traditional notion obstinately held, even though it is unreasonable.

23 LPFD, vol. VIII, p. 227.

24 BL Cotton MS Cleopatra E iv, fol. 129. See also LPFD, vol. VIII, p. 365.

25 Ling, or cobia, *Rachycentron canadum*, is a deepwater, long, slim-bodied fish of the cod family found in North Atlantic waters.

26 BL Cotton MS Cleopatra E iv, fol. 35.

27 BL Cotton MS Cleopatra E iv, fol. 36.

28 BL Cotton MS Cleopatra E iv, fol. 26. See also LPFD, vol. IX, p. 172.

29 Surviving menus for the Charterhouse brethren for a few days in October 1535 indicate a frugal board. Sunday dinner for each monk was 'frumenty [hulled wheat boiled in milk and flavoured with sugar and spices], a hot pie of lampreys [an eel-like fish] and three eggs'; the lay brothers had salt fish and cheese. On Monday, all had a pottage of herbs, 'plenty of Suffolk or Essex cheese and three eggs'. Tuesday's menu was frumenty, oysters and a piece of ling for each monk; on Wednesday they ate a pottage of herbs, a great whiting and two eggs. The proctor of the house was urged to search foreign ships and 'all the wharves between London Bridge and the Tower for . . . salt lampreys, onions, oranges, lemons, pomegranates, vinegar, sardines, dolphins and olive oil'. See LPFD, vol. IX, p. 200.

30 The last to die in Newgate was William Johnson on 20 September. The tenth Carthusian, William Horne, was executed at Tyburn on 4 August 1540.

31 NA E 322/133.

32 Knowles, p. 116.

33 He did not do any work: this was done by Thomas Watson.

34 The first published work from Syon was probably *A Profitable Treatise to Dispose Men to be Virtuously Occupied*, written by Thomas Betson and printed by Wynkyn de Worde in Fleet Street in 1500. See Christopher de Hamel, *Syon Abbey: The Library of the Bridgettine Nuns*, Roxburghe Club, privately printed, Otley, 1991.

35 LPFD, vol. VIII, p. 441.

36 BL Cotton MS Cleopatra E iv, fol. 125.

37 He died on 21 October 1537 as a result of the squalor of the prison.

38 LPFD, vol. XI, p. 197.

39 Syon was finally suppressed in November 1539 with generous pensions granted to the abbess, fifty-three choir nuns, four lay sisters, twelve brothers and five lay brothers on the day they were expelled. The abbess, Agnes Jordan, received a pension of £200 a year. Her monumental brass remains over her grave in Denham Church, Buckinghamshire. The famous library was dispersed, itself a major crime to lay against Henry and Cromwell.

40 The word 'convent' was used in the sixteenth century to refer to an entire community of monks, nuns and friars living in a single house, not to the building in which they lived. Only later was the word's use adapted to describe the home of nuns.

41 27 Henry VIII cap. 28.

42 27 Henry VIII cap. 27.

43 NA SP 1/239/298. See also Elton, 'Police', p. 246.

44 Eliot was also keen that Cromwell should be aware of his full support for religious reform: 'I would to God that the king and you might see the most secret thoughts of my heart, surely you should then perceive that . . . I have in as much detestation as any man living [of] all vain superstitions, superfluous ceremonies, slanderous jugglings, counterfeit miracles, arrogant usurpations of men called spiritual and masking religions and all other abuses of Christ's holy doctrine and laws.' Cook, p. 111.

45 Knowles, p. 181.

46 BL Cotton MS Cleopatra E iv, fol. 234, also printed in Cook, p. 90 and Wright, pp. 119–20. The chantry chapel survives today. The priory was suppressed in 1537 and was granted to Delawarr for £125 13s. 4d. He held it for four years but was then ordered to exchange it with the crown for the abbey of Wherwell in Hampshire. Today, the monks' choir is the parish church of Boxgrove, the nave having been partially demolished after the dissolution.

47 BL Cotton MS Cleopatra E iv, fol. 122. Letter from Richard Wharton to Cromwell on behalf of Edward Calthorpe.

48 BL Cotton MS Cleopatra E iv, fol. 269, also printed in Cook, pp. 118–19 and Wright, pp. 72–3.

49 Cook, p. 127.

50 Croyland was eventually surrendered on 4 December 1539, with annual revenues of £1,217 6s. 8d.

51 The roads of England and Wales must have sometimes been packed with carts moving tombs and the bodies they contained to other churches of safety. The huge monumental brass of Thomas Nelond, a fifteenth-century prior of Lewes, was dragged 15 miles (24 km) as the crow flies to Cowfold Church in West Sussex. The sculptured tombs of Richard Fitzalan, Second Earl of Arundel (d.1376) and his wife Eleanor (d.1372), Joan de Vere (d.1293) and the monument commemorating the heart burial of Maud, Countess of Surrey, were also taken from Lewes before its suppression on 16 November 1537 to Chichester Cathedral. At Abingdon, Berkshire, the brass to a local benefactor, Geoffrey Barbour, was removed from the local Benedictine abbey to the parish church by the mayor and council. In Gaimster and Gilchrist (eds.), see 'Tombs of Brass are Spent', Robert Hutchinson, pp. 452–6.

52 LPFD, vol. XI, p. 26.

53 27 Henry VIII cap. 25.

54 28 Henry VIII cap. 7. Elizabeth was also declared a bastard. This second Succession Act created three new treasons: to speak, write or act against the marriage to Jane Seymour; by 'words, writing, imprinting or any other exterior act, directly or indirectly' to 'accept or take, judge or believe' the Aragon and Boleyn marriages were lawful; and finally to refuse to take an oath to answer questions concerning the Act or, having taken the oath, refusing to answer. See Tanner, p. 380.

55 Wilding, p. 102.

56 Cook, pp. 101–3.

57 Cook, pp. 119–20. The abbot and the canons escaped execution but spent several months in jail. See Dickens, pp. 51–2.

58 LPFD, vol. XI, pp. 323–4.

59 LPFD, vol. XI, p. 390.

60 An untrue rumour suggested that Bellow had been blinded, sewn up in a bull's hide and torn apart by dogs 'with many vigorous words against Cromwell'. See Moorhouse, p. 50. Millicent was also said to have been hanged, but this was also untrue. See LPFD, vol. XI, p. 225.

61 Moorhouse, p. 53.

62 NA SP 1/106/250.

63 BL Cotton MS Vespasian F xiii, fol. 116.

64 LPFD, vol. XI, pp. 218 and 220.

65 The Virgin Mary.

66 LPFD, vol. XI, p. 221.

67 LPFD, vol. XII, pt i, p. 37.

68 Hoyle, p. 133 and Moorhouse, p. 57.

69 LPFD, vol. XII, pt i, pp. 38–9.

70 LPFD, vol. XI, p. 222.

71 LPFD, vol. XI, p. 226.

72 LPFD, vol. XI, p. 246.

73 LPFD, vol. XI, p. 230.

74 LPFD, vol. XI, p. 244.

75 LPFD, vol. XI, p. 258.

76 Hoyle, p. 173.

77 LPFD, vol. XI, p. 264.

78 LPFD, vol. XI, p. 280.

79 LPFD, vol. XI, p. 332.

80 John Gostwyck told Cromwell on 1 December that £6,470 8s. 2d remained in the Mint. 'I have paid some of the greedy persons today and mean to pay the rest tomorrow.' LPFD, vol. XI, p. 492.

81 LPFD, vol. XI, p. 282.

82 LPFD, vol. XI, pp. 304–5.

83 From the translation of the Greek word for 'Jesus'.

84 BL Add. MS 38,133, fol. 9 has an account of his expenses as Percy's servant in 1527. An account of a law case involving Aske as a lawyer is on fol. 7.

85 LPFD, vol. XI, pp. 360–1. The reference to 'butt' means an arrow range.

86 LPFD, vol. XI, p. 354.

87 Hoyle, p. 375.

88 He had written to Cromwell the previous July, begging for his compassion 'else I shall be undone . . . and utterly shamed this day if there come not comfort' from him. Bigod's 'friends, or rather foes are driving me from post to pillar' despite his 'large efforts to be out of debt'. See LPFD, vol. XI, p. 14.

89 LPFD, vol. XII, pt i, p. 227.

90 LPFD, vol. XII, pt i, p. 234.

91 Ellis, 'Original Letters', 3rd series, vol. III, p. 60.

92 LPFD, vol. XII, pt i, p. 441.

93 Ellis, 'Original Letters', 3rd series, vol. III, p. 60.

CHAPTER SIX: **In a Glass Darkly**

1 'State Papers', vol. II, p. 551, fn.

2 Holbein the Younger (*c.*1497–1543), the son of a painter, was born in Augsburg, Bavaria. He came to England in 1526 with a letter of introduction to Sir Thomas More from the humanist Erasmus, and spent two years there before returning to Basel, Switzerland. Holbein came back to England in 1532 and was appointed court painter four years later. Cromwell gave him £2 as a New Year's gift in January 1538. Holbein died of the plague in London in 1543.

3 In 1538, Cromwell had spectacles to help him read. His accounts for 18 July of that year record the purchase of 'a lace for his spectacles, four pence'. See LPFD, vol. XIV, pt ii, p. 337.

4 NPG 1727. The oil on panel measures $30\frac{3}{4} \times 24\frac{1}{4}$ in. (781×619 mm). Another contemporary version of the portrait is in the Frick Collection, East 70th Street, New York. The National Portrait Galley in London also has two miniatures of Cromwell either attributed to Hans Holbein the Younger, or from his studio. One (NPG 6310), measuring $1\frac{3}{4}$ in. (44 mm) in diameter and painted in 1532–3, is similar to the larger portrait. The other (NPG 6311), exactly the same size, was painted around 1537 and shows Cromwell wearing a chain of office, probably that of Lord Privy Seal.

5 Galton, p. 81 and Stow, vol. I, p. 189.

6 LPFD, vol. X, p. 513.

7 Ellis, 'Original Letters', 3rd series, vol. III, p. 91.

8 Bearing a design portraying plants.

9 LPFD, vol. IV, pt ii, pp. 1,454–7.

10 The building was destroyed in the Great Fire of London in 1666. A new hall was built between 1667 and 1671 to designs by Edward Jarman, but this in turn was damaged by fire in 1772. John Gorham built a replacement which was re-fronted by Herbert Williams in the 1860s and again altered in 1898–9 by Sir Thomas Graham Jackson.

11 LPFD, vol. X, p. 131.

12 LPFD, vol. VI, p. 179, Chapuys to Charles V, 27 April 1533.

13 LPFD, vol. VII, p. 233. Henry had appointed him provincial of the order in April that year. He declared his obedience to the King as supreme head of the Church on 14 May 1534. See also p. 255.

14 LPFD, vol. VII, p. 617.

15 For an account of the priory, see *Victoria County History of England: London*, vol. I, London, 1909, pp. 510–13. The nave of the priory church was granted to Dutch Protestant refugees by the government of Edward VI in July 1550, with another part being used as a granary and coal store. This part was pulled down in 1603 and the whole church was later destroyed by fire. It was rebuilt in 1865, but this church was bombed during the Second World War Blitz of 1940. A new church was completed in 1950, with the foundation stone being laid by ten-year-old Princess Irene of the Netherlands.

16 A boundary fence of thin, split wooden stakes or pickets, from the Old French word *pal*.

17 Stow, vol. I, p. 179. This was probably not the Stow family home, which was most likely in the nearby parish of St Michael, Cornhill, as John Stow was born in that parish in the summer of 1525 and his father Thomas, a tallow chandler, was buried in the cloister of that church in 1559.

18 Hackney is contained in a list of the Knights' property in BL Cotton MS Nero E vi, fol. 64-64B. See the Revd Daniel Lysons, *The Environs of London*, 5 vols., London, 1800–11, vol. II, pt i, 'Middlesex', p. 297.

19 LPFD, vol. XI, p. 185.

20 The arms of the now defunct Wimbledon Borough Council borrowed the Cornish choughs from Cromwell's arms for use in its crest.

21 London Metropolitan Archives ACC/1720. See also Owen Manning and William Bray, *History & Antiquities of the County of Surrey*, 3 vols., London, 1804–14, vol. III, pp. 350–1.

22 Stow, vol. I, p. 89.

23 LPFD, vol. XIV, pt ii, pp. 330 and 336.

24 The State Papers record a case of embezzlement by one of Cromwell's servants called William Body in 1535. The stolen items included a 'standing cup with a cover from Mr Wither's plate [Dr John Withers, d.1534], a gilt spoon of Mr Plimer's [probably Christopher Plummer], a gold Garter saved at the melting of Lord Dacre's gold, [and] a pearl coronet which his wife has taken'. See LPFD, vol. VIII, p. 79.

25 Cited by Weir, p. 307.

26 CSP, vol. V. pt i, p. 569.

27 Cromwell's accounts for 11 July 1538 record the '[payment] to Richard Trapes for two dozen each of platters, dishes, saucers and trenchers of silver at 3s. 9d the ounce: £359 18s. 1d and for burnishing the same: £2 11s. 8d'.

28 Cited by Williams, 'Cardinal', p. 150.

29 LPFD, vol. XIV, pt ii, pp. 328–44.

30 Such as his perjured testimony during the trial of Sir Thomas More.

31 Falconbridge was paid £20 'by my lord's command' on 23 December 1538.

32 Thomas Avery, who kept the accounts, had real problems spelling 'lute', then, as now, a stringed instrument. He wrote first 'lutte', then tried 'lowtt' and finally 'lwwtt'. Unfortunately for him, dictionaries had not yet been invented.

33 For information on Somers' unique relationship with Henry, see Hutchinson, pp. 144–8.

34 John Hussey told his mistress, Honor, Viscountess Lisle, on 14 December 1537 that 'when the wine . . . comes [it] shall be delivered and your thanks given to the serjeant of the cellar'. See LPFD, vol. XIII, pt ii, p. 426.

35 Sir Brian Tuke, Treasurer of the Privy Chamber.

36 Sir Walter Kingston, Vice-Chamberlain of the Household.

37 LPFD, vol. XIII, pt i, p. 9.

38 See Maria Hayward, 'Gift-Giving at the Court of Henry VIII: The 1539 New Year's Gift Roll in Context', *Antiquaries Journal*, vol. 85 (2005), pp. 125–75.

39 John Graynfield told Lord Lisle that Cromwell 'keeps his chamber, much vexed with ague. He has been very ill fourteen days and few have spoken to him.' See LPFD, vol. VIII, p. 125.

40 CSP, vol. V, pt i, pp. 411, 436 and 452.

41 Cited by Williams, 'Cardinal', p. 151.

42 Membership is limited to twenty-six, chosen by royal prerogative.

43 ?John Lord Scrope.

44 'Life', p. 16.

45 'Life', pp. 19–21. The story was earlier recounted by Drayton, p. 22.

46 LPFD, vol. VIII, pp. 147 and 204.

47 LPFD, vol. IX, p. 156.

48 LPFD, vol. XI, pp. 55–6.

49 Cromwell was not popular amongst the monks of Lenton. The sub-prior reported in April 1537 that he had heard the monks 'speak ill of the king and queen and Lord Privy Seal whom they love worst of any man in the world'. See LPFD, vol. XII, pt i, p. 398.

50 LPFD, vol. VIII, p. 387.

51 See, for example, Elton, 'How Corrupt was Thomas Cromwell?' In contrast, Muriel St Clare Byrne calls Cromwell a 'looter and freebooter' (Byrne, *The Lisle Letters*, vol. I, p. 96).

52 Cromwell may have had a sweet tooth. His grocer William Gardiner sent him 'all the fine treacle of Cairo that I have and you shall pay nothing for it'. See LPFD, vol. XI, p. 13.

53 LPFD, vol. VIII, p. 189.

54 34 Henry VIII cap. 31.

55 LPFD, vol. VIII, p. 226.

56 CSP, vol. V, pt ii, p. 263.

CHAPTER SEVEN: **A Merry Widower Thwarted**

1 BL Harleian MS 282, fol. 233.

2 'Waites' comes from the Anglo-Saxon word *wacian* meaning 'to guard' and described official night watchmen. It later came to mean pipers or musicians.

3 A form of flute or oboe, named from the French *chalemie*. A number were recovered from the wreck of Henry's 700-ton warship *Mary Rose*, sunk during an engagement with the French fleet off Portsmouth, Hampshire, on 20 July 1545.

4 'Wriothesley', vol. I, pp. 66–7.

5 The signet bears the arms of England and France, impaling the quartered arms of Seymour under a royal crown.

6 The letter to Cromwell is in BL Cotton MS Nero C x, fol. 1. Another copy is in BL Harleian MS 283, fol. 155. Tyrrell, the queen's gentleman usher who brought the letter to Cromwell, was paid ten marks for his pains (LPFD, vol. XIV, pt ii, p. 332). Cromwell also repaid Wriothesley the £20 he had borrowed from him to tip the 'ladies that attend on my lord Prince'.

7 BL Harleian MS 282, fol. 211.

8 The Lord High Admiral, Sir William Fitzwilliam, told Cromwell on 12 October that 'three or four persons a day are dying of the plague' in Croydon. Two persons were sick in the Dowager's house. See LPFD, vol. XII, pt ii, p. 311.

9 'State Papers', vol. I, pp. 570–1.

10 'State Papers', vol. I, p. 571.

11 No duke was allowed to bring more than six persons; no marquis more than five; earls, four; barons, three; no bishop or abbot more than four; 'and none of the king's or queen's chaplains above two'. See BL Harleian MS 442, fol. 149 and LPFD, vol. XII, pt ii, p. 311.

12 Throgmorton (c.1489–1552), a religious conservative, had been arrested in 1536 for showing a misplaced interest in the grievances of the Pilgrimage of Grace rebels and again the following year because his younger brother Michael had been sent to spy on Cardinal Pole but was suborned into becoming his servant.

13 DNB2, vol. 14, p. 373.

14 LPFD, vol. XII, pt ii, pp. 332–3.

15 Throgmorton's wife immediately wrote to Sir William Parr, seeking help in obtaining his release: 'Not that I desire you to speak to my lord Privy Seal for him, but merely to give me your best counsel what to do for the help of him, myself [and my children]'. See LPFD, vol. XII, pt ii, p. 332.

16 BL Add. MS 6,113, fol. 81. Another version, in a later hand, is in BL Egerton MS 985, fol. 33. He was proclaimed Prince of Wales on 18 October.

17 A sweet liqueur wine from Smyrna, flavoured with aromatic spices.

18 For details of Henry's doctors and sixteenth-century medical treatments, see Hutchinson, pp. 131–7.

19 'State Papers', vol. I, p. 572.

20 'State Papers', vol. I, pp. 573–4.

21 LPFD, vol. XII, pt ii, p. 339.

22 LPFD, vol. XII, pt ii, p. 348.

23 LPFD, vol. XII, pt ii, p. 372.

24 Letter from Sir John Wallop to Lord Lisle, Deputy of Calais, 3 November 1537. See LPFD, vol. XII, pt ii, p. 358.

25 LPFD, vol. XII, pt ii, p. 339.

26 BL Royal MS 7C xvi, fols. 18–32.

27 A listing of property, assessing its value, from the medieval Latin meaning 'value' or 'worth'.

28 BL Royal MS 7F xiv, fol. 78.

29 'Mistress Jak' was appointed as the baby's wet nurse. See 'State Papers', vol. VIII, p. 2.

30 'State Papers', vol. VIII, p. 2.

31 She was aged fifteen. Madeleine, her sister, had married the Scottish king, James V, at the Cathedral of Notre Dame on 1 January 1537, before dying from a

viral infection in June 1537, only weeks after landing at Edinburgh's port of Leith. James kept her substantial dowry.

32 Marie de Guise, aged twenty-two in 1537, had recently lost her husband, Louis d'Orléans, Second Duc de Longueville.

33 LPFD, vol. XII, pt ii, p. 348 and 'State Papers', vol. VIII, p. 2.

34 A funeral for a 'good and lawful' queen had not been staged since that of Henry's mother, Elizabeth of York, in 1503. Then, Norfolk told Cromwell, there were 'seven marquis and earls, sixteen barons, sixty knights and forty squires, besides the ordinary of the king's house, which is more than we be certain of. Therefore we have named more persons, that you may choose them and others at the king's pleasure.' See LPFD, vol. XII, pt ii, p. 355. Norfolk also arranged for 1,200 masses to be said in the London churches for Jane's soul in early November. See BL Cotton MS Nero C x, fol. 2.

35 Lewes Priory, which owned lands in Sussex, Norfolk, Suffolk, Surrey, Kent, Essex, Hertfordshire, Cambridgeshire, Middlesex, Wiltshire, Devon, Leicestershire, Lincolnshire and Yorkshire, was surrendered on 16 November 1537 by the prior, Robert.

36 LPFD, vol. XII, pt ii, p. 360.

37 Cromwell's 'remembrances' for November include a prompt to establish the 'true value' of the priory's estate at Castleacre in Norfolk 'for my part thereof' and to 'set order for making ready of Lewes and to have a book made of the stuff'. See BL Cotton MS Titus B i, fol. 437.

38 BL Cotton MS Titus B i, fol. 390. See also LPFD, vol. XII, pt ii, pp. 341–2.

39 BL Cotton MS Titus B i, fol. 389.

40 HMC 'Rutland', p. 26.

41 About £2,700 in 2006 money.

42 LPFD, vol. XII, pt ii, p. 477.

43 LPFD, vol. XII, pt ii, p. 378.

44 34 Henry VIII cap. 40.

45 LPFD, vol. XII, pt ii, p. 388. A month later, Thompson was still in trouble. He pleaded that he was using 'all diligence' as surveyor and overseer of the King's works, but if 'he had knowledge of the expenses and the choice of labourers, it would be to the king's advantage'. He begged Cromwell to give him this authority, or else 'would gladly be dismissed'. Ibid., p. 432.

46 Henry habitually expelled those in court who wore mourning for their friends. He was to continue to wear mourning himself throughout the Christmas festivities at Greenwich and up to Candlemas, 2 February 1538. It was the only time he paid this tribute to a dead wife.

47 LPFD, vol. XII, pt ii, pp. 414–15 and 'State Papers', vol. VIII, p. 5. The Duchy of Cleves is in modern Germany and covers today's districts of Cleves, Wesel, Duisburg, Jülich and Berg. In the mid-sixteenth century, it was a Protestant ducal state.

48 Count William of Ravestein was the son of the Duke of Cleves.

49 'State Papers', vol. VIII, pp. 6–7.

50 LPFD, vol. XII, pt ii, p. 419.

51 Kaulek, p. 5.

52 Kaulek, p. 9. James V had briefly wooed her in 1536.

53 Cromwell's instructions to Mewtas are in 'State Papers', vol. VIII, pp. 10–12.

54 Kaulek, p. 13, letter dated 31 December 1537.

55 Fraser, p. 289.

56 Kaulek, pp. 17–19 and 23–4, Teulet, pp. 131–4.

57 'State Papers', vol. VIII, pp. 39–40.

58 'State Papers', vol. VIII, p. 146.

59 The oil painting, 70.5 × 32.5 in. (179.1 × 82.6 cm), survives in the National Gallery, London (NG 2475). It was purchased by the National Art Collection Fund, with the aid of an anonymous donation, in 1909.

60 Byrne, *Letters of King Henry VIII*, pp. 192ff.

61 Kaulek, pp. 48 and 51–3.

62 LPFD, vol. XIII, pt ii, p. 111.

63 LPFD, vol. XIII, pt ii, pp. 110–11.

64 Kaulek, pp. 80–1 and LPFD, vol. XIII, pt ii, p. 28.

65 Strickland, vol. III, p. 170.

CHAPTER EIGHT: **Reformation and Retribution**

1 BL Cotton MS Cleopatra E iv, fol. 226. See also Cook, pp. 200–1 and Wright, pp. 224–5, where the recipient is wrongly identified as Sir Richard Riche. John London (1486–1543), another of Cromwell's commissioners, was responsible for dissolutions in Reading, Oxford, Warwickshire and Northamptonshire after 1538. He was a priest and notary public and had come under threat in 1533 after one Richard Jones, arrested and imprisoned in the Tower for his involvement in alchemy and prophecy, promised he would reveal things about London 'that would make him smoke and others too of his affinity'. See Elton, 'Police', p. 56 and DNB2, vol. 34, pp. 351–2.

2 When all her teeth were collected by order of Edward VI's Protestant government in the early 1550s, they filled a whole wine tun. See Fuller, p. 331. The saint, who died in AD 249, had all her teeth knocked out.

3 BL Cotton MS Cleopatra, E iv, fol. 120.

4 'Wriothesley', vol. I, p. 88.

5 LPFD, vol. IX, pp. 154–5.

6 A Catholic church, dedicated to Our Lady of the Taper, was consecrated in Cardigan on 23 July 1970.

7 Cook, pp. 165–6 and 263–4.

8 Ellis, 'Original Letters', 3rd series, vol. III, p. 79.

9 Ellis, 'Original Letters', 3rd series, vol. III, p. 100.

10 A gorget was a collar, worn below the neck.

11 Ellis, 'Original Letters', 3rd series, vol. III, p. 107.

12 A tablet with a representation of the Crucifixion kissed by the priest during mass.

13 Ellis, 'Original Letters', 3rd series, vol. III, pp. 79, 100–1 and 107.

14 Ellis, 'Original Letters', 3rd series, vol. III, pp. 168–9 and Cook, p. 144.

15 Bernard, p. 331.

16 'Wriothesley', vol. I, p. 75.

17 Fuller, p. 333.

18 The old Roman road.

19 Ellis, 'Original Letters', 3rd series, vol. III, pp. 223–4 and Cook, pp. 206–7.

20 LPFD, vol. XIII, pt ii, p. 74 (letter from Latimer to Cromwell, 25 August) and pp. 272–3.

21 Ellis, 'Original Letters', 3rd series, vol. III, pp. 250–1.

22 The Abbot of Hailes talked in a letter to Cromwell in February 1538 of his fears of condemning himself as 'guilty of misusing it, as changing and renewing it with drake's blood'. See LPFD, vol. XIII, pt i, p. 119.

23 'Wriothesley', vol. I, p. 90 and Holinshed, p. 807.

24 These included two pieces of the Holy Cross; St James's hand; the stole of St Philip; a bone of St Mary Magdalene; an arm bone of St Edward the Martyr; the jawbone of St Ethelmold; a bone of St Andrew and two pieces of his cross; and a 'piece' of St Pancras's arm. For the full inventory, see BL Cotton MS Cleopatra E iv, fol. 223. See also Cook, p. 202; the inventory is also reproduced in Wright, pp. 226–7.

25 LPFD, vol. XIV, pt i, p. 156.

26 NA SP 1/133, fols. 51–53.

27 LPFD, vol. XIII, pt i, p. 516, March 1538.

28 Ironically, Walsingham is still a busy place of devout pilgrimage for both Anglican and Catholic pilgrims. A replacement statute of Our Lady of Walsingham was carved for a new Anglican shrine in 1922, copied from the seal of the medieval religious house there. The Catholic shrine was re-founded by Pope Leo XIII in 1897 and the Slipper Chapel dedicated as the National Shrine to Our Lady in 1934.

29 Ellis, 'Original Letters', 3rd series, vol. III, pp. 162–3, 20 January 1540.

30 An order of Franciscan monks. The reformers nicknamed them 'Friars Obstinate'.

31 'Wriothesley', vol. 1, p. 78, fn., and pp. 78–9.

32 Ellis, 'Original Letters', 3rd series, vol. III, pp. 203–4.

33 Born c.566, died 660. St Derfel was said to be one of King Arthur's warriors before turning to religion after the Dark Ages Battle of Carnlan, in Snowdonia, when legend says only seven survived the carnage. Such was the reputation of Bardsey that, during the Middle Ages, three pilgrimages to the island were reckoned equal to one to Rome. The ruins on the island are of the thirteenth-century Augustinian monastery of St Mary, dissolved in 1537. Today, Bardsey remains a popular site of religious retreat.

34 The remains of what is said to be a carving of St Derfel's horse can be found in the porch of Llandderfel. In reality, it depicts a red stag, which formed part of the shrine.

35 5 April was the saint's feast day.

36 BL Cotton MS Cleopatra E iv, fol. 55, letter from Price to Cromwell, 6 April 1538. See also Wright, pp. 190–1.

37 Price wrote to Cromwell reporting that after he rejected their offer, they planned to come to London to see the Lord Privy Seal 'not only to make suit . . . but also to make . . . complaints on me. Therefore I purpose . . . to give attendance upon your lordship within this fortnight that I may answer to such complaints [about] me.' Ellis, 'Original Letters', 3rd series, vol. III, pp. 194–5.

38 Darvell Gadarn, or Derfel Cadarn, from the Welsh meaning 'valiant' or 'strong'.

39 Hume, p. 80.

40 Hume, p. 81.

41 Hall, pp. 826–7. Forrest was amongst fifty-three English martyrs to be beatified by Pope Leo XIII on 9 December 1886.

42 Hall, p. 827.

43 The church took its name from the makers of pattens, or over-shoes, who worked in the parish. The church was burnt down in the Great Fire of London in 1666 and rebuilt by Sir Christopher Wren in 1684–7. It is now the home of the Anglo-Filipino Charismatic Episcopal Church.

44 'Wriothesley', vol. 1, p. 81.

45 The right to present a priest to an ecclesiastic benefice.

46 Portinari, 'a native of Italy', was granted denization – the right of a foreigner to reside in England – on 14 February 1537. See LPFD, vol. XII, pt i, p. 252. He was to fulfil a number of missions for Cromwell and later worked on the unfinished tomb of Henry VIII in the late 1540s. For more information on Portinari, see L. White, 'Jacopo Aconcio as an Engineer', *American Historical Review*, vol. 72 (1967), no. 2.

47 Cook, pp. 138–9.

48 Cook, p. 140.

49 LPFD, vol. XIII, pt ii, p. 291. Henry Courtenay was first cousin to Henry; Henry Pole, Lord Montague, was a second cousin. See also BL Add. MS 33,514, fol. 5.

50 This aspect of the story seems likely to be apocryphal, as the book was not published until 1532. Machiavelli wrote it in 1513, but copies may have been circulated around the courts of Europe before publication.

51 LPFD, vol. XI, pp. 34–5.

52 LPFD, vol. XI, p. 44.

53 LPFD, vol. XI, p. 181.

54 Merriman, vol. I, p. 204.

55 BL Add. MS 30,662, fol. 246 (copy).

56 BL Add. MS 25,114, fol. 262, 25 April 1537.

57 LPFD, vol. XII, pt i, p.xxxix, fn.

58 LPFD, vol. XII, pt i, p. 561.

59 'State Papers', vol. VII, p. 703.

60 LPFD, vol. XII, pt i, p. 570.

61 See Wilding, pp. 195–8 and LPFD, vol. XII, pt ii, pp. 280–1.

62 'State Papers', vol. II, pp. 551–4, fn.

63 LPFD, vol. XIII, pt ii, p. 91.

64 Henry suffered from varicose ulcers in the legs and probably chronic osteitis, a very painful bone infection. See Hutchinson, pp. 127–9. Predicting the death of Henry was now treason under the law.

65 LPFD, vol. XIII, pt ii, p. 418.

66 The Somerset butcher John Howell claimed Courtenay's arrest was because of a personal quarrel between him and Cromwell and he boasted he would recruit a group to rescue him. See NA SP 1/121/67.

67 LPFD, vol. XIII, pt ii, pp. 422–5.

68 'Wriothesley', vol. 1, p. 91. The others arraigned on 4 December were Dr George Croft, Chancellor of the Diocese of Chichester; Montague's chaplain, who denied the King's supremacy; and one of his servants, Hugh Holland.

69 She was beatified in 1886. It took eleven blows to finally kill her.

70 LPFD, vol. XIII, pt i, p. 72.

71 Foxe, vol. V, pp. 229ff.

72 Burnet, vol. 1, pt i, bk iii, p. 186.

73 Foxe, vol. V, pp. 181–234.

74 Burnet, vol. 1, pt i, bk iii, p. 187 and Foxe, vol. V, p. 236.

75 'Wriothesley', vol. 1, p. 90.

76 These included the ceremonies of 'holy bread, holy water, processions, kneeling and creeping to the Cross on Good Friday and Easter Day; setting up of lights before the Corpus Christi; bearing of candles upon the day of the Purification of Our Lady and all other laudable ceremonies yet be not abolished nor taken away by the king's highness'.

77 The name given to the followers of John Wyclif, a heretical, anti-clerical group, numerous in England in the later fourteenth and first half of the fifteenth centuries and ruthlessly suppressed.

78 Henry II is more likely to have cried out: 'What a parcel of fools and dastards have I nourished in my house that not one of them will avenge me of this one upstart clerk!' He was taken at his word and Becket was murdered in the north-west transept of Canterbury Cathedral on the night of 29 December 1170 by four knights: William de Tracey, Reginald Fitzurse, Hugh de Morville and Richard le Bret.

79 See TRP, vol. I, pp. 275–6; Elton, 'Police', p. 257, fn.; and also Wilkins, vol. III, pp. 847–8. There has been much debate amongst historians over claims that a mock trial of the dead Becket was staged by Cromwell in the Court of King's Bench, the hearing beginning on 11 June 1539. The legend has it that, unsurprisingly, Becket did not appear in person and was assigned counsel to speak for him – but he was subsequently convicted of rebellion and treason after an enthusiastic prosecution by the Attorney General, John Baker. See 'Wriothesley', vol. I, p. 90, fn.; J. F. Lewis, 'Lollards, Reformers and St Thomas of Canterbury', *University of Birmingham Historical Journal*, vol. IX (1963), pp. 1–15; and Fred Levy, *Tudor Historical Thought*, San Marino, California, 1967, p. 86. Despite some cogent arguments supporting the reality of the trial, it seems likely the event was a fairy tale concocted in the seventeenth century.

80 The position of the shrine is today normally marked by a lighted candle. The monument was so heavy that it has left an indentation in the floor of the chapel.

81 The shrine is depicted on a pilgrim's badge – a medieval tourist souvenir – of c.1400, 3.125 in. (7.9 cm) in height, now in the Metropolitan Museum of Art, New York (Accession Number 2001.310).

82 Holinshed, pp. 806–7. Wriothesley describes how the Canterbury monks had earlier enclosed another skull in silver 'for people to offer to, which they said was St Thomas's skull, so now the abuse was openly known that they had used many years afore'. See 'Wriothesley', vol. I, pp. 86–7. The official account of religious changes during this period, written in 1539 by Thomas Derby, Clerk of the Privy Seal, casts doubts on the fate of Becket's remains. He wrote: 'His shrine and bones are . . . taken away and bestowed where they will cause no superstition . . .' The following section of that sentence is struck out: 'as it is indeed amongst other of that sort conveyed and buried in a noble tower.' See LPFD, vol. XIV, pt i, p. 156. A skeleton found in 1888 below the floor of the eastern crypt seems unlikely to be that of Becket. Five theories on what happened to the saint's remains are discussed in John Butler's *The Quest for Becket's Bones*, New Haven, 1995, but the mystery remains.

83 John Hussey, the agent in London for the conservative Lord Lisle, jokes, with heavy humour, in a letter of 8 September, that 'Mr Pollard has been so busy night and day in prayer with offering unto St Thomas's shrine and hearse . . . that he could have no idle worldly time' for other business. This is a reference to a report that Pollard spent many hours in prayer before defacing the shrine. Pollard, appointed King's Remembrancer of the Exchequer in May 1535, purchased the dissolved Cistercian abbey at Forde, near Chard, Somerset, in 1540. The following year his income from lands and fees amounted to £230, or £85,000 in today's money. He died in 1542.

84 'Wriothesley', vol. I, p. 86, fn. The ring appears amongst the diamonds fitted to the golden collar worn by Henry's daughter, Mary, when queen after she ascended the throne of England in 1553. It may have been given as a gift when she married Philip of Spain the following year. See Arthur P. Stanley, *Historical Memorials of Canterbury*, London, 1887, p. 254, fn.

85 She accompanied the French King's Madeleine to Scotland for her very brief marriage to James V and remained there until his second marriage to Marie de Guise. She was now making her return to France.

86 'State Papers', vol. I, pp. 583–4. This was presumably the fake skull (see note 82, above). After her tourist's visit to the church, the prior sent her a generous present of rabbits, capons, chickens and fruit – so much food that she exclaimed: 'What shall we do with so many capons?' The answer was easy: she invited him to dinner.

87 'Wriothesley', vol. I, p. 87. The church claimed to be built on the site where Becket was born. See Thomas Fuller, *History of the Worthies of England*, London, 1662, p. 203. After surrender, the church was sold to the Mercers' Company, which later built its livery hall on the site. For a history of the church and hospital, see Sir John Watney, *Some Account of the Hospital of St Thomas Acon*, London, 1892. On 21

October 1538, the hospital was suppressed 'and the master and brethren put out and all the goods taken to the king's treasury', ibid., p. 88.

88 Muller, 'Reaction', pp. 76–7.

89 See Frederick Bussby, *Winchester Cathedral 1079–1979*, Ringwood, 1979, p. 46. A conjectural reconstruction of the shrine is on p. 49.

90 Knowles, p. 238.

91 Cook, p. 199.

92 Wilkins, vol. III, p. 840.

CHAPTER NINE: **The Distant Sound of Conflict**

1 Muller, 'Letters', p. 399.

2 Beaton (1494–1546) was appointed Archbishop of St Andrews in 1539 and became Chancellor of Scotland in 1543, as well as protonotary apostolic and legate *a latere*. He was assassinated three years later in revenge for his condemnation of George Wishart, one of the most popular Scottish religious reformers, who was burnt for heresy at St Andrews in 1546.

3 Halliwell, vol. I, pp. 359–60.

4 The French ambassador Louis de Perreau, Sieur de Castillon, departed without his successor being named. The Spanish envoy Chapuys was not withdrawn until his replacement arrived.

5 'State Papers', vol. I, p. 593.

6 Elton, 'Police', p. 261.

7 Merriman, vol. II, pp. 151–5 and Burnet, vol. II, p. lxxix.

8 NA SP 1/136 fols. 226–8.

9 NA SP 1/144 fols. 93, 135. The rumour originated with sixty-year-old Margaret Ede, of the same town, who had misheard a sermon as she lacked 'a great part of her hearing'.

10 'State Papers', vol. I, pp. 612–13.

11 Elton, 'Police', p. 260.

12 NA SP 1/144 fol. 128.

13 'State Papers', vol. VIII, p. 590.

14 The Act for the Advancement of True Religion (34 and 35 Henry VIII cap. I) of 1543 withdrew permission for everyone to read the English Bible, limiting the privilege to noblemen, gentlemen and merchants (who could peruse it in private). Low-born women, workers and apprentices were strictly prohibited from reading it publicly or privately.

15 Ribier, vol. I, pp. 357–9.

16 Byrne, *The Lisle Letters*, vol. V, p. 1,415.

17 See A. F. Pollard, 'Thomas Cromwell's Parliamentary Lists', *Bulletin of the Institute of Historical Research*, vol. XI (1931–2), pp. 31ff.

18 Muller, 'Letters', p. 399. Letter from Gardiner, written in the Fleet Prison, 14 October 1547. His phrase 'turned the cat in the pan' probably means that Cromwell had deviously later reversed their roles in his account of the conversation.

19 See E. R. Adair, 'The Statute of Proclamations', *English Historical Review*, vol. XXXII (1917), p. 35.

20 31 Henry VIII cap. 8. See 'Lords Journal', p. 123.

21 Tanner, p. 534.

22 Cromwell was still interrogating her. On 19 April 1539 he informed Henry: 'I shall assay to the uttermost of my power and never cease till the bottom of her stomach [her innermost thoughts] might be clearly opened and displayed and to that I shall not be slack.' See BL Cotton MS Titus B i, fol. 265.

23 The Countess of Salisbury's attainder is 31 Henry VIII cap. 15.

24 31 Henry VIII cap. 10.

25 Holinshed, p. 810.

26 A long edged and hooked weapon, used against attacking horsemen. The name 'morris' comes from 'Moorish', supposedly describing the origin of the weapon.

27 Bill, or pole, weapons included halberds (with an axe head and spear point), partisans (spear point), and glaives, a long edged weapon with protruding hooks.

28 The arms of the City of London are *Argent, a cross gules, in the first quarter, a sword in pale, point upwards, of the last.*

29 'Wriothesley', vol. I, pp. 95–6.

30 Cromwell also paid out 23s. 8d to John ap Richards for gunpowder fired as a salute at Stepney before the muster began. See LPFD, vol. IX, p. 340.

31 Sir Thomas Audley.

32 Umbrellas were not widely used in England until the early seventeenth century.

33 The King's Bridge was at the eastern end of the Palace of Westminster, a short distance from Old Palace Stairs. It was a landing stage rather than a bridge.

34 'Wriothesley', vol. I, p. 100.

35 BL Royal MS 18 A.L., a twenty-five-page quarto volume. It may have been read by Henry himself. The original draft, with autograph corrections, is in BL Cotton MS Faustina C ii, fols. 5–22. See also Sydney Anglo, 'An Early Tudor Programme for Plays and other Demonstrations Against the Pope', *Journal of the Warburg and*

Courtauld Institutes, vol. XX (1957), pp. 176–9, for further discussion of Morison's propaganda proposals.

36 See Anglo, pp. 266–7.

37 Bale (1495–1563) was educated at the Carmelite convent in Norwich and Jesus College, Oxford, and became an embittered religious reformer. On Cromwell's death in 1540, he fled to Germany and stayed there for seven years before returning to England during the reign of Edward VI. He became vicar of Swaffham, Norfolk, in 1551 and was appointed Bishop of Ossory (the oldest Irish bishopric) two years later. On Mary's accession, he again fled to Europe and finally ended his days as a prebendary canon at Canterbury.

38 Anglo, p. 267. See also McCusker, p. 5.

39 LPFD, vol. XIV, pt ii, pp. 337 and 339.

40 See J. H. P. Pafford (ed.), introduction to *Kynge Johan*, Oxford, 1931, p. xvii.

41 McCusker, p. 75. John Murray, *English Dramatic Companies 1558–1642*, 2 vols., London, 1910, vol. II, p. 36 lists the known performances staged by Cromwell's troupe of actors. There is a reference to 'the Secretary's players' in payments to actors in Leicester in 1537–8. See Mary Bateson (ed.) et al., *Records of the Borough of Leicester 1103–1603*, 4 vols., Cambridge, 1899–1923, vol. III, pp. 41 and 58.

42 LPFD, vol. XII, pt i, p. 244 and Anglo, p. 266.

43 Printed by Thomas Berthelet of Fleet Street, the King's printer 1530–47, royal bookbinder and stationer. Printed 1539, STC 18111–2.

44 The second edition was also printed by Berthelet. See Elton, 'Police', pp. 202–4.

45 Also printed by Berthelet, STC 18110.

46 LPFD, vol. XIV, pt ii, p. 340.

47 LPFD, vol. XII, pt ii, p. 478. Morison wanted Cromwell's help in arranging a £400 loan to the owner of a 'fair house' in Norwich, which property would be given to Morison on receipt of the advanced cash. 'If you would get him this money to get me this house, you should put me in such credit that, with a little more help, I might attain to a marriage worth two of the house,' he told Cromwell.

48 NA SP 3/5/93 (Lisle Letters).

49 Cited by Elton, 'Police', pp. 134–5.

50 31 Henry VIII cap. 13. Cromwell had earlier written to the heads of monasteries in the King's name telling them they should not listen to idle rumours of further suppressions: '[The King] does not intend in any way to trouble you or devise for the suppression of any religious house that stands.' See Knowles, p. 239.

51 Cook, p. 217, letter to Cromwell, 2 December 1539.

52 At Jervaulx Abbey, Yorkshire, the lead 'pigs' had been stacked at the west end of the nave, but before they could be taken away, the vaulting of the roof collapsed,

burying the pile. They were found during excavations of the site in 1923 and later re-used for re-leading the Five Sisters window in the north transept of York Cathedral. See Cook, p. 137, fn.

53 See Gaimster and Gilchrist, Richard K. Morris, 'Monastic Architecture: Deconstruction and Reconstruction', p. 240. At St Alban's, Hertfordshire, the excavation of the chapter house site in 1978 uncovered wheel ruts leading through its west door and into the cloister garth.

54 Cook, pp. 241–2.

55 He had asked Cromwell for a leave of absence from the session of Parliament in spring 1539 because of his physical infirmity. See Knowles, p. 262.

56 He was a friend of the conservative Arthur Plantagenet, Lord Lisle, and had educated his stepson James Basset at Reading Abbey.

57 Holinshed, p. 811.

58 All these men were amongst the English martyrs beatified by Pope Leo XIII on 13 May 1895.

59 BL Cotton MS Cleopatra E v, fols. 313–320. Unsurprisingly, all his amendments were included in the final text, including the description of his title in the preamble. This he changed from 'Supreme Head of this Church in England' to 'by God's law, Supreme Head of this church and congregation of England'.

60 'Wriothesley', vol. I, p. 103.

61 Writing in code.

62 He married Margaret, niece of the Lutheran divine Andreas Osiander, at Nuremburg during the period when he was ambassador in Germany in 1532, a year before becoming Archbishop of Canterbury. Clerical marriage was illegal then.

63 Byrne, *The Lisle Letters*, vol. V, p. 1,425.

64 31 Henry VIII cap. 14.

65 Burnet, vol. I, pt i, bk iii, p. 195.

66 John Cox, *The Works of Thomas Cranmer*, 2 vols., Cambridge, 1844–6, vol. II, pp. 394–5.

67 Scarisbrook, 'Henry', pp. 421–2.

68 A light shallow-draught rowing boat that conveyed passengers.

69 Burnet, vol. I, pt i, bk iii, p. 195. See also Nichols, p. 237.

70 Burnet, vol. I, pt i, bk iii, p. 195.

71 Mori and Vivis, bk i, letter 28, cols. 22–9.

72 Strype, vol. I, pt ii, p. 438.

CHAPTER TEN: **The Royal Neck in the Yoke**

1 Hatfield House, CP 1/27.

2 On France's north-east coast. The town and the immediate surroundings (the 'Pale of Calais') were held by England between 1347 and 1558 as a bridgehead on the European mainland.

3 Hall, p. 832.

4 His father had given him £40 for his expenses in going to Calais, but he had to borrow a further £10 from one of his servants when he was there. 'Bruges' the tailor was paid £9 for Gregory's new 'apparel' and for coats for his two companions, Wadham and Conisby. Cromwell also paid out £100 to his nephew Richard 'against the coming of the queen'. See LPFD, vol. XIV, pt i, p. 344.

5 Holinshed, p. 811.

6 *Sweepstake*, 300 tons, was built in 1535, and *Lion*, 140 tons, the following year. See Geoffrey Moorhouse, *Great Harry's Navy*, London, 2005, p. 323.

7 A carrack was an ocean-going ship design developed in the fifteenth century with three or four masts and an aftcastle over the high rounded stern and a forecastle over the bows.

8 'State Papers', vol. VIII, p. 208.

9 See Carl W. Bouterwek, 'Anna von Cleve, Gemahlin Heinrich VIII, König von England', *Zeitschrift des Bergischen Geschichtsvereins*, 9 vols., Bonn, 1863–73, vol. IV, pp. 374ff.

10 The English name was derived from the player gaining 100 points to win. Piquet was established from the early sixteenth century and was popular in Spain and France before being played in England. The game involves two players and a deck of thirty-two cards.

11 'State Papers', vol. VIII, p. 213.

12 LPFD, vol. XIV, pt ii, p. 260.

13 It had been suppressed the previous year.

14 Sir Howard Colvin, *History of the King's Works 1485–1660*, vol. IV, London, 1982, p. 39. The surveyor, James Needham, had 350 men working on the site and had to order 372 candles so they could work at night to finish in time. Needham must have been grateful for the delay in Anne of Cleves' departure from Calais.

15 Now the site of the Old Royal Naval College on the banks of the River Thames. King Henry V gave Greenwich to his brother Humphrey, Duke of Gloucester, who built a defensive tower there from 1427, as well as a large riverside house called Bella Court. Henry VIII's father substantially upgraded and extended the house and Henry was born there on 28 June 1491. He later built stables, a new banqueting hall and set up armouries attached to the palace, as well as a tilting yard

for jousting. Placentia – the name means 'a pleasant place' – was used as a royal palace until the Civil War in 1642. It was demolished by Charles II in the 1660s.

16 Strype, vol. I, pt ii, p. 455.

17 Strype, vol. I, pt ii, p. 457.

18 Ibid.

19 The official version of the meeting was somewhat different. Both Wriothesley and Holinshed talk of warm embraces between the betrothed pair: 'After [Henry] had spoken to her and welcomed her, she with loving countenance and gracious behaviour him received and welcomed him on her knees, whom he gently took up and kissed. All that afternoon [he] communed and devised [planned] with her, supped that night with her and the next day he departed to Greenwich.' See Holinshed, p. 811. Cromwell's propagandists had been at work again.

20 Strype, vol. I, pt ii, p. 455. In the Tudor period, it was unfashionable for women to be suntanned.

21 'State Papers', vol. II, pp. 551–2, fn.; SP 1/121/67; and LPFD, vol. XIII, pt i, p. 171.

22 Holinshed, p. 812.

23 Hume, p. 91.

24 Hall, p. 834.

25 Holinshed, p. 812.

26 LPFD, vol. XIV, pt ii, pp. 360 and 505.

27 The remains of the chapel were uncovered during archaeological excavations in 2006. The foundations of the banqueting house that overlooked the palace's great tiltyard were discovered by Museum of London archaeologists in 2002.

28 Hall, p. 836.

29 The headboard is on display in the Tudor room of the Burrell Collection, Glasgow Museums (registration no. 14.236). It was purchased by Sir William Burrell in 1938 for £800 from the dealer in antiquities John Hunt. My thanks to Patricia Collins, Curator, Medieval and Renaissance Collections, for this information. The headboard is illustrated in Simon Thurley, *The Royal Palaces of Tudor England: Architecture and Court Life, 1460–1574*, New Haven, 1993, p. 237.

30 Burnet, vol. II, p. lxxxvi.

31 Strype, vol. I, pt ii, p. 458.

32 Holinshed, p. 814.

33 Hall, p. 837.

34 Strype, vol. I, pt ii, p. 462.

35 Strype, vol. I, pt ii, p. 461.

36 Hatfield House, CP 1/22, deposition of Dr William Butts.

37 'Wriothesley', vol. 1, p. 112. At the time, the Thames was almost destitute of fresh water because of an excessive drought, and the river was salt above London Bridge.

CHAPTER ELEVEN: **No Armour Against Fate**

1 Roper, p. 56.

2 LPFD, vol. XV, p. 250. The title came with an annuity of £20 from the county of Essex.

3 The office of Lord Great Chamberlain was established by Henry I in 1133 and was hereditary. Today, the office-holder has nominal charge over the Palace of Westminster and is entitled to bear the Sword of State at the opening and closing of Parliament, although the work is often delegated to another member of the House of Lords. Previously the role also involved the supervision of the dressing of a new monarch on coronation day and investing the sovereign with the insignia of rule.

4 BL Harleian MS 6,074, fol. 57B.

5 Their appointment must have been early in April as Wriothesley signed his name as Chief Clerk of the Signet on a writ of Privy Seal – NA C 82/764/77 – on 30 March 1540 and was succeeded by Thomas Knight on 14 April. Wriothesley had served as secretary to Cromwell; Sadler, as a gentleman of the privy chamber, acted as his go-between with Henry.

6 The warrant for their appointment is undated but must have taken effect before 14 April 1540, when Sadler wrote to Cromwell as one of the King's two principal secretaries. The warrant states that Henry 'is pleased and ordains that all such times as the Lord Privy Seal shall be present in the Court, the said Thomas Wriothesley and Ralph Sadler shall accompany him at his table, and when he shall be absent . . . then they shall have his diet [daily subsistence] for themselves'. See 'State Papers', vol. I, p. 623. Both secretaries were knighted during the ceremony creating Cromwell Earl of Essex.

7 Elton, 'Revolution', p. 315.

8 'Life', p. 30.

9 LPFD, vol. XV, p. 308, 7 May 1540.

10 See the letter from Richard Hilles to the reformer Henry Bullinger written after Cromwell's death, LPFD, vol. XVI, p. 270.

11 De Vere, born before 1490, was appointed Lord Great Chamberlain on 19 December 1526. He was bearer of the crown at Anne Boleyn's coronation in 1533 and was one of the peers who tried her three years later.

12 The rose window in the western gable of the great hall, minus its glass, remains

today, after being rediscovered following a fire in a later building on the site in 1814. Winchester House, the London home of the Bishops of Winchester from c.1145, was turned into a prison for Royalist prisoners by Parliament on 16 November 1642 (*House of Commons Journal*, vol. 2, 1802, p. 848). For information on the palace in its heyday, see Martha Carlin, 'The Reconstruction of Winchester House', in *London Topographical Record*, vol. 25 (1985), pp. 33–57. On 18 April 1540, a reformist, evangelical priest hanged himself while imprisoned in Winchester House. He was due to be interrogated by Gardiner. See 'Wriothesley', p. 115.

13 Edmund, second son of Thomas, Second Duke of Norfolk, had commanded the English right flank at the Battle of Flodden on 9 September 1513 when the Scots army was cut to pieces. He died in 1538.

14 Catherine Howard was a first cousin to Anne Boleyn. She had spent her childhood and teens living with her pious step-grandmother, Agnes, Duchess of Norfolk, at Horsham St Faith, near Norwich in Norfolk. She was not so pure as she seemed, as Henry was to find to his cost later. She had been seduced at the age of fourteen and already had two lovers. See Robinson, p. 32.

15 L. B. Smith, *A Tudor Tragedy*, p. 103.

16 Nichols, p. 259.

17 Strype, vol. I, pt ii, p. 460.

18 Byrne, *The Lisle Letters*, vol. IV, p. 1,663, letter from Norfolk to Sir John Wallop, the English ambassador in France.

19 A short staff weapon with an axe blade and a spear point, used in fighting on foot.

20 The names of the first Pensioners are provided in LPFD, vol. XIV, pt ii, p. 345.

21 The Pensioners were formally set up in December 1538 (see BL Harleian MS 6,807, fol. 25) in addition to the eighty Yeomen of the Guard, but Cromwell's 'remembrances' show in November and December that much still needed to be decided, and they were not fully instituted until a year later, under their captain, Sir Anthony Browne, later Master of the King's Horse (see LPFD, vol. XIV, pt ii, pp. 192, 266, 275). In February 1540, Cromwell was still working out whether they should be paid their daily wage of 3s. 4d (17 pence) monthly or quarterly (LPFD, vol. XV, p. 71) and full details of their organisation were not settled until the following month. On 5 April, Cromwell authorised pay increases for them ('Ordinances', p. 213). Each Pensioner was to be equipped with 'three great horses' and be accompanied by one or two archers and another horseman armed with a lance – a handy, quickly mobilised military force. Henry VII had a similar bodyguard, but this had lapsed and the new force was an entirely new creation. See Thiselton, pp. 2–5 and 12–13, and Sandeman, p. 24. The Pensioners became the Honourable Corps of Gentlemen-at-Arms on 17 March 1834, and their forty members today still accompany the sovereign on state occasions. Their captain is now a political appointment and is normally the government Chief Whip in the House of Lords.

22 Barnes had returned to London from exile in Antwerp at Cromwell's invitation in 1535. On Christmas Day 1537, Bishop Latimer had reported to Cromwell about a preaching tour by Barnes in Worcestershire: 'Surely, he is alone in handling of a piece of Scripture and in setting forth of Christ, he has no fellow.' See LPFD, vol. XII, pt ii, p. 442.

23 The structure is shown in a diptych of 1616 depicting Old St Paul's, owned by the Society of Antiquaries of London. See Pamela Tudor-Craig, *Old St Paul's: The Society of Antiquaries Diptych*, London Topographical Society Publication No. 163, London, 2004.

24 Holinshed, p. 815.

25 Burnet, vol. I, pt i, bk iii, p. 216.

26 Garret did penance by carrying a 'faggot in open procession from St Mary's Church to St Friswides, Garret having his red hood on his shoulders like a master of arts'. See Nichols, p. 294.

27 Cited by Williams, 'Henry VIII', p. 193.

28 Byrne, *The Lisle Letters*, vol. VI, no. 1,663.

29 Wilson, p. 452.

30 Both were prominent religious conservatives. Tunstall (1474–1559), a former Keeper of the Privy Seal, had prohibited Protestant books and took a leading role in the passing of the Six Articles in 1539. Clerk (d.1541) was Master of the Rolls in 1522–3 and tried to obtain the papacy for Wolsey in 1523.

31 LPFD, vol. XV, p. 206.

32 'Wriothesley', vol. I, p. 115.

33 Byrne, *The Lisle Letters*, vol. V, no. 1415.

34 LPFD, vol. XV, p. 190.

35 LPFD, vol. XV, p. 196.

36 LPFD, vol. XV, p. 239.

37 LPFD, vol. XV, p. 249.

38 Burnet, vol. I, pt i, bk iii, p. 201.

39 The Enabling Act (32 Henry VIII cap. 26) authorised two committees of bishops to define religious doctrine and to produce a book of approved liturgy.

40 Wilding, p. 291.

41 Nearly £3 million at 2006 monetary values.

42 Elton, 'Revolution', pp. 401–3.

43 The last monastery to surrender was Waltham Abbey, on 23 March. The Hospitallers had refused to yield up their revenues to the King at the dissolution of the monasteries.

44 32 Henry VIII cap. 24. The Act says that the knights 'unnaturally and contrary to their duty of their allegiance sustained and maintained the usurped power and authority of the Bishop of Rome and have not only adhered themselves to the said Bishop, being common enemy to the king, our sovereign lord and to his realm, untruly upholding, knowing and affirming maliciously and traitorously the said Bishop to be Supreme Head of Christ's Church by God's Holy Words'.

45 The mutilated accounts are in BL Cotton MS Appendix XXVIII, fol. 52 and partially reprinted in LPFD, vol. XV, p. 302.

46 A list of those taking part is in BL Harleian MS 69, fol. 18. The challengers included Henry's favourite, Thomas Culpeper, a gentleman of the privy chamber, who was defeated on foot in mock combat with Richard Cromwell on 5 May, doubtless with much injury to his pride. Gregory, Cromwell's son, was amongst the defenders during the tournament. See also 'Wriothesley', p. 117–18 and Stow, vol. II, p. 99.

47 This thirteenth-century palace was annexed to the Palace of Westminster by Henry in July 1536 in an exchange of property with Cuthbert Tunstall, Bishop of Durham.

48 'Wriothesley', vol. I, p. 117.

49 Holinshed, vol. I, p. 816.

50 'Lords Journal', p. 134.

51 32 Henry VIII cap. 50.

52 LPFD, vol. XV, p. 221.

53 Wilding, p. 293.

54 32 Henry VIII cap. 50.

55 BL Cotton MS Titus B i, fol. 406. Reprinted in 'State Papers', vol. I, pp. 628–9.

56 Hall, p. 816.

57 Kaulek, p. 186.

58 '*Que bien peut s'en faillit qu'il ne feyt ung sault* . . .' Kaulek, p. 187 and LPFD, vol. XV, pp. 350–1.

59 LPFD, vol. XV, p. 336.

60 BL Cotton MS Cleopatra E v, fol. 300.

CHAPTER TWELVE: **A Traitor's Cry for Mercy**

1 LPFD, vol. XV, p. 377 (letter from the French ambassador Marillac to Annede Montmorency, Constable of France, 23 June 1540); Kaulek, p. 193; Hume, pp. 98–9; Wilding, pp. 298–9.

2 Hume, p. 99.

3 'Lords Journal', p. 143.

4 Kaulek, p. 189 and LPFD, vol. XV, p. 363.

5 T. B. and T. J. Howell, *Complete Collection of State Trials*, London, 1828, vol. I, p. 455 and LPFD, vol. XV, p. 364.

6 LPFD, vol. XV, p. 377 and Hutchinson, p. 32. Some of the choicest items in the spoil unsurprisingly found their way into Henry's personal possession. An inventory of his plate and jewels, drawn up *c*.1545, includes nine silver spoons engraved with the arms of Thomas Cromwell. See BL Egerton MS 2,679, fol. 4B. The 1547 inventory also includes some of Cromwell's possessions appropriated by his king: a glass cup, garnished with silver; a pair of gilt pots; a pair of flagons of glass with black leather, garnished with silver gilt; a gilt table salt and a crystal salt, decorated with a lion 'standing upon three deer or wild beasts'. There were also a number of cushions, including twelve in yellow satin and black velvet, embroidered with the initials 'T. C.', a chair covered in crimson velvet and bearing Cromwell's arms, and two arras hangings, one depicting the Virgin Mary and Christ as a small child. For further information, see Starkey.

7 Kaulek, pp. 193–4.

8 Hall, pp. 838–9.

9 BL Arundel MS 97, fol. 132B and LPFD, vol. XVI, p. 187. Vincent, Edward Lloyd and Humphrey Orince, by special command of the King, rode from Hampton Court to Austin Friars in early August 'and there busy at the late Earl of Essex's house, at the Tower of London, at Westminster, for the furniture of the lady Anne of Cleves, four days, 32s'. BL Arundel MS 97, fol. 142B.

10 LPFD, vol. XV, pp. 454 and 488.

11 Kaulek, p. 193.

12 Kaulek, p. 189.

13 Kaulek, p. 191 and LPFD, vol. XV, p. 369.

14 Throgmorton was not only a member of the religiously conservative faction at court, but moreover was involved in a legal dispute with Cromwell over land in Warwickshire.

15 LPFD, vol. XV, p. 366 suggests that Cromwell was speaking to John Lord Russell, later Earl of Bedford, but he was not appointed Lord Admiral in succession to the Earl of Southampton until 28 July 1540, sixteen days after this letter to Henry.

16 A law against retainers was brought in by Edward IV in 1486 but it was not rigorously enforced. Henry VII, the King's father, fearful of insurrection, was more careful to enforce it.

17 BL Cotton MS Titus B i, fols. 267–273; Merriman, vol. II, p. 348; and Ellis, 'Original Letters', 2nd series, vol. II, pp. 163–9.

18 Burnet, vol. II, pt i, bk iii, pp. lxxxii–iv; LPFD, vol. XV, p. 376; and BL Add. MS 48,028, fols. 160–165.

19 'Lords Journal', vol. I, p. 145.

20 LPFD, vol. XV, pp. 216–17.

21 'Lords Journal', p. 149, Act of Attainder, 32 Henry VIII cap. 62. Later copies of the Act are in BL Lansdowne MS 515, fol. 44 and Cotton MS Titus B i, fol. 503.

22 Ellis, 'Original Letters', 2nd series, vol. II, pp. 160–2.

23 BL Cotton MS Otho C x, fol. 241.

24 BL Cotton MS Otho C x, fol. 246.

25 Strype, vol. I, pt ii, p. 452. The promise was never kept and those papers that eventually were sent were judged not to 'be authentic'.

26 The eight-page original is Hatfield House CP 1/27. See also Burnet, vol. II, pt i, bk ii, pp. lxxxv–vii, an inaccurate version, and BL Cotton MS Otho C x, fol. 242. Notarial copies are in BL Add. MS 10,451 and Harleian MS 1,061.

27 'Lords Journal', vol. I, pp. 152 and 155. The Act of General Pardon (32 Henry VIII cap. 49) was passed on 13 July.

28 'State Papers', vol. I, p. 635.

29 The original eight-page testimony is Hatfield House CP 1/23. See also BL Cotton MS Otho C x fol. 242.

30 Hatfield House CP 1/22.

31 The Act dissolving the marriage is 32 Henry VIII cap. 25.

32 Ellis, 'Original Letters', 2nd series, vol. II, pp. 158–9. The interpreter, the deputation reported, 'did his part very well'.

33 'State Papers', vol. I, p. 638.

34 BL Cotton MS Otho C x, fol. 240.

35 'State Papers', vol. I, p. 642.

36 Wilson, p. 466.

37 See Ridley, p. 242 and Foxe, vol. V, pp. 402–3.

38 Hume, p. 103.

39 Foxe, vol. V, p. 438 and Bell, p. 113.

40 Letter from Richard Hilles to Henry Bullinger, LPFD, vol. XVI, p. 270.

41 Ibid.

42 In the next century, Bishop Burnet was convinced that Cromwell died a Lutheran. Many concluded at the time that his use of the word 'catholic' implied

that he died in the communion of the Church of Rome, but Cromwell probably used the word as a demonstration of his opposition to the more superstitious aspects of the Catholic faith. See Burnet, vol. I, pt i, bk iii, p. 206.

43 He used the word 'imp' in the sense of 'outcome'.

44 Holinshed, p. 817.

45 BL Harleian MS 3,362, fol. 17.

46 The poet. He died in 1542. His son, also called Thomas, was later leader of the rebellion in Kent against Queen Mary in 1554.

47 Hume, p. 104.

48 Galton, p. 156. During an execution by beheading, it is likely that the victim becomes unconscious within a few seconds and dies from shock and anoxia, due to loss of blood pressure, within less than a minute. Because of the muscles and vertebrae in the neck, decapitation often required more than one blow by the axeman. Beheading is retained as a method of capital punishment in some Middle Eastern nations.

49 Cited by Weir, p. 435.

50 The dedication means 'St Peter in Chains' – an allusion to the prisoners held in the Tower. The chapel was rebuilt in 1520 and contains the bodies of those executed either on Tower Hill or on Tower Green, a few short yards away.

Epilogue

1 Holinshed, p. 818.

2 A Middle English word meaning to sing out in a carefree and jovial spirit.

3 'Rumelow' means a refrain or chant sung by sailors when rowing. 'Broadsides', fol. 4.

4 A courtier who waited on the King's dining table.

5 'Broadsides', fol. 5. It bears the imprint 'Printed: London at Lombard Street, near unto the Stocks Market at the sign of the Mermaid by John Gay'.

6 Foxe, vol. V, pp. 434–8.

7 Bindoff, p. 728.

8 The Fourth Earl's daughter, Lady Elizabeth Cromwell, assumed the title of Baroness Cromwell on the death of her father in the mistaken belief that the barony was not entailed in the male line, as it was. However, she walked as a peeress both at the funeral of Queen Mary II and at the coronation of Queen Anne. She died of consumption on 31 March 1709, at which point the assumption ceased.

9 LPFD, vol. XVI, p. 284, 3 March 1541. The King was probably suffering from a severe infection caused by fistulas in his legs closing up and his life was briefly thought to be endangered. For a detailed discussion of Henry's medical problems, see Hutchinson, chs. 5 and 9.

Bibliography

PRIMARY SOURCES

Manuscript sources

BRITISH LIBRARY

Add. MS 6,113, fol. 81 – Contemporary account of the christening of Prince Edward, Hampton Court, 15 October 1537.

Add. MS 8,715, fol. 53 – Letter from Ridolfo Pio, papal nuncio in France, expressing horror at the execution of the Carthusian priors and priests in London, 17 May 1535.

Add. MS 25,114, fol. 262 – Letter from Henry VIII to his envoys in France regarding the apprehension of Cardinal Pole, Greenwich, 25 April 1537.

Add. MS 28,587, fol. 81 – Spanish Privy Council memorandum to Emperor Charles V, reporting that Henry was 'weary and tired' of Queen Anne Boleyn, 1534.

Add. MS 28,588, fol. 149 – News of Catherine of Aragon's death sent to Cromwell by Sir Edward Chamberlain and Sir Edmund Bedingfield, Kimbolton Castle, 7 January 1536.

Add. MS 30,662, fol. 246 – Copy of Pope Paul III's bull appointing Cardinal Pole papal legate to England, Rome, 31 March 1537.

Add. MS 32,091, fol. 121 – Copy of the commission to Cromwell for visitation of churches, monasteries and clergy, 21 January 1535.

Add. MS 33,514, fol. 5 – Letter from the French ambassador Castillon to Montmorency regarding Henry VIII's attitude to the surviving families of the Yorkist faction in England, Chelsea, 5 November 1539.

Add. MS 38,133:

> fol. 7 – Account of two law cases, one involving Robert Aske, 1525–7.
>
> fol. 9 – Account of expenses of Robert Aske, servant to Henry Percy, Sixth Earl of Northumberland, 1527.

Add. MS 48,022, fols. 83–96 – Extracts from proceedings of Cromwell's Court for Ecclesiastical Causes from 14 October 1535.

Add. MS 48,028 (Yelverton MS 32), fols. 160–165 – Act of Attainder of Thomas Cromwell, Earl of Essex, 29 June 1540.

Arundel MS 97, fol. 132B – Charges for taking away Cromwell's household 'stuff', June 1540.

Arundel MS 152, fol. 294 – Account of interrogation of Sir Thomas More by Cromwell, Tower of London, 31 April 1535.

Cotton MS Cleopatra E iv:

> fol. 21 – Injunctions to commissioners during visitation of monasteries, January 1535.

> fol. 26 – Order creating governors of the Charterhouse in London, October 1535.

> fol. 35 – Letter from Jaspar Fylolle to Cromwell describing the finances of the London Charterhouse and detailing the brethren's loyalties, 5 September 1535.

> fol. 36 – Letter from Jaspar Fylolle to Cromwell describing the discovery of heretic books at the Charterhouse, 2 October 1535.

> fol. 55 – Letter from Ellis Price to Cromwell regarding the image of Darvell Gadarn in North Wales, 6 April 1538.

> fol. 75 – Letter detailing the prophecies of Elizabeth Barton, the 'Holy Maid of Kent', 25 November 1533.

> fol. 79 – Thomas Goldwell, Prior of Christchurch, Canterbury's account of Elizabeth Barton, 25 November 1533.

> fol. 81 – Apology by monks of Christchurch, Canterbury, for their involvement in the episode of the 'Holy Maid of Kent', 25 November 1533.

> fol. 84 – Inventory of Elizabeth Barton's goods, 16 February 1534.

> fol. 84B – Prophecies of Mrs Amadas, widow of Robert Amadas, former Keeper of the King's Jewels, July 1533.

> fol. 85 – Letter from Cromwell to Bishop Fisher of Rochester regarding his encouragement of the 'Holy Maid of Kent', 27 February 1534.

> fol. 99B – John, Lord Russell's, letter to Cromwell, providing an account of the abbot and two monks of Glastonbury, 16 November 1538.

> fol. 120 – Letter from John ap Rice to Cromwell regarding the relics at Bury Abbey, Suffolk, 5 November 1535.

> fol. 122 – Letter to Cromwell from Richard Wharton on behalf of Edward Calthorpe with a bribe to buy the priory of Ingham, Norfolk, 7 November 1536.

> fol. 125 – Letter from Richard Layton regarding the nocturnal escapades at Syon, 12 December 1535.

fol. 127 – Richard Layton's account to Cromwell on his visitation of Langdon Abbey, Kent, 22 October 1535.

fol. 129 – Account of an apparition of a Carthusian monk, London Charterhouse, 27 June 1535.

fol. 131 – Layton's report of his visitation to Chicksands and Harrold Priories, Bedfordshire, December 1535.

fol. 134B – Letter from John Bartelot to Cromwell reporting the discovery of the Prior of Crossed Friars in bed with his concubine, Lent, 1535.

fol. 178 – Letter from Ralph Sadler to Cromwell reporting on his discussions about finding him a member's seat in the House of Commons, November 1529.

fol. 223 – Letter from John London to Cromwell describing surrender of the Greyfriars of Reading, Berkshire, with an inventory of holy relics, 28 September 1538.

fol. 226 – Letter from John London to Cromwell concerning the image of Our Lady of Caversham, 27 September 1538.

fol. 234 – Letter from Thomas, Lord Delawarr, to Cromwell about his 'poor house' at Boxgrove, West Sussex, Halnaker, 'Lady Day', 25 March 1536.

fol. 249 – Letter from Dr Layton to Cromwell describing the human frailties of Richard Jenyn, Abbot of Maiden Bradley, Wiltshire, 'Saint Austin's without Bristol', 24 August 1535.

fol. 269 – Letter from Nicholas Austen, Abbot of the Cistercian abbey at Rewley, Oxfordshire, to Cromwell, offering £100 for his house to be spared, September 1536.

Cotton MS Cleopatra E v:

fol. 300 – Letter from Richard Sampson, Bishop of Chichester, to Cromwell, Tower of London, 7 June 1540.

fols. 313–320 – Corrections and amendments in Henry VIII's hand to proposals for the Act of Six Articles, 1539.

Cotton MS Cleopatra E vi:

fol. 149 – Letter from Sir Thomas More to Cromwell, vindicating himself in matters of religion, Chelsea, 5 March 1534.

fol. 161 – Letter from John Fisher, Bishop of Rochester, to Cromwell, complaining that his letters have been misconstrued, 31 January 1534.

fol. 162 – Letter from John Fisher, Bishop of Rochester, to Henry VIII, exculpating himself over the matter of the 'Holy Maid of Kent', Rochester, 27 February 1534.

fol. 178B – Indictment of John Fisher, Bishop of Rochester, for not acknowledging the King's supremacy in matters of religion, 17 June 1535.

Cotton MS Cleopatra F ii:

> fol. 131 – Commission to Cromwell for visitation of churches, monasteries and clergy, Westminster, 21 January 1535.

> fol. 249 – Petition from the Commons against practices of the clergy, November 1529.

Cotton MS Faustina C ii, fols. 5–22 – Original draft, with autograph corrections, of Richard Morison's 'Persuasion to the King that the Laws of the Realm should be in Latin'.

Cotton MS Nero B vii, fol. 93 – Letter from Edmund Harvel in Venice, reporting Italian anger at the execution of the Carthusians, 1535.

Cotton MS Nero C x:

> fol. 1 – Circular letter signed with Queen Jane Seymour's signet, announcing the birth of Prince Edward, 12 October 1537.

> fol. 2 – The Duke of Norfolk's arrangements for 1,200 masses to be said in London churches for the soul of Queen Jane Seymour, 8 November 1537.

> fol. 406 – Henry VIII's summons to Cromwell, Westminster, 9 May 1540.

> fol. 503 – Later copy of Act of Attainder of Thomas Cromwell.

Cotton MS Nero E vi, fols. 64–64B – List of properties of the Knights of St John, late 1530s. Another copy is in BL Royal MS 18 A.L.

Cotton MS Otho C x:

> fol. 159 – Licence from Henry VIII to Thomas Cranmer, Archbishop of Canterbury, to examine and determine the matrimonial cause between him and Catherine of Aragon, 1532.

> fols. 164B and 166B – Letters from Thomas Bedyll to Cromwell detailing the progress of the divorce proceedings against Catherine of Aragon, Dunstable, 10 and 17 May 1532.

> fols. 168–170 – Arguments to be used to persuade Catherine of Aragon to forgo the title of queen and accept a new title of dowager, 1533.

> fols. 199–203B – Reports of a meeting between Catherine of Aragon and Henry VIII's privy councillors at Dunstable, July 1533.

> fol. 209B – Letter from Sir Edward Baynton declaring that only Mark Smeaton would confess anything against Queen Anne, May 1536.

> fol. 213 – Letter from Thomas Bedyll to Cromwell, reporting that Catherine of Aragon's servants were still addressing her as queen, 10 October 1534.

> fols. 216–216B – Will of Catherine of Aragon in English and French, 7 January 1536.

> fol. 221 – Henry Percy, Sixth Earl of Northumberland, to Cromwell, denying any marriage pre-contract with Anne Boleyn, Newington Green, 13 May 1536.

fol. 222 – Letter from Sir William Kingston to Cromwell reporting on Anne Boleyn's behaviour and speech in the Tower of London, 3 May 1536.

fols. 222–225 – Letter from Sir William Kingston to Cromwell on Anne Boleyn's arrival at the Tower of London and three other letters regarding her behaviour while imprisoned, 3 May 1536.

fol. 225 – Letter from Archbishop Cranmer to Henry VIII consoling him about Queen Anne's misconduct, 3 May 1536.

fol. 228 – Letter from Queen Anne Boleyn to Henry VIII protesting that she is innocent of the charges against her, May 1536.

fol. 232 – Order for an inquiry into the 'pretended' marriage of Henry VIII with Anne of Cleves, 1540.

fol. 240 – Anne of Cleves' letter to her brother, Duke William of Cleves, 1540.

fol. 241 – Questions to be put to Cromwell, written (in his own hand) by Henry VIII, 1540.

fol. 241B – Henry's deposition to the Clerical Convocation on his marriage with Anne of Cleves, 1540.

fol. 242 – Cromwell's letter to Henry VIII regarding his marriage to Anne of Cleves, Tower of London, 30 June 1540.

fol. 246 – Cromwell's signed copy of Henry's questions on his marriage to Anne of Cleves, 1540.

Cotton MS Titus B i:

fol. 71 – Sentence of divorce between Henry VIII and Catherine of Aragon (in Latin), 23 May 1533.

fol. 265 – Letter from Cromwell to Henry VIII on his interrogation of the Countess of Salisbury, 19 April 1539.

fol. 267–269 – Cromwell's letter to Henry VIII, Tower of London, 12 June 1540.

fol. 275 – Letter from William Capon, Dean of Cardinal's College, Ipswich, to Wolsey, 26 September 1528.

fol. 365 – Letter in Italian from Wolsey's doctor, Augustine de Augustinis, to Cromwell, seeking leeches for his master's medical treatment, Esher, Surrey, 19 January 1530.

fol. 389 – Letter from Elizabeth, Duchess of Norfolk, to Cromwell, Redbourne, Herts., 10 November 1537.

fol. 390 – Letter from Elizabeth, Duchess of Norfolk, to Cromwell, Redbourne, Herts., 24 October 1538.

fol. 437 – Cromwell's 'remembrances' for November 1537.

fol. 481 – Instructions from Henry VIII to Cromwell for parliamentary business, St Michael Term, 1531.

fol. 503 – Copy of the Act of Attainder brought against Thomas Cromwell.

Cotton MS Vespasian B v – quarto volume of ninety-one folios, with the grounds for the divorce of Henry VIII and Catherine of Aragon written in Latin in Cranmer's hand.

Cotton MS Vespasian F xiii:

fol. 91 – Letter from Cecily, Marchioness of Dorset, to Cromwell, 14 August 1522.

fol. 116 – Letter from John, Lord Hussey, to the Mayor of Lincoln, urging the suppression of rebels, Sleaford, Lincolnshire, 3 October 1536.

fol. 157 – Letter from Elizabeth Cromwell to Henry VIII, appealing for pity for herself and her husband Gregory, after July 1540.

Cotton MS Vitellius B xiv, fol. 220B – A Frenchman's account of the wax candles around Catherine of Aragon's tomb 'lighting of their own accord', June 1536.

Cotton MS Vitellius B xxi:

fol. 178 – Nicholas Wotton and Richard Berde to Cromwell reporting their negotiations regarding Henry's marriage to Anne of Cleves, Cleves, 3 May 1539.

fol. 186 – Nicholas Wotton to Henry VIII giving an account of Anne of Cleves, Düren, 11 August 1539.

Cotton MS Appendix XXVIII:

fol. 52 – Details of the spoil from the Church of St John, Clerkenwell, May 1540.

fol. 68 – Bill, dated 17 July 1540, for one month's work maintaining the gardens at Cromwell's home at Austin Friars, after his arrest.

fol. 76 – Letter from Wolsey to Cromwell asking him to come 'urgently without delay', Esher, Surrey, 2 December 1529.

Cotton MS Appendix XLVIII, fol. 25 – Wolsey's letter to Cromwell, distraught at the dissolution of his colleges, July 1530.

Egerton MS 2,679 – Inventory of plate and jewels belonging to Henry VIII, including spoons engraved with the arms of Thomas Cromwell, Earl of Essex, c.1545.

Harleian MS 6, fols. 6 and 148ff. – Appearance of Elizabeth Barton before a special commission, 1533.

Harleian MS 69, fol. 18 – List of those taking part in the May Day celebrations joust at the Palace of Westminster, 1540.

Harleian MS 282:

> fol. 211 – Cromwell's letter to Sir Thomas Wyatt, English ambassador to Charles V, informing him of the birth of Prince Edward, St James's Palace, 12 October 1537.

Harleian MS 283:

> fol. 75 – Letter from Queen Anne [Boleyn] to Lord Cobham, her chamberlain, announcing the birth of a princess, Greenwich, 7 September 1533.

> fol. 158 – Letter from John Clerk, Bishop of Bath, to Cromwell, on his appointment as Dean of Wells Cathedral, 26 September 1537.

Harleian MS 442, fol. 149 – Mandate to Mayor and Sheriffs of London to make proclamation limiting access of persons to the court for the christening of Prince Edward, Westminster, 12 October 1537.

Harleian MS 530, fol. 54 – Privations of three London Carthusian monks: Exemere, Newdigate and Middlemore, June 1535.

Harleian MS 3,362, fol. 17 – Cromwell's last words on the scaffold, 28 July 1540.

Harleian MS 6,074, fol. 57B – Creation of Cromwell as Earl of Essex, Palace of Westminster, 18 April 1540.

Harleian MS 6,807, fol. 25 – Order establishing 'The Spears' or Gentlemen Pensioners, the new bodyguard for Henry VIII, December 1538.

Lansdowne MS 515, fol. 44 – Act of Attainder of Thomas Cromwell, June 1540.

Royal MS 7C xvi, fols. 18–32 – 'The Book of the Queen's [Jane Seymour's] Jewels', October 1537.

Royal MS 7F xiv, fol. 78 – *Valor* of Queen Jane Seymour's lands in Hertfordshire, Hampshire, Surrey and Berkshire, October 1537.

Royal MS 18 A.L. – Twenty-five-page quarto treatise 'Persuasion to the King that the Laws of the Realm should be in Latin' by Richard Morison, Old Royal press-mark 'No. 1249'.

Royal MS Appendix 89 – Memoranda of the return of jewels to the King by Cromwell, as Master of the Jewel House, 4 and 7 October 1532.

HATFIELD HOUSE, HERTFORDSHIRE

Manuscripts of the Marquis of Salisbury: CP prefix denotes Cecil Papers.

CP 1/22 – Deposition of Henry VIII's chief physician, Dr William Butts, to the commission investigating the validity of the marriage to Anne of Cleves, 1540.

CP 1/23 – Deposition of Henry VIII to the commission inquiring into the validity of his marriage to Anne of Cleves, 1540.

CP 1/27 – Letter from Thomas Cromwell to Henry VIII, Tower of London, 30 June 1540.

LONDON METROPOLITAN ARCHIVES, LONDON EC1

ACC/1720 – Records of Dunford Manor, Surrey, recording sale from Charles Brandon, Duke of Suffolk, to Thomas Cromwell in 1539 and, on his attainder, its passing to the crown.

E/NOR – Records of the Manor of Canonbury.

NATIONAL ARCHIVES, KEW, SURREY

'C' series –   Records of Court of Chancery, Westminster.
'E' series –   Records of the exchequer and related bodies, including the Office of First Fruits and the Court of Augmentations.
'KB' series – Records of the Court of King's Bench, Westminster.
'SP' series – State Papers.
'STAC' –   Records of the Star Chamber court.

C 1/218/49–52 – Alexander, son of Edmund Fognall Esq., deceased, v. Thomas Grene concerning the manor of Frognall and lands, rents and services in Teynham, Tong, Linstead and Bapchild, Kent, conveyed to Sir Thomas Wyatt, deceased, under a threat by Grene and Cromwell to hang the complainant's son, then in sanctuary.

C 1/1,063/75 – John Stokes of Fulham, Middlesex, committed to Newgate Prison by command of the Recorder of Middlesex, for saying that Cromwell 'should at the hour of his death depart very sorry and penitent and die like a Christian man', c.1538.

E 24/23/1 – Wolsey's commission to Sir William Gascoigne, William Burbank and Thomas Cromwell to survey five monasteries and their possessions which were about to be converted to the use of Cardinal's College, Oxford, 4 January 1525.

E 25/82/2 – Renunciation of papal supremacy and acceptance of the King as supreme head of the Church of England by the prior and convent of the London Charterhouse, 18 May 1537.

E 36/77 – *Black Book of the Forests*, an account of the forests north of the River Trent, taken by order of Cromwell, 1539.

E 36/85 – Inventory of the King's jewel house, late in the custody of Robert Amadas, deceased, and now under care of Cromwell, late 1532.

E 36/113 – Method of deposing or removing a Knight of the Order of the Garter, and letter to Cromwell, Earl of Essex, on the same subject, 1540.

E 36/139 – Catalogue of deeds, petitions and other papers in the custody of Cromwell, 1530–4.

E 36/191 – Indenture between Sir Richard Weston and Cromwell regarding documents delivered into the Treasury of Receipt for safe keeping, 1530.

E 101/421/8 – Indenture concerning transactions by Cromwell relating to Wolsey's debts, 1532–3.

E 101/518/14 – Cromwell's account book of moneys spent on behalf of Cardinal Wolsey, 1528–9.

E 163/10/19 – Warrant under the Signet to Cromwell, Keeper of the Hanaper, for the delivery of letters patent to Lady Anne Rochford, creating her Marquis of Pembroke, September 1532.

E 344/1 – E 344/21/8 – *Valor Ecclesiasticus*, Cromwell's survey of Church property in 1534/5.

KB 8/7:

> Part One: Special Oyer and Terminer roll, defendants and charges: Robert Feron, alias Fern, and John Hale, clerks, alleging high treason, exciting sedition and rebellion; and the Carthusian priors of London, Axholme, Beavale and Syon, alleging high treason and denying the King's supremacy, 29 April 1535.
> Part Two: Similar roll, defendants and charges: John Fisher, Bishop of Rochester, and three monks of the London Charterhouse, alleging high treason and denial of the King's supremacy, April 1535.

KB 29/162/12 – Indictment of praemunire against fifteen clerics, September 1530.

SP 1/65/132 – Letter to Cromwell from Reynold Littleprow of Norwich, 6 February 1530.

SP 1/77/203 – Report of seditious words by William ap Lli, priest of Wales, July 1533.

SP 1/82/151 – Reports of statements by the Colchester monk Dan John Frances, 22 January 1534.

SP 1/106/250 – Letter from Sir Robert Tyrwhit, Sir Edward Maddison, Thomas Portington and William Ainscough, lay subsidy commissioners and local gentry, held by the commons of Lincolnshire, to Henry VIII, 3 October 1536.

SP 1/116/187 – Reports of seditious words uttered by John Tutton of Mere, near Glastonbury, Somerset, March 1537.

SP 1/121/67 – Interrogation of George Paulet, June 1538.

SP 1/128/110 – Questioning of John Raven, January 1538.

SP 1/129/73 – Report of conversation between John Hampson and Richard Hore, Boarstall, Buckinghamshire, February 1538.

SP 1/132/163 – Report of seditious songs being taught to schoolboys by Edward Eland, chaplain to the Vicar of Wakefield, May 1538.

SP 1/133/51 – Case of Thomas Cowley, Vicar of Ticehurst, East Sussex, June 1538.

SP 1/136/226 – Interrogation of Lewis Herbert on rumours that parish registers were a tax-gathering measure, September 1538.

SP 1/144/93 and 135 – Rumours in Horsham, West Sussex, that the establishment of parish registers would involve new taxes, March 1539.

SP 1/144/128 – Account of sermon of Richard Mawde, of Whatcote, Warwickshire, March 1539.

SP 1/162/157 – Interrogation of Thomas Molton about his seditious words concerning Cromwell, July 1540.

SP 1/239/298 – Letter from Cromwell to heads of monastic houses earmarked for dissolution, 10 May 1536.

SP 3/5/93 (Lisle Letters) – Letter from John Hussey to Lord Lisle reporting his conversation with Cromwell about the dismissal of a soldier of the Calais garrison, 1539.

STAC 2/7 – Action of Christopher Burgh, Parson of Spennethorne, Yorkshire, alleging that Cromwell, late servant of Cardinal Wolsey, extorted £20 from him, ?1530.

SURREY HISTORY CENTRE, WOKING, SURREY

Loseley MS (LM): papers relating to the offices and estates of Sir Thomas Cawarden.

LM/128/11 – Declaration by Mr Cawarden of 'stuff' received for the King's timber house at Whitefriars out of the Earl of Essex's house, no date – ?c.1543.

LM/1,802 – Receipt from Henry VIII to John Ryther for 'household stuff' left in Austin Friars, home of the late Earl of Essex, 1 April 1543.

Printed sources

'Broadsides' – Bound folios of printed broadsides, vol. 1 – *Henry VIII to Elizabeth*, Society of Antiquaries of London.

Byrne, M. St Clare, *Letters of King Henry VIII: A Selection*, London, 1936.

———, *The Lisle Letters*, 6 vols., Chicago and London, 1981.

'Cavendish' – *Life of Cardinal Wolsey by George Cavendish, his Gentleman Usher*, Samuel W. Singer (ed.), London, 1827.

Cook, G. H., *Letters to Cromwell and Others on the Suppression of the Monasteries*, London, 1965.

CSP – *Calendar of Letters, Dispatches and State Papers relating to the Negotiations between England and Spain*, vol. IV, pts i (1529–30) and ii (1531–3), Pascual de Gayangos (ed.), London, 1879–82; vol. V, pts i (1534–45) and ii (1536–8), Pascual de Gayangos (ed.), London, 1886–8.

Dickens, A. G., *Clifford Letters of the Sixteenth Century*, Surtees Society Publications, vol. 172, Durham and London, 1962.

Drayton, Michael, *The Historie of the Life and Death of the Lord Cromwell, sometime Earl of Essex and Lord Chancellor of England*, London, 1609.

Ellis, Sir Henry, 'Original Letters', *Original Letters Illustrative of English History*, 2nd series, 4 vols., London, 1827; 3rd series, 4 vols., London, 1846.

Foxe, John, *Acts and Monuments*, G. Townsend and S. R. Cattley (eds.), 8 vols., London, 1837–41.

Hall, Edward, *Hall's Chronicle Containing the History of England from the Reign of Henry IV . . . to the Reign of Henry VIII*, London, 1809.

Halliwell, James, *Letters of the Kings of England*, 2 vols., London, 1846.

Harpsfield, Nicholas, *Life and Death of Sir Thomas More*, Elsie Hitchcock and R. W. Chambers (eds.), Early English Text Society, vol. 186, London, 1932.

HMC – Historical Manuscripts Commission: 'Rutland': MSS of the Duke of Rutland preserved at Belvoir House, vol. I, London, 1888.

Holinshed, Raphael, *Chronicles of England, Scotland and Ireland*, London, 1807–8.

Hume, Martin A. Sharp, *Chronicle of King Henry VIII of England . . . Written in Spanish by an Unknown Hand*, London, 1889.

Kaulek, J. (ed.), *Correspondance Politique de MM. de Castillon et de Marillac, Ambassadeurs de France en Angleterre 1537–1542*, Paris, 1885.

'Lords Journal' – *House of Lords Journal*, vol. I, 1509–77, London, 1802.

LPFD – Letters and Papers, Foreign and Domestic, Henry VIII: vol. III, pts i and ii, 1519–23, J. S. Brewer (ed.), London, 1867; vol. IV, pts ii and iii, 1526–8, J. S. Brewer (ed.), London, 1872–6; vol. V, 1531–2, J. Gairdner (ed.), London, 1880; vol. VI, 1533, J. Gairdner (ed.), London, 1882; vol. VII, 1534, J. Gairdner (ed.), London, 1883; vol. VIII, 1535, James Gairdner (ed.), London, 1885; vol. IX, 1535, James Gairdner (ed.), London, 1886; vol. X, 1536, James Gairdner (ed.), London, 1887; vol. XI, 1536, James Gairdner (ed.), London, 1888; vol. XII, pt i, 1537, James Gairdner (ed.), London, 1890; vol. XII, pt ii, 1537, James Gairdner (ed.), London, 1891; vol. XIII, pt i, 1538, James Gairdner (ed.), London, 1892; vol. XIII, pt ii, 1538, James Gairdner (ed.), London, 1893; vol. XIV, pt i, 1539, James Gairdner and R. H. Brodie (eds.), London, 1894; vol. XIV, pt ii, 1539, James Gairdner and R. H. Brodie (eds.), London, 1895; vol. XV, 1540, James Gairdner (ed.), London, 1896; vol. XVI, 1540–4, James Gairdner and R. H. Brodie (eds.), London, 1898.

Muller, James Arthur, 'Letters', *Letters of Stephen Gardiner*, Cambridge, 1933.

Nichols, John Gough (ed.), *Narratives of the Days of the Reformation*, Camden Society, London, 1859.

'Ordinances' – *A Collection of Ordinances and Regulations for the Royal Household*, Society of Antiquaries, London, 1790.

Roper, William, *Life of Sir Thomas More*, Elsie Vaughan (ed.), Early English Text Society, vol. 197, London, 1935.

'State Papers', 11 vols., London, 1830–52.

Stow, John, *A Survey of London*, Charles Kingsford (ed.), 2 vols., Oxford, 1908.

Strype, John, *Ecclesiastic Memorials Relating Chiefly to Religion*, 6 vols., Oxford, 1832.

Teulet, Alexandre, *Papiers d'État, Pièces et Documents Relatifs à l'Histoire de l'Écosse au XVIe Siècle*, Paris, 1851–60.

Toller, T. Northcote (ed.), *Correspondence of Edward, Third Earl of Derby, during the years 24–31 Henry VIII*, Chetham Society, vol. 19, Manchester, 1890.

TRP – *Tudor Royal Proclamations*, Paul L. Hughes and James F. Larkin (eds.), 3 vols., New Haven and London, 1964–9.

Tyndale, William, *Doctrinal Treatises and Introductions to Different Portions of the Holy Scriptures*, Parker Society, Cambridge, 1848.

Vergil, Polydore, *Anglica Historia 1485–1537*, Denys Hay (ed.), London, 1950.

Wilkins, David, *Concilia Magnæ Britanniæ et Hiberniæ*, 3 vols., London, 1737.

Wright, Thomas, *Three Chapters Relating to the Suppression of the Monasteries*, Camden Society, London, 1843.

'Wriothesley' – *A Chronicle of England during the Reigns of the Tudors 1485–1559 by Charles Wriothesley, Windsor Herald*, William Douglas Hamilton (ed.), 2 vols., Camden Society, London, 1875.

SECONDARY SOURCES

Calculations of modern monetary values were derived from McCusker, John, 'Comparing the Purchasing Power of Money in Great Britain . . .', Economic History Services, 2001. URL: http://www.measuringworth.com.

Anglo, Sydney, *Spectacle, Pageantry and Early Tudor Policy*, Oxford, 1969.

Bell, Doyne, *Notices of the Historic Persons Buried in the Chapel of St Peter ad Vincula in the Tower of London*, London, 1877.

Bernard, G. W., 'The Making of Religious Policy 1533–46: Henry VIII and the Search for the Middle Way', *Historical Journal*, vol. 41 (1998), pp. 321–49.

Bindoff, S. T., *History of Parliament*, vol. I, 'The House of Commons 1509–58', London, 1982.

Brigden, S., 'Thomas Cromwell and the Brethren', *Law and Government under the Tudors*, C. Cross, D. Loades and J. J. Scarisbrook (eds.), Cambridge, 1988.

Burnet, Gilbert, *History of the Reformation of the Church of England*, 2 vols., London, 1841.

Bush, Michael and David Bownes, *The Defeat of the Pilgrimage of Grace*, Hull, 1999.

Collier, Jeremy, *Ecclesiastical History of Great Britain, Chiefly of England*, 2 vols., London, 1714.

'Complete Peerage' – *Complete Peerage of England, Scotland and Ireland*, Vicary Gibbs et al. (eds.), 14 vols., London and Stroud, 1910–88.

Devereux, E. J., 'Elizabeth Barton and Tudor Censorship', *Bulletin of the John Rylands Library*, vol. 49, Manchester, 1966.

DNB2 – *Dictionary of National Biography*, new edn, H. G. G. Matthews and Brian Harrison (eds.), 60 vols., Oxford, 2004.

Ellis, James, 'Cromwell', *Thomas Cromwell*, London, 1891.

Elton, G. R., 'How Corrupt was Thomas Cromwell?', *Cambridge Historical Journal*, vol. 36 (1993), pp. 905–8.

———, 'Police' – *Policy and Police: The Enforcement of the Reformation in the Age of Thomas Cromwell*, Cambridge, 1972.

———, 'Revolution' – *The Tudor Revolution in Government*, Cambridge, 1953.

Fletcher, Anthony and Diarmaid MacCulloch, *Tudor Rebellions*, 4th edn, London, 1997.

Fraser, Antonia, *The Wives of Henry VIII*, New York, 1992.

Fuller, Thomas, *Church History of Britain*, London, 1655.

Gaimster, David and Roberta Gilchrist (eds.), *The Archaeology of Reformation 1480–1580*, Leeds, 2003.

Galton, Arthur, *The Character and Times of Thomas Cromwell*, Birmingham, 1887.

Guy, John, *Thomas More*, London, 2000.

Haas, Stephen W., 'Simon Fish, William Tyndale and Sir Thomas More's "Lutheran Conspiracy"', *Journal of Ecclesiastical History*, vol. 23 (1972), pp. 127–33.

Hoyle, R. W, *The Pilgrimage of Grace and the Politics of the 1530s*, Oxford, 2003.

Hutchinson, Robert, *The Last Days of Henry VIII*, London, 2005.

Ives, Eric W., *Anne Boleyn*, Oxford, 1986.

Knowles, David, *Bare Ruined Choirs*, Cambridge, 1976.

Lee, Frederick G., *Reginald Pole, Cardinal Archbishop of Canterbury*, London, 1888.

Lehmberg, S. S., 'The Religious Beliefs of Thomas Cromwell', *Leaders of the Reformation*, R. L. DeMolen (ed.), London, 1984.

Lemon, Robert, *Catalogue of a Collection of Printed Broadsides in the Possession of the Society of Antiquaries of London*, London, 1866.

'Life' – *Life of Thomas Lord Cromwell, A Blacksmith's Son, Born at Putney*, Anon., London, 1715.

MacColl, Alan, 'The Construction of England as a Protestant "British" Nation in the Sixteenth Century', *Renaissance Studies*, vol. 18, pt ii (December 2004), pp. 582–608.

McCusker, Honor, *John Bale, Dramatist and Antiquary*, Bryn Mawr, Pennsylvania, 1942.

MacNalty, Sir Arthur S., *Henry VIII: A Difficult Patient*, London, 1952.

Marius, Richard, *Thomas More, A Biography*, London, 1984.

Merriman, Roger, *Life and Letters of Thomas Cromwell*, 2 vols., Oxford, 1902.

Moorhouse, Geoffrey, *The Pilgrimage of Grace: The Rebellion that Shook Henry VIII's Throne*, London, 2002.

Mori, Thomas and Ludovic Vivis, *Epistolae Philipi Melanchthonis*, London, 1652.

Mottram, Stewart, 'Reading the Rhetoric of Nationhood by Richard Morison and Nicholas Bodrugan', *Renaissance Studies*, vol. 19, pt iv (September 2005), pp. 523–40.

Muller, James Arthur, 'Reaction' – *Stephen Gardiner and the Tudor Reaction*, London, 1926.

Paul, John E., *Catherine of Aragon and her Friends*, London, 1966.

Phillips, John, 'The Cromwell Family', *The Antiquary*, vol. II (1880), pp. 164–9.

Pollard, A. F., *Wolsey*, London, 1929.

Raine, James, *St Cuthbert, with an Account of the . . . Opening of his Tomb*, Durham, 1828.

Rex, Richard, 'The Crisis of Obedience: God's Word and Henry's Reformation', *Historical Journal*, vol. 39 (1996), pp. 863–94.

Ribier, Guillaume, *Lettres et Mémoires d'Estat des Roys, Princes et Ambassadeurs sous les Regnes de François Ier, Henri II et François II 1537–59*, 2 vols., Blois, 1666.

Ridley, Jasper, *Henry VIII*, London, 1984.

Robinson, John Martin, *The Dukes of Norfolk*, Chichester, 1995.

Sandeman, John Glas, *The Spears of Honour and the Gentlemen Pensioners*, Hayling Island, Hampshire, 1912.

Scarisbrook, J. J., 'Henry' – *Henry VIII*, New Haven and London, 1997.

———, 'Pardon' – 'The Pardon of the Clergy, 1531', *Historical Journal*, vol. 12 (1956), Cambridge, pp. 25ff.

Shagan, Ethan, *Popular Politics in the English Reformation*, Cambridge, 2003.

Smith, Lacey B., *A Tudor Tragedy: The Life and Times of Catherine Howard*, London, 1961.

Smith, R. B., *Land and Politics in the England of Henry VIII: The West Riding of Yorkshire, 1530–46*, Oxford, 1970.

Starkey, David (ed.), *The Inventory of King Henry VIII: The Transcript*, London, 1998.

Strickland, Agnes, *Lives of the Queens of England from the Norman Conquest*, 8 vols., reprinted London, 1972.

Sylvester, Richard S. and Davis P. Harding (eds.), *Two Early Tudor Lives*, New Haven and London, 1962.

Tanner, J. R., *Tudor Constitutional Documents*, Cambridge, 1951.

Taylor, Rupert, *The Political Prophecy in England*, New York, 1911.

Thiselton, William Matthew, *Regal Insignia or an Account of the King's Honourable Band of Gentlemen Pensioners*, London, 1819.

Weir, Alison, *Henry VIII: King and Court*, London, 2002.

Whatmore, L. E., 'The Sermon Against the Holy Maid of Kent and her Adherents, Delivered at Paul's Cross, 23 November 1533 and at Canterbury 7 December', *English Historical Review*, vol. 58 (1943), pp. 463–75.

Wilding, Peter, *Thomas Cromwell*, London and Toronto, 1935.

Williams, Neville, 'Henry VIII' – *Henry VIII and his Court*, London, 1973.

———, 'Cardinal' – *The Cardinal and the Secretary*, New York, 1975.

Wilson, Derek, *In the Lion's Court: Power, Ambition and Sudden Death in the Reign of Henry VIII*, London, 2002.

Index